BECOMING A PA

The contexts for becoming a parent are ever-changing, bringing new opportunities and new challenges. *Becoming a Parent* examines the transition to parenthood from diverse perspectives – it is about becoming, rather than being a parent. Drawing on a large body of theory and research, the book explores universal psychological journeys as well as the specific challenges faced by those whose pathways to parenthood are non-traditional or medically complicated. It also examines the unprecedented reproductive choices in contemporary society and provides a comprehensive overview of the personal and social impact of reproductive technologies. Pregnancy, childbirth, and early parenthood (the so-called "fourth trimester") are discussed in detail and illustrated with case anecdotes and personal stories of people with "high-risk" pregnancies, fathers as well as mothers, adoptive parents, and LGBTQ as well as heterosexual adults. It concludes with social and policy initiatives that can better support positive adaptation during this crucial life transition.

CATHERINE A. MCMAHON is Honorary Professor at the School of Psychological Sciences in Macquarie University, Australia. Her research focuses on psychological adaptation during the transition to parenthood, and she has published extensively on perinatal mood disorders, infertility and assisted conception, and the parent–infant relationship. Her current collaborative work with community-based services aims to build an evidence base for programmes to support parenting in the early years.

BECOMING A PARENT

*Contemporary Contexts and Challenges
during the Transition to Parenthood*

CATHERINE A. McMAHON

Macquarie University, Sydney

CAMBRIDGE
UNIVERSITY PRESS

CAMBRIDGE
UNIVERSITY PRESS

University Printing House, Cambridge CB2 8BS, United Kingdom

One Liberty Plaza, 20th Floor, New York, NY 10006, USA

477 Williamstown Road, Port Melbourne, VIC 3207, Australia

314–321, 3rd Floor, Plot 3, Splendor Forum, Jasola District Centre,
New Delhi – 110025, India

103 Penang Road, #05–06/07, Visioncrest Commercial, Singapore 238467

Cambridge University Press is part of the University of Cambridge.

It furthers the University's mission by disseminating knowledge in the pursuit of
education, learning, and research at the highest international levels of excellence.

www.cambridge.org
Information on this title: www.cambridge.org/9781108836050
DOI: 10.1017/9781108870641

© Catherine A. McMahon 2023

First published 2023

A catalogue record for this publication is available from the British Library.

ISBN 978-1-108-83605-0 Hardback
ISBN 978-1-108-79928-7 Paperback

To my husband, my children, and my grandchildren

Contents

Preface

Becoming a parent is transformative: life affirming, and life changing. Every expectant parent confronts the fundamental processes of life itself – joy, pain, fear, echoes from the past, and the challenges of a radically different future. The transition to parenthood provides a window of opportunity to promote adult mental health and wellbeing, and positive developmental trajectories for children. This book examines this monumental rite of passage from diverse perspectives. Universal psychological journeys are explored, as well as the unique challenges faced by those whose pathways to parenthood are non-traditional or medically complicated. The aim is to provide a contemporary, integrative understanding of the holistic processes involved in becoming a parent in the twenty-first century.

Human reproduction is in a state of flux and the human family continues to evolve. The development of the contraceptive pill in 1960 meant that women could reliably control their fertility for the first time in human history. In the decades since then, astounding advances in biomedical technologies, and radical changes in social values and demographic realities have led to unprecedented choice and unprecedented challenges when it comes to reproduction. Contemporary babies are generally highly planned, and long anticipated. A pervasive 'risk management' mindset casts becoming a parent as a 'high-stakes' undertaking, with prospective parents seeking certainty that the expected baby is normal, and that an optimal environment is in place to guarantee the child will flourish. Writing about becoming a mother is ubiquitous – blogs, memoirs, 'how to' guides. The process of becoming a father has received scant attention. Even less attention has been directed to those whose transitions to parenthood are not mainstream (single parents, LGBTQ parents, adoptive parents) and those with complicated and painful reproductive histories of infertility, medical risk, and loss. This book addresses these gaps.

Shared psychological processes (anchored in developmental theory) provide a coherent unifying framework. Different chapters explore variability and diversity – the ways in which the experience of becoming a parent can be influenced by gender, culture, and context (particularly mode of conception and medical risk). Throughout, the book takes a bio-psycho-social perspective, exploring the complex interactions of biological, psychological, and socio-cultural influences. Childbearing pits biological realities against the constraints, norms, and demographic shifts of developed societies, most striking in the well-established trend to delay partnering and postpone first-time parenthood. Technological advances have made it possible to bypass and overcome many biological barriers to becoming a parent, but these options are finite. In a world characterised by global mobility, traditional cultural beliefs about birth, mothering, and gender roles rub up against the lifestyle and career goals of contemporary women, and expectations that contemporary men will be involved in the day-to-day care of their young children. In high-income societies, workplace demands clash with a pervasive parallel ideology of intensive parenting.

While the book is grounded in scholarship, even the most rigorous research is selected and presented in a subjective way. My goal has been to present a broad and balanced 'big-picture' view of the transition to parenthood, integrating the perspectives of colleagues and scholars in different disciplines: sociology, feminist scholarship, psychoanalysis, paediatrics, among others. Inevitably, however, the book will reflect my own experiences and biases, my personal philosophy of parenthood, my cultural background (white, middle-class, Western), and my education and career as a developmental psychologist.

During my own transition to parenthood my personal and professional lives were intertwined. An early career as a developmental physiotherapist enabled me to appreciate the extraordinary commitment of parents of atypically developing infants, and the ways in which they supported their infants' developmental vulnerabilities. I had no comprehension, as an ingénue at the time, of the scale of the challenges they faced. Participation in a classic psycho-analytically informed 'infant observation' was a rare privilege. I became a 'fly on the wall' observer of baby Rose for an hour every week for the first year of her life. This extraordinary experience activated a sense of wonder about newborn infants, a quiescent longing for a baby of my own, and a fascination with the parent–child relationship. Working as a Childbirth Educator during my childbearing years, I found myself enthusiastically advocating natural childbirth (very much the thing at the time), whilst enduring a traumatic instrumental delivery and subsequent caesarean sections with my own babies. I completed my dissertation on the transition to parenthood, whilst transitioning to parenthood myself. Fortunate in having a settled first baby, I was an enthusiastic advocate of maternal intuition and baby-led mothering, convinced I didn't need any 'mothercraft' advice at all, sceptical (indeed naïve) about postnatal depression, and intolerant and judgemental about expressed ambivalence. I had much to learn.

Decades later, I am grateful to countless research participants who have shared their experiences of becoming a parent. They have helped me to appreciate the variability as well as the common ground, the ways in which parenting adapts to meet particular social contexts and cultural expectations, and the importance of a perspective that neither idealises nor denigrates this extraordinary, yet ordinary life pursuit. Becoming a grandmother (a recent development) has enabled me to savour the rewards of renewed closeness with adult offspring, and to re-experience the anxious anticipation of childbirth, the delight and wonder of newborn infants, the fragility of new parents, and the unique feelings of helplessness a tiny baby can engender when she won't stop crying, won't go to sleep, and pointblank refuses to be strapped in her car-seat.

Men and women who have struggled with involuntary childlessness, infertility, perinatal loss, postnatal depression, have helped me to understand how context, life history, and grief confer vulnerability during the transition to parenthood, but also intensify the rewards. Researching educational and therapeutic interventions for prospective and new parents has confirmed the importance of a flexible, non-judgemental stance towards both parents and infants, and shown that a relationship lens can transform perceptions, build empathy, and promote self-compassion, self-worth, and confidence in parents.

Research has its limitations and its blind spots. There is a pervasive middle-class bias. In general, participants in published studies of the transition to parenthood are well-off, educated, white, heterosexual women who have choices and resources. While this book, like the research from which it is drawn, focuses predominantly on the experiences of English-speaking parents in high-income countries, each chapter acknowledges cultural diversity and the ways in which cultural values and beliefs challenge the assumptions of universality implicit in foundational theories of parenting. Recent interviews with new parents from diverse backgrounds illustrate how culture and context influence the experience of becoming a parent. The interviews were faithfully transcribed, word for word, with participating parents invited to review and comment. Most made only minor changes to the first drafts. I thank them all for their generosity and their candour.

Acknowledgements

There are many people to thank, in both professional and personal domains. Several influential books were published on the Transition to Parenthood in the latter decades of the twentieth century. Some were classic texts that set the parameters for subsequent research, including my own. These books anticipated the radical impact of technological and social change on family formation, nascent then, commonplace now. The following were particularly influential: Barbara Katz Rothman's (1986/1993) incisive feminist analysis of the ways in which technology changes the experience of pregnancy and has the potential to commodify both women and offspring; Susan Golombok's rigorous body of research challenging discriminatory myths and unfounded assumptions about parenting in the non-traditional families enabled through reproductive technologies; Sarah Blaffer Hrdy's (1999) scholarly integration of evolutionary and anthropological perspectives on mothering, infant needs, and maternal ambivalence; psychotherapist, Joan Raphael-Leff's (2005) wise and compassionate model of different orientations to motherhood that explores the intra-psychic origins of competing (and polarised) positions, and the different vulnerabilities that each confers; Robyn Barker's (2014) humane, common-sense guide for new parents, grounded in years of hands-on support of mothers and their infants.

I am also indebted to many writers of literary memoirs on becoming a mother. I am especially grateful to classical pianist and writer, Anna Goldsworthy and to BlackInc Publications for permission to quote from her (2014) book *Welcome to Your New Life*. Thanks also to Academic and Writer, Charles Fernyhough for permission to reproduce his moving account of miscarriage from a father's perspective; to Writers Jamila Rizvi, Annabel Crabb, and Amelia Lester for permission to quote from their work; and to Jennifer Senior whose wise and entertaining (2015) book on the paradox of modern parenting reminds us of the need to keep in mind the bigger picture – the deeper philosophical dimension to becoming a parent, that is so difficult to capture empirically. Special thanks are due to documentary director and writer, Vanessa Gorman. Her courageous documentary film and book about the loss of her first-born daughter, Layla, provide a confronting, honest, heart-warming, and ultimately hopeful exploration of grief, and the life-enhancing joys of becoming a parent.

Thanks to the postgraduate research students who were a joy to work with and deepened my understanding of the transition to parenthood in different contexts: Jeanette Lightfoot's study of older first-time fathers, Anna-Lisa Camberis and Nikki Johnson for their work on the transition to parenthood for older-first time mothers; Michelle McCarthy's illuminating study of women with severe postnatal depression who didn't receive the support they needed; Wendy Roncolato's exploration of how different orientations to motherhood influence the experience of early parenthood, and Anne-Marie Maxwell's research on what helps contemporary parents to feel effective, confident, and connected with their babies. Among many wonderful colleagues two warrant special mention: Frances Gibson, for her friendship, her wisdom, and her profound understanding of infant development, and Jacky Boivin, for her feisty and inspiring theory-driven research on fertility and infertility and her commitment to implementing evidence-based interventions that empower informed fertility decision making.

Thanks to my commissioning editor at Cambridge University Press, Janka Romero, for her encouragement and guidance, and to friends and family who read drafts. They were generous with their time and from their different personal and professional perspectives, they provided encouragement, and constructive suggestions: Anne-Marie Maxwell, Margot Cunich, Colleen Canning, and my husband, Andrew Bowes. This book is dedicated to him, to my three adult children, Thomas, Julia, and Dominic, and my two grandchildren, Colin and Quinn. Thanks to my talented niece, Sophie Pontikis, for the artwork on the cover. Finally sincere thanks to the parents who shared their personal stories with me. They are neither typical, nor extraordinary – each provides a unique snapshot of a contemporary context for becoming a parent.

Permissions

Thanks are due to the following:

Black Inc Publications and Anna Goldsworthy for permission to quote from *Welcome to Your New Life*.

Penguin Random House Australia, and authors Vanessa Gordon and Jamila Rizvi for permission to quote from 'The Motherhood' and 'Layla's Story', respectively.

CHAPTER I

Contemplating Parenthood
Why Children?

Adults today have more choice than ever before regarding whether they will become parents, when they will do so, and under what circumstances. Surveys indicate that most young adults intend to have children (Prior et al., 2019), yet birth-rates are falling across the globe. They are well below replacement level in most industrialised countries (Guzzo & Hayford, 2020). This population trend is particularly strong in East Asian countries, where, despite strong pro-family cultural values and expectations, gender inequities present significant challenges for women trying to reconcile family and workplace demands (Rafferty, 2017). Birth rates are also very low and falling in Nordic countries, despite well-established family friendly social and workplace policies (Bodin et al., 2021).

Trends in Childbearing Choices

Childbearing trends in the decade between 2007 and 2017 indicate that the number of adults choosing not to have children is greater than ever before, but so is the number who intended to have children, but find themselves childless (Guzzo & Hayford, 2020). The educationally advantaged are most likely to have fewer (or no) children, as higher education and greater financial resources offer more life choices, and alternative forms of self-realisation. At the same time, liberal progressive social attitudes about relationships and sexuality, advances in reproductive technologies, and more equitable access to fertility treatments has led to unprecedented diversity and choice in family timing and family structure. Single women, lesbian couples, gay couples, previously excluded from parenthood by social and biological barriers, can now embark on complex and expensive pathways to parenthood with the assistance of reproductive technologies, surrogacy, or adoption (Inhorn, 2020).

About 10 per cent of those who want children will encounter difficulties conceiving. Fertility problems are intertwined with well-established demographic trends for adults in high-income developed countries to spend longer in education, and to delay partnering and considering parenthood until they are well into their thirties or early forties (Gameiro & Finnigan, 2017; Hammarberg et al., 2017a). Women can and do fall pregnant when they are older, but there are biological limits. Older age is associated with lower fertility for men and women, and women's age is the strongest predictor of successful conception, both spontaneously and with fertility treatment (Prior et al., 2019).

This book examines the process of becoming a parent and the complex ways in which biological, psychological, and social factors interact to influence the decision to have a child, the mode of conception and gestation, and the experience of pregnancy and first-time parenthood. Biological processes of conception, pregnancy, birth, and lactation are shared with other mammals – but humans are more complex beings, unique in being able to consciously plan their pregnancies, and avoid them altogether. Medical and scientific advances have made it possible to separate sexual intercourse from procreation: contraception enables sex without pregnancy and assisted reproductive technologies (ART) enable pregnancy without sex. This chapter explores individual motivations and cultural pressures to parent, the psychological impact when the desire for a child is thwarted through life circumstances or infertility, and the decision to live a childfree life.

Fertility Control

For most of human history having children was not a choice, rather it was viewed as an expected duty, a misfortune, or an unavoidable sacrifice. The 'default mode' for women was to have experienced pregnancy, lactation, and nurturing (perhaps of several children) by the time they were in their early twenties (Rotkirch, 2007).

Contraception

The development of the oral contraceptive ('the Pill') was a major scientific breakthrough that radically changed the lives of women by allowing them to reliably control their fertility for the first time. By 1963, millions of women around the world were taking the Pill, and it was the most frequently used method of birth control by the late 1960s (Eisert, 2012). Access to a simple and reliable way to prevent unwanted pregnancies liberated women from the biological constraints of unplanned pregnancy and childbirth, enabling a greater participation in employment and public life.

From the outset, however, there was disquiet about contraception. Social conservatives and religious groups worried that the decoupling of sex and reproduction would lead to promiscuity and the breakdown of the traditional family. Many women worried about the side-effects and long-term implications for their health. Some feminists argued that the Pill enabled, indeed required, male control of women's bodies – for the first time, women had a long-term dependence on (mostly male) medical practitioners to prescribe it and pharmaceutical companies to manufacture and market it (Eisert, 2012).

Feminists have long argued passionately for women's rights to control their bodies and their fertility through contraception and through termination of pregnancy. While opponents of abortion vociferously advocate for the 'right to life' of the developing foetus, and strive to prevent access to abortion on demand, most contemporary women in high-income countries have access to both contraception and legal, safe, termination of pregnancy (Guzzo & Hayford, 2020; Jones & Jerman, 2017). Abortion rights and access are complicated in the United States; they vary from state to state. The landmark *Roe v Wade* decision in 1973 meant that American women achieved the legal (constitutional) right to terminate an unwanted pregnancy in a medically regulated environment. Five decades later, in the context of contentious and highly politicised views about abortion, the overturning of this judgement in June, 2022 by the US Supreme Court means that women in many US states may not be able to procure legal and safe abortions in the future.

Unintended Pregnancies

Unintended pregnancies still occur, mostly, but not exclusively in young women. Estimates of prevalence in the last decade range from 26 per cent in an Australian population survey (Taft et al., 2018) to 45 per cent in England (Wellings et al., 2013) and in the United States (Finer & Zolna, 2016). About two-thirds of unintended pregnancies are carried to term (Finer & Zolna, 2016). Not all are unwanted; some are better described as mis-timed, happening earlier than expected (Taft et al., 2018). Ambivalence is common (Wellings et al., 2013). Depending on the circumstances, women can experience strong emotional and moral dilemmas regarding whether to continue with the pregnancy, particularly if they come from cultural backgrounds where having children is highly valued and expected. Unintended pregnancies can also bring economic challenges, interfering with educational, career, and work plans. They may also provoke

relationship change, fracturing some relationships and bringing other couples closer together (Raphael-Leff, 2005).

Infertility

Sexually active women live with the prospect of parenthood, and they
need to take active steps if they wish to avoid becoming pregnant before
they are ready. Indeed, contemporary women spend a large proportion of
their adult lives trying to avoid pregnancy. When they decide they want
to become parents, most couples conceive within nine months of stopping
contraception, but this is not the case for everyone (Mansour et al., 2011).
Estimates vary, but between one in six and one in ten couples experience fertility problems. The World Health Organization (WHO, 2016)
views infertility in heterosexual couples (the failure to establish a clinical
pregnancy after 12 months of regular unprotected sexual intercourse) as a
global public health issue. The causes are equally likely to be attributed to
women and men (about 30 per cent of cases each). A combination of male
and female problems is implicated in about 20 per cent of cases; and for
the remaining 20 per cent (approximately) the cause of infertility is not
known (Winston, 2015). Hormonal problems (producing eggs or ovulation) and/or structural difficulties (e.g., blocked fallopian tubes, endometriosis, problems with the uterus) are common causes for women. For men,
fertility problems generally relate to quantity or quality of sperm. Fertility
declines with age. The number and quality of eggs (ova) is determined
embryologically and begins to decline in women in their thirties, with
an accelerating decline from the age of thirty-five (Winston, 2015). Male
fertility declines from the age of forty (Ali & Parekh, 2020). Modifiable
lifestyle factors also play a part; those who are over- or underweight and
those using alcohol, cigarettes, or performance enhancing drugs are more
likely to experience difficulties conceiving (Sharma et al., 2013).

Most (about 56 per cent) couples in high-income countries who are
diagnosed with infertility will choose to undergo fertility treatment (Boivin
et al., 2007). Reproductive technologies have made it possible for many with
biologically based infertility, and also for those who are unable to conceive
a child due to having a same-sex partner, or no partner, to become parents. Nonetheless, many couples who undergo fertility treatment are not
successful (da Silva et al., 2018). When the life goal of becoming a parent
is derailed, it can be experienced as a significant life crisis that challenges
identity and alters expectations of the future (Burns, 2007). The stresses
related to infertility and infertility treatment are existential, physical,

emotional, interpersonal, and financial (Gerrity, 2001). Infertility and infertility treatment are discussed in detail in Chapter 2 and the impact on adjustment to pregnancy is considered in Chapter 5.

Individual Differences in Desire for a Child

Becoming a parent is so culturally embedded and 'normative' that the motivations and perceived benefits can be difficult to articulate. Encountering unexpected obstacles can highlight implicit motivations and intensify a nascent desire. It is only as fertility levels have begun to fall, that societies have begun to interrogate fertility choices, and consider social policies to encourage childbearing (Foster, 2000; Rotkirch, 2007). The decision to have children is a fluid and dynamic one, evolving over time. It is influenced by social and cultural expectations, a cumulative series of life decisions, and personal opportunities and circumstances, particularly relationship status (Blackstone & Stewart, 2016). The notion of an innate drive to reproduce is contentious. It is certainly the case that some women describe feeling overwhelmed by an instinctive, fundamental urge to have a baby, while for others, becoming a parent is a more distant and negotiable objective (Maher & Saugeres, 2007). For many, there is no clear, explicit process of decision making; rather, adults simply assume they will have a child one day, and the question is about when. Sometimes not making the decision inadvertently becomes the decision (Berg & Wiseman, 2019).

From an evolutionary perspective there is a clear biological imperative to reproduce, but there is debate about whether individual men and women experience a biological drive to do so. Indeed, there is surprisingly little academic discourse and research evidence about the biological underpinnings of the motivation to have (and nurture) children, individual differences in the desire for a child, and the interactions between social, psychological, and biological variables (Foster, 2000). If such a biological drive does exist, it is neither universal nor automatic (Hrdy, 1999), and it is largely subsumed as a by-product of the sex drive. Cultural influences and individual choice play a large part in childbearing choices and, in so doing, differentiate us from our primate ancestors. Moulet (2005) argues that a false dichotomy of biologically versus culturally deterministic positions can fragment thinking about becoming a parent. This book takes an integrated approach that acknowledges the biological influences on reproduction, and then examines how they interact with variations in individual psychology and social circumstances. Individuals who choose parenthood generally do so because they desire both the biological and the social experience.

Biological Perspectives

Women and men vary in their desire to become parents and in their nurturing feelings towards young children (Hrdy, 1999). Some women are aware of a desire for a baby during childhood. Documentary director and writer, Vanessa Gorman recalls 'a primal and intense longing' even as an eight-year-old: 'I wanted to be holding and caring for my own child, even though I knew it was impossible at my age. I wasn't sure how I could wait, I wanted it so much' (Gorman, 2005, 2006, p. 74). As things turned out, Vanessa had to wait until her mid-thirties to have a child. By then, the biological drive felt potent, compelling, and all-consuming. She describes a powerful physical longing for a baby that grew stronger and stronger as she moved through her thirties:

> I wanted it all. I wanted to feel the tug of mouth on breast, the slobbering suck on my face, the feel of down beneath my chin, the weight of a sleeping head on my shoulder. The sheer animal attraction of mother and baby. (Gorman, 2006, p. 94)

While there are clearly many cultural factors influencing the desire for a child, Hrdy (1999) argues that these do not negate the underlying biology. Higher cortical functions can over-ride biology, (using contraception is one obvious example), and technology can compensate when biology is problematic, but they do not erase ancient predispositions to nurture that are derived from our evolutionary past.

Reproductive Desires: Baby Lust?
Finnish population researcher Ana Rotkirch was intrigued by the lack of research on the phenomenon she called 'baby fever' – a visceral longing for a baby. She wondered if it might provide an incentive for childbearing that served a compensatory purpose in low-fertility societies. Ethologists have established that the unique configuration of infant facial features is powerful in eliciting emotional responses and a desire to provide care and protection (Bowlby, 1957). As Hrdy (1999) puts it: 'Infants are delectable, which makes mothers and fathers willing to be consumed by them' (p. 535). Strong brain responses to infants have been confirmed with neuro-imaging techniques in women and in men (Kuo et al., 2018).

In 2007, Rotkirch wrote a newspaper article about 'baby fever' and invited her readers to respond. Over 100 women and seven men provided written testimonies. She analysed the women's responses. Several described a primal experience – 'a sudden, surprising, physical longing' (Rotkirch, 2007, p. 97), that ran contrary to prevailing social norms and, in many cases, to their own plans to defer childbearing while they pursued other goals and opportunities. Women compared their longing for a baby with their experiences of body forces and sexual needs, using phrases like 'empty arms', 'womb demands', and 'a physical, compelling, painful need to be pregnant' (p. 98). Several found themselves seeking proximity to infants, even to infant toys and clothing in retail stores, and raising the topic of pregnancy with partners. Some respondents, for whom pregnancy was simply not possible at the time, consciously avoided pregnant women and children to reduce their own cognitive dissonance and distress. A similar avoidant coping strategy has been frequently described in women diagnosed with infertility (Burns, 2007).

Advancing age acted as a trigger. As one woman put it: 'and then I turned 35, and it was like "bing" – the biological clock or some inner voice that said: "It's now or never" and that was it ...' (Rotkirch, 2007, p. 99). Others experienced 'baby fever' in parallel with sexual attraction in the early stages of a relationship: 'Our baby fever builds on our hopes and plans to become a family, on the one hand, and on the other, on our immense infatuation and love for each other' (p. 99). Observing pregnancies among peers (or even unknown women) was also a catalyst. Rotkirch (2007) acknowledged the selection bias in those who responded and a lack of clarity regarding how representative the experience was.

Intrigued by these findings, Brase and Brase (2012) conducted a quantitative study in the United States to further explore 'baby fever' and its prevalence. They recruited two large samples (one comprised of undergraduate students and the other a community sample of adults). Their findings confirmed that a visceral desire for a child was indeed a real phenomenon, present in men as well as women, but stronger in women. Interestingly, it was largely independent of traditional gender role identification, general nurturance traits, and sexual desire. They speculated about a variable biological element that contributes to bearing and rearing children, activated in part by exposure to 'attractive' infants. Brase and Brase acknowledged that translation of 'baby fever' into a conscious intent to have a child would inevitably be influenced by multiple biological and social factors including partner status, individual differences in personality, attachment history, and normative expectations from immediate family and society at large.

Even if one accepts the premise of an underlying biological drive to procreate, humans differ from all other primates in being conscious of such predispositions; in being able to imagine what it might be like to be a parent; in their capacity to make a rational decision about the costs and benefits; and in being able to choose whether they will become pregnant, and when (Hrdy, 1999). The overlay of human consciousness and rational thinking precludes simple biological determinism and enables choice. Individual choices are a function of continuing and reciprocal interactions between genetic/biological predispositions, environmental conditions, cultural conditioning, and life goals. There are substantial individual differences in the propensity to reproduce and to nurture.

Psychological Perspectives: Rational Decision Making?

The high costs of childbearing and childrearing for contemporary women can be calculated, and there is a genuine choice regarding whether to become a parent. The emotional and physiological contribution to caregiving required of human mothers is more pronounced and more protracted than in any other mammal (Hrdy, 1999). It is mothers whose bodies experience the nine-month gestation, the birth process, and lactation (Buss, 2015). The social and economic costs of reproducing (discussed later) are also greater for women. It is challenging to reconcile these biological predispositions with modern lifestyles, workplace demands, and life goals. Those who choose not to procreate can find less-costly outlets for any nurturance predispositions – young children for whom they are not completely responsible, pets, or plants, for example (Foster, 2000).

Modern China presents an intriguing example of these choices in action. In the last fifty years birth rates in China have declined dramatically, largely as a consequence of the one-child policy introduced in 1980, which removed individual choice regarding the number of children women could have. Feng (2017) points out that a change to a two-child policy in 2016 made little difference to plummeting fertility rates, and he is sceptical about the likely impact of a more recently implemented three-child policy, as more and more women are choosing not to have more than one child, and many are choosing not to have any children at all. This trend has been attributed to better education, higher income, more career options, and to workplace practices that are unsupportive of, or discriminatory towards, childbearing women.

Why choose to become a parent, given many alternative lifestyle options, legitimate concerns about the wellbeing of the planet, and substantial opportunity costs? Childbearing choices are hard to pin down: motives are complex, elusive, and operate at different levels, ranging from mundane practicalities to deep reflections on the meaning of life.

Childbearing Decisions: Existential Meaning
and Cost–Benefit Analyses

A rational approach to fertility decision making requires accurate and meaningful predictions about the negative and positive consequences of parenthood. An empirical understanding of childbearing choices and consequences has proven challenging, however. Berg and Wiseman (2019) point out that for previous generations, becoming a parent was quite simply a necessary and expected part of a life well lived; something people did for its own sake, and to please their parents and extended family. This still remains the case in many traditional cultures (Akesson, 2017). The desire for a child may seem so 'obvious' that it is not articulated. Studies using open-ended questions about costs and benefits generate helter-skelter lists. On any simple balance sheet, the costs clearly outweigh the benefits, but the calculation is not straightforward: costs are immediate, tangible, easier to name and count. Capturing the benefits is not easy: they are elusive, conditional, abstract, may take years to be realised, and are difficult to quantify and measure (Hoffman & Hoffman, 1973; Senior, 2015). The very notion of a cost–benefit balance sheet can be viewed as an internalising of prevailing capitalist and corporate world views of the human condition (Sussman, 2019).

The costs of becoming a parent have been well documented – in motherhood memoirs, and empirically. A non-exhaustive list includes increased daily hassles and stress (repetitive chores, housework, and seemingly endless caring tasks), disrupted sleep, exhaustion and burnout, relationship conflict, reduced sexual relations, role strain and couple conflict, the loss of freedom and spontaneity in lifestyle, career and financial sacrifices, and economic costs (Hansen, 2012; Hoffman & Hoffman, 1973; Nomaguchie & Milkie, 2020). The list goes on, and many studies draw bleak conclusions about the detrimental effects of having children on life satisfaction (Luhmann et al., 2012; Nomaguchie & Milkie, 2020). In addition, there are growing concerns, particularly among millennials, about the negative impact of a growing population on climate and environment (Berg & Wiseman, 2019), and opportunity costs, especially for women, in relation to career development and social engagement (Hrdy, 1999).

On the plus side, modern evolutionary psychologists argue that becoming a parent sits at the top of a hierarchical pyramid of human needs, that it is central to human life and uniquely life-affirming (Kenrick et al., 2010). Longer-term benefits of caring for one's own child include the fulfilment of a developmental need for immortality through leaving an enduring positive legacy (Erikson, 1994), personal growth and maturity through developing new insights and competencies (Taubman-Ben-Ari, 2019), and a sense of existential (eudaemonic) wellbeing due to a renewed meaning and purpose in life and a tangible investment in the future (Brandel et al., 2018; Erikson, 1994; McAdams, 2013). On a day-to-day level, while the hassles and stresses noted earlier are indisputable, there is also the stimulation, joy, and quiet wonder of seeing something of oneself in another, and watching the baby develop (Hoffman & Hoffman, 1973; Hrdy, 1999; Senior, 2015). One participant in Hoffman and Hoffman's landmark study, a young woman, who was living in impoverished circumstances, saw becoming a parent as a hopeful investment in the future:

> To me, having a baby inside is the only time I'm really alive. I know I can make something, do something, no matter what color my skin is, no matter what people call me. When the baby's born I see him and he's full of life; or she is; at least now we've got a chance; or the baby does. You can see the little one grow and get larger and start doing things, and you feel there must be some hope, some chance that things will get better; because there it is, right before you, a real, live, growing baby ... (Interview from Coles, 1967, quoted in Hoffman & Hoffman, 1973, p. 35).

Clearly, it is difficult, if not impossible to capture such rewards in a quantitative study. In general, studies that have attempted to compare subjective wellbeing in parents and non-parents have yielded mixed results. Whether findings are positive or negative, effect sizes are at best small to modest, leading Hansen (2012) to conclude that it would be unwise to base the decision to have a child on existing empirical data. Philosophers have noted the limits of rationality; many of the most significant decisions in life are made with little reference to rational thought and number crunching, rather they are emotional and primordial (Berg & Wiseman, 2019). When over-scrutinised, the magic, the drama, and the transcendent nature of an experience can be lost.

Social and Cultural Perspectives

While biological, psychological, and social motivations are intertwined in complex ways, the social and cultural pressures to become a parent are so profoundly embedded that becoming a parent may not feel like a choice at all.

Pronatalist Social Norms

Most societies are pronatalist and a family that includes children remains the social and economic cornerstone of most cultures and most institutions (Gottlieb & DeLoache, 2017). Having children is considered a public good from an economic perspective, most religions explicitly encourage couples to procreate, and many governments in high-income countries have socio-economic policies to 'nudge' procreative intentions and increase fertility rates (Feng, 2017; Guzzo & Hayford, 2020). The social value assigned to parents allows them to occupy normative and prestigious positions within social hierarchies (Hoffman & Hoffman, 1973; Riggs & Bartholomaeus, 2018). Achieving the developmental milestone of parenting is a rite of passage that 'formalises' adult status and social identity in most cultures (Erikson, 1950; Hoffman & Hoffman, 1973) and facilitates greater affiliation and social connectedness with other adults, with family of origin, and with community organisations (Nomagushi & Milkie, 2020). In cultures where becoming a parent is considered imperative and inevitable, choosing not to have a child can elicit moral outrage, judgement, stigma, and social exclusion (Akesson, 2017; Bodin et al., 2021; Smith et al., 2019).

Demographic Influences
In industrialised countries, the significant rise in the economic and opportunity costs of becoming a parent in the last few decades has become an important consideration in weighing up decisions about parenthood (Berg & Wiseman, 2019; Cannold, 2005; Feng, 2017). Since reliable contraception and first-wave feminism enabled greater participation of women in the workforce and public life, the difficulties of reconciling career ambition and the expectations of the workplace with the demands of becoming a parent have become a major focus of public discourse. These tensions are front and centre for contemporary women and attention is increasingly being directed to similar challenges for men.

As noted earlier, the following entrenched demographic trends have made becoming a parent more difficult or less likely: a delayed transition to adulthood related to longer periods in education, fluctuating relationship status and fewer marriages (a declining propensity for committed long-term relationships), the growing participation of women in the workforce, and the normalising of workplace expectations of long hours to achieve professional advancement. Becoming a parent may be viewed as one potential life project among many. Perceived costs have intensified relative to perceived benefits, but the ratio varies depending on social status and cultural context (Glass et al., 2016; Guzzo & Hayford, 2020). Endorsing the view that women need to have children to be fulfilled is inversely related to education (Hansen, 2012) and women with higher education in high status jobs are the most likely to delay marriage and childbirth (Feng, 2017; Hansen, 2012; Hrdy, 1999).

Data are more inconsistent for men. Unlike women, highly educated men are more likely to have children than their less educated peers (Guzzo & Hayford, 2020), perhaps because they face less role incompatibility, have fewer opportunity costs, and have a wife at home who is sustaining the day-to-day care of children and household functioning (Crabb, 2015). This too is shifting, however, with recent data showing that men with egalitarian gender views are the most likely to delay childbearing and be childless (Guzzo & Hayford, 2020). While numbers are still small, more men are joining with women in complaining about irreconcilable tensions between modern workplace demands and committed engagement with parenting (Petre, 2016). While the media focus is on the work/family conflict of high profile and successful parents in professional occupations, it is disadvantaged parents living in under-resourced communities, and those likely to be employed in jobs that lack the flexibility of home-based work, who struggle most (Manne, 2018). This inequity has been clearly exposed through the COVID-19 pandemic.

Becoming a parent is the default position for many: 'It's just what you do' (Riggs & Bartholomaeus, 2018). Many of the young middle-class Australian adults interviewed by Riggs and Bartholomaeus struggled to explain their motivation to become parents. Rather than a conscious choice, social expectations and prescribed roles were gradually assimilated, to comply with a pre-determined life-course plan. They described becoming a parent as 'innate and inevitable', 'something they had always assumed they would do', 'a natural progression over time in a relationship' (pp. 380, 381). Several noted the pressure, sometimes explicit, always implicit, from extended family and a sense that they 'owed' their parents a grandchild.

Thinking about whether to have children may span a long period of adult life, and unfold in a series of vacillations, revisions, and postponements of earlier plans. Acceptance of lifestyle choices that don't conform to prevailing social norms is growing, enabling more adults to choose not to have children and pursue alternative pathways to self-development and meaning in life (Guzzo & Hayford, 2020; Hansen, 2012).

Childless or Childfree?

An adult life without children can be a disappointing outcome after pursuing infertility treatment, a passive 'non-decision', an unintended outcome related to life circumstances beyond the individual's control, or an active and conscious choice.

Delayed Childbearing and Involuntary Childlessness

Although the number of adults choosing not to have children has doubled since the 1970s, intentional childlessness remains uncommon (Guzzo & Hayford, 2020). Through a series of postponements related to personal, relational, and economic circumstances, many adults just don't get around to becoming parents (Hansen, 2012). Reasons to delay include waiting until economically stable and secure (which means different things to different people), and a growing number of lifestyle, self-expression, and personal-development goals, colloquially referred to as bucket lists (Bodin et al., 2021). The fertility window is finite, however, and adults may unwittingly find themselves in a transition from 'becoming a parent one day' to an acceptance that they will not have children.

Late childbearing is rarely a conscious plan. While women with high levels of education and strong career investment are the most likely to find themselves in this situation (Guzzo & Hayford, 2020; Hrdy, 1999), partnership status is key. Not having a partner, having a partner who does not want children (or 'not yet'), or being in a relationship deemed unlikely to survive the stresses of parenting are all major contributing factors to involuntary childlessness (Hammarberg et al., 2017a; Koert & Daniluk, 2017). In their mid-late thirties, awareness of the 'biological clock' can elicit a sense of urgency for women. The number of eggs is declining, and remaining eggs are increasingly likely to have abnormal chromosomes. In addition, uterine problems such as fibroids and endometriosis are more common as women get older (Winston, 2015). While there is undoubtedly scaremongering about the reduced likelihood of achieving pregnancy as women age, many women have unrealistic expectations regarding the extent to which reproductive technologies can overcome age-related fertility problems (Miron-Shatz et al., 2020). Success rates for older women using reproductive technologies to conceive remain low, and many will find themselves unintentionally childless (Koert & Daniluk, 2017).

Studies exploring how women adjust to permanent (involuntary) childlessness indicate that many experience a sense of powerlessness, grief, and exclusion from the 'normative' world of mothers, and that these feelings that can be compounded by a sense of anger and injustice (da Silva et al., 2018; Gameiro & Finnigan, 2017; Koert & Daniluk, 2017). Writer, musician and broadcaster, Sian Prior poignantly describes a profound and persistent regret – a series of decisions both small and large, miscarriages, failed IVF treatment, that meant she was never able to see herself (her features, quirks, talents) in another, and enjoy the lifelong connection a child would bring – ever present in someone else's mind (Prior, 2022).

The Canadian women in Koert and Daniluk's (2017) study felt judged and stigmatised. They were particularly sensitive to inaccurate assumptions that they had not wanted children. The process of adjustment involved making sense of their fate, acknowledging the circumstances that led to their predicament, and taking responsibility for their own actions and decisions (Koert & Daniluk, 2017). Some reflected ruefully that trying to build a life structure that would be perfect for a child (financial and career stability, the 'right' partner) had prevented them from becoming a parent at all. It is challenging to re-orient life goals and forge a new identity in a world where the ideology of parenthood is normative and pervasive. Deconstructing idealised notions of motherhood by acknowledging the many negative aspects of being a parent can be helpful (da Silva et al., 2018; Moulet, 2005).

Choosing a Childfree Life

The distinction between involuntary and voluntary childlessness can be blurred. In some cases, ambivalence contributes to indefinite postponing of childbearing, and 'not making a decision' becomes the decision. For others, questioning and ultimately rejecting dominant social norms and expectations about parenthood is a clear and active choice and their numbers are growing. These adults prefer not to have children, and may have always done so, preferring the term *childfree* to *childless* (Blackstone & Stewart, 2016). 'Childfree' adults are increasingly speaking out about their motivations, challenging stigmatising stereotypes, and proactively subverting dominant discourses linking childbearing with fulfilment for women (Berg & Wiseman, 2019; Gillespie, 2003; Smith, 2018). Parenthood is seen as incompatible with other valued life goals that focus on personal freedom, career opportunities, and creative spontaneity. The costs clearly outweigh the benefits. Observing the lifestyles of friends or siblings with children and their perceived negative impact on adult wellbeing and partner relationships can be a powerful deterrent (Blackstone & Stewart, 2016; Smith et al., 2019). Reasons for avoiding parenthood are as individualised, complex, multi-determined, and difficult to pin down as motives for having children. Some view themselves as unsuited to parenting. Their decision may be grounded in memories of negative early family experiences and a related worry about inflicting psychological damage on offspring. For others, broader social and environmental concerns and worries about the state of the world are paramount.

Interestingly, the decision not to become a parent can be related to idealised views about what children need, and a reluctance to make the onerous sacrifices 'good parents' ought to make. Maher and Saugeres (2007) explored the decision-making process in young women who had chosen to be parents and those who had chosen not to have children. Those who became parents expressed a flexible and pragmatic view of mothering; they were at pains to demystify and challenge idealised definitions of 'good mothers', and they sought to negotiate motherhood on their own terms in the context of other life goals. In contrast, women who chose not to have children expressed the view that mothers should be ever-present and completely available to their children. Based on this representation, they had made a rational choice: meeting these standards of 'intensive parenting' (Hays, 1998) was not for them, as it was not compatible with other important personal goals. These women feared the loss of identity associated with all-encompassing motherhood and were not prepared to make the fundamental changes to identity and lifestyle that they believed were necessary.

Very little research has considered men's motivations for parenthood, or their reasons for choosing to remain childless. The role of procreator is a dominant one in representations of masculinity, but significantly less so than for women. Contrary to expectation based on gender norms, research indicates that choosing to be childfree is more accepted in women than men, and associated with more positive wellbeing for women, for whom the opportunity costs of childbearing and childrearing are greater (Rijken & Merz, 2014). Smith and colleagues (2019) conducted in-depth interviews with Australian men in their thirties, regarding their fertility motivations and found their attitudes were fluid, rather than fixed. Most were unwilling to commit to a position; preferring to keep their options open. They were strongly influenced by their partner's views, and many acknowledged they had avoided the topic and had not really engaged in serious conversations about it.

There were some men, however, who were unequivocal in their commitment to a childfree life: they viewed themselves positively as unconventional and 'outside the norm'. They were keen to proactively endorse voluntary childlessness as a valid life choice, rejecting the notion that procreation was central to adult identity. Proud of challenging normative expectations, these men took the view that many couples had children simply to conform with social expectations and meet the needs of their own parents for grandchildren. Aware of the social stigma regarding selfishness, several pointed out that there were other ways in which they could express generativity and nurturance, through coaching, mentoring, or philanthropy. Some men expressed concerns about reconciling the lifestyle changes and responsibility of parenthood with their personal goals. Others cited worries about the state of the world and the wisdom of bringing children into it. Some reported a difficult childhood and problems with their own fathers, or worried about passing on a vulnerability to mental health problems.

Adults who choose not to have children are often stigmatised and stereotyped as selfish, materialistic, unnatural. They typically experience pressure and disapproval from their own parents, and do not feel supported in their decision (Bodin et al., 2021). Hazel Smith (2018) argues for a more nuanced understanding and respect for the choice to be childfree, including the right to express mixed feelings, just as many parents do.

Becoming a Parent: Contemporary Contexts and Challenges

Childbearing choices are deeply personal, but also profoundly social; they are influenced by personal life experiences, current circumstances, intergenerational traditions, and culture-specific rules. Beliefs about the importance of children and rituals around pregnancy, childbirth, and parenting are socially constructed. There are significant cultural differences regarding the importance of parenthood and differences within pluralistic societies, among different minority and ethnic groups, those who are well off with those who are poor, and between generations. Some contemporary parents and parents-to-be are in transition from traditional beliefs, yet remain strongly connected to the extended family (Akesson, 2017). Others are extending and redefining the boundaries of traditional definitions of family and family relationships as discussed in Chapter 6.

Childbearing choices are fluid and dynamic. Almeling (2015) argues that reproduction should be viewed as a process that spans the life course, and one that includes phases of not having and having children. Different motives take precedence at different times, depending on cognitive appraisals of circumstances and opportunities. There is currently more choice than ever before, however choice varies depending on cultural values, life circumstances, and socio-economic resources. Some become parents unintentionally and reluctantly; for others, parenting is untimely, but welcome. There are significant barriers to becoming a parent for some who wish to do so, and there is significant stigma and judgement for those who choose not to become a parent. Overall, however, the trend is toward a growing tolerance for a wide variety of adult choices regarding parenthood.

The contexts for becoming a parent are ever-changing, bringing new opportunities and new challenges. This book is about *becoming*, rather than being a parent: the experience of pregnancy, childbirth, and very early parenting (the so-called 4th trimester). A synthesis of scientific theory and research regarding the process of becoming a parent is enriched with examples of lived experience from literary memoirs, qualitative studies, and individual accounts. Interviews with mothers and fathers whose stories are neither typical nor extraordinary illustrate various contemporary contexts for becoming a parent: unplanned pregnancies, highly valued pregnancies after reproductive loss, cultural diversity, global mobility, disability, premature birth, and the disruptions of the global COVID-19 pandemic.

Reproductive technologies have radically changed options regarding who can become a parent and the subjective experience of the transition to parenthood. Chapter 2 provides an overview of what is available, what is involved, and what remains controversial. Research on how diagnostic tests and screening procedures have influenced the experience of pregnancy is reviewed and the social impact of reproductive technologies on individuals, couples, and the broader community is discussed.

Chapter 3 considers theory and research on how women adapt to pregnancy – the changes in their own bodies, the developing baby within, the integration of a maternal identity, and the need to renegotiate relationships with partners and others. Challenging pregnancy contexts are examined – unplanned pregnancies, disability, and 'off-time' pregnancies.

Men's experiences of pregnancy have received limited theoretical and research attention. Are theories of the transition to parenthood developed about mothers applicable to fathers? How engaged do fathers feel with pregnancy and with antenatal services? Chapter 4 reviews research on how expectant fathers come to terms with the reality of pregnancy, develop a relationship with the unborn baby, and restructure their social relationships and networks in anticipation of becoming a parent.

Chapter 5 examines the experience of pregnancy when high investment is juxtaposed with high risk. The impact of infertility, conception involving ART, pregnancy loss (miscarriage, termination, or perinatal death) is examined in depth, as well as evidence regarding the most effective ways to support parents who experience perinatal loss.

Chapter 6 considers the more complicated process of becoming a parent when one or both parents is not genetically related to the child, and there is a third party (donor, relinquishing parent, or surrogate) involved. Research evidence on the experience of these less conventional transitions to parenthood is reviewed: for heterosexual couples conceiving with donor

sperm, eggs, or embryos, for women who choose to parent alone and conceive with donor sperm, for lesbian couples, gay couples, and those who
adopt a child.

Chapter 7 takes a bio-psycho-social perspective on the experience of
childbirth and first contact with the infant. Historical and contemporary
debates about medical interventions in childbirth are discussed, as well as
evidence for the effectiveness of different approaches to preparation for
childbirth and pain management, the role of fathers and support persons,
the effects of different birth settings, and the experience of premature
birth. The final two chapters (8 and 9) explore the 4th trimester (the nature
of the newborn infant, challenges to the couple relationship and parenting in the first three months), contemporary work/family challenges, and
the ways in which social policies and interventions can better support the
process of becoming a parent.

Individual stories capture idiosyncratic and atypical experiences often
overlooked when broad research trends are aggregated: Daisy (Chapter
3) describes the challenges faced by new parents bridging traditional cultural practices and modern lifestyles, and the complexities of extended
family involvement; Aisha (Chapter 8), extends this theme, adding a
grandmother's perspective; Annie (Chapter 5) highlights the importance
of social connection and support when moving countries with infant
twins. Vanessa and Michael (Chapter 5) tell a moving story of their different journeys through loss and grief after losing their firstborn daughter. Katrina (Chapter 8) describes a Deaf woman's experiences during the
transition to parenthood, and the barriers she encountered. Meg and Kym
become a two-mother family, adopting their baby daughter through the
welfare system. Josh and Sean become fathers of twins with the help of a
surrogate (Chapter 6). Jamila recounts how her life-course was changed
by an accidental pregnancy (Chapter 3); Kate describes a birth that didn't
unfold according to plan (Chapter 7). Finally, this book has been written
as the COVID-19 pandemic has unfolded and wreaked havoc across the
world. Grace (Chapter 7), Christopher (Chapter 4), and Ben (Chapter 4)
reflect on how the backdrop of the pandemic influenced their experiences
of becoming a parent.

CHAPTER 2

Reproductive Technologies

In 1932, Aldous Huxley famously anticipated the advent of reproductive technologies, describing incubators with racks of ova (eggs) combined and immersed 'in a warm bouillon containing free swimming spermatozoa' (Huxley, 1932, p. 276). More than thirty years later, in February, 1969, the first scientific paper about in vitro fertilisation (IVF) in humans was published. The IVF technique was developed to overcome female infertility caused by blockage in the fallopian tubes that connect the ovaries with the uterus. The technique enabled the mechanical barrier that prevented sperm and eggs coming together to be bypassed. Eggs were harvested from the ovaries, sperm were collected, and conception occurred outside the body, 'in vitro', in the laboratory. The world was on the precipice of a reproductive revolution, according to *Life Magazine* in the United States. Later that year, in a special issue entitled 'Science and Sex' (Life Magazine, 13 June 13 1969), the editors surveyed community responses to this radically different imagined future. Readers were open-minded about the new reproductive technologies and the opportunities they offered. At the same time, they anticipated with great prescience many of the social and bio-ethical dilemmas and controversies that still accompany reproductive technologies today: Could the traditional family survive? Would parents conceiving through IVF be able to love their babies? Would virgin births become common? Could women's bodies be commercialised and exploited through womb-leasing and surrogacy? Would favoured men father thousands of children? The purpose of this chapter is to provide a broad overview of assisted reproductive technologies (hereafter ART), their application to medical infertility, and broader applications that have enabled single women and same-sex couples to become parents. The chapter focuses on the biological, psychological, and social implications of reproductive technologies for the experience of becoming a parent.

Milestones in Reproductive Technologies

On 25 July 1978, the world's first baby conceived through IVF was born in Oldham, Lancashire, in the United Kingdom (Steptoe & Edwards, 1978). As he made his way to the hospital, pioneering obstetrician Patrick Steptoe predicted that the birth of Louise Brown would be considered a more significant event than man's landing on the moon (Fishel, 2019). The birth was indeed hailed with enormous fanfare and widespread media coverage, as one of the most momentous events of the twentieth century. The success of the IVF technique revolutionised the treatment of infertility, and it laid the foundations for numerous ground-breaking advances in molecular biology, embryology, diagnostic imaging, cloning, and stem-cell research.

Each subsequent decade has seen significant advances. The first live birth after transfer of an embryo that had been frozen in the laboratory was reported in Melbourne, Australia, in 1983 (Trounson & Mohr, 1983). The capacity to freeze and store fertilised embryos had significant implications: it reduced the treatment burden and cost for couples, but also raised new dilemmas regarding embryo ownership and dominion. Embryo freezing was a precursor to embryo donation, and in 1984, a successful conception using a donated embryo was reported (Lutjen et al., 1984). For the first time it was possible for a woman to become pregnant and give birth to a child to whom she was not genetically related.

Conception through artificial insemination (without sexual intercourse) can be achieved without medical intervention and has been reported since ancient times. It was first described in the scientific literature at the end of the eighteenth century. The first babies born in medical settings after conception with thawed frozen sperm were reported in scientific journals in the middle of the twentieth century (Davis, 2017). In 1992, in response to the growing recognition of male causes of infertility, a new treatment technique was launched that reduced the need to use donated sperm in cases of male infertility. A single sperm could be directly inserted into a mature egg in the laboratory. This procedure, called intra-cytoplasmic sperm injection, or ICSI (Palermo et al., 1992), has increased successful conceptions even in cases where sperm counts are very low. More recently, ICSI has had applications beyond male infertility, in cases where other attempts with IVF have not been successful.

Pre-Implantation Genetic Diagnosis involves a biopsy of embryonic tissue soon after fertilisation to enable the identification of genetic and chromosomal abnormalities before embryos are implanted in the mother's womb (Handyside et al., 1989). More controversially, PGD can be also used to select embryos by sex (for non-medical reasons) and to screen for 'desirable' genetic characteristics, discussed in more detail later in this chapter. Since the late 1990s, techniques for freezing eggs (oocyte cryopreservation)and ovarian tissue have been refined. Originally developed to enable women having chemotherapy for cancer to preserve their fertility, egg freezing is now offered commercially to women so that they can increase their chances of having a genetically related child at an older age, after their social requirements for becoming a parent are met (Argyle et al., 2016). In this chapter these techniques (and their many acronyms) will be collectively referred to using the broad term 'Assisted Reproductive Technology' (ART).

Third Party Reproduction

Reproductive technologies were developed to deal with internal physical impediments to conception in women (IVF) and later in men (ICSI), as described earlier. Couples who are known carriers of genetic diseases may also choose to conceive through ART, even if they have no fertility problems, to enable genetic diagnosis prior to implantation of the embryo.

From the beginning, however, it was clear that the application of the technologies could be broadened to include those who wanted a child and were unable to reproduce because they were not in a heterosexual relationship. This generally requires the involvement of 'third parties' who donate sperm, eggs, or embryos. Single women and lesbian couples can conceive using donor insemination (DI), often, but not necessarily, with the assistance of IVF. Male couples can use donated eggs to achieve a child who is genetically related to one of them. A surrogate is required to carry the pregnancy.

Surrogacy, the most ethically and legally complex application of reproductive technologies (Golombok, 2020), involves a woman agreeing to carry and give birth to a baby, with the intention that she will give the baby to another person or couple after birth. Heterosexual couples may seek surrogacy if a woman is unable to be pregnant for medical reasons (for example, if she does not have a uterus, or pregnancy is considered too medically risky). Single men or male couples can commission a surrogate to carry a child for them. Traditional surrogacy involves the biological mother carrying the child as the surrogate (she may become pregnant through intercourse or through donor insemination using sperm from the biological father and her own egg). Gestational surrogacy involves the implantation of an embryo in the surrogate. The resulting child is not genetically related to her (Brinsden, 2003). Arrangements regarding donated eggs, sperm, embryos, and surrogacy may be altruistic (for example a relative or friend offers to assist), or commercial if an agency or broker is involved, and donors and surrogates are reimbursed for medical costs and paid for their donation or for gestating the pregnancy, respectively. There are different regulations in different jurisdictions. Commercial surrogacy is not legal in most Western industrialised countries, so commissioning parents engage in complex and expensive trans-national gestational surrogacy arrangements (Söderström-Anttila et al., 2016).

Biological, Psychological, and Social Impact of Reproductive Technologies

In this section the impact of ART on individuals and the broader society is introduced. The experience of becoming a parent after infertility, reproductive loss, and complicated conceptions is examined in more depth in Chapter 5. Chapter 6 focuses on the experience of becoming a parent using donated sperm, eggs, or embryos, as well as surrogacy and adoption.

Physical Consequences

There are many invasive diagnostic investigations prior to commencing fertility treatment. For women, these include blood tests and ultrasound examinations to confirm ovulation, and tests for tubal patency and uterine normality. The male partner will undergo semen analysis to assess sperm numbers and quality (Winston, 2015). The IVF treatment process for women involves daily injections with synthetic hormones to stimulate ovulation, followed by ultrasound imaging, and monitoring of egg development and maturity from blood samples. Hormonal stimulation is ongoing, with daily injections. 'Egg pick-up' takes place under ultra-sound guidance. The procedure involves a light anaesthetic during a hospital day procedure at mid-cycle, and the eggs are collected via the vagina. (When donated eggs or embryos are used, the woman does not require hormone injections to stimulate ovulation, but hormones are taken for several weeks to prepare the lining of the uterus). The male partner attends the laboratory to provide a sperm sample through masturbation (or sperm from a donor is used). The harvested eggs are placed in a culture medium in a Petrie dish in the laboratory and sperm are then introduced. If fertilisation is successful and an embryo develops, it is transferred through a catheter into the woman's uterus between two and five days after fertilisation (another day surgery procedure), and there is a final blood test about two weeks later to confirm pregnancy. Any surplus fertilised embryos can be frozen and stored in the laboratory.

IVF treatment is physically demanding. Side-effects of hormone treatments vary. They interfere with daily functioning for some; and there are concerns about long term health effects (Hammarberg et al., 2001). The invasive nature of the procedures (lots of needles!) is stressful and some women also experience significant discomfort, including ovarian hyperstimulation syndrome (Ellis, 2018; Hammarberg et al., 2001). Compared to women conceiving spontaneously, women conceiving through IVF are likely to undergo more screening and diagnostic procedures after a pregnancy is achieved, and this is particularly the case for older women who have a greater likelihood of medical complications during pregnancy and around the time of birth.

Psychological Consequences

Long-term infertility is associated with lower quality of life and wellbeing for men and women. Salient feelings of lack of control are common due to uncertainty about outcomes in the face of repeated setbacks (Burns, 2007). The grief, confusion, and devastation when the life goal of becoming a parent is threatened or blocked contributes to a high emotional investment in ART treatment as a solution, often accompanied by unrealistic expectations of success (da Silva et al., 2018; Miron-Shatz et al., 2020). A rollercoaster metaphor has frequently been invoked to describe the emotional ups and downs of the treatment cycle. Women oscillate between hope that medical intervention will provide a longed-for pregnancy, worry that something will go wrong, elation as each stage in the process is successfully negotiated, and despair when treatment cycles fail (Raphael-Leff, 2005).

Success Rates and Treatment Failure

Despite significant advances in the technology, success rates are low to moderate. Numbers are difficult to interpret; success rates vary markedly in relation to the woman's age, cause of infertility, use of fresh or frozen embryos, and from one clinic or setting to another. When treatment succeeds it often happens relatively quickly. Recent Australian and New Zealand figures indicate that for an individual woman, the likelihood of conceiving and achieving a live baby is about 25 per cent if conception occurs in the first treatment cycle, reducing to 13 per cent on the eighth treatment cycle (Newman et al., 2021). Older maternal age is associated with less likelihood of conception and greater likelihood of miscarriage, and there are also lower success rates associated with older paternal age (Practice Committee of American Society of Reproductive Medicine, 2017). To summarise, there is the potential for failure at every stage of the treatment process: eggs may not develop or be successfully retrieved, fertilisation may not be successful, transferred embryos may not implant in the woman's uterus, and even when implanted successfully, a miscarriage may follow; approximately 20 per cent of clinical pregnancies end in miscarriage (Newman et al., 2021).

It is hardly surprising, then, that a large body of research demonstrates that ART treatment is associated with considerable psychological distress for women and men. Anxiety and depression symptoms fluctuate as couples move through the treatment cycle, peaking with treatment failure, and improving over time (Martins et al., 2016). Interestingly, despite anecdotal views that anxiety and stress may compromise treatment outcomes, research evidence for this proposition is equivocal. There is no question, however, that treatment-related anxiety, depression, and stress compromise relationships and quality of life. Recent screening tools indicate that patients who are likely to adapt poorly to the stresses of the ART treatment process can be identified in advance and offered targeted support (Boivin, 2019).

Repeated treatment failure can take a significant emotional and financial toll, as couples are forced to re-evaluate their own motives and how much they are prepared to endure to achieve their goal of biological parenthood. The treatment process itself, and the hope that it offers with each 'throw of the dice' is compelling, even addictive. It begins to feel like a game of probabilities, where surely persistence will be rewarded (da Silva et al., 2018). As Melanie (aged 34) expressed it after seven unsuccessful treatment cycles:

> What I am doing to my body is probably not the best, but I have to do it. It's compulsive. It's like next time I'll get it. … Am I doing this because I want a baby? Or am I doing it because I don't want to be beaten? It's almost as though I've lost sight of the baby. (McMahon et al., 2000, p. 132)

Deciding to Stop Treatment   As noted earlier, when IVF treatment works, it may happen quite quickly. Couples who are less fortunate are faced with difficult decisions. When is 'enough' enough? In general, it is only when the physical, psychological, and financial costs of continuing become unsustainable that a decision to discontinue is even considered (Gameiro et al., 2012). A fear of future regret if they give up too soon stops many couples coming to terms with treatment failure (da Silva et al., 2018).

An Israeli study noted a high prevalence of irrational 'magical thinking' – despite being presented with statistics indicating an extremely low probability of success, women in their forties who were trying to conceive ignored this prognostic advice when deciding to continue treatment. They believed the statistics did not apply to them, and many had no plan for when they would stop (Miron-Shatz et al., 2020). Persisting with treatment and repeated treatment failure is emotionally debilitating and can prevent couples from exploring other avenues to becoming a parent (for example using donated sperm, eggs, embryos, adoption, or fostering) or adapting to a childfree life.

Retired Australian netball team captain and broadcaster Liz Ellis had a daughter in her late thirties after a successful international sporting career. When she wanted a second child, conception didn't happen spontaneously, so she and her partner embarked on the IVF journey. As Ellis (2018) explains, they made the decision that enough was enough after five cycles in which pre-implantation screening indicated that the embryos were irreparably compromised, and three miscarriages in a two-year period. They were emotionally debilitated – it was time to focus their emotional energy on their three-year-old daughter.

Social Consequences

Engagement with ART treatment takes a significant toll on a couple's relationship and lifestyle – both emotionally and financially.

The Couple Relationship

To say that infertility is challenging for couples is an understatement. First, there is the diagnosis – attributed to male or female factors, the infertile person faces the confronting fact that their partner could conceive with someone else, and guilt and blame can surface. The couple may also struggle with the loss of spontaneity when sexual intercourse is goal focused and scheduled on a timetable, potential disagreement on whether they want to pursue ART at all, and on their openness to different treatment options (including third party donations) if they do. Once couples do embark on ART treatment, the unequal burden on women is striking. It is the woman's body and lifestyle that is on the line.

Some couples will face ethically complex and personally confronting decisions regarding the use of donor eggs or sperm, and the ways in which relationships with third parties and disclosure to offspring will be managed. They will also need to consider alternative pathways to parenthood or a childless future if a pregnancy is not achieved. Challenges related to third-party reproduction and non-biological parenthood are discussed in more depth in Chapter 6.

Treatment failure is disappointing; repeated treatment failure is devastating. Many men leave the responsibility for treatment decisions to their partners, as they believe women carry most of the treatment burden (da Silva et al., 2018). While the negative impact of treatment failure is certainly greater for women, men also struggle, particularly when infertility is attributed to sperm problems (Martins et al., 2016). Despite all these challenges, however, there is evidence that when couples communicate effectively and jointly manage the stresses of the infertility diagnosis and treatment in a mature way, their relationship can grow closer and deeper as a result (Leiblum et al., 1998).

Lifestyle Implications.   There are numerous day-to-day lifestyle challenges. The treatment timetable may be difficult to reconcile with work demands, particularly work-related travel, as both partners need to be in the same geographical location at the same critical time. Daily life must be re-organised to accommodate early morning blood tests and collection of sperm samples. Support networks in the extended family and friendship network can be compromised; particularly if couples choose not to disclose that they are involved in ART. Socially, couples struggling with infertility treatment may find themselves out of synchrony with friends and family who are having children. Attending social events where there are lots of pregnant women and babies may be painful, leading to self-imposed social isolation.

Cultural, Religious, and Economic Barriers

The perception that infertility represents an adult life crisis is universal. While ART offers hope, cultural, religious, economic, and legislative barriers can render the process complex or impossible (Burns, 2007; Faircloth & Gürtin, 2018). In some cultural groups, engagement with ART provokes religious or spiritual conflict and stigma, particularly for infertile women in societies where the social pressure to have a child is intense and non-negotiable (Inhorn, 2020; Ombelet & Goossens, 2017).

While costly ART treatment could be viewed as an indulgence of affluent societies compared with problems of overpopulation or extreme poverty (Faircloth & Gürtin, 2018), the pressure to have children, especially male children, has led to high uptake of ART in low-income countries. In India, for example, 'to beget, bear and rear children is a must; the family is incomplete without a male child; and regarding the number of children, the more the better' (Parikh, 1999, p. 441). Infertility can lead to social ostracism, intimate partner violence, or divorce (Rouchou, 2013). At the same time, many religions, notably Catholicism and Islam, officially forbid the use of ART. This seems contradictory, and it is. In practice, many couples give precedence to their own personal needs over the dictates of their religion, leading to dissonance between individual action, public discourse, and the views of extended family and friends (Zegers-Hochschild, 1999). If they feel they need to keep their involvement with ART treatment secret – and this is even more the case if donated gametes are involved – they will face the demands of the treatment process without the buffer of social and family support.

Legislative and financial obstacles to accessing ART compound stress in both low-and high-income countries (Inhorn, 2020). Public funding subsidies vary markedly; same sex-couples are excluded from them in some settings, and regulatory restrictions of commercialised third-party reproduction have led to 'Reproductive Tourism' whereby couples or individuals travel to different jurisdictions to achieve their goal of having a child, generally at great expense, and sometimes without any legal oversight or protection. We return to this issue in Chapter 6. We turn now to risk-screening and diagnostic technologies and examine the ways in which they influence the experience of pregnancy.

Windows on the Womb: Imaging, Screening, and Diagnostic Testing

Swedish photojournalist Lennart Nilsson caused a sensation when his colour photograph 'Foetus 18 weeks' was published in Life Magazine in April 1965. Hailed by some as the greatest photograph of the twentieth century, it was the first example of a photography-enriched biological study. Since then, remarkable technological advances in photography and ultrasound imaging have proceeded in parallel with ART, allowing scientists to make systematic observations of foetal development, behaviour, sensitivity, and intelligence (Chamberlain, 2013; Nilsson et al., 1965). As historian Sara Dubow (2011) points out, these advances have also made the foetus a subject of public controversy regarding beliefs about personhood, motherhood, women's rights, and termination of pregnancy. Ultrasound, used to guide egg collection and embryo transfer in IVF, has been the foundational technology in tandem with other tests that screen for risk, or test for developmental anomalies by sampling foetal tissue.

Ultrasound

Ultrasound was first used to monitor pregnancy in the 1970s and became standard obstetric practice for pregnancies classified 'high risk' during the 1980s. Ultrasound scanning is now almost ubiquitous, profoundly changing the subjective experience of pregnancy (Dowdy, 2016; Rothman, 1986/1993), and challenging traditional theories of psychological adjustment to pregnancy (discussed in detail in Chapter 3). Ultrasound uses sound waves which are converted to electrical impulses to create a visual image. The primary medical application is the precise determination of gestational age (based on foetal weight and length), but there are additional diagnostic benefits including identifying structural foetal anomalies and facial deformities and identifying sex (more on this later). Two dimensional (2D) images in the early days of ultrasound technology yielded blurred shadowy forms that most parents couldn't make sense of without explanation from experts. Contemporary real-time images, on the other hand, capture the movements of the foetus (4D ultrasound) and enable parents to clearly see the foetus – heartbeat, facial features, sex organs, movements, perhaps even thumb-sucking, from quite early in pregnancy. This has changed the experience from a diagnostic medical procedure (with some attendant anxiety) to entertainment (Edvardsson et al., 2015). What could be more compelling for expectant parents? It's hardly surprising then, that a non-medical industry of 'keepsake ultrasound' has emerged: a hybrid of ultrasound imaging and photography with images and video clips that expectant parents can circulate through social media and post on Instagram. Information about the sex of the infant has led to the common contemporary practice of 'gender reveal' parties (Dowdy, 2016). While ultrasound has an excellent safety record, new versions of the technology, and the widespread practice of scanning at every antenatal visit need ongoing evaluation, with some experts recommending that scans should be carried out only when there is clinical need and that evidence does not support them being routinely offered after 28 weeks' gestation (National Institute for Health Care Excellence [NICE], 2021a).

Risk Screening and Diagnostic Testing

In addition to ultrasound, an array of screening and diagnostic tests is available to detect chromosomal, genetic, and developmental abnormalities, generally with a view to providing couples with the information they need in order to decide whether to continue with a pregnancy.

Down Syndrome, caused by having three copies of chromosome 21, is the most common condition tested for. The relative risks of chromosomal abnormalities like Down Syndrome are related to maternal age, with mothers over 35 years almost twice as likely as those aged 30 and under to have a child with Down Syndrome, although the absolute risk is still quite low (Gabbe et al., 2007). Other rarely occurring chromosomal conditions can also be detected. Skilled counselling is important regarding the implications, options, timing, benefits, and limits of all antenatal tests. Women should always be offered a choice.

Non-invasive Pregnancy Screening Tests in the First Trimester
Recent developments in the application of non-invasive ultrasound technology (nuchal screening) combined with screening blood tests in the first trimester (often referred to as the 'combined test') have been revolutionary (Thomas et al., 2021). They have changed obstetric practice and invasive diagnostic tests are now much less frequently used than in the past (Oster, 2019). Non-invasive screening tests do not yield a definite diagnosis, as foetal tissue is not sampled. Rather they provide a relative risk statistic regarding the likelihood of having a particular condition, which can guide decisions about whether to undergo future invasive diagnostic testing. Importantly, this information is available early in the pregnancy. A blood test to detect infectious diseases is offered early in the first trimester (8–10 weeks) and the First-Trimester Combined Test between 10 and 14 weeks. Women may also be offered the Quadruple Screening test for Down Syndrome in the second trimester (NICE, 2021a).

The First Trimester Combined Test   There are two steps. First, the mother's blood is tested for two pregnancy specific proteins: associated plasma protein and human chorionic gonadotropin (HCG). The second step is an ultrasound examination that examines the translucency (thickness) of fluid (the clear space) in the back of the neck of the developing foetus. Thickness scores can be compared with normal values. Results of these two tests are then considered in the context of maternal age to calculate the relative risk of carrying a baby with Down Syndrome (Trisomy 21) (Thomas et al., 2021). (Routine screening targets vary in different health systems; the test may also screen for Trisomy 18 and Trisomy 13, less common than Down Syndrome.)

When relative risk is elevated, women are advised to seek genetic counselling and they have the option to undergo further invasive diagnostic testing in the second trimester of pregnancy (amniocentesis, discussed

further later). Sensitivity statistics (or accurate detection rates for chromosomal abnormalities) are in the range of 90–95 per cent and false positive
rates (results suggesting a chromosomal abnormality when there is not
one) are in the range of 2.5–5 per cent (Kagan et al., 2019).

Cell Free DNA Technology (cfDNA)   This technique involves genome
sequencing of foetal cells that are circulating in the maternal blood
stream during pregnancy (Wong & Lo, 2015). cfDNA tests have a higher
detection and lower false positive rate than the first trimester combined
test described in the previous sub-section (Kagan et al., 2019). Nonetheless,
a positive test result is still only an indication for further testing. While
confidence about accuracy is a clear advantage, the cost of this test is a
limitation. It is generally not available as a public health option, so it is
currently out of reach for many women, particularly in the United States
(Oster, 2019).

Invasive Diagnostic Tests
It is only when foetal tissue is sampled (biopsied) that a definitive diagnosis
can be made to inform decisions about whether to terminate or continue
with a pregnancy. A diagnostic test is offered when a woman receives a
'high chance' result in the screening test or unexpected findings on the
ultrasound.

Pre-implantation Genetic Diagnosis (PGD)   The earliest possible
diagnostic test is one conducted prior to the pregnancy being established.
Couples known to be at risk for chromosomal and genetic disorders
can use IVF to create several embryos that then undergo genetic
testing, with the intention that only embryos where genetic disorders
have been excluded will be implanted. The procedure is complex and
expensive, especially for couples who are not experiencing infertility
and would not otherwise need to be engaged with IVF. While clinical
guidelines and protocols vary, couples generally undergo DNA testing
and non-directive genetic counselling prior to embarking on PGD
(Karatas et al., 2010a). A related technique, Pre-Implantation Genetic
Screening (PGS) can be used to screen the quality of embryos obtained
through IVF/ICSI, with the goal of improving pregnancy rates and
reducing the likelihood of miscarriage in couples, particularly in cases
of advanced maternal age, repeated pregnancy loss, and repeated IVF
failure (Handyside, 2020).

Chorionic Villus Sampling (CVS)   The CVS test involves retrieval of a small quantity of tissue from the chorionic villi in the uterus. Tissue is sampled using a fine needle through the abdominal wall or through the vagina and cervix under ultrasound guidance. The test is generally conducted around 9–10 weeks' gestation. The tissue, which has exactly the same DNA as the developing embryo, can then be tested for chromosomal and genetic abnormalities. Miscarriage is the main concern, although the rate is low, and not significantly different from miscarriage rates in the first trimester in women who do not undergo the test. Miscarriage rates vary, however, related to the skill, precision, and experience of the practitioner performing the procedure (Akolekar et al., 2015).

While there are clear benefits of a definitive first trimester diagnostic test for the mother, CVS does not test for neural tube defects characteristic of Spina Bifida, which are diagnosed based on alpha-fetoprotein levels in the second trimester. Amniocentesis (discussed later) may be preferred if other ultrasound and blood screening results have been abnormal, or the parents have a family history of genetic disorders. Indicators for CVS and amniocentesis include abnormalities identified on non-invasive screening tests, described earlier, older maternal age (as older mothers are more at risk of chromosomal abnormalities, particularly Down Syndrome), parents who have known genetic conditions, and those who are known carriers for a genetic condition.

Amniocentesis   The use of amniocentesis was first reported in the middle of the twentieth century. Like IVF and ultrasound, the procedure became more commonly used from the 1980s. During amniocentesis, cells from the foetus are sampled from the amniotic fluid that surrounds it in the uterus, and the cells are then cultured in the laboratory. This reveals chromosomal abnormalities, genetic diseases, and alpha-fetoprotein levels as risk indicators for neural tube defects (Spina Bifida). The procedure is generally conducted between 16 and 20 weeks of pregnancy. The woman is required to lie on her back and ultrasound reveals the position of the placenta and foetus. A needle is introduced to aspirate the amniotic fluid through the abdominal wall. Results may take several weeks, and this varies depending on the clinic, and the fees paid (Oster, 2019). Although there is a small risk of injury to the foetus or miscarriage, this complication is rare with a recent systematic review indicating a rate of less than 1 per cent of all procedures, comparable to background rates of second trimester pregnancy loss in the community (Akolekar et al.,

2015). The timing of the test relatively late in the pregnancy, with results not available until even later, when the mother may be feeling foetal movements, are disadvantages.

Finding Out the Sex of the Foetus

While the screening and diagnostic techniques described in the previous section were developed to identify medical risk, they also provide information to expectant parents about the sex of the child, either through chromosomes from foetal tissue or cells in maternal blood samples, or through seeing the genitals on an ultrasound screen. Speculation about foetal sex has a long history in both scientific and social contexts. Plato, Aristotle, and Hippocrates theorised about the origins of human sex almost 400 years BC. Since then, numerous folkloric theories have proliferated in every culture about how to determine the sex before an infant is born and how to conceive one sex or the other (generally related to the timing of intercourse in the menstrual cycle). Emily Oster (2019) reviewed the research evidence for several of these popular theories and concluded they could be neither confirmed nor rejected, with about a 50:50 chance of being correct! When given the opportunity to find out the sex during pregnancy, most parents are unable to resist (Oster, 2019; Rothman, 1986/1993).

Impact of Antenatal Screening and Diagnostic Testing

Biological Impact

The medical and health implications of antenatal screening and testing have been far-reaching. Ultrasound allows more accurate dating of gestational growth and age, important if the birth needs to be induced, or a caesarean section planned. Ultrasound also allows the detection of structural anomalies such as Spina Bifida and cardiac defects. In these cases, parents can be given the choice to terminate the pregnancy or to continue, perhaps with the option of intrauterine foetal surgery or surgery immediately after birth. A worldwide increase in the number of pregnancies affected by Trisomy 21 and Trisomy 18 due to older maternal age at first birth has been offset by a parallel increase in antenatal screening. The termination of affected pregnancies has meant that the prevalence of these disorders has remained relatively stable (Moorthie et al., 2018). PGD remains controversial, but the exclusion of affected embryos prior to implantation has allowed parents at known risk of genetic disorders to avoid becoming pregnant with an affected child, whilst enabling them to give birth to unaffected children. Findings regarding the benefits of PGS to improve IVF outcomes in older mothers (when there is no known history of genetic disorders) are equivocal, with debate amongst obstetricians about whether benefits justify the additional costs (Ledger, 2019).

Psychological Impact

Screening and tests in pregnancy always engender some anxiety, but they can also provide a great deal of reassurance. They increase the predictability, controllability, and in some cases, the modifiability of adverse pregnancy outcomes. The risk-to-benefit ratio is a personal one for couples, depending on their own circumstances, history, and beliefs (Oster, 2019). Karatas and colleagues (2010a) conducted in-depth interviews with women at known genetic risk who were interviewed about their experience of PGD. Unsurprisingly, they had mixed reactions. They found the procedure intensely stressful and emotionally draining, worrying about the possible diagnosis, about discarding embryos, and about the possibility of failure inherent in conceiving through IVF. Nonetheless, after a history of reproductive failures, most were glad they had undergone PGD as it gave them a positive sense of empowerment due to more certainty about the pregnancy outcome. Because they didn't have to undergo a test during pregnancy and the potential trauma of a late termination, they felt able to invest emotionally in the pregnancy and anticipate a healthy child.

While there are solid grounds for couples with a medical history of genetic disorders to undergo PGD, and clear benefits in being able to select unaffected embryos, recent trends to offer extended first trimester screening for a wide panel of aneuploidies and chromosomal anomalies can come with a cost. Informed consent and genuine shared decision-making models are crucial. Doctors need to make sure that couples understand the nature of the testing and the implications of false positive and uncertain results, before they undergo screening procedures (National Institute for Clinical Excellence [NICE], 2021a; Thomas et al., 2021). There are also ethical dilemmas about the expanding panel of genomic sequences that can be identified with cell-free DNA tests. The clinical implications of many positive results are not clear. Thomas and colleagues (2021) have expressed concerns that cell-free DNA tests may evolve into a screen for 'normality' posing significant ethical challenges for practitioners and parents, alike.

Psychological Impact of Ultrasound

The capacity to see the unborn baby, enabled through ultrasound imaging is generally a positive experience. As images have become more engaging and accessible, and women and their partners have been included more in the process, ultrasound has become a normalised, integral, and unquestioned examination in pregnancy (Edvardsson, et al., 2015) There are clear benefits with respect to early diagnosis of structural developmental anomalies, and reassurance about normal foetal development (in most cases). Indeed, the experience can be a turning point in antenatal bonding for both parents, with research evidence of stronger feelings toward the unborn baby and more positive maternal health behaviours after ultrasound (Sedgmen et al., 2006). Fathers and extended family (grandparents) can be included in the previously secret world of the unborn baby much earlier than was previously possible, promoting feelings of closeness, connection with the pregnancy, and enthusiastic preparation for the new parental and grandparental role (Harpel & Gentry Barras, 2018). Writer and psychology researcher Charles Fernyhough (2008) describes the impact of seeing his first-born daughter Athena:

> When we saw Athena for the first time on the day of her 12-week scan, she became powerfully, unquestionably real. We gave her foetal form a name, and graced her movements on the ultrasound with all sorts of intentional nuances, alternating bouts of exuberance and thoughtfulness. (p. 222)

Being able to see the developing baby very early in gestation can have its downsides, however (Oster, 2019). Any scanning experience always brings with it the prospect of exposing a problem. Classical pianist and writer Anna Goldsworthy (2014) felt she was intruding on the secret life of her unborn baby as she watched an early scan:

> It is both awesome and terrifying: why must there be so many component parts, so many places where things could go wrong? Next we dive down your torso in cross-section, past your two dormant lungs and the black cavity of your stomach to the great motor of your heart. It is so private in here. Surely we should not be looking. (p. 25)

Even when all is well, confirming the reality of the foetus as a developing autonomous individual can make early miscarriages (or seeing an embryo that isn't growing or developing as it should) more poignant and painful. Implications of attribution of personhood so early in pregnancy, prior to viability, are discussed in more detail in relation to psychological adaptations to pregnancy (Chapters 3 and 4) and the special case of high-risk pregnancies (Chapter 5).

Social Impact

Reproductive technologies have raised fundamental questions about relationships between science and society: the meaning of pregnancy and childbirth, kinship, gender, sexuality, and family making (Faircloth & Gürtin, 2018; Inhorn, 2020). Scholars from diverse disciplines (women's studies, philosophy, anthropology, bioethics, theology) have argued that the proliferation of antenatal testing has medicalised a natural, indeed primal, life experience. The focus on diagnosing problems, reframes pregnancy as a medical condition to be problematised and scrutinised, and shifts the focus from the wellbeing of the mother to the wellbeing of the foetus (Dubow, 2011; Faircloth & Gürtin, 2018; Rothman, 1986/1993). External images may override an embodied knowledge of the developing pregnancy (Harpel & Gentry Barras, 2018). The early personification of the foetus through the proliferation of accessible images is hotly contested and has contributed to legal claims in the United States, including claims against pregnant women on behalf of foetal rights, and complex public debates about abortion (Dubow, 2011).

Knowing the Sex of the Foetus

Antenatal screening and testing provide early information about foetal sex. Couples generally choose to know the sex because they can, and are unable to tolerate not knowing something if someone else does (Oster, 2019; Rothman, 1986/1993). Along with 'keepsake ultrasound', the routine practice of informing parents about foetal sex has contributed to the commercialisation of pregnancy and the 'gendering' of unborn children. Many contemporary expectant couples hold gender reveal parties (pink or blue balloons, cakes), purchase gendered infant clothing, and decorate nurseries in pink or blue. Rothman argued that this can entrench gender stereotypes at the very beginning of a child's life when abstract *maleness* or *femaleness* is the only known characteristic, and therefore ripe for attributions and fantasies, without the balance of individuality. After birth, the infant's gender can be contextualised, as just one of many infant characteristics. Many parents, perhaps because pregnancy represents so many unknowns, feel empowered by knowing the sex – it bestows personhood on the foetus, who can be named, and is somehow easier to relate to (see Jamila's story, Chapter 3, and Christopher's story, Chapter 4). While some parents prefer to wait, knowing the gender of the baby in advance is considered a normative contemporary pregnancy experience (Oster, 2019). Some of the more disturbing social consequences of sex selection are discussed later in this chapter.

Benefits of Reproductive Technologies and Ongoing Controversies

Enthusiasm about the potential benefits of medical breakthroughs have always co-existed with a fear that reproductive technologies have the potential to tamper with the natural order; that they can be misapplied and cause social harm, inequities, and exploitation (Inhorn, 2020; Jones & McMahon, 2003). As theological scholar Anthony Fisher (1989) put it, very early in the evolution of IVF treatment 'It would be surprising, in fact, if there were not psychological ill effects from the IVF program' (p. 73).

Making parenthood possible for adults who want a child and are unable to conceive is a self-evident and profound benefit of reproductive technologies, and arguably the key outcome against which they should be evaluated. More than eight million babies have been born worldwide after conception through ART (Crawford & Ledger, 2020). Application of the technology for non-medical limitations has expanded the reproductive options for adults from sexual minority groups, enabling a broad range of possible family structures: comprised of various combinations of genetic, gestational, and social parents. Given the radical nature of these changes to family forms, it is not surprising that questions have been raised regarding potential negative consequences. What does research tell us about consequences of reproductive technologies for the children conceived in this way, and their parents?

Impact on Parenting and Offspring

More than forty years after the birth of Louise Brown, some social and bio-ethical concerns (particularly around third-party reproduction and surrogacy) remain the topic of vigorous debate, but many others have been shown to be baseless. In the early days, anecdotal case studies and sensationalised media reports about 'test tube babies' predicted inevitable problems. A 'messianic child' born after so much effort, investment, and unrealistic parent expectations could only disappoint. Overprotective, over-involved parenting was considered inevitable (Fisher, 1989). Further, it was assumed that infertile couples would struggle to parent effectively due to the residual emotional and financial strains following their infertility diagnosis and the demands of the treatment process, and that social stigma could further compromise their parenting capacity and the child's wellbeing.

Susan Golombok (2019, 2020) summarises three decades of research that has debunked concerns that conception using ART (and the different family forms that have been enabled) is associated with problematic parenting or compromised child development and wellbeing. Her comprehensive reviews conclude that there are more similarities than differences when children conceived through ART are compared with those conceived spontaneously, irrespective of family structure, and genetic relationships with parents. These findings are consistent with Lamb's (2012) proposition that it is the quality of family relationships, rather than family structure per se that is crucial for child wellbeing. These findings are extended by a longitudinal follow-up examining quality of life in ART-conceived adults (average age 21). Hammarberg and colleagues (2022) report that compared to young adults conceived spontaneously, and controlling for relevant confounding variables, those conceived through ART report comparable physical health and better quality of life related to social relationships, a better relationship with their parents, and a better financial situation. It seems, then, that '*The kids are all right.*' (Cholodenko, 2010).

Some study limitations are acknowledged. Many studies have small samples, and likely sample biases (those families who are struggling or experiencing most stigma or difficulty may not participate in research) so the findings may be mainly applicable to a self-selected group of high-functioning families. While some studies rely on parental report, with the potential for socially desirable responding, a substantial number of longitudinal studies have included observations of parent–child interaction, in-depth interviews with children and parents, and ratings by teachers, who are blind to mode of conception. A key limitation in studies involving donated sperm, embryos, or eggs is that those families who have kept the details of the child's conception (and genetic origins) secret are unlikely to participate. Open disclosure to the child of their genetic origins is recognised as an important issue for child wellbeing (Nuffield Council on Bioethics, 2013). Keeping such a fundamental secret can be a source of stress that compromises family functioning (Berger & Paul, 2008). We return to the issue of disclosure in Chapter 6 when we discuss becoming a parent through adoption, as well as through ART involving third parties. We now consider two other consequences of ART that remain contentious and unresolved: the increased likelihood of multiple births and dilemmas regarding surplus frozen embryos.

Multiple Births: Perinatal Health

From the outset, conception through IVF has been associated with a higher prevalence of multiple births. Although it is widely believed that the success rate of IVF treatment is higher after implanting multiple embryos, most current evidence does not support this view (El-Toukhy et al., 2018; Human Fertilisation and Embryo Authority (HFEA), 2020). Indeed, El-Toukhy and colleagues argue that multiple births are the greatest avoidable risk of IVF treatment for both mother and offspring, and they pose an unjustified public health burden. Higher multiple birth rates due to multiple embryo transfer are associated with a greater likelihood of premature birth and the need for special care treatment. Practices regarding how many embryos are transferred vary in different countries and clinics and they are influenced by several factors, including the cost of treatment cycles, and the extent to which treatment is publicly subsidised (El-Toukhy et al., 2018).

A self-regulation policy of single embryo transfer (as the safest option for patients of all ages) has led to significant decreases in the rate of multiple births conceived through ART in the last two decades, in Australia (Newman et al., 2021), the United Kingdom, (HFEA, 2020) and the United States (Practice Committee of the Society for Reproductive Endocrinology and Infertility, Quality Assurance Committee of the Society for Assisted Reproductive Technologies, and the Practice Committee of the American Society for Reproductive Medicine [ASRM, 2022]). One key motivation for multiple embryo transfer is the desire to reduce the financial burden of treatment. Having twins (an instant family) and only having to go through the arduous and expensive treatment process once may be appealing (see Josh's story, in Chapter 6). Related practices aimed at boosting success rates by stimulating production of multiple eggs, and then fertilising more embryos than the mother intends to use with the intention of freezing those that are surplus to need, have also raised complex unresolved dilemmas about what to do with surplus frozen embryos.

Surplus Frozen Embryos

As noted earlier, the freezing of embryos has provided many benefits in terms of reducing treatment burden and cost. But what should be done with those that are surplus to need? It is difficult to get a clear indication of numbers, but estimates suggest hundreds of thousands (if not millions) of embryos are in frozen storage throughout the world. This unintended and unwelcome consequence of IVF treatment presents ongoing ethical and legal dilemmas, which pose a significant logistical and resource challenge to clinics. For couples, the challenge is personal, emotional, and financial (McMahon & Saunders, 2009). They have four options regarding their surplus embryos: they can continue to store then as a future treatment option (which becomes problematic if they have as many children as they want); they can opt to have the embryos destroyed; they can donate the embryos for medical research; or they can donate to other infertile couples. A fifth option, to do nothing and avoid the decision, is the most common. A recent survey exploring the intentions of couples with stored embryos had a response rate of just 21 per cent (Zimon et al., 2019).

Couples generally think about the embryos as potential children (indeed siblings of their existing children) and this may be intensified through the experience of 'seeing them' in the laboratory, prior to implantation. A study conducted by McMahon and colleagues (2003a) showed that couples were aware of the potential benefits of donating the embryo for medical research. The idea that the embryo may contribute to more effective IVF treatment, as well as breakthroughs in stem cell research and the treatment of debilitating diseases was appealing, as they felt it had improved their own chances to conceive. Nonetheless, a relatively small number choose to donate for this purpose. Many used emotional language and vivid imagery to describe their concerns. As one woman put it 'I feel I should, but the reality is, it's hard to know my possible baby is a specimen'. Another said: 'I wouldn't feel comfortable with the idea of them cutting up and study-ing something that would have been a baby had nature been fair to us' (p. 875). A more recent Belgian study also found that just a small number (10–15 per cent) choose to donate surplus embryos for medical research. Provoost and colleagues (2012) suggest that counselling that provides details about the nature of the medical research, whilst acknowledging and addressing clients' emotional attachment to the embryos, could make this option more acceptable.

While donating embryos appeals to an altruistic desire to help oth-ers who are also struggling with infertility, most do not consider this option, and just 10–15 per cent opt to do so (Daniels, 2020; Zimon et al., 2019). This has led to a stark shortage of donated embryos relative to demand. Again, studies show that reluctance relates primarily to the meaning of the embryo for the couple: 90 per cent view the embryo as their own child, or potential child, and feel an ongoing responsibil-ity for its wellbeing, sometimes coupled with a desire to control who the recipient is. Examples of written respondent comments in a survey study of 99 women with stored frozen embryos (who had opted not to donate) included: 'I don't want someone else raising my flesh and blood'; 'I worry about the calibre of the people and their parenting abil-ity'; 'I would always wonder if the child was OK and being cared for' (McMahon & Saunders, 2009, p. 144).

Millbank and colleagues (2017) point out that most of the available research focuses on those who choose *not* to donate, with scant information about those who do. Their small study, which followed 26 potential embryo donors, concluded that those who chose to donate found the process straightforward, and did not view it as analogous to adoption. Rather, donors de-emphasised genetic relatedness, and focused on gestation and caregiving as markers of 'real parents'.

Clearly there is much to be resolved. Clinics are grappling with growing numbers of abandoned embryos; some embryos are stuck in legal limbo. There have been court cases regarding custody and ownership of stored embryos after one genetic parent dies, when there is divorce, when legislation regarding consent changes, or when couples simply can't agree what to do with them. If embryos are stored indefinitely, the responsibility will pass to the next generation. There are debates about commercialisation, and whether the regulatory frameworks that surround adoption should be applied, with widespread consensus that more education, support, and research are needed (Zimon et al., 2019).

Costs, Equity of Access, and Commercial Exploitation

Who should fund fertility treatment and costly antenatal screening? Some suggest there are more deserving priorities for public health budgets, while others express concerns that the high cost of IVF treatment to individuals (even when there is a public contribution) raises broader issues of equity of access. They advocate for more affordable ART in low-income countries (Crawford & Ledger, 2020; Inhorn, 2020). In some high-income countries, notably the United States, there are marked disparities in access to healthcare in general, and to ART more specifically (Faircloth & Gürtin, 2018; Guzzo & Hayford, 2020). There is clear evidence that uptake of ART treatment varies in relation to affordability, when comparing within and between countries (Inhorn, 2020). In Australia where there is a relatively high uptake, the out-of-pocket cost for a single treatment cycle represents 6 per cent of average annual disposable income; compared with 12 per cent in Japan, 13 per cent in the United Kingdom and 44 per cent in the United States, where treatment uptake is the lowest in the world (Raymer et al., 2020). Low-cost IVF (with a focus on affordable protocols through avoiding excessive investigations) offers some hope of addressing inequity of access in low-income countries (Bahamondes & Makuch, 2014). Meanwhile in the United Kingdom and Australia, there is heated debate about the proliferation of so-called 'add-on' treatments. There is currently limited evidence of success for techniques such as screening for embryo quality using pre-implantation genetic diagnosis, which has the potential to greatly increase costs to both individuals and health systems (Handyside, 2020).

Cultural acceptance of ARTs and broader regulatory frameworks are also important determinants of treatment access and uptake (Raymer et al., 2020). In some jurisdictions single women and gay couples are not able to access treatment (or public subsidies for treatment), and in many commercial surrogacy is illegal. This has led to complex and expensive transnational reproductive care known as 'reproductive tourism', whereby individuals travel to other countries to receive treatment, as well as an international market in sperm, eggs, and embryos and the contracting of women (often living in developing countries) to act as surrogates. These practices have the potential to aid and abet the exploitation of women living in poverty. We return to these issues in Chapter 6.

The Egg Freezing Debate

The trend across all developed countries to postpone childbearing is a major contributor to involuntary childlessness, infertility, the need for ART, and high multiple birth rates. While discussion tends to focus on maternal age, with the implicit assumption that women are choosing to prioritise their career or social life over childbearing, evidence shows that one of the main explanations women provide for postponing childbearing, and for choosing to freeze eggs is that they either haven't found a partner or they have a partner who is not willing to commit to parenthood, as discussed in Chapter 1 (Hammarberg et al., 2017a, 2017b; Inhorn, 2020). It is women who bear the brunt of responsibility for fertility decision making, the demands of infertility treatment, and the challenge of reconciling the demands of work and family when trying to juggle caring for children with a career.

Egg freezing has been presented as a potential game changer (Argyle et al., 2016). Originally developed to preserve fertility in women undergoing chemotherapy treatment for cancer, egg freezing for non-medical reasons is increasingly common, but still controversial. Some argue that it increases autonomy and choice for women and reduces the likelihood of involuntary childlessness. Other potential benefits include lessening the pressure that many women experience in their early thirties to find a suitable partner, and the opportunity to establish a career or pursue career goals that might be constrained by having a baby (Mertes, 2015). There are concerns, however, that the technology offers false hope, as success rates are relatively low and highly dependent on the age of the woman when the eggs are frozen: 15–25 per cent for those aged 25–35, and 6–10 per cent for those who freeze their eggs after the age of 37 (HFEA, 2018). Given these success rates, presenting egg freezing as an insurance policy against age-related infertility may encourage women to postpone childbirth, with the consequence that they ultimately fail to achieve the personal goal of parenthood (Hammarberg et al., 2017b).

There is a clear risk of commercial exploitation unless women are fully informed about costs, risks, and age-related outcomes. The procedure is expensive (between $10,000 and $15,000 in Australia and the United States), and this does not include ongoing costs of storage and IVF treatment, if, and when, the eggs are thawed for use (Hammarberg et al., 2017b; Beilby et al., 2020). Egg freezing is generally not publicly funded so access is restricted to high-income women. There has been scant research on the experiences of those who do freeze their eggs, but current evidence suggests that only about 10–15 per cent of women ultimately go on to use them (Hammarberg et al., 2017b). Perhaps most concerning is the fact that currently most women who do freeze eggs do so at an age when it is unlikely to result in a successful conception. While it is recommended that women freeze eggs when they are under the age of 35, most do so when they are 37 or older (HFEA, 2018).

Interestingly, while the technology has been commercially available for approximately twenty years, few women consider it, and those who do generally don't proceed (Sousa-Leite et al., 2019). Sousa-Leite and colleagues argue that women should be informed by primary health care practitioners about egg freezing as an option for fertility preservation. According to Hammarberg and colleagues (2017b), however, any such suggestion implemented as routine care would need to be accompanied by detailed individualised counselling. Fully informed consent requirements include disclosure about benefits, risks, diverse outcomes related to age at freezing, and evidence-based information about the numbers of women who ultimately return to use their frozen eggs to ensure that only those for whom it is genuinely the best available option take this path.

The Commodification of Life?

As discussed earlier, feminist scholars have argued that reproductive technologies have contributed to a view of women's bodies as sites for foetal growth – 'gestational environments' that are a potential threat to foetal wellbeing. Eggs, wombs, sperm, and embryos can become products for sale, with attendant testing technology ensuring 'quality control' and possible litigation for damaged goods. It is certainly common practice in jurisdictions that allow a commercial market for eggs, sperm, and embryos that donors are paid, with prices and marketing focused on the desirability of their physical and intellectual attributes. Taken to its extreme, pregnancy could be viewed as a production value chain leading to a society structured around a small number of expensive, precious children conceived as investments in the future. This harks back to the dystopian future first envisaged by Huxley in 1932, and further explored with respect to exploitation of women as reproductive 'handmaids' by Margaret Atwood in 1985. Perhaps the most salient concerns about commodification of women's bodies arise in the context of surrogacy. Popular films *Baby Mama* (Michaels, 2008) and *Juno* (Reitman, 2007), both explore the power relationships between commissioning mothers (usually older and well-off) and young (generally poor) surrogate mothers, and the potential for the young women's bodies to be viewed as baby incubators, with genetic parents seeking to control the surrogate mother's lifestyle and diet.

Court-ordered pregnancy behaviour and a mandated caesarean birth were described in the landmark Baby M custody case in the United States when surrogate Mary-Beth Whitehead did not want to hand over the baby after birth (Whitehead & Schwartz-Nobel, 1989). Ultimately, the commissioning mother, Elizabeth Stern, was awarded custody, with Whitehead having visitation rights. A different complication emerged in the more recent 'baby Gammy' case in 2014. Pattaramon Janbua, a surrogate mother living in rural Thailand, was left to care for a twin with Down Syndrome after the commissioning parents from Australia elected to accept only his typically developing twin sister. A follow-up media report (Cochrane, 2017) found Gammy was doing well at preschool, assisted by charitable donations achieved through crowdfunding sourced in Australia, but his mother was still struggling financially and worried about his future.

Highly publicised cases defined by conflict are the exception rather than the rule, however. Dystopian cautionary tales about reproductive technologies have generally been a far cry from current mainstream practice, and the sensationalised negative scenarios that were anticipated to flow from conception through ART have generally not come to pass. As noted earlier, evidence regarding psychological development and adjustment in ART families suggests normal development of offspring and positive family functioning. Likewise, despite a more complicated context, a recent systematic review indicates generally positive psychological wellbeing in surrogate mothers, and the children produced through surogacy, although the research is sparse and most studies have significant methodological limitations (Söderström et al., 2016) While these findings are reassuring, concerns about commercial and emotional exploitation cannot be dismissed and more research is needed (see Chapter 6 for further discussion of this issue).

Designer Babies: A 'Slippery Slope'?

From the earliest days of IVF there were fears that the science underpinning reproductive technologies could be misapplied. This debate intensified with the advent of PGD, which enabled selection of embryos with specific genetic characteristics. Jones and McMahon (2003) surveyed young adults in Australia and found that fears that ART had the potential to devalue and commodify life were commonplace. Threatening dystopian scenarios co-existed with more rational evaluations of the benefits of the technology. Respondents were particularly concerned about scientists 'playing God' and 'tampering with nature', concerns raised by theologians and bioethicists from the inception of ART. Some expressed concerns about the potential for long-term impacts on evolution should particular genotypes be selected or eliminated.

One ethically challenging consequence of the widespread use of antenatal testing is a broader intolerance of human imperfections, atypical development, and disability (Rothman, 1986/1993), as well as a reduction in social structures that support alternative choices (for example choosing to raise a child with a disability). PGD also raises the possibility of selection of embryos with socially desirable traits (intelligence, sporting ability, height, or sex), however with the exception of sex selection, this remains largely beyond the capability of present-day medicine, at least in the case of PGD. PGD is applicable to monogenic (single gene) traits, but complex traits like intelligence are multigenic. In many countries, the United Kingdom and Australia, for example, regulatory bodies have specified that PGD should be restricted to chromosomal or genetic conditions that can affect the likelihood of a live birth or those that result in a serious medical condition (Crawford & Ledger, 2020). There are concerns, however, about trends for PGD (originally implemented with a specific diagnostic objective) and recent expansions in applications of cell free DNA technology in the first trimester to evolve into pre-genetic screening for overall 'quality and sex' (Inhorn, 2020; Thomas et al., 2021). What constitutes a 'serious medical condition' remains an open question: Autism? Deafness? Gene mutations that predispose to bowel and breast cancer?

Sex Selection and Gendercide

Should parents be assisted to select the sex of their child? Many clinics and regulatory bodies do not condone the use of PGD for the purpose of family balancing (selection of embryos for implantation based on their sex), nonetheless the practice is widespread (Bhatia, 2018). Indeed, PGD for sex selection is a multi-million-dollar industry in the United States (Sharma, 2008). PGD aside, many parents can now access information about child sex earlier and earlier in pregnancy which means a pregnancy can be terminated based on child sex. Together these screening techniques have contributed to a significant and growing gender imbalance in the world population, most marked in societies where male gender is privileged (or required, for a firstborn). This application of reproductive technologies has long-term and profound social implications (Inhorn, 2020). There is ongoing debate; some bioethicists and scientists argue that the right to information about child sex is a fundamental reproductive freedom, while others believe it represents the ultimate commodification of human life and a threat to population demography through disruption of male–female sex ratios.

The Technological Imperative

Just because we can do something, should we? Some feminist scholars have argued that the availability of ART has consolidated pronatalist views, and that it pressures couples (women in particular) to become parents, rather than make a positive decision to be childless or adopt. There is an undeniable pressure to know the knowable – surprise discoveries at the time of birth may soon be a thing of the past. Tymstra (1989) pointed out that most patients feel they cannot refuse a medical opportunity when it is offered to them, and that they are usually willing to accept any side-effects and financial drawbacks. He called this phenomenon 'anticipated decision regret', a reluctance to turn down diagnostic or therapeutic possibilities – evident in the difficulties couples experience terminating IVF treatment, despite a poor prognosis (da Silva et al., 2018).

Screening technologies have far-reaching consequences for individuals, families, societies, and the public health budget. There are serious implications of false positives (when a problem is incorrectly identified) and false negatives (where a problem is not identified). Despite advances that have increased the accuracy of antenatal tests, some couples have to deal with ambiguous results and make difficult choices. In the case of adverse results, the decision to terminate to prevent the birth of a child with a disabling condition is profoundly challenging and distressing. Earlier (first trimester) testing has made this easier, but early imaging has added intensity and grief to the relatively common experience of first trimester pregnancy loss. As ultrasound during pregnancy has become normalised, some women will feel pressured and not able to decline for fear of being considered alternative, or irresponsible (Edvardsson et al., 2015). In 1989, Tymstra anticipated the public-health implications of screening all pregnant women for age-related risks such as Down Syndrome. Thirty years later, Oster (2019) describes a suite of available tests that is limited only by financial capacity.

Science and technology are a package deal. Once available and established, it is difficult to cherry pick and judge some to be acceptable and others not. Allowing contraception and life-saving interventions for premature babies, implies acceptance that science can and will over-ride nature. Rather like the case of mobile phones, the technological genie is out of the bottle. Further, individuals seem prepared to experiment with the tools at their disposal – taking their chances and using new technologies when they don't have rigorous evidence of effectiveness, and sometimes at great personal cost. Egg freezing is a case in point.

From the outset, advances in ART have outpaced attempts to evaluate their impact, to understand their social and cultural meaning, and to address concerns about ethical and legal consequences. Inhorn (2020) argues that ART is 'good to think with' (p. 47) and she urges social scientists to actively engage with the impact of ART in social and family life. Who should bear the burden of proof? If a technology does have proven benefits, who should pay? Who should have access to the technology? Should treatment be publically subsidised? Proponents of individual rights to engage with whatever science can offer argue that in the absence of evidence of harm, individuals should have an unfettered opportunity to take advantage of new scientific advances. The precautionary principle, on the other hand, would suggest that when technologies have the potential for far-reaching individual and social consequences, the onus in on the scientists and practitioners (particularly when there are large profits to be made) to prove no harm, as is the case with new developments in pharmaceuticals.

New Frontiers and New Challenges
To date ART has not delivered all that its proponents claim it can deliver. Nor has it delivered all that its opponents fear. Golombok (2015, 2020) questions whether it is important or even feasible to try to regulate the range of reproductive technologies on offer across different borders and

legal jurisdictions. There are new frontiers and new challenges on the horizon, including children being born through mitochondrial DNA transfer, who would have genetic material from three people, a father, a mother, and a woman who donates her mitochondrial DNA (Dimond, 2015); and ectogenesis whereby embryos would be fully gestated in an artificial womb (Romanis, 2018). Oocyte cryopreservation, combined with ectogenesis, has the 'revolutionary potential' to extend reproductive capacity to transgender men (Inhorn, 2020, p. 53). There is talk of uterine transplantation for transgender women (Winter, 2019). Families can be arranged online, including a plan to co-parent without any face-to-face engagement or commitment (Golombok, 2020).

In some ways ART is deceptively simple – science and technology have provided the means for a diverse range of people to become parents and to overcome the fertility problems and social barriers that have been a cause of anguish and stress for many. Ethical debates about potential future developments may sound remote from the concerns of the infertile adult who just wants to become a parent, but deciding to embark on conception using reproductive technologies requires engagement with these issues: Would they consider egg freezing? What are their views on donated eggs or sperm? Disclosure to the child? What will they do with surplus embryos? For those considering becoming a parent using ART, findings regarding overall typical developmental outcomes for children conceived through IVF are reassuring. The large numbers of children who have been conceived in this way has 'normalised' the process, but this should not blunt sensitivity to this special and complicated pathway to parenthood (McMahon & Gibson, 2002). Reproductive technologies are taxing on women's bodies, on emotions, on relationships, and on finances, as discussed earlier in this chapter. Reproductive technologies have opened new possibilities for forming families, but they have also changed the subjective experience of conception, pregnancy, and birth. The ways in which conception using reproductive technology can influence the subjective experience of pregnancy and the transition to parenthood is a key focus of this book and is discussed in more depth in the following chapters, particularly Chapters 5 and 6.

CHAPTER 3

Becoming a Mother

Becoming a mother is a momentous rite of passage (Rich, 1986). Being pregnant changes everything: a woman's body, her appearance, her primary occupation, her understanding of herself in relation to other people, and her autonomy. For the foreseeable future, she will be responsible for someone else's wellbeing (Laney et al., 2015). There are obvious costs – physical discomfort, personal time, sense of competency – but resolving inevitable conflicts, developing new skills and a new relationship can also engender feelings of personal growth and a new sense of meaning in life (Benedek, 1959; Morse & Steger, 2019).

For much of the twentieth century, the transition to motherhood was viewed as an existential 'crisis' (LeMasters, 1957), and many heart-felt personal accounts emphatically endorse this perspective. More recently, psychological theorists have preferred to characterise the transition as a 'normal', but complex period of adaptation involving transformation and re-organisation physically, psychologically, and socially (Nelson et al., 2014). In this chapter the biological, intra-psychic, and developmental processes involved in becoming a mother are discussed, taking account of the social context in which the pregnancy unfolds (Belsky, 1984; Bronfenbrenner & Morris, 2006). Theory and research are reviewed to explore why the transition to motherhood is relatively smooth for some women, yet overwhelmingly difficult for others. The chapter concludes with an overview of research on psychological wellbeing and mood problems in pregnancy. A historical perspective on theories regarding the transition to motherhood is informative in understanding how representations of motherhood have evolved over time. We begin with influential developmental theories.

A Developmental Perspective on Becoming a Mother

Life-course theorists describe a series of developmental tasks across the lifespan (Billari et al., 2011). Socially prescribed normative ages for key life transitions represent a pervasive set of '*shoulds*' defined by family models, culture, and gender (Neugarten, 1979). Neugarten's 'social clock' theory proposes that development is more likely to proceed smoothly when the socially endorsed life-course is not interrupted. Problematic adjustment is more likely for 'off-time' events, for example a teenage pregnancy or a first pregnancy when a woman is in her forties (Billari et al., 2011; Neugarten, 1979). The social clock varies in relation to culture, social class, and economic resources. Longstanding social norms for adult developmental milestones are being challenged, however. As discussed in Chapter 1, the 'normative' time for becoming a parent has shifted significantly in recent decades, in part due to broader demographic changes and the difficulties women encounter reconciling career and childbearing goals. This has led to significant conflicts between biological and social clocks (Daly & Bewley, 2013). For many contemporary women, the decision to become a mother represents a deeply willed and epic commitment, rather than a natural or automatic life-course progression (Wolf, 2003).

In the mid-twentieth century, women theorists from a psychoanalytic tradition proposed an influential developmental theory to explain the process of becoming a mother, and this theory has had a pervasive and enduring influence on social representations of motherhood. Becoming a mother was considered a normal and a necessary stage of development for women – one that would provoke significant psychological and physiological re-organisation and precipitate personal growth. If successfully negotiated, becoming a mother would enable new levels of maturity, psychological integration, and fulfilment. On the other hand, not becoming a mother would stunt adult development. Failure to resolve inevitable conflicts, formulate new insights, and integrate the new role would lead to adjustment problems and less responsive parenting, with negative consequences that could echo across generations. Many aspects of this theory have been challenged, particularly the idea that women need to have a child to achieve meaning in life and fulfilment (as discussed in Chapter 1).

Psychoanalytic Theory: Developmental Tasks of Pregnancy

Psychoanalytic theorists describe sequential tasks that need to be mastered during pregnancy as pre-requisites for healthy mothering: adaptation to the biological reality of pregnancy; integration of a new identity as a mother; the development of a relationship with the unborn baby; and renegotiation of relationships with partner, extended family, and the outside world, in order to create an accepting space for the baby (Benedek,

1959; Bibring, 1959; Deutsch, 1945). Becoming a mother is viewed through an intergenerational lens: past and present representations of caretaking relationships need to be reconciled during the transition to parenthood.

Adjusting to the Biological Changes of Pregnancy

> All human life on the planet is born of woman ... the one unifying incontrovertible experience shared by all women and men is the months' long period we spent unfolding inside a woman's body (Rich, 1976, p. 11)

Pregnancy is a quintessentially female experience (Rich, 1976/1986). Women live the transformative process through their bodies. While life goals and options have changed dramatically over the last fifty years, the biological condition of women remains largely unaltered. This is nowhere more apparent than during pregnancy and lactation. The profound impact of a woman's biological legacy has defined and limited her social roles and opportunities, and her physiological states have governed her day-to-day existence (Kitzinger, 1978). Becoming a parent does not impact on the father's body and may be only minimally disruptive to his lifestyle. Woman shoulder most of the physical and emotional responsibility.

The first challenge for a pregnant woman is to acknowledge the reality of her pregnancy and its implications, a process often accompanied by a preoccupation with the self and with changes in body functions (Deutsch, 1945; Raphael-Leff, 2005). These changes are all encompassing – body shape, sleep patterns, energy, fitness, exercise tolerance. There are also changes to blood volume and cardiac output, hormonal fluctuations that influence metabolic, cognitive, and psychological functioning, and long-term changes to the brain and neuro-endocrine systems (Hoekzema et al., 2017). Changes to the oxytocin system and surges in levels of oestrogen and progesterone in late pregnancy are believed to contribute to heightened emotionality and sensitivity that prepare women to become attached to and protect their developing infants (Kohlhoff et al., 2017). The pregnant woman must manage these changes in her body and her own reactions to them, as well as the reactions of the people around her.

In almost all societies there is a collective social commitment to ensuring the safe passage of infants, and this can make a pregnant woman feel that her body is public property: both vulnerable, and dangerous. There are numerous cultural taboos regarding what a pregnant woman should and should not do. They represent a public recognition of the importance of pregnancy and childbearing to individual parents and the broader community, but they can also be experienced as intrusive, restrictive, patronising, and judgmental (Kitzinger, 1978; Wolf, 2003). To promote the health of the unborn baby, pregnant women are encouraged to change the way they eat (restrict certain foods and eat more of others), exercise (avoid high core body temperatures), and socialise (alcohol, caffeine, and smoking are strongly discouraged). As the baby grows and the pregnancy advances, women gain weight and move further and further away from socially prescribed body ideals of thinness as attractive that are pervasive in high-income Western countries (Fuller-Tyszkiewicz et al., 2012).

The numerous 'normal' discomforts during pregnancy are legend: nausea, fatigue, and painful breasts in the first trimester; backache, ligament pain, and heartburn (reflux) as the pregnancy progresses. Childbirth educator Judith Lothian (2008) contends that these changes should be regarded as indicators of health and femininity; a reassuring confirmation that the pregnancy is progressing as it should, rather than unfortunate symptoms and side-effects. In her view, these body changes help the woman to negotiate the transition in her body and in her mind. Lothian is critical of contemporary highly medicalised pregnancy care, arguing that it can undermine a woman's intuitive harmony with the normal physiological changes of pregnancy.

Women differ in how they respond to these body changes and the meanings they attach to them. There is generally some ambivalence, but some embrace the changes. Vanessa Gorman, finally pregnant after years of longing for a child, was enthusiastic about her changing body shape. She saw it as an endorsement of her femininity and sexuality: 'The tender pride of being round and soft in a hard-bodies world ... I am in love with the shape she makes, and secretly steal glances at myself in the mirror, both alarmed and proud of this enormous swelling.' (Gorman, 2005; 2006, p. 125). There may be a sense of alienation, however, from a radically changing body. As pianist and writer Anna Goldsworthy (2014) writes: 'I view my new body in the mirror. Somewhere within it lies my old body, as scaffolding for these giant, rude appendages: this bulge that contains you, these bulbous breasts' (p. 47).

Research on body image in pregnancy is surprisingly limited. Clark and colleagues (2009) conducted a longitudinal study of Australian women during the transition to parenthood and found that most adapted positively to the body changes and weight gain of pregnancy, especially in the second and third trimesters, with more negative feelings in the first trimester and the first few months after birth. These researchers suggest that in the context of relentless social pressure towards thinness, pregnancy may represent a unique time when the functionality of the female body can be appreciated, rather than objectified. For once, weight gain has a purpose and can be viewed as acceptable, even desirable. A minority do struggle with body image concerns, of course, but it was not clear in this study whether these concerns were more prevalent than in non-pregnant cohorts of women. Body satisfaction in pregnancy was lower for women who had experienced body image problems in the past and for those with depressed mood during pregnancy and after the birth.

Psychosocial Challenges: Taking on a Maternal Identity
Being pregnant changes how a woman sees herself, how she sees the world around her, and how others see her. People she hardly knows may treat her as though she is fragile, others cross personal boundaries, asking her if they can touch her swelling stomach. She is on the threshold of a new identity and a new life role: the 'taken for granted infrastructure of her life ... is questioned and begins to crumble' (Hartrick, 1997, p 271). The pregnant woman is challenged to rework her sense of self so that she can form a clear and confident image of herself as a mother (Mercer, 2004). These identity shifts take time and require a constantly evolving reconciling of the new identity with the old.

According to theorists from a psychoanalytic perspective, imagining a future as a mother involves reflecting (sometimes unconsciously) on one's own past as a needy infant (Fraiberg et al., 1975) as well as current views of self and future life goals (Raphael-Leff, 2005). This reflective process is influenced by a woman's current state of mind regarding her early child-hood relationships with her own mother (Chodorow, 2004; Huth-Bocks et al., 2004). Research suggests the identity shift is easier for those who recall their mother as a compassionate and supportive caregiver (Rholes & Paetzold, 2019). The process is more complicated for those with memories of maternal rejection or unpredictable emotional availability. Some will be determined to be a different mother to the one they had, while others may struggle with unrealistic perfectionistic expectations based on representations of an idealised mother (Snell et al., 2005).

Social Constructions of Motherhood. The pregnant woman must also consider the extent to which she is willing to accept socially constructed scripts of femininity and idealised images of mothers (Faircloth & Gürtin, 2018; Oakley, 1986). Feminist scholarship highlights the burdens imposed by powerful, culturally endorsed ideals of what a 'good' mother should be: selfless, unconditionally loving, always present, fully devoted to the wellbeing of her child. These representations fail to acknowledge the mother as a subject in her own right, and, if embraced inflexibly, they can lead to a loss of self and autonomy (Chodorow, 2004; Hays, 1998). Mauthner (1999) argues, however, that contemporary pregnant women have agency; they can do more than passively internalise social constructs and prescriptive roles. Several recent qualitative studies confirm this. Women's narratives about becoming a mother indicate that they actively construct their own maternal subjectivity and identity, whilst at the same time reclaiming and maintaining crucial aspects of who they were before the pregnancy. Culturally sanctioned images are influential and prevalent in women's narratives of motherhood, but modern women can and do flexibly integrate multiple identities; they are able to combine personal aspirations with anticipated mothering activities; autonomy with interdependence; and project an extended sense of self into the future (Maher & Saugeres, 2007; Sheridan & Bain, 2020).

Some women believe their identity will be enhanced and enriched by pregnancy and motherhood; for others, pregnancy is a threat to their sense of self and independence. For most it is both. The transformation can be exhilarating and daunting at the same time. Whether welcomed or not, the transition to motherhood for most women involves some sense of loss, fracturing, and redefinition (Laney et al., 2015). The sense of self is crucially changed by the presence of a very particular and dependent 'other' (Sheridan & Bain, 2020), and the reality of a lifetime commitment. Writer and documentary maker, Vanessa Gorman experienced this impending identity change as exhilarating: 'A deep peace settled over me, even as heart and mind raced ahead, reconfiguring myself as a parent' (p. 123). For many women, however, there is ambivalence. Naomi Wolf (2003) describes a process of quiet mourning for the demise of her former identity as a carefree and independent individual, and the challenging process of rebirth as a messier, interdependent mother.

The development of a maternal identity is a complex, fluid, and continuous process that interweaves who the woman was in the past, her current pregnant state, and the future goals that are important to her sense of self. The pregnant woman is challenged to redefine aspects of herself, and her past and future relationships, whilst salvaging those parts of her former identity she values most. These profound changes in self-definition, thinking, and emotions are difficult to capture empirically. Most of the 'data' about the process come from literary reflections about becoming a mother (motherhood memoirs) and clinical anecdotes from the therapist's couch. Perhaps unsurprisingly, prospective studies using in-depth interviews (Leifer, 1977; Shereshefsky & Yarrow, 1973) and self-report questionnaires

(Camberis et al., 2014) have shown that women who are more positively engaged with the process of maternal identity formation during pregnancy report a smoother transition to parenthood and more positive psychological adjustment in the early months after birth.

Camberis and colleagues (2014) explored how the process of taking on a maternal identity influenced the transition to motherhood in a large sample of pregnant women in Australia. Consistent with findings from an earlier study in the United States (Heinicke, 2002), these researchers found that those with a more positive response to taking on a maternal identity scored higher on personality measures of ego resiliency and hardiness, and that this cluster of personality traits predicted less vulnerability to depression after childbirth. Both constructs capture a sense of agency and internal control and an adaptive flexibility when faced with changing environments or circumstances – a tendency to view change as an opportunity rather than a threat (Gramzow et al., 2000).

Some limitations need to be acknowledged. Adaptation to motherhood was assessed by mothers' own reports, so the results may reflect socially desirable responding and/or an unquestioning attitude to traditional views on women and motherhood. Narrative interviews allow women to tell their stories in a nuanced way, and they enable a more sophisticated assessment of the ambivalence that typically characterises the messy process of identity transformation. Interviews can also reveal defensive responses. A *highly* positive identification with motherhood based on idealised views of pregnancy, young infants, and self as parent can leave women vulnerable to violated expectations, guilt, and disappointment – something much discussed in experiential writings about early motherhood. The context of the pregnancy is important. Research has shown that women who have struggled to achieve a pregnancy, for example after infertility, are more likely to report highly positive identification with motherhood (see Chapter 5 for more discussion of this topic).

Representations of self as mother that acknowledge ambivalence and negative aspects of the new role are adaptive (Raphael-Leff, 2005). In this regard, it is interesting to note that in the study by Camberis and colleagues (2014), women who were older during their first pregnancy and those with higher levels of education reported *lower* scores for identification with motherhood. Perhaps these women felt they had more to lose in becoming a mother, with more established independent lifestyles and a greater investment in their occupational role. This is consistent with Oakley's (1986) findings thirty years earlier – women who endorsed and embraced a traditional feminine identity were more likely to have a smooth transition to motherhood, while the sense of self was more threatened and disrupted for those with strong career goals.

According to Rubin (1984) taking on a maternal identity and forming an attachment to the foetus are interdependent coordinates of the same process. As Anna Goldsworthy (2014) writes, directing her comments to her unborn baby: 'this pregnancy is changing more than just my body. Who am I, if not my preferences and characteristics? Am I still myself, or have I metamorphosed permanently into something else, some tandem being of me-you?' (p. 30).

Developing a Relationship with the Unborn Baby
As the pregnancy progresses, the expectant mother becomes increasingly aware that she is no longer alone. 'Quickening', the time in the second trimester when a woman is first aware of the movements of the unborn baby, has traditionally been viewed as a pregnancy milestone when the foetus is recognised as a separate living being, albeit a mysterious and not quite human one. As discussed in Chapter 2, however, the widespread use of ultrasound screening earlier and earlier in pregnancy has meant that expectant mothers (and fathers) are aware of the presence, appearance, and viability of the unborn baby long before the baby's movements are perceptible. After her ultrasound at 10 weeks, Goldsworthy (2014) wrote:

> And there you are, a frantic beating inch. Obscured by my tears you are blurry as a distant galaxy, except for the insistent flashing of your heart. I feel such tenderness for that heartbeat, for its certainty, its dogged commitment to life. It is the good that trumps everything. (p. 8)

Just a few weeks later, the image is more differentiated, and the process of attributing personality and feelings is more elaborated:

> At twelve weeks, you have grown fingernails and a pancreas. Pain has been switched on. Sometimes you cry silently in the womb. But what do you have to cry about, little bean? Are you lonely in there with your unseen, unknown face? (p. 14)

As the intense physical side-effects of the first trimester abate, the expectant mother's attention is increasingly divided between the demands of the external world and the foetus within. She draws on her imagination, her experience of ultrasound images, and her growing awareness of foetal movements and biorhythms to elaborate a representation of this largely unknown being – she may converse with the foetus, stroke her abdomen, or play music to soothe it.

Some ambivalence is inevitable, indeed ubiquitous, however much the baby is wanted. At times, the expectant mother will wait eagerly for signs of activity and life; at others, reminded that she is no longer her own person, she will wish for quiet and a reprieve from the presence of this hostile stranger (Raphael-Leff, 2005) who looks and feels like an alien, not yet human, and not yet lovable (Wolf, 2003).

Maternal-Foetal Attachment.   The emergence of fantasies about the foetus is viewed by psychoanalytic theorists as a sign of emotional investment in the pregnancy. Markin (2018) describes a process of prenatal reverie – the expectant mother uses her mind as a play-space in which she can practice thinking about herself as a mother and about her unborn baby. These reflections are driven by a desire to know, understand, love, and care for the developing baby. Images and beliefs about the foetus become more elaborated as the pregnancy progresses and these images form the underpinnings of the developing caregiving system (Slade et al., 2009).

Women differ in the extent to which they engage in conjecture about the unborn child, and they also differ in the kinds of thoughts they have. Mental representations of the infant may be highly elaborated or vague; positive or negative. In the absence of any 'solid evidence' beyond ultrasound and foetal movements, the expectant mother projects both her desires and her fears onto the unborn foetus (Slade et al., 2009). These differences can arise from the circumstances of the pregnancy, whether it was planned and wanted, the effort to conceive, and the medical risk status (see Chapter 5 for a detailed discussion), or the woman's own early attachment history, so called 'ghosts in the nursery' (Fraiberg et al., 1975). Measures of maternal–foetal attachment aim to capture thoughts and behaviours that express affiliation, affection, and a desire to protect the foetus (Cranley, 1993). Research has shown that maternal–foetal attachment is enhanced by ultrasound, particularly 4D ultrasound, and that it increases over the course of the pregnancy, indicating a developmental process (Sedgmen et al., 2006).

Studies have shown that lower scores on questionnaires assessing maternal–foetal attachment are related to an insecure attachment style (Alhusen et al., 2013), elevated anxiety (Hart & McMahon, 2006), and depression symptoms (Alhusen et al., 2013; Brandão et al., 2019) and fewer self-care and health behaviours during pregnancy (Alhusen et al., 2012). There is evidence that higher scores for attachment to the foetus predict more positive adaptation after birth, including responsive maternal behaviour toward the infant (Siddiqui & Hägglöf, 2000), lower parenting stress, and less likelihood of postnatal depression (Alhusen et al., 2013). One systematic review noted emerging evidence that low maternal–foetal attachment predicts less optimal developmental outcomes for the infant, including more difficult temperament and colic (Branjerdporn et al., 2017). Possible explanatory pathways include fewer health promoting (protective) behaviours during pregnancy, the contribution of mood problems in pregnancy to the development of infant temperament and stress reactivity, and less responsive parenting postnatally.

As in the case of maternal identity acquisition, discussed earlier, studies using narrative interviews allow a more nuanced assessment. Open-ended invitations to describe the unborn baby can capture the flexibility of the pregnant woman's expectations, compared with more rigidly held projections, which may be idealised or exclusively negative. For writer Rachel Cusk (2008) the internal baby is inevitably idealised; it is not until after birth that the baby will become human, misbehave, and cry. Anna Goldsworthy (2014) also questions whether a mother can love such a vague and undefined image, and she is hesitant about projecting her fantasies and expectations on to what is, essentially, a blank slate.

Research indicates that *balanced* representations (coherent descriptions that convey respect for the infant's individuality and an openness to both positive and negative traits) are associated with secure attachment with the baby after birth, while distorted representations (inflexible, disengaged, or idealised), have been associated with insecure mother–child attachment (Huth-Bocks et al., 2004). Maternal ambivalence is a normal phenomenon; one that can provoke a creative process of reflection on the differences between the baby and herself, and engender more attuned mothering (Raphael-Leff, 2005).

Social Challenges: Renegotiating Relationships
Anthropologist and childbirth educator Sheila Kitzinger (1978) points out that in most societies, pregnancy is a ritualised state – the pregnant woman has a special place, and relationships with the father of her child, and extended kin groups visibly change in response to her becoming a mother. Birth is significant because it links generations and has a wider social meaning. Rubin (1984) argued that the expectant mother needs to create both a psychological and a physical space for the baby; fantasies about the unborn child are shared with partner and family members, to ensure their acceptance of the child. Opportunities for fathers and other family members to see ultrasound images has made this process easier, and expectant mothers frequently encourage their partners to feel the baby's

movements. The quality of the partner relationship in an important deter-minant of the mother's adjustment during the transition to parenthood (Slade et al., 2009), but making room for a third party in a relationship can be complicated. Expectant fathers may struggle to share their partner's attention as she becomes increasingly preoccupied with the anticipated baby, and there may be changes to the sexual relationship if intercourse is perceived as a threat to the baby (Raphael-Leff, 2005). Relationship sat-isfaction is higher when both partners feel positive about the pregnancy, and more problematic if one or other is depressed or anxious. Father's reactions to pregnancy are discussed in more detail in the next chapter, and in Chapter 6.

Relationships with other women are also important. As noted earlier, many women will seek to re-enact or repair their relationship with their own mother when expecting a first baby. Most societies collectively sup-port the pregnant woman – other women pass on the wisdom of their experiences and try to make her feel safe and cherished (Kitzinger, 1978; Raphael-Leff, 2005).

Challenging Contexts for Becoming a Mother

Every pregnancy takes place against the backdrop of a unique set of life circumstances and a network of relationships with family, commu-nity, and culture. Based on her clinical experience, psychotherapist Joan Raphael-Leff (2005) outlines some of the contextual factors that can make the transition more challenging: the 'wrong mother' (a woman who never wanted a child becomes pregnant); the 'wrong father' (in the worst case, a conception following rape or sexual assault, but also an irresponsible, uncommitted, or absent father), the 'wrong time' (in terms of the mother's development, education, career goals, finances, or the timing in her cur-rent relationship). Sometimes all of these occur together. There are unique challenges becoming a parent for women with a disability. The next section explores how different contexts can shape the experience of pregnancy.

Biological and Social Clocks: 'Off-Time' Pregnancies

There has been a significant shift in the age at which women have a first baby in high-income countries over the last three decades with a decline in the proportion of women becoming pregnant in their teens, and fewer women having babies in their twenties (Weinraub & Kaufman, 2019). The number having a first baby over the age of thirty-five (considered 'older first-time mothers' from an obstetric point of view) has doubled, while the number having a first baby in their forties has tripled in high-income countries (Guzzo & Hayford, 2020). This shift has been attributed to a broad range of social and demographic factors, including access to reliable contraception and abortion, longer periods in education, later partnering, and expectations (sometimes misguided) that access to reproductive technologies will offset fertility problems if childbearing is postponed, discussed in detail in Chapter 1.

Having a first baby at either end of the 'normative' reproductive window has traditionally been viewed by the wider society as 'off-time' and potentially problematic (Neugarten, 1979). 'Off-time' pregnancies pose significant additional challenges. For many decades, substantial public health resources have been directed to preventing teenage pregnancy. More recently, public health campaigns have warned women about the fertility implications of delaying childbearing. The social context and related risk and protective factors are vastly different. For the very young mother, the physical and psychological demands of pregnancy are superimposed on the emotional turmoil of puberty, often in the context of significant social disadvantage. The older first-time mother faces fertility and medical risks, and the potential loss of a well-established identity and lifestyle, but these difficulties are generally cushioned by socio-economic advantage.

Becoming a Mother as a Teenager

While the prevalence of teenage pregnancies is on an established downward trajectory, WHO figures indicate more than 12 million young women aged fifteen to nineteen years give birth every year in low-income developing countries (WHO, 2020). Rates vary markedly in high-income, industrialised countries compared with low-income countries, but adolescent pregnancy, particularly unplanned pregnancy, is a cause and a consequence of social and financial disadvantage in all societies (Weinraub & Kaufman, 2019). Weinraub and Kaufman note that the prevalence of births in adolescent women remains significantly higher in the United States compared to other Western industrialised nations, and there are marked racial and ethnic disparities. While most young women, even those in socially disadvantaged circumstances, are aware of contemporary social norms against early childbearing, they may have limited access to contraceptives and high-quality family planning services, low self-efficacy about controlling their own fertility, and fewer alternative life options (Guzzo & Hayford, 2020).

The negative consequences of adolescent pregnancy have been extensively documented; they are not inevitable, however (Easterbrooks et al., 2019; Weinraub & Kaufman, 2019). Many are attributable to the risky living conditions that gave rise to teenage pregnancy in the first place, rather than the age of the mother, or the pregnancy per se. Insufficient support from the co-parent and poor access to healthcare also contribute to negative outcomes (Conn et al., 2018). For some young women, the pregnancy is a turning point providing an impetus to change to a more positive life path, and new sense of meaning and purpose. For most, however, especially those who have had adverse experiences during childhood themselves, there are significant ongoing challenges for the mother and for her child (Weinraub & Kaufman, 2019).

Biological Challenges. From an obstetric perspective, teenagers may be better suited physically to pregnancy and childbirth than older parents (Drife, 2004). In their review of epidemiological data, Paranjothy and colleagues (2009) found, however, that adolescent mothers in the United Kingdom have higher rates of pregnancy and childbirth complications than mothers over the age of 20. Although much less likely than older mothers to have an elective caesarean, teenage mothers have a high incidence of instrumental deliveries that can be experienced as traumatic. There is also a significantly higher risk of premature birth, low birth weight, and of infants being born small for gestational age. These pregnancy and perinatal complications are largely attributed to lifestyle factors including obesity, smoking, alcohol, recreational drugs, and exposure to domestic violence, all more prevalent in adolescent pregnancies, particularly if young women do not receive antenatal education.

The overlay of pregnancy hormones on adolescent hormones can intensify the emotional lability and fragility that is typical during adolescence. It can be challenging for young women to accept the body changes of pregnancy during a life-stage when body image and peer approval are central to self-evaluation (Easterbrooks et al., 2019). In turn, body-image problems during pregnancy can contribute to depression symptoms and negative eating behaviours that could be harmful to the developing baby (Conti et al., 1998). Findings from a recent review of research are consistent with findings from the broader population of pregnant women: while there is an exacerbation of body-image disturbance for some teenage pregnant women, particularly those who had body-image problems prior to pregnancy, the majority have a positive body image and appreciate a context where weight gain is necessary and purposeful (Zaltzman et al.,

2015). Zaltzman and colleagues note, however, that there is scant research on young women, studies are of poor quality, and more research is needed.

Psychological Challenges. Psychoanalyst Erik Erikson is perhaps best known for his extensive writings about the development of identity in adolescence, and for coining the term 'identity crisis'. Although he paid very little attention to women, Erikson's writings (1950) on adolescent identity struggles in the context of a 'physiological revolution within' are particularly pertinent to the young woman who is pregnant and facing a significant interruption to her expected developmental trajectory. She is faced with the daunting developmental task of separating from parents whilst becoming a parent herself (Raphael-Leff, 2005). Male partners are often absent in teenage pregnancies, but when the father of the child is present, it may be difficult for the young woman to negotiate a relationship with him if the pregnancy has occurred before a commitment is established.

As noted earlier in this chapter, taking on a maternal identity can reactivate early childhood memories. Compared with their older counterparts, teenage mothers are significantly more likely to have been raised in a single parent household themselves, often by a teen mother, and to have suffered adversity, domestic violence, and traumatic events in early childhood (Meade et al., 2008). They are more at risk of Post-Traumatic Stress Disorder (PTSD) (Easterbrooks et al., 2017), and elevated depression and anxiety symptoms during pregnancy, with rates reported to be twice as high as for adult pregnant women (Schmidt et al., 2006). There is extensive evidence that trauma, depression, and anxiety can compromise the capacity to negotiate the developmental tasks of pregnancy (Hart & McMahon, 2006).

Developing a relationship with the unborn baby (including feelings of affiliation, and interactive and protective behaviours) can be difficult for young expectant mothers. The cluster of risks that make adolescent pregnancy likely are all recognised as impediments to foetal attachment (Alhusen, 2008). Alhusen notes a striking lack of research on maternal–foetal attachment in young pregnant women, those from minority groups, and those living in adverse circumstances more broadly. Research with adolescent mothers indicates that, compared with older mothers, they are more likely to have unrealistic expectations of their infants after birth, and these can contribute to negative attributions about 'normative' infant behaviour. They may, for example, feel that an unsettled baby is trying to make their life difficult (Easterbrooks et al., 2017). As foetal attachment is strongly associated with positive health practices during pregnancy and more positive adaptation after the birth, a better understanding of how young mothers develop representations of their unborn infant, and supportive antenatal education that helps them to reflect about their unborn infant as an individual could have useful clinical applications.

Social Challenges. Becoming pregnant as a teenager is a life event with many long-term consequences. While it opens some opportunities, it closes many others, often entrenching health and social inequalities. Becoming a mother can derail the mainstream social markers of attaining adulthood: completing education, gaining employment, and achieving financial independence. Women pregnant in adolescence are less likely than their peers to complete their education and more at risk of facing a lifetime of welfare dependency. As noted earlier, it can be difficult to disaggregate these social consequences from the social risk factors that predispose to adolescent pregnancy in the first place (Easterbrooks et al., 2019).

In high-income Western countries, teenage pregnancy is generally perceived as 'deviant': a social and economic problem, arising from and contributing to inter-generational cycles of poverty and disadvantage (Weinraub & Kaufman, 2019). Teenage pregnant women are likely to face stigma and judgement, sometimes compounded by racial and class stereotyping (Conn et al., 2018), which may be detrimental to their mental health, undermine their confidence in parenting, and make them less likely to attend childbirth classes and social support networks where they could learn adaptive skills to cope with pregnancy and motherhood.

Early marriage and childbearing are considered desirable and encouraged in some cultural and religious groups, and in these community settings teenage pregnancies may be welcomed and supported by extended family (Weinraub & Kaufman, 2019). While it cannot be assumed that the pregnancy is unplanned, even when 'planned', the young woman herself may have limited choice in the matter and limited access to contraception (Easterbrooks et al., 2019). Even when socially endorsed, however, teenage pregnancy is associated with fewer educational and career opportunities. In their recent review, Easterbrooks and colleagues point out that teenage pregnancies in high-income countries are more prevalent in ethnic and migrant communities and in marginalised communities living in poverty, where there are limited educational and employment opportunities.

The experience of teenage pregnancy is not necessarily negative, but shaming, stigma, negative stereotypes, and low expectations can become self-fulfilling prophecies (Sheeran et al., 2021). With support, particularly flexible school options that enable young mothers to complete their education, and access to quality parenting classes designed with the needs of young women in mind, teenage mothers can overcome challenges, experience personal growth and enhanced meaning in life, and help their children to thrive (Easterbrooks et al., 2019). Support services need to be engaging (including social media, social networking and telehealth platforms), welcoming, inclusive, strengths-based, and include skills training and practical help (Conn et al., 2018; Deeb-Sossa & Kane, 2017), discussed further in Chapter 9.

Older First-Time Mothers

In stark contrast to the social context for teenage motherhood, socially advantaged women tend to have a strong sense of efficacy about controlling the timing and context of becoming a mother, and many more opportunities to find identity and purpose outside motherhood (Guzzo & Hayford, 2020). While the demographic correlates and consequences of delayed childbearing are the subject of extensive and ongoing public discussion (see Chapter 1), the personal consequences for women and men have received less attention. Like teenage mothers, older first-time mothers are stigmatised and stereotyped, but in very different ways. They are frequently described by clinicians as 'anxious', 'selfish' and 'difficult', negative views that are generally unsubstantiated (Carolan, 2005; Shaw & Giles, 2009). The 'selfish' label is based on a perception that older first-time mothers have prioritised a 'bucket list' of life projects and lifestyle goals ahead of fertility, pregnancy health, and the best interests of the child. Research shows, however, that many individual influences and circumstances can contribute to delayed childbearing, that it is often neither a deliberate nor a preferred choice (Cooke et al., 2012), and that not having a willing partner is the most frequently cited contributing factor (Hammarberg et al., 2017a).

Biological Challenges.   Falling pregnant is, of course, the crucial first step, and older first-time mothers are significantly more likely to need medical assistance to conceive. It can be difficult, therefore, to disentangle the risks associated with infertility and its treatment from the risks related to age. In general, compared with younger women, older pregnant women have a greater likelihood of miscarriage, hypertension, diabetes, premature labour, low infant birthweight, and caesarean birth (Cohen, 2014). Offsetting these risks, socio-economic protective factors can enable greater choice in healthcare, and participation in antenatal education and health-promoting activities (Fisher et al., 2013). Reporting on a large Australian sample of first-time mothers stratified by maternal age, Fisher and colleagues (2013) found no evidence that negative physical pregnancy symptoms were more common in older, compared with younger pregnant women. The authors concluded that while some pregnancy health problems (pre-eclampsia and placenta praevia) were related to older maternal age, any adverse consequences with respect to subjective wellbeing were ameliorated by access to high-quality multi-disciplinary health care. In this study, pregnancy health and service use were determined more by socio-economic factors than by mode of conception or maternal age.

Hammarberg and colleagues (2013) examined the subjective experience of pregnancy (hassles vs. uplifts) in the same sample and found that older maternal age and conception using ART were both associated with a more *positive* experience of pregnancy. Once again, this difference was accounted for by socio-demographic protective factors. More positive responses were associated with higher socio-economic status. The process of adjusting to pregnancy after the experience of infertility and conception through ART is discussed in more depth in Chapter 5.

Psychological Challenges.   While teenage mothers may struggle to establish an independent identity, older first-time mothers may be concerned about relinquishing theirs, even if only temporarily. The threat becoming a mother poses to an established, autonomous identity as a successful career woman is an existential dilemma extensively explored in motherhood memoirs. From a developmental perspective, the cognitive and coping styles acquired with maturity and life experience (more flexible thinking, reflective functioning, and perspective taking) may help older women to assimilate a new identity and lifestyle without losing a coherent sense of self (Camberis et al., 2014; Raphael-Leff, 2005). Experience managing earlier challenges in personal life or intractable problems in the workplace can contribute to generic problem-solving skills that are adaptive in any new challenge context (Maddi et al., 2011). When asked to reflect on how their age influenced their adjustment to becoming a mother, older first-time mothers have explained that emotional preparedness, patience, self-awareness, resilience, and a more philosophical understanding of the juxtaposition of happiness and suffering helped them to adapt (Camberis et al., 2014; Carolan, 2005).

There are relatively few quantitative studies to date to test these propositions. As discussed earlier in relation to taking on a maternal identity, there is some evidence that older mothers (over 37 years) may be less inclined than those aged 35 or less to enthusiastically endorse identification with motherhood during pregnancy (Camberis et al., 2014). Contrary to pejorative stereotypes of older mothers, a maternal identity that is reality based and acknowledges both negative and positive aspects of the maternal role, and mature self-regulatory capacities can be adaptive when faced with the day-to-day reality of early parenting (Camberis et al., 2014; Carolan, 2005; Raphael-Leff, 2005).

When it comes to establishing a relationship with the unborn baby, older first-time mothers, mindful of age-related medical risk, may be anxious about the survival and wellbeing of the developing embryo, and concerned that something will go wrong around the time of birth. Rothman (1986/1993) has written extensively about 'tentative pregnancies' describing the ways in which a fear of disappointment and loss can lead to a defensive strategy of holding back from attachment to the unborn baby. Fisher and colleagues (2013) speculate that older first-time mothers may have thought long and hard, and also read extensively about the needs of the foetus during pregnancy, contributing to fewer health-compromising and more health-promoting behaviours, which are viewed as behavioural indices of maternal–foetal attachment. We explore how infertility and medical risk influence the development of a relationship with the foetus in more depth in Chapter 5.

Social Challenges. Financial security including established career, secure housing, access to health insurance, and paid help if needed, is highly protective when embarking on motherhood, and in stark contrast to the ecological context of teenage pregnancy. Nonetheless, there are challenges. The likelihood that older women may experience more tension reconciling a maternal identity with a career identity has been noted previously. Women who have a baby at an older age may have less access to support from their own parents, who are also older – the so-called 'sandwich' generation caught between the needs of young infants on the one hand and ageing parents on the other. Other social challenges include being out of synchrony with friends (whose children may be teenagers), and the timing of the birth of the child in the context of the couple relationship. For some couples who meet at an older age, there is pressure to try for a baby in the early days as a couple, before the relationship is consolidated.

To summarise, findings from the most in-depth analysis of age-related adaptation to pregnancy to date (Camberis et al., 2014), indicate that even after taking account of socio-economic benefits, psychological maturity is a key protective factor. Older first-time mothers in this large study were more psychologically mature, and maturity, rather than chronological age per se, predicted positive adaptation to pregnancy and early motherhood, including better mental health. Negative stereotypes predicting problematic psychological adjustment for older mothers have not been supported by empirical evidence. Nonetheless, a medical perspective continues to focus, appropriately, on age-related fertility challenges (including the possibility of involuntary childlessness), the personal and financial burden of Assisted Reproductive Technologies, and age-related risks of adverse perinatal outcomes. We return to these issues in Chapter 5.

Becoming a Mother: Challenges for Women with a Disability

Approximately 9 per cent of women of childbearing age have a disability (ABS, 2018). A statement from the WHO (2011) noted the tendency for healthcare providers to overlook or fail to understand the needs of pregnant women with disabilities, often presumed (incorrectly) to not be sexually active and less likely to have children. As a result, women with disabilities may have limited access to sexual health and reproductive health services, and they may feel invisible in the health system.

Defining disability is complex; people with disability are a heterogeneous group, with diverse needs. In its simplest form, disability can be defined as functional activity and participation restrictions that reflect the interaction between an individual's body and their social setting (WHO, 2011). Challenges for women with disability during pregnancy include physical barriers in accessing services, lack of specialised services, information barriers, problems with communication, and attitudes of health service providers, in particular a lack of flexible, respectful, and responsive care. Pregnant women with disabilities require support through the transition to motherhood that focuses on their abilities rather than disabilities; empowering them, supporting their decision-making, and providing effective strategies to help them overcome practical hurdles in caring for a young infant (Malouf et al., 2017). We return to these issues in Chapter 8, where Katrina, a Deaf mother discusses the obstacles she encountered during the transition to parenthood and Chapter 9, which focuses on inclusive support services for expectant and new parents.

Alternative Pathways

More tolerant attitudes to diverse family forms and more equitable access to reproductive technologies have enabled women to become mothers without a partner, or with a woman partner, either through adoption or the use of donated sperm to conceive. While the psychological processes of adapting to pregnancy are shared by women, irrespective of context and mode of conception, those who become a mother as a single person, or with a woman partner may experience social stigma and exclusion, that makes the process more challenging. Chapter 6 focuses on alternative pathways to becoming a parent. Here, we briefly consider the challenges of being a single parent, either through circumstance or choice.

Becoming a Mother as a Single Woman

Becoming a mother as a single woman can be an unintended or a highly planned event, and the social context and consequences are markedly different.

Unintended Pregnancies. Most women who have an unplanned pregnancy as a single person are teenagers, from disadvantaged social circumstances. The pregnancy is not planned; the father may be unknown, or he may not be willing to take responsibility. The negative social consequences related to financial stress and lack of support for teenage pregnancies have been discussed earlier in this chapter, and they can be further exacerbated if there is no-one to help with the day-to-day practical chores of parenting (Weinraub & Kaufmanm, 2019). Raphael-Leff (2005) suggests that the embracing of a maternal identity may happen more rapidly in young single mothers, when there is no partner to provide companionship. However, we know little about this process, as so few studies of the transition to parenthood focus on young mothers in these circumstances.

Planning to Become a Parent Alone. When the choice to conceive and rear a child alone is carefully planned, the psychological processes of pregnancy are more likely to follow the typical pattern. It is certainly the case that some teenage pregnant women make an active choice to parent alone, judging the partner to be unworthy or unable to support them or contribute in a positive way to the child; perhaps due to a risk of domestic violence. This suggests a sense of agency and self-efficacy, a positive representation of the baby, and a commitment to care for and protect it (Weinraub & Kaufman, 2019).

For the most part, however, women who choose to embark on pregnancy alone are older, and acutely conscious of a ticking 'biological clock'. This is a growing demographic. Weinraub and Kaufman point out that in the United States, the proportion of births to 'unmarried' women under twenty has declined from 50 per cent in 1970 to 13 per cent in 2015, while the percentage aged over thirty increased from 8 per cent to 25 per cent in the same period. There are several ways to achieve a pregnancy as a single woman: having intercourse with a man who will not act as a father; organising self-insemination using sperm from a donor in a known social network, or an anonymous donor (usually through a commercial sperm bank); engagement with a fertility clinic to organise and implement donor insemination; or adoption. The decision to embark on parenthood alone implies a willingness to make significant lifestyle changes and this may be easier for women who are mature and financially stable. The choice sometimes reflects feminist concerns, including a desire to live independently of men and traditional family structure, and a strong commitment to nurturing (Weinraub & Kaufman, 2019). The transition to parenthood for women who plan to have a baby alone is discussed in more detail in Chapter 6.

Wellbeing during Pregnancy: Positive Adaptation and Mental Health

There is debate about what constitutes positive adaptation to motherhood. 'Classic' longitudinal studies (Heinicke, 2002; Leifer,1977; Shereshefsky & Yarrow, 1973) have been informed by psychoanalytic theories that view pregnancy as a crucial stage in the development of women. Positive adaptation to early motherhood is indexed by the mother's psychological wellbeing in early parenthood, her capacity to be responsive to the cues and needs of her infant, and her sense of fulfilment and meaning in life. Findings indicate that prior experience caring for young children, an acceptance of and engagement with the developmental tasks of pregnancy, ease of visualising oneself as mother, and personality characteristics of ego strength, nurturance, flexibility, and hardiness are associated with more positive wellbeing during the transition to parenthood. Scholars from a feminist perspective point out that these indices of 'adjustment' reflect an implicit and uncritical endorsement of traditional, idealised, representations of motherhood. They reify intensive engagement with infant-focused mothering, and they fail to acknowledge the role conflict and relentless demands of combining work outside the home with parenting, and the gendered burden that falls predominantly on mothers (Faircloth & Gürtin, 2018; Oakley, 1986). The construct of parenting stress (Deater-Deckard & Panneton, 2017) focuses on situational, role related, and relational stressors as well as intrapersonal struggles with identity and offers a broader perspective on the challenges in adapting to the demands of early parenthood.

Perinatal Distress

Women are more vulnerable to psychological distress during the perinatal period than at any other time in their lives (O'Hara & Wisner, 2013). Indeed Oakley (1986) contended that the question to be answered by researchers was not why some women get depressed during the transition to parenthood, but why so many women don't! Stress, anxiety, and depression symptoms are to be expected during such a challenging life transition, especially in the context of current heightened expectations of maternal care and overwhelming social scrutiny of parenting, with many new mothers vulnerable to feeling they are not good enough (Faircloth & Gürtin, 2018; Hays, 1998).

Most women do not have a diagnosable mental illness during the transition to motherhood, but many feel emotionally fragile, with intermittent distress and anxiety. It is important to identify mood problems in pregnancy, given evidence that at least half of all postnatal mood disorders are present before birth (Austin et al., 2017; Taubman-Ben-Ari et al., 2019). Unfortunately, many cases of depression and anxiety in pregnancy are not identified and treated. Rather, they are dismissed as part and parcel of the expected emotional and physiological upheaval of pregnancy. Further, women may be reluctant to report their symptoms due to stigma about negative emotions during a time when they are expected to be happy. Psychotherapist Barbara Almond (2010) points out that while the feminist movement of the 1960s and 1970s effectively advocated for a more open expression of ambivalence about motherhood, 'it was never *really* acceptable then, nor is it now' (p. 3).

Mood Disturbances: Perinatal Depression and Anxiety

A large body of international research confirms that about one in ten women experience clinically significant mood disturbances during pregnancy with negative consequences for themselves, their important relationships, their day-to-day to functioning, and the developing infant (Austin et al., 2017; National Institute for Clinical Excellence [NICE], 2014b). Large scale longitudinal studies have identified risk factors for perinatal mood problems, and they closely overlap with the predictors of pregnancy adjustment and parenting stress discussed earlier. A bio-psycho-social framework is useful. Women are most vulnerable when there is genetic vulnerability (for example, a family or previous personal history of depression or anxiety), and/or when there is an imbalance between the demands of the pregnancy and their internal (personality, maturity, coping styles) and external (partner relationship quality, social support, financial stability) resources (Austin et al., 2017). A woman's own early childhood experiences and state of mind regarding attachments in her family of origin are important. Recall of adverse caretaking in childhood and current insecure attachment styles are associated with increased risk of the onset, severity, and persistence of clinically significant mood problems in the perinatal period (McMahon et al., 2005; Rholes & Paetzold, 2019).

Perinatal mood disorders can compromise a woman's subjective wellbeing, her day-to-day functioning, and her capacity to negotiate the developmental tasks of pregnancy, particularly forming an attachment to the unborn baby (Alhusen et al., 2013; Brandão et al., 2019). Maternal mental health problems can impact directly on the developing foetus. There is a growing body of evidence that anxiety and depression in pregnancy predict low birthweight and pre-term birth (Dunkel-Schetter, 2011) and later problems in child self-regulation and social and emotional wellbeing (Korja et al., 2017). It is important to note, however, that adverse sequelae of stress in pregnancy are more likely when mothers live in adverse psychosocial circumstances, emphasising the importance of clusters of risk, the social determinants of health, and the fact that the 'gestational environment' is broader than the womb – it is the social environment in which the person gestates (Lyerly, 2022).

Various explanatory models are proposed to explain the impact of pregnancy mood on the child. These include genetic transmission, whereby a mother's genetic vulnerability to anxiety or depression is inherited by the child, physiological effects of maternal stress hormones on placenta functioning and the child's developing brain and endocrine systems, and caregiving. Pregnancy mood problems predict postnatal mood problems, which, in turn, can compromise caregiving capacity, especially in a context of socio-economic adversity and low support (Goodman & Gotlib, 2002)

The early identification of women who are experiencing difficulties adjusting to the biological and psychological demands and social upheaval of pregnancy is crucial. Early intervention can enhance a woman's experience of pregnancy, her capacity to develop a relationship with her unborn baby, and her relationships with significant people in her life. Social support networks can be activated. Screening and early intervention can encourage women to report when they are struggling and to effectively access social support both before and after the birth (Austin et al., 2017). Naomi Wolf (2003) argues for a need to speak more openly about the dark aspects of the journey to motherhood, as well as the positives, to promote better understanding and empathy and enable better support. Perinatal mood problems are discussed in more depth in Chapter 8, and supportive interventions in Chapter 9.

Different Orientations to Motherhood

Psychotherapist and researcher, Joan Raphael-Leff (2005), developed a model for understanding individual differences in adaptation to motherhood that has intuitive and theoretical validity and practical clinical application. In essence, the model proposes that motherhood has different meanings for different women, that they are vulnerable in different ways, and that they therefore need different types of support at different stages in the process. Supportive interventions that may be 'game-changers' for one woman, won't work at all for another. The model is grounded in psychoanalytic theory, with a focus on two fundamental psychological defensive strategies: idealisation, on the one hand, and avoidance, or derogation on the other. Raphael-Leff explains how early childhood caretaking experiences influence the development of these defensive styles, but the model also takes account of contemporary social constructions of motherhood and the context and circumstances of the pregnancy.

At its heart, Raphael-Leff's model captures the competing contemporary representations of motherhood. While 'categorising' individual women can be overly simplistic and reductionist, she argues that women tend toward one or other of two polarised positions, both of which are maladaptive if adopted in an inflexible way. The *facilitator* orientation (in its extreme form) is one that idealises pregnancy and motherhood as the ultimate fulfilment of femininity, consistent with traditional psychoanalytic representations of motherhood. Women who embrace this orientation are eager to take on a maternal identity; they revel in the body changes of pregnancy, they are preoccupied with fantasies about the unborn baby, and they may form an intense attachment prior to birth. Childbirth is positively anticipated as a natural process; there is a strong commitment to avoiding interventions, and breastfeeding is seen as a crucial way to reinforce a desired exclusive maternal bond, viewed as fundamental to the psychological wellbeing of the infant. Expectations of parenting are highly positive, and there is an unqualified commitment to infant-led care. Negative feelings and ambivalence are neither acknowledged nor tolerated. In short, this orientation aligns with traditional social representations of selfless motherhood, and the view that infants need intensive and exclusive care from their mothers.

In contrast, the *regulator* orientation is characterised by a strategy of minimising the threats that pregnancy and motherhood pose to a well-established, autonomous adult identity. The woman who embraces this orientation is likely to hide the physical changes of pregnancy and avoid maternity clothes for as long as possible. She tries to limit her think-ing about the unborn baby, who is experienced as an intruder likely to deplete her physical resources and change her body in negative ways, and whose relentless demands will threaten her autonomous adult existence. Childbirth is approached with trepidation and planning, and medical intervention is welcomed. Women with a regulator orientation are likely to experience wariness about exclusive breastfeeding, and an intention to include other caretakers (father, grandmother, paid carers) from the outset so they can quickly resume aspects of 'normal life'. Put simply, the facilita-tor enthusiastically embraces the maternal role and plans to unreservedly adapt to the needs of her infant, while the regulator is ambivalent about the changes mothering will bring, intends that her infant will adapt to her, and is focused on maintaining her autonomous identity and lifestyle.

Rigid adherence to either of these orientations confers vulnerability dur-ing the transition to motherhood (Raphael-Leff, 2005). A balanced third 'mid' position is considered the most adaptive. *Reciprocators* can acknowl-edge and tolerate ambivalence about mothering, recognising that there are both losses and gains in taking on a maternal identity. They develop real-istic (balanced positive and negative) representations of the unborn baby; and they plan a flexible approach to infant care that meets their own needs, as well as those of their infant and other family members.

Perhaps the most useful contribution of the model is the explicit acknowledgment of positives and negatives about becoming a mother. For those working with women during the transition to parenthood, the model facilitates a non-judgmental understanding that different women are vulnerable in different ways, and a respect for different coping strate-gies. A woman with a facilitator orientation may be strongly committed to a natural childbirth and to breastfeeding on demand, and therefore par-ticularly vulnerable if her baby is unexpectedly born prematurely, (perhaps an emergency caesarean section), there is separation straight after birth, and breastfeeding is not possible. On the other hand, a woman with a regulator orientation will prefer a more predictable and medically man-aged birth and may plan to leave the baby in the care of a nanny and return early to work. In her case, an unexpected or precipitate labour that precludes use of pain relief, or a change in circumstances requiring her to stay at home with her baby with limited support, rather than returning to work, may be particularly threatening and distressing. Women with a regulator orientation tend to be more vulnerable to depression in the early months of parenting (Raphael-Leff, 2005), a time that tends to be dominated by the almost exclusive maternal care that breastfeeding requires. The model also has useful application in understanding individual differences in how women cope with the challenges of early parenting. We return to these issues in Chapter 8.

Summary Comments

In summary, the experience of pregnancy is life changing, challenging for all, and profoundly disorienting and distressing for some. Many will experience subclinical symptoms of depression and anxiety and a substantial number (about 10 per cent) will experience mood disorders that are personally and functionally debilitating (Austin et al., 2017; NICE, 2014a). Some anxiety is appropriate and potentially adaptive in a first pregnancy, and there can be a fine line between making sure the pregnancy distress is adequately identified and treated, if appropriate, and over-pathologising the inevitable disequilibrium that accompanies adjustment to a major life transition. Different women are vulnerable in different ways, and they need different types of individualised support. This chapter concludes with two women's stories of becoming a mother. Jamila describes how an unexpected pregnancy changed the course of her adult life, and the identity struggles she faced in becoming a mother; Daisy describes the process of reconciling traditional Chinese and modern views on childbearing and the complexities of extended family support.

Jamila's Story: An Unexpected Pregnancy

Jamila was 28 years old, recently engaged to her partner, and on an exciting upward career trajectory, when she discovered she was pregnant.

> It was an enormous shock because I was on the pill. It just hadn't occurred to me that pregnancy was a possibility. I had imagined I'd be well into my thirties before I had children. I knew I wanted them, but it wasn't something that was on my radar for the next five years.

At first, she could think only about what was immediately in front of her: 'I was focused on what being pregnant would be like. I wasn't thinking about the birth; I wasn't thinking about raising a child. I was just thinking about getting through the next eight months'. The first trimester was very challenging. Jamila experienced significant nausea which peaked each morning, at exactly the time she had to lead a busy team meeting. The fatigue and lethargy were unlike anything she had ever experienced before, and they were compounded by a requirement to commute by plane between two city offices every week. She pushed through, but on weekends, she found she could do little other than sleep.

The middle trimester was easier. Jamila felt physically better, stronger, and she began to enjoy some of the changes to her body: 'all the pregnancy clichés: glowing hair, healthy fingernails; a swelling body. Before I'd felt uncomfortable with my body, but now I could say – here's the reason I'm gaining weight and looking different. I could point to my belly'. By the time she reached the third trimester, however, she started to feel more and more uncomfortable, and frustrated about the physical limitations imposed by pregnancy: 'I wasn't good at pausing to be impressed at what my body was doing. I focused on all the things my body couldn't do instead of marvelling at the fact that it was doing a whole lot of amazing things'.

From the outset, Jamila was curious about the sex of the baby. She was convinced she was having a boy, and felt frustrated at having to wait for confirmation:

> I was used to being in control. I was running a big team at work. I had a busy life, but it was a controlled life, and I'm someone who gets a lot of confidence from feeling in control. I felt so out of control when I was pregnant. Having my instinct that it was a boy confirmed was really very important to me. I felt like it legitimised a sense of control over this one thing. I was happy when I found out, and happy that I was right. I'm surprised how important it was to me. It gave me some concrete sense of what I was preparing for.

When asked to reflect on when she first felt a connection with the baby, Jamila pauses and reflects:

> To be honest, it was probably a good ten weeks after he was born. I really didn't feel connected during the pregnancy. I did a lot of planning, but my planning was functional, and it was very focused on my work. I was more focused on

preparing my workplace to be without me, than on preparing myself to be with my baby.

Jamila's partner had an immediate and strong emotional response to the baby. Within an hour of the birth, he turned to her: 'Don't you just love him?' The process was more gradual, and more tentative for Jamila:

> I remember thinking … hmmm, 'he's alright'. I quite liked him, but I didn't have that overwhelming sense of love. That just didn't come for a while … Once he started smiling and cooing, around five to six weeks, I started to feel a relationship with him and that's when I began to settle in. It started to feel like a human connection, rather than me just trying to keep something alive.

Taking on a maternal identity was also a gradual process, partly attributable to her 'off-time' pregnancy. As Jamila explains:

> I had never been someone who wanted to hold other people's babies. I've always liked little kids, but babies have never really interested me, until I had one. Most of my friends hadn't had babies. It wasn't what the people around me were doing. That made it harder. I felt like I was on my own.

After the birth, she felt disconnected from her former self for some time:

> Previously I had always defined myself by my work. If I wasn't working, then who was I? I experienced quite a strong dislocation of purpose. Around three to four weeks after birth, I remember feeling quite distressed, and wishing I could go back to my life before. It didn't last a long time … I was willing to take on this new job and do the work. I just couldn't see how the previous version of my life in anyway fitted into the current version.

In the end, becoming part of a community of mothers was a turning point. Jamila was living in an inner-city location, away from family, and none of her close friends were mothers. Then they moved to a suburban neighbourhood where several of her partner's friends were living. They all had babies and young children, and they made Jamila feel welcome:

> It started to feel like there was a community that I wanted to be part of; a status: 'I get to be one of these; I'm part of this'. That really helped me. A lot of the challenge for me was around identity and feeling lonely and isolated.

Despite her enthusiasm for her career and her strong work ethic, going back to the workplace she had invested so much in was difficult and confusing:

> When I went back to work – and I had loved that workplace – I felt like the whole place had moved on from me. I was back – same title, same salary. I just didn't belong. I tried to carve out a place for myself again, but I ended up leaving after a couple of months because I couldn't seem to reconcile the new version of me in the shadow of the old version of me.

Jamila's relationship with her partner didn't change much during pregnancy, but there was a huge shift from the night she gave birth.

> I assumed I would be competent during labour, the way I am in life. It would be straightforward, I would be in charge; it would be hard work, but I'd be able to get through it. But it wasn't like that at all. I was like a really frightened little girl. I needed it to be over. I depended entirely on J. He was extra-ordinary.

After that she felt much more willing to lean on J. for support, confident he would look after her in a crisis. He'd had more experience with babies, growing up with siblings who were a lot younger:

> I had a sense that everything was going to be alright because he had it in hand, rather than I had it in hand. This was a big change. The baby has meant we have more fun together. We've welcomed the most entertaining little person you can imagine into our home. And he's there twenty-four hours a day. We can be funny and joyful and silly together.

When asked to reflect on how becoming a parent has changed her, Jamila pauses for some time and then explains:

> It's helped me to take a step back from my professional self and value my whole self. I lean more into family and friendships than I used to. Rather than prioritising just one version of myself, I want to wear all of those different hats.

She didn't know it at the time, but the unexpected pregnancy changed the course of her life:

> I can't have more children. So, I still marvel every single day that I got to do this. A surprise pregnancy, and then finding out I was unable to have more children not long after that. It's changed me – it's made me more grateful. It's been the biggest privilege of my life to be R's Mum and it could easily have not happened at all, but for the incredible luck of the Pill not working.

Daisy's Story: 'The Traditional Way is the Right Way for Me'

Daisy* grew up in the South-West region of China. In her early twenties she travelled to Edinburgh, Scotland, where she studied for her Masters' degree and doctorate. It was a radical change and a brave move. After returning to China, she visited Australia, to explore graduate employment and research opportunities, and met her future husband, Joe, on a ferry on Sydney harbour. (Joe had emigrated to Australia, was training as a chef, and came from a large family in Borneo, Indonesia.) Daisy begins her story of becoming a parent by explaining the intensity of her desire for a child, heightened by cultural and peer pressure:

> I had wanted to become a mother since I was very young. I always loved chil-
> dren. When I returned to China to work [after studying abroad], I felt a lot
> of pressure. Between the ages of 27 and 32, I was single and working, and I
> had a long-distance relationship with Joe. All around me, friends had become
> mothers. All my peers, my cousin who I had grown up with, they all had very
> cute babies. I wanted to become a mother too. I wanted it so much, that for six
> months I could hardly sleep because of this pressure and longing.

In the same month that she and Joe were married, Daisy became pregnant. She was surprised and delighted, as she had expected it would take some time. At first, she felt hesitant to tell her mother. 'When I became pregnant, I felt that my identity changed – I had become another person's mother. I felt I couldn't yet accept this new identity, and I couldn't share it with my mother. But then I did tell my mother, and she was very happy.' The news was welcomed by her family and friends, with great celebration.

Daisy was content during the pregnancy: 'I felt like my wish had come true. I really wanted to become a mother. I was so looking forward to having this baby. Every day I was talking to him'. She spent the first trimester with her family in China. In Chinese culture, family support is fundamental during pregnancy. The first trimester is viewed as very risky, vigilant care is the norm, and her mother was very attentive. Daisy wasn't to do any housework at all, she was not to exercise, nor walk too much. Her mother took her to the hospital if there was even the slightest twinge or discomfort:

> We have lots of taboos – what you can and cannot eat. We cannot eat any cold
> food during the pregnancy - no crab, no raw fish. Children mean a lot to the
> Chinese family – it is your heritage, your bloodline, from your family, it is your
> parents' grandchild. And it is also important for your parents-in-law. They all
> care very much for your baby. They will buy clothes for the baby; they will want
> to look after you. You become the most important person in the family.

In the second trimester, Daisy flew to Australia to join her husband, Joe. At the first ultrasound scan, they were able to find out the sex of the child. Joe wanted a boy, but Daisy had very much wanted a girl. According to Chinese folklore, having a girl meant she should eat strategically – lots of fresh fruit and absolutely no spicy food. This would ensure a daughter with beautiful skin. When she learned the baby was a boy, she was initially disappointed, but this was soon offset by being able to enjoy a big bowl of 'hotpot' (Joe was a chef, very attentive, and the food was good – and spicy!)

The second half of the pregnancy was a lonely time. New to Australia, Daisy didn't have many friends, and she relied heavily on Joe for support. Luckily, it was forthcoming, and Joe prioritised her every need. He cooked the dishes she was 'permitted to eat', accompanied her to the doctor, and even when she went for walks, to exercise. He explained that Daisy was the number one person in the family and that he needed to organise his life around her wellbeing.

Daisy's parents joined her in Australia later in the pregnancy, as she was beginning to focus on the birth. She had a strong desire for a natural childbirth:

> From my knowledge I think labour is the best way for the baby. The child's brain will get more stimulus during the birth process. Giving birth to a baby is a natural thing for all animals, so I wanted to do it in the most natural way.

A scan about four weeks before the due date, however, suggested the baby was growing very big and he had a large head. Daisy was small, and her doctor advised her to opt for an elective caesarean section. She was very disappointed and keen for a trial of labour. Her mother intervened. She was emphatic that Daisy should have a caesarean section. Daisy reluctantly acquiesced.

Joe was with her for the caesarean birth, holding her hand, and he was astonished by how quick it was. Just five to six minutes in the theatre and he was a father. He felt overcome with emotion, elated. For Daisy, the birth experience was bewildering. When they put the baby on her chest in the operating theatre, she just felt tired; she didn't feel ready. It was some hours later, back in her room when she was alone with her baby, that a deep sense of contentment and joy gradually surfaced. Once home, her parents looked after her according to the Chinese tradition; she was not allowed to do anything at all during the confinement period:

> I think that was quite correct for me. Even though I had Western education for a few years, I still think that's the right way; the traditional way. If other people look after you, and you look after yourself, you will have good health into the future. I deeply believe the first month after you give birth will shape your body immunity. If I was not careful to avoid washing my hands with cold water, to avoid wind, to do no work for the first month, I would have problems in my body in the future.

While Daisy strongly endorsed these traditional practices and extended family involvement, she is open about her unresolved feelings about the birth, and the challenges she experienced taking on a maternal identity:

> My parents were always helping me, so I didn't have a chance to take the role of mother. The mother should make the decisions for the baby, how to look after

him. But for me, my own mother dominated. I did not have much say. I just had to listen to what she thought was right. For example, how I should give birth. My mother made me have a caesarean. Sometimes I think, that because I did not let Aydan come out naturally. I am not a very good mother ... He came out very quickly. I felt like I prepared for nine months, I prepared for so long, and he came out in just five minutes. C-section makes everything so easy and quick. If you watch a drama, you want to have a very dramatic ending that you will remember for a life-time. I felt the C-section was not the ending I expected. I cannot redo it. It caused unhappiness and conflict with my mother. She explained to me that she had experienced a very difficult delivery and didn't want her daughter to suffer as she had done. That makes me feel less resentment.

And after the birth, I felt like I was an assistant in how to look after my own baby. I know that this is common in Chinese culture – the grandparents will have lots of involvement in the first two years. Then, when my parents had to leave Australia, I felt completely overwhelmed with the responsibility. Looking after the baby, house-chores, my milk had dried up, I felt very, very tired. One day when the health visitor came, I just cried, and cried, and cried. I was overwhelmed.

More than a year after the birth, Daisy reflects on how becoming a mother has changed her:

Becoming a parent has changed me a lot. But in my mind, I still want to be the person I was before. I love the relationship I have with Aydan. I am the one to feed him, to look after him, to give him the stimulation, to comfort him. To take responsibility for him. To choose childcare for him. I always think of his best interests. In the longer term, he is an independent boy. I want to give him freedom to follow his interests. I want to encourage that. Every time I see Aydan, I see he is so happy, so carefree. He looks very content. I am proud of Aydan and proud that I have cared for him. Yet, fundamentally I still want to be a person who has other parts of life. Who still has independent dreams, I want to work, I want to become an independent woman who can have a career; I want to do both.

* Names have been changed.

CHAPTER 4

Becoming a Father

From the moment that sperm hits egg, we treat mothers as the proper parents and fathers as their gormless accessories.

(Crabb, 2019, p. 6)

Expectant fathers have always been viewed as the 'support act' when it comes to caregiving. Across history and across cultures, men have been largely excluded from the rituals of pregnancy and birth. When they were finally invited into the labour ward in the 1970s, they were generally deprived of the opportunity to provide meaningful support and frequently ridiculed (cartoons featured nurses looking after fainting husbands). Writing in 1978, anthropologist and childbirth educator Sheila Kitzinger (1978) pointed out that in Western culture there were almost as many expectant father jokes as there were mother-in-law jokes. Almost fifty years later, there is incremental (albeit very slow) progress toward gender equity with respect to men's involvement in the lives of their infants and young children, and there is a growing scholarship of fathering. Most expectant fathers now attend the birth of their child and accompany their partner at preparation for childbirth classes. Nonetheless fathers are still marginalised, and stereotyped as inept 'buffoons' (Crabb, 2019; Sturrock, 2020). They frequently feel excluded and patronised by antenatal education and perinatal health services, and this limits their emotional engagement with the pregnancy process (Kowlessar et al., 2015).

The discourse around fathering is evolving in parallel with a more nuanced understanding of gender and masculinity (Preisner et al., 2020; Thomas et al., 2018). Still, fathers who want to be equal co-parents actively involved in the nurturing of their infant face many barriers – low caregiving knowledge/skills, ill-defined and gender stereotyped role expectations (Fillo et al., 2015), and social and work structures that don't support their day-to-day involvement with the child (Crabb, 2019).

There is extensive evidence that fathers make an important contribution to children's development (see Lamb & Lewis, 2010, for a comprehensive review) and support their partner's mental health and wellbeing during the transition to parenthood (Fletcher et al., 2020). There is relatively little written *about* fathers, and even less *by* fathers (Sturrock, 2020). There is a significant gap in research and theory focused on understanding the impact of becoming a parent on men themselves (Parke & Cookston, 2019). Men are under-represented in the transition to parenthood literature, and even more so in the broader genre of parenting memoirs. Indeed, most early research about fathers focused on the impact of father absence, followed by studies with a very narrow focus on quantitative measures of father involvement – namely hours or minutes per day spent with children (Lamb, 2010). Most of the information about fathers has been provided by the child's mother, with men given little opportunity to describe their own experiences (Draper, 2003). This chapter focuses on how men navigate the transition to fatherhood. Why do some men enthusiastically embrace the experience while others are disengaged? Why do some thrive, and others develop mental health problems? Theory and research are reviewed to explore the interaction of biological, psychological, and social influences on the experience of becoming a father. The chapter concludes with two fathers' accounts of their transition to parenthood.

Theoretical Perspectives on Becoming a Father

Compared with the transition to motherhood, the paternal rite of passage is less clear. In most cultures, men have seen little place for themselves; and the meaning of fatherhood has remained tangential and elusive, perhaps because physical pregnancy and childbirth are so visible and dramatic (Rich, 1976/1986). Few studies have examined the subjective experience and unique features that characterise the process of becoming a father. Those that have done so show that feeling like an outsider or third party, detached and excluded, is a recurring theme. Theories about mothers have provided templates that have been adapted for fathers and there are few theoretical models specific to men (Roggman, 2004). Most studies employ comparative approaches contrasting the experiences of mothers and fathers; some focus on the role that fathers play in supporting the couple relationship, and the mother's capacity to nurture the infant, with origins in psychoanalytic theory.

Traditional Psychoanalytic Theory on Fathering

Jones (2005) reviews the role of the father in psychoanalytic theory, and he notes an almost exclusive focus on mothering and the mother–infant relationship. The father's primary duty is to protect a necessarily enmeshed mother–child dyad during pregnancy and lactation, and, after that, to gradually support the process of separation. This has contributed to an over-emphasis on maternal and under-emphasis on paternal contributions to healthy and pathological development, as well as a tendency to 'mother-blaming' for any and all child problems, a view that has permeated wider society.

From this perspective, the father's role during pregnancy is containment of the pregnant mother's inevitable emotional upheaval, in other words 'dealing with the environment for the mother' (Winnicott, 1960, p. 43), in order to 'help mother feel well in her body and happy in her mind' (p. 114). Taking on a paternal identity in pregnancy is indexed by the man's capacity to manage his own feelings of exclusion whilst providing a supportive environment for his partner (Cenerini & Messina, 2019; Winnicott, 1960). Interestingly, the experiences of Ben and Christopher, whose stories of becoming a father conclude this chapter, both resonate with this.

The mother-father-child triangle was first articulated in the psychoanalytic tradition: the Oedipus complex positioned the father as the person with whom the child competed for possession of the mother (Freud, 1924). Psychoanalytic theory posits that some fathers may feel similarly competitive with the child for the mother's attention during the transition to parenthood. The framework for parenting is grounded in traditional gender role stereotypes with the father's role viewed as instrumental (provider) rather than emotional (nurturer). The father archetype in Freud's writings was dominant, assertive, a good provider, and remote from the child. Modern psychoanalysts have called for a reconsideration, noting that the attached father can and should provide functions previously associated exclusively with the mother–child connection, such as holding, nurturing, and comforting the infant (Jones, 2005).

Louise Emanuel (2008) proposes a synthesis of gender stereotyped roles, arguing that each parent needs to integrate both maternal and paternal functions. Nonetheless, what she identifies as the 'paternal function' remains gendered, both in language and in focus.

> … each of the parents embodies within him or herself both a paternal and a maternal function, a combined internal parenting couple … The 'paternal function' is characterized by benign but firm boundary and limit-setting, a

capacity for 'penetrative' insight (new ideas and initiatives); the 'maternal function' is characterised by tender receptivity to a child's communication of both pleasure and distress. The combination of these qualities of firmness and receptivity provides a containing framework within which children in both single- and two-parent families are able to flourish. (pp. 187–188)

Attachment Theory and Fathering

Attachment theory has its origins in psychoanalytic theory. Developmental psychologist and psychoanalyst John Bowlby developed the theory following his seminal study of the negative effects of maternal deprivation on children. Attachment theory focuses on the importance of a predictable, emotionally responsive caregiver (usually explicitly the mother) who provides protection and comfort to the infant when threatened or distressed (a safe haven) and also supports the infant's developing autonomy and exploration through providing a secure base (Bowlby, 1982). According to this influential theory, attachment relationships begin as specific affectional bonds with evolutionary significance for survival. The infant distinguishes the primary caregiver from others and engages in caregiver-directed attachment behaviours, leading to an attachment hierarchy, with the mother at the apex. This has contributed to a single-minded focus on mothers, undervaluing or ignoring the potential influence of fathers (Lamb & Lewis, 2010).

In fact, a meta-analysis of thirty years of research has shown that the same relational dynamics can be observed for father–child as for mother–child attachment – sensitive responsive caregiving on the part of the father contributes to the development of secure attachment in the child (Lucassen et al., 2011). Further, it is possible for an infant to be securely attached to the father, while insecurely attached to the mother (Bretherton, 2010), meaning fathers can provide a corrective attachment experience in situations where the mother's caregiving capacity is compromised.

Meta-analyses synthesising a large body of research indicate that inter-generational influences on parenting play out in the same way for fathers as for mothers (Bretherton, 2010; Verhage et al., 2016). Early attachment experiences with parents are organised and stored as internal working models theorised to influence behaviour in the context of intimate relationships across the lifespan. These dynamic, relationally based mental representations of early attachment experiences are strongly activated and particularly salient during the transition to parenthood (Rholes & Paetzold, 2019). Contemplation and reflection on the meaning of parenting and parenthood can activate unresolved early attachment issues for expectant fathers (Palkovitz, 2002). In practical terms, some men are likely to seek close involvement with their children because they are emulating the behaviour of their own fathers, while others are driven by a desire to be a better or more present father (Lamb & Lewis, 2010).

Social Constructions of Fatherhood

Throughout history, family forms, beliefs, and practices have been constantly under revision (Pleck, 2004). In most cultures, the transition to parenthood tends to push couples towards traditional stereotyped gender roles (mother nurturer, father provider), irrespective of the equity of their roles before the pregnancy (Cowan et al., 2010). Breadwinning (or providing financially) has traditionally been viewed as central to a father's role, with caregiving contributions optional (Lamb & Lewis, 2010). It has only been in recent decades that the direct contribution fathers make as nurturers to young children has been recognised and studied (Preisner et al., 2020). Consequently, there is less agreement about what constitutes 'good fathering' compared with 'good mothering', probably to the detriment of both.

The recognition that fathers can and should be involved in nurturing *and* providing has largely been driven by feminist critiques of the gender inequities perpetuated by traditional parenting roles, as women have become more economically productive, career focused, and engaged in public life. A growing scholarship of fathers and fathering in high-income Western cultures in recent years is reflected in public discourse and popular literature. Representations of a 'new' more involved father are evident in films, in media accounts of celebrity fatherhood (Lupton & Barclay, 1997), and in social media campaigns for parental leave equality championed by high profile 'celebrity' ambassadors. A growing number of social media platforms and software applications (apps) are now directed at fathers; they aim to support and encourage their involvement during the transition to parenthood. Thomas and colleagues (2018) conducted a critical discourse analysis of the content of these apps and concluded that they provide user-friendly, accessible information on pregnancy and parenthood. They noted, however, that limited and stereotyped representations persist – of modern fathers 'who are supportive and involved, but who simultaneously embody the position of inept and secondary figures, thus following culturally and historically specific "scripts" that portray fathers as floundering, feckless and flawed' (p. 768).

While women in high-income countries have changed their lives beyond recognition in the last 50 years, men's lives (and particularly their contribution to childrearing and housework) have scarcely changed at all (Crabb, 2019). Social policies in some countries, notably Scandinavian countries and Germany, have made explicit and purposeful attempts to promote and facilitate father involvement (Preisner et al., 2020). In most, however, the tension between breadwinner and caregiver remains largely unresolved – with men increasingly expected to be 'provider-caregiver-all-rounders' in the absence of any meaningful social change to support this (Preisner et al., 2020, p. 39). The gap between public discourse and structural workplace change remains, and a coherent alternative model of fathering has not been fully articulated. We return to these issues in Chapter 9.

In some cultures (notably Italy and France) tensions have been revealed between the social construction of hegemonic masculinity and the emotional availability and physical closeness of involved fatherhood (Sellenet, 2005). Sellenet points out fathers in France who have rejected traditional gender role prescriptions are often ridiculed and caricatured. For example, the French term 'papa-poule' (father-hen), is frequently used as a derogatory description of stay-at-home fathers who are emasculated – viewed as overly maternal and providing inadequate guidance to their sons.

In summary, father involvement in pregnancy and parenting is multiply determined: by cultural background, social constructions of gender roles, workplace structures and expectations, early childhood experiences with parents (particularly fathers), and the quality of the partner relationship (Crespi & Ruspini, 2016). While men are increasingly seeking more involvement, they struggle to achieve this due to inequities in access to parental leave and flexible work practices (Crabb, 2019; Sturrock, 2020). But change is afoot.

A Developmental Perspective

While there are extensive theoretical writings (mostly from a psychoanalytic tradition) on the developmental tasks of pregnancy for women, there is limited theorising on the comparable process for fathers. Confirmation of the reality of the pregnancy is crucial in activating the process, but the biological changes of pregnancy can only be experienced vicariously. Like women, men need to need to acquire a new identity and sense of competence as they transition to parenthood; they need to develop a relationship with the unborn child; and they need to negotiate and manage changes to the couple relationship and their lifestyle – the process of two becoming three (Boyce et al., 2007). This involves an acceptance of loss and change with respect to old friends and lifestyle, and a willingness to adopt new parenting and domestic responsibilities and explore ways of restructuring their workplace demands to make this possible. (Draper, 2003).

Coming to Terms with the Biological Reality of the Pregnancy

Kitzinger (1978) points out that the term to 'father' refers to providing the sperm, while to 'mother' a child suggests a continuing presence for nine months at the very least, and generally for half a lifetime. All the pregnancy action takes place in the woman's body, meaning experiences of pregnancy for men are second-hand, leaving them feeling 'one step removed' (Draper, 2003, p. 565). There are few natural indicators to help a father orient himself in taking on his new role. Many theories on fathering adopt *deficit* perspectives and paradigms – what fathers can't do, and don't have (Palkovitz, 2007), and this is nowhere more pertinent than in relation to biological aspects of pregnancy. Fathers are unable to experience pregnant embodiment and have no direct somatic experience of the developing infant. This can contribute to a sense of unreality, confusion, and alienation (Harpel & Gentry Barras, 2018)

Because of paternal 'disembodiment', the significance of scientific evidence of the pregnancy and the wellbeing of the foetus is amplified for men. Confirmation through sharing the pregnancy test experience, actually seeing the pink line, is particularly important (Draper, 2002). In her ethnographic study of British men during the transition to parenthood, technology and science made the pregnancy real. The pregnancy test provided 'physical evidence', then the bump, then the image on the scan. Draper found that fathers expressed a desire to be involved in the pregnancy, while at the same time struggling to engage with the reality of what was going on. They achieved contact by proxy; frequently touching their partner's body as the pregnancy progressed in order to gain access to the foetal form and movements.

While men don't carry the baby and undergo the dramatic body transformation of pregnant women, there is evidence that hormonal changes prepare them for caregiving. Recent research confirms hormonal oscillations during the various phases of their partner's pregnancy with higher concentrations of prolactin and cortisol in the third trimester and declines in testosterone levels as the pregnancy progresses (Corpuz & Bugental, 2020; Feldman, 2019). Further, despite the absence of body cues, men tend to reduce risky health behaviours when their partner is pregnant, and this can be viewed as an indication of early protective caregiving (Boyce et al., 2007). Brain changes have also been documented. There is more fMRI activation when expectant fathers look at photographs of infants compared with photos of objects, and activation of the amygdala in the emotion processing areas of the brain when they are exposed to the sounds of crying infants (Swain et al., 2014).

Taking on a Paternal Identity

The process of becoming a parent is not defined for men; there are few rituals to serve as external markers Cultural practices and rituals (maternity clothes, avoiding certain foods, medical appointments) and social structures (maternity leave) provide a framework through which women's emerging identities as mothers are externally validated. Maternal identity is socially recognised by default, while fathering has traditionally formed a much less significant part of the masculine identity (Nešporová, 2018). Draper notes that stereotyped images of smoke-filled waiting rooms with anxious expectant fathers nervously pacing up and down the corridor, and the public ceremony of wetting the baby's head, are now outdated. A new generation of fathers are redefining representations of fatherhood and psychological engagement in pregnancy.

Men's identity, role definition, self-esteem, and sense of meaning in life all change when their partner is pregnant. There is ambiguity – men feel they are in a no-man's land, with no fixed role or place (Draper, 2003). Some feel jealous of the intimate, physical connection between the mother and the unborn infant –that they are interlopers in a woman's world (Rowe et al., 2013). Feeling like an outsider – separate, and excluded, is a prevalent theme in men's accounts of pregnancy (Deave & Johnson, 2008; Draper, 2003; Kowlessar et al., 2015), as evident in G's comments when attending a 'men only' group of expectant fathers in Italy:

> I am 40 years old and we are in the 33rd week ... I think the problem is to understand what they feel but also how important we are at this stage ... I could even disappear ... you see her beautiful and beaming while rubbing her belly ... In one thing I'm useful, thank goodness, I'm a musician, and when I'm home she always asks me to play for 'them' – she says, using finger quotes and a bitter smile – for God's sake, of course I do it willingly, but sometimes it seems that I'm not seen anymore. (Cenerini & Messina, 2019, p. 155)

Men are challenged to integrate their own gender identity, their experience of being parented, and their beliefs about what fathers should be, before they can imagine themselves as fathers (Palkowitz, 2002). This requires in-depth psychic work and reflection on the impact of past experiences in early childhood (Cenerini & Messina (2019). Those who lack a relatable model derived from the parenting they received from their own fathers may struggle to develop a model of fatherhood from scratch. A study of Canadian fathers of pre-term babies during the transition to parenthood illustrates the impact of early caregiving experiences. One man reported he was 'worried about being a terrible father like mine. My dad was never around ... I want to be there for my baby when he needs me ...' (Benzies & Magill-Evans, 2015, p. 82).

There is evidence that through becoming parents, men develop a broad sense of generativity; they become more affiliative and empathic with a better capacity to understand self and others (Parke & Cookston, 2019). One of the fathers attending Cenerini and Messina's group reported that becoming a father 'changed everything including my feelings about life, the way I live my life, my expectations for the future – I am more hopeful' (p. 82). Another recent study of Italian first-time parents examined eudaemonic wellbeing (a sense of meaning in life) and found significant improvements across the transition to parenthood with a greater positive change for men than for women (Brandel et al., 2018).

Cultural context and the influence of prevailing gender role stereotypes can still be barriers, however. In Nešporová's (2018) study of Czech couples during the transition to parenthood she noted that Czech expectant fathers had 'hazy' and vague thoughts about becoming a father; they emphasised the provider over the nurturer role and only a few described significant lifestyle changes and meaning in life. She commented on the striking difference in the narratives of expectant fathers and those of their female partners who described their transition to motherhood much more vividly and viewed it as significantly more distinct. The differences were attributed to realistic appraisals of likely changes to everyday life (far greater for women) and traditional (and restrictive) cultural definitions of femininity and masculinity.

The prominence assigned to different components of paternal identity varies in relation to individual, family, and cultural factors. The 'pie-chart' methodology has been used to explore how central a man's 'father-to-be' status is to his sense of self. Participants are asked to assign 'portions' of different sizes to a drawn circle of the self, for example 'caregiver', 'economic provider', and 'partner/lover'. Habib and Lancaster (2006) used this methodology with first-time Australian expectant fathers and found that they viewed themselves as both breadwinners and caregivers – 'partner/lover' was clearly in decline. The prominence assigned to involved father (caregiving) status was related to their feelings of attachment to the unborn baby – the more intensely preoccupied the expectant father was with the foetus, the larger the portion of his identity he assigned to 'involved father'. In a longitudinal study, Cowan and colleagues (2010) also reported that as men in the United States moved through the transition to parenthood, the partner/lover aspect of their self-definition decreased and the 'involved father' proportion increased. Being a 'provider' remains important, but it is just one of several identities that contemporary fathers hold (Fletcher & StGeorge, 2011; Preisner et al., 2020).

Developing a Relationship with the Unborn Baby

Developing a mental representation of the unborn child enables the earliest form of fathering intimacy and, as noted earlier, is an important precursor to bonding with the child after birth (Habib & Lancaster, 2006). Evidence suggests that fathers are keen to develop strong emotional responses to their unborn child (Brandâo et al., 2019; Condon et al., 2008; Habib & Lancaster, 2006). As the experience of the developing foetus is disembodied for men, 4D ultrasound confirms the reality of the pregnancy, reassures them regarding foetal wellbeing, and makes it easier for them to imagine a future with the baby. Knowing the sex of the baby also assists this process, as described by Christopher at the end of this chapter. The ultrasound experience promotes excitement about the impending birth, feelings of closeness, and a tendency to talk to and touch the unborn baby (Harpel & Gentry-Barras, 2018).

Paternal Foetal Attachment

Paternal foetal attachment, like maternal-foetal attachment, is the emotional tie or bond between a father and his unborn baby and is comprised of two dimensions: a subjective feeling of affiliation, love, and protection, and the time the expectant father spends thinking about the unborn baby (Condon et al., 2008). In depth interviews in qualitative research capture this experience for fathers. Rich data emerged from Cenerini and Messina's 'father-only' groups. At thirty weeks' gestation, 'C' was already anticipating separation anxiety and felt resentful of social structures that required him to work early in the postpartum period, limiting his time with his baby:

> I'm convinced I will want to be there right away. I feel bad about leaving him (the baby) to go back to work when I should like to be with him as much as possible and build a close relationship and depth of confidence from the beginning … but it seems that society never thinks about putting fathers in the position to be able to do that … I don't want to become one of those fathers who, on return from work, is left with the job of just saying no and stopping him having or doing things. (Cenerini & Messina, 2019, p. 151)

Two weeks later, C. elaborated further about his enthusiastic preoccupation with the unborn baby:

> I can't wait for my baby to be born – [silence] … it's a baby boy. I'm always thinking about it, how he will turn out, what we can do to make him love us as much as we love him … if it were possible … I imagine him being very similar to my partner, much more beautiful than me, and above all much more intelligent … Lately I sleep lightly, I wake up for nothing, and even F. – my partner – does the same … I don't know if we are 'practising' to become the parents ready to hear the baby's cry … or [it's] just our strong emotional reaction and nothing more. (Cenerini & Messina, 2019, p. 151)

Like mothers, fathers' feelings of attachment to the foetus are compromised if they have elevated depression symptoms in pregnancy (Brandâo et al., 2019). In an unexpected finding, however, Brandâo and colleagues reported that fathers' anxiety symptoms were *positively* correlated with paternal foetal attachment. They noted that the anxiety symptoms were within the normal range, and speculated that the anxiety may have reflected a strong (and perhaps adaptive) concern for the wellbeing of the unborn baby. Christopher's story, at the end of this chapter, is consistent with this interpretation. Similar associations (high anxiety and high attachment) have been found in parents conceiving through Assisted Reproductive Technologies, discussed further in Chapter 5 (Hammarberg et al., 2008).

Paternal foetal attachment is associated with a positive identity as a father as caregiver, coach, and breadwinner (Habib & Lancaster, 2006), and with higher quality partner relationships (Brandâo et al., 2019) and better relationships with parents in the family of origin (Bouchard, 2011). There is evidence that, like mothers, paternal attachment to the foetus increases over the course of the pregnancy, is stable across the transition to parenthood, and predicts more positive perceptions of the child after birth (Condon et al., 2008).

While the available evidence suggests fathers' attachment to the foetus resembles that of mothers, there is scant research. Notably, studies have yet to report on fathers' representations of the unborn baby using more sophisticated discourse analysis of narrative interviews. Interview measures are less likely to be confounded by socially desirable reporting and allow a more nuanced assessment of defensive responding, including the presence of idealised or inflexible representations, or a defensive resistance to reverie and fantasies about the unborn baby.

Two Becomes Three: Renegotiating the Couple Relationship

The couple relationship plays a key role in providing spouses with the emotional resources needed to deal with pregnancy. The quality of the couple relationship influences the extent to which expectant fathers feel they are part of the pregnancy, and this in turn influences the father–child relationship more than the mother–child relationship (Slade et al., 2009). It works both ways: the quality of the couple relationship is both a determinant and a consequence of paternal involvement during the transition to parenthood (Pleck, 2012).

As noted earlier, the focus on how fathers manage the new relationship dynamic – the need to share their partner with the unborn baby, feelings of exclusion and alienation as they are unable to experience the intense connection the pregnant woman has with the unborn child – has its origins in psychoanalytic theory. As 'M', one of the men in the group studied by Cenerini and Messina (2019) commented: 'Yes, I go with her to every visit … but I know that it's useless … it only serves me to feel I am part of it, when I often feel that I'm pushed out, just sitting there.' (p. 155). According to Cenerini and Messina, it is important that men learn to manage these feelings and to stay in supportive contact whilst feeling like an outsider.

Research suggests that secure attachment styles with the family of origin are linked with more adaptive functioning in intimate relationships in adulthood, and specifically with greater marital satisfaction for fathers and mothers prior to birth (Bernier & Matte-Gagné, 2012). There is consistent evidence that for both fathers and mothers, both *avoidant* attachment styles (characterised by discomfort with closeness, dependency, and emotional intimacy) and coping strategies based on emotional distancing, and *anxious* attachment styles (characterised by anxiety about abandonment and negative self-image) are associated with less positive adaptation during the transition to parenthood, evident in higher vulnerability to depression symptoms, lower relationship satisfaction, and more negative views of the baby (Rholes & Paetzold, 2019). We return to this research later in this chapter.

Challenging Contexts for Becoming a Father

In addition to the influence of family of origin attachment experiences, the context for fathering varies in relation to age, sources of support, socio-economic resources, daily life hassles, and work–family conflict (Belsky, 1984; Heinicke, 2002). The couple relationship, discussed earlier is the most proximal, and perhaps the most critical contextual influence. The life-course context is also important.

The Timing of Fatherhood

The timing of fatherhood can profoundly influence the life course trajectory for men, depending on their own developmental stage. Compared to older men, the transition to parenthood during adolescence may be experienced as a life crisis (Cabrera et al., 2000). Adolescent pregnancies are often unintended (though not necessarily unwanted), and, young fathers, like young mothers, are more likely to live in adverse socio-economic conditions. At the other end of the age-span, as discussed already in Chapters 1 and 3, a wide range of life options and changing demographics have contributed to an established trend to embark on first time parenthood at an older age, often referred to as the 'postponement' transition (Hansen, 2012). While the media and public health focus has been almost exclusively directed to older first-time mothers, due to well documented age-related declines in female fertility, research discussed in Chapter 1 shows that one of the key factors in delayed childbearing for women is not having a male partner who is willing to commit to parenting (Hammarberg et al., 2017a).

Teenage and Young Fathers

The typical age for becoming a father varies with marital status, education, and ethnic and cultural background (Eickmeyer, 2016). Teenage fathers have been largely absent from public discourse, with scholars and social policy experts focusing almost exclusively on young mothers (Mollborn & Lovegrove, 2011). Compared to older fathers, teenage fathers are more likely to be unemployed, have low levels of education, and be socially disadvantaged (Berger & Langton, 2011). Financial and educational readiness and emotional maturity are important prerequisites for successful adaptation to fatherhood. Interruptions to education, financial stress, unstable couple relationships, and stigma contribute to lower life satisfaction for teenage fathers. Apart from the broader social consequences for their own development, men who become fathers early in life are less likely than their older counterparts to have contact and cohabit with their partners during pregnancy, and to live in the same household with their children (Cabrera et al., 2000; Guzzo & Hayford, 2020; Mollborn & Lovegrove, 2011).

As is the case with teenage mothers, it is challenging to disentangle the risk factors that predispose to teenage parenthood from the consequences for the young men themselves, and for their offspring. Becoming a father early in life can lead to negative impacts on men's psychological adjustment, and stunt their adult development, even after controlling for their pre-existing disadvantage (Lau Clayton, 2016). While statistical trends are clear for young fathers as a group, Mollborn and Lovegrove found that teenage fathers drawn from a large national birth cohort in the United States were a heterogenous population living in a wide variety of life circumstances. Overall, there were negative consequences of an early transition to parenthood for health and development for the young men and their children, however these negative outcomes were clearly related to social disadvantage and marital status. When young fathers were married to the mother of the child and lived in the same household, outcomes were strikingly more positive. They reported the same challenges and joys during the transition to parenthood as older fathers. Indeed, there were surprisingly few age-related differences in father involvement or attitudes to parenting, nor were there differences in the quality of the father–child relationship. Like teenage mothers, young fathers experience discriminatory attitudes and stigma (Conn et al., 2018). Sheeran and colleagues (2021) argue that negative stereotypes fail to recognise the diversity among teenage fathers, who are collectively belittled and devalued as incompetent parents. When these attitudes are internalised, young fathers are likely to feel alienated from support services (Paranjothy et al., 2009), and disengaged from parenting (Lau Clayton, 2016). We return to these issues in Chapter 9.

Older First-Time Fathers
The public health and social discourse regarding older first-time parenthood has been almost exclusively focused on fertility implications for women, and as a consequence, male experiences of infertility and becoming a parent at an older age remain poorly understood (Fisher & Hammarberg, 2012). Male fertility declines from about the age of forty, although the decline is slower than for women (Ali & Parekh, 2020). Lightfoot (2012) studied the experience of the transition to parenthood for a cohort of older (over the age of thirty-five) first-time fathers, where couples conceiving through ART were over-represented, relative to prevalence in the community. Neither

age, nor infertility and ART conception were related to a broad range of indices of psychological adjustment in pregnancy and early parenthood. Irrespective of age, a secure state of mind related to early childhood attachment experiences was a key predictor of positive adjustment in this sample of fathers during pregnancy and after the birth. See Chapter 5 for a more detailed discussion of the impact of infertility and ART conception on both men and women during the transition to parenthood. Alternative pathways to becoming a father, for example through adoption, or as part of a male couple are discussed in Chapter 6.

Wellbeing and Mental Health

Mastering the strains and challenges typically encountered during the transition to parenthood has the potential to stimulate personal growth and contribute to an enhanced sense of meaning in life. Declines in wellbeing are generally greater for women than for men, Intriguingly, as noted earlier, a recent study reported that compared with women, men experience a greater increase in eudaimonic wellbeing (sense of meaning in life) in response to becoming a parent (Brandel et al., 2019). Positive psychological adjustment in the perinatal period is predicted by general life adaptation, the quality of the couple relationship in pregnancy (Gross & Marcussen, 2017), and a secure state of mind about early childhood relationship experiences (Rholes & Paetzold, 2019).

The experience is not always positive for men. Some expectant fathers experience significant emotional distress in pregnancy including depression (Condon et al., 2004; Paulson & Bazemore, 2010), generalised anxiety (Boyce et al., 2007), and pregnancy specific anxiety (Cameron et al., 2021). Adjustment difficulties for men are also expressed through externalising behaviours, including aggression and increased alcohol consumption (Boyce et al., 2007; Condon et al., 2004). Meta-analytic reviews indicate a prevalence of approximately 5–10 per cent for depression, about half the prevalence generally reported for pregnant women (Paulson & Basemore, 2010) and 5–15 per cent for anxiety (Leach et al., 2016). As is the case for women, postnatal mood problems are predicted by pregnancy mood problems (Paulson & Basemore, 2010). There is some evidence of different patterns of distress for men and women across the transition to parenthood. Several studies have found that while emotional vulnerability peaks in the early months after birth for women, men are likely to experience more distress during pregnancy (Boyce, et al., 2007; Condon et al., 2004) and that men's mood problems after birth may occur later in the postpartum period (Paulson & Basemore, 2010).

Longitudinal studies indicate that men are more vulnerable to mood problems during pregnancy if they have an insecure (avoidant), attachment style and if they report low care from their fathers during childhood (Lightfoot, 2012; Lowyck et al., 2009; Rholes et al., 2006). Boyce and colleagues (2007) found that immature defence styles and neurotic personality traits also confer more vulnerability. Men tend to have less prior experience with children than women do (Leerkes & Burney, 2007), and are likely to feel ill-prepared for becoming a father (Condon et al., 2004; Gross & Marcussen, 2017). Perceived skill deficits and anxiety about their capacity to cope in their new role are significant contributors to postpartum mood problems (Biehle & Mickelson, 2011). This may be particularly the case for young fathers (Lau Clayton, 2016).

Men are less likely to present to perinatal mental health services (Darwin et al., 2017). They typically have more limited social networks, and negative perceptions of help-seeking (Benzies & Magill-Evans, 2015). Feeling guilty about complaining may be a contributing factor. Darwin and colleagues (2017) found that British fathers questioned the legitimacy of their distress and their right to seek help. They felt it could detract from their partner's needs, so they tended to minimise their own difficulties and emphasise the challenges their partner faced. In some cases, these views were linked to concerns about adding strain to already overstretched mental health resources, with men indicating that 'it's not about me' and tending to just 'hold it in': 'I'm always conscious that [partner]'s got it a lot worse, so I just sort of get on with it' (Father 2, p. 5).

Services need to find effective ways to engage and include men, who may feel marginalised and ignored by perinatal health providers working in services that have been developed with mothers' needs front of mind (Kowlessar et al., 2015). Feeling excluded, ignored, or that their distress is not justified or legitimate can contribute to under-reporting of psychological distress, which, in turn, contributes to a failure to implement timely interventions during pregnancy, that could prevent postnatal difficulties. Pregnancy provides a window of opportunity to engage with expectant fathers. They need targeted psychological support and education about parenting during pregnancy, so that they can build knowledge, skills, and confidence (Benzies & McGill-Evans, 2015; Deave & Johnson, 2008). There is promising evidence that social media and online forums can be effective for men who feel excluded, or who feel that information is not tailored to their needs (Fletcher & StGeorge, 2011; Fletcher et al., 2020). We return to this issue in Chapters 8 and 9.

As fathers have become more involved in nurturing their young infants, more attention has been directed to their adjustment during the transition to fatherhood. This chapter has focused on men becoming fathers with a female partner who is pregnant. Recent liberalised attitudes to gay marriage have meant that growing numbers of men are choosing to become parents with gay male partners, through adoption or surrogacy. We discuss these pathways to parenthood in Chapter 6. The chapter concludes with Ben's and Christopher's accounts of becoming a father.

Ben's* Story: A New Depth and Purpose to Daily Life

Ben* was thirty-seven years old when he and his wife, Yumi* (thirty-three), learned they were expecting their first baby. At the time both were working long hours in busy jobs in Japan. When asked when he first started to think about having a child, Ben explained:

> It was something I always thought I would do. My mother worked with babies, and I always enjoyed being around them and learning about how they develop. As I grew older, I enjoyed life without a baby, especially with a busy job, but increasingly felt something was missing – I was ready for responsibility and had love and care to give.

Once they were married, Ben and Yumi were open to idea of having a baby, but there was no explicit timeline. Life was good, professionally and socially. Nonetheless, the confirmation of the pregnancy, when it happened, was welcome. For Ben, the fact that the baby was due around New Year put a clear demarcation point on the transition to parenthood:

> I started imagining life with a baby very early on – this year will be pregnancy, next year will be baby. My parents and friends were very excited, and it was difficult not to share the news widely in the first trimester. Yumi's morning sickness gave the first real sense that the pregnancy and baby would lead to conflicting responsibilities and challenges with work. While home life preparing for the baby was very enjoyable, she had a lot of challenges and worries related to her job, which was stressful.

Because of restrictions related to COVID-19 public health measures, Ben was excluded from face-to-face meetings at the hospital, but he could see the ultrasounds online. There was one with every doctor's visit and he found the scans reassuring:

> Early on, the experience was mainly a sense of wonder at how tiny the foetus is and its growth. Later, there was a great sense of relief that the baby was still growing, as we had had a miscarriage previously.

From Ben's perspective, despite all the scans, the baby didn't feel like an individual during the pregnancy. At that time, he felt primarily connected with his wife, and what she was going through. It was at birth that his own emotional connection with the baby began:

> I don't think I developed a relationship with the baby through looking at the scans, I saw them more as medical milestones. Of course, we joked about the baby expressing himself with kicking and turning in the womb, but during that time I don't think I thought of the baby as an individual. I thought more of my wife and how she was undergoing a transformational experience. But once the baby was born, you could see in retrospect that even in pregnancy he was trying to express himself and was eager for interaction.

Throughout the pregnancy, Ben worried most about the physical and emotional demands Yumi was experiencing.

> She was very busy at work, and she was not well supported in her workplace. This was by far the toughest challenge. She also had a sense of unfairness that all the burdens of becoming a parent fell on her, which was challenging from my perspective. Material matters, preparing the house and so forth, were not so challenging, perhaps because we had a baby relatively late in life, and we were financially secure.

Because of public health restrictions, Ben's opportunities for formal preparation for childbirth were limited:

> I had much less [preparation] than most fathers because I was excluded from the hospital until birth due to COVID-19 restrictions and the materials and classes were in a language I don't speak. My wife was keen to take control of the process herself and was ready to tell me what she wanted from me. There was not much effort on the part of the hospital to include fathers prior to birth.

When he recalls the birth, Ben describes a room set up with everything focused on his wife, 'she was the centre of the world'. He saw his role as making sure that Yumi was OK, and that she felt in control of what was happening. The birth unfolded more or less as they expected. The contractions started early in the morning and Yumi took a taxi to hospital without him (as he wasn't allowed to enter). Early labour was confirmed, her membranes had ruptured, and Ben was permitted to join her at the hospital later in the afternoon, by which time the birth was imminent, and the pain had intensified. The hospital was well prepared. Yumi had an epidural, as planned, and in the early evening their son (a very large baby boy!) was born.

Ben recalls intense emotions when he first saw his newborn infant: 'It was exciting! He was very cute, and quite mature. I felt mainly a great sense of relief that he made it out and my wife was still OK'. He was pleased to be able to hold the baby's hand while the nurses carried out a series of invasive checks and tests straight after the birth: 'It made it easy to understand his existence and his needs and our relationship. I could use my touch to support him through these procedures in his first minutes in the world'.

It was during that evening, when the three of them were left alone in the room, that Ben first began to feel that he was a father and that the baby belonged to him. Yumi was at times too exhausted to stay awake, so Ben appreciated the opportunity to sit there, and quietly hold his son. The hospital was very helpful and supportive in the early days:

> We didn't have to worry about medical basics, just about forming a relationship with the baby and learning his rhythms and needs. The baby was so cute and responsive – he seemed to know how to ensure that his parents would love and care for him.

Ben sees many positives in the changes to his life since becoming a parent, but the twenty-four-hour responsibility of parenthood was the biggest challenge in the early weeks. 'We had to think ahead to ensure that he would be safely cared for, no matter what else we had to do or manage'. Overall, he found becoming a parent profoundly life-affirming: 'It provides depth and responsibility to my existence and a new purpose to my daily life'.

*Names have been changed.

Christopher's Story*: A 'Hands On' Dad from the Start

Christopher was in his early thirties when his daughter was born. He had always known he wanted to become a parent. He and partner Phoebe* (also in her early thirties) had decided to wait until they had a stable base – financial, social, extended family. When the time felt right, they were fortunate to fall pregnant straight away.

His excitement about the pregnancy was tempered by a sense that he needed to protect himself emotionally:

> That first three months is incredibly exciting, and it is also a little bit scary, because you're waiting till you've made it over that three-month hump before you can start communicating the news. At one level, you're emotionally protecting yourself and trying not to get too attached.

Phoebe had severe morning sickness and watching her struggle was hard:

> Males become 'maternal' and protective as well. It's hard for women. You feel quite helpless as a man. You can't stop morning sickness; you can't help her balance the hormones. You just have to do the best you can do and be there. I realised that there were times when Phoebe just needed to vent her frustration, and that I would need to absorb that. It comes with the territory. The helplessness is the hardest thing for men.

He and Phoebe were both in demanding jobs. Christopher's work was particularly challenging at the time, and he felt bad about coming in late each night. It didn't seem fair that Phoebe had to work, prepare his dinner, and also manage the physical demands of pregnancy.

> It occurred to me that I needed to make some really major changes to be able to contribute and help her get through this. I resigned from that job. It was a good opportunity; I ended up taking on all the household chores, so Phoebe could just work and grow a baby.

As the pregnancy progressed, the morning sickness eased, and the baby began to feel more real: 'It was really when I saw her moving on the scan, that I thought there is a person inside, a human form, that had somehow been magically created'. They named the baby as soon as they found out the sex.

> We weren't traditional. We really wanted to know, and we had always known what we would call her if it was a girl. Naming her early gave the developing baby an identity: 'Maggie is making Phoebe sick, she's already up to mischief'. Monitoring her movements and patterns of activity and sleep made her seem like a person.

Even late in the pregnancy, Christopher found himself keeping a lid on his expectations:

> I'm naturally cautious. We really wanted to have a kid and it meant a lot. I was instinctively protecting myself a little bit. You hear stories about things going wrong ... I went through the nesting process with Phoebe, but I didn't feel as connected as she did. I was holding back a bit, just to make sure the baby was OK.

Although he attended classes, Christopher was sceptical about over-preparation: 'I'd had a lot of exposure to babies and for me it wasn't scary. I knew how to hold a baby; I knew the process of looking after a baby'. Thinking ahead to the labour, he was concerned that he would be very anxious, but also confident he'd be a good 'coach', especially when it came to the breathing. Unlike most men, he had seen a baby born:

> When I was 10, I saw my little brother come out of my mother. I'd actually witnessed a birth! So, I knew for sure I didn't want to watch that part. I was going to stay top end and be whatever support I could be from that position.

Unexpected medical complications after the birth, for Phoebe and for baby, Maggie, meant Christopher was catapulted immediately into a hands-on caregiving role:

> It was an emotional roller-coaster for me, that I'm sure I'll never forget. Phoebe [who had a postpartum bleed] had to be rushed off to surgery straight after the baby was born … and I was left there holding Maggie, skin on skin, for 35 minutes without knowing that Phoebe was going to be OK. That was really scary. Then Phoebe had quite an extensive recovery period, so I had to take the lead with the baby over the next 24 hours. Just as Phoebe was becoming more active, medical concerns emerged about the baby. She was transferred to neonatal intensive care, and then had to be transferred to a specialist paediatric hospital.

Christopher moved to the specialist hospital with the baby while Phoebe stayed in the maternity hospital and recovered:

> That was really scary. We had twenty-four hours without her Mum on her second day of being alive. It was certainly not a normal experience, and it was very scary. Then Phoebe was able to join us, which was great. Maggie was fine, but she had to stay in intensive care for tests and monitoring for several days.

It was a rocky start, and not what they had anticipated. Christopher and Phoebe were not able to take the baby home for seven days, but the upside was that they received a lot of support and guidance in baby-care tasks from the nursing staff. The early weeks at home were intense. Christopher was starting a new business, and working from home, due to the Covid-19 pandemic, which meant he had complete flexibility during the day, to hold and be with the baby and give Phoebe some time out. There were lots of benefits:

> I got to spend time with the baby when she was at her best, I wasn't just there for the evening crying, as a lot of men are. Phoebe had another adult to talk to; Maggie became attached to both of us … not just dependent on one person. That crying phase is just so hard; we did shifts.

Christopher took on the 8.00 pm. to midnight shift, every night, when Maggie had her most intense crying period. He was glad he had learned some skills caring for his younger brother: 'I had options – the pouch, the pram, walking, cuddling, but a crying baby hurts you – it really cuts through. It's so much easier with two, working together'.

The delight the baby brought to the whole extended family was the highlight for Christopher: 'We wanted to make sure that we weren't too nervous and over-protective, and we wanted to share her around with everyone. We wanted everyone to hold her. She is the first grandchild'.

He sums up his experience of becoming a parent:

> There is no way you can be prepared for the impact of having a baby on your life – everyone told me, but there was nothing anyone could have said that would have prepared me for the fact that you had to be focused on her and ready to do something for her every minute of the day. You need to give each other time out, because otherwise you're on. We have no pride. We accept whatever help is offered. And we recharge with the power that gives us, and that makes it work.

---

*Names have been changed.

CHAPTER 5

High Stakes Pregnancies
The Impact of Infertility, Risk, and Loss

All pregnancies involve emotional upheaval, uncertainty, and re-organisation, but some are more challenging than others. Pregnancies characterised by intense emotional investment juxtaposed with height-ened risk have been described as 'over-valued' (Raphael-Leff, 2005). There is a great deal at stake: perhaps the pregnancy was difficult to achieve; the couple are older, and they feel this may be their only chance for a baby. There may have been a miscarriage, or a stillbirth in the past; sometimes, all of these. Medical risks in pregnancy can be real or imagined. Either way the perception of risk changes the subjective experience of pregnancy.

Tentative Pregnancies

'Expecting' has long been the colloquial term for pregnancy, a nine-month period of anticipation, preparation, and hope, with a healthy baby as the final reward. Rothman (1986/1993) coined the term 'tentative pregnancy' to describe pregnancies encumbered with uncertainty about the outcome. The couple is hyper-vigilant, seeking one external indica-tor after another to confirm that their quest for a baby will succeed, waiting each time with trepidation for results and reassurance. Tentative pregnancies are plagued with the fear that something will go wrong. In order to protect themselves from disappointment, couples may engage in 'emotional cushioning' (Côté-Arsenault & Donato, 2011) actively containing their expectations and holding back from reverie about the unborn baby. In extreme cases, this can take the form of denying the physical and psychological changes of pregnancy. Reluctant to assume a maternal identity, in case things go wrong; women may choose to keep the news of the pregnancy quiet, and refrain from thinking about the unborn baby – a baby they fear they may never hold in their arms (McMahon et al., 1999).

Does pervasive anxiety during pregnancy have a lasting impact? Theoretical models of adjustment during the transition to motherhood, discussed in Chapter 3, suggest that a defensive approach to pregnancy could lead to problematic adjustment after birth, and compromise the evolving parent–child relationship. This chapter considers the research evidence for this proposition. Tentative pregnancies can also be explored and understood in the context of a growing body of research examining the impact of maternal anxiety and stress during pregnancy on the developing foetus.

Pregnancy-Focused Anxiety

Pregnancy focused anxiety refers to fears and worries specific to the experience of being pregnant, the health of the baby or mother during pregnancy, medical complications of childbirth, and their impact on the mother or the baby. Pregnancy-focused anxiety (sometimes called pregnancy-specific anxiety) has consistently been shown to be a distinct construct, only modestly related to more general anxiety in mothers (Huizink et al., 2004; McMahon et al., 2013).

Questionnaire measures of pregnancy-focused anxiety present direct statements expressing concern about whether the baby is developing normally, or whether something might happen to compromise the baby's survival during childbirth. Respondents are asked to indicate the intensity or frequency of these concerns. Researchers have also used delays in so called 'nesting behaviours' – telling others about the pregnancy; choosing a name for the baby; preparing a nursery – as behavioural indicators of pregnancy-focused anxiety. Longitudinal studies suggest pregnancy-focused anxiety is most intense in the first and third trimesters (Figueiredo et al., 2018).

Chapter 3, presented a model of individual orientations to pregnancy, suggesting that women respond differently based on their early life experiences and the current context of their pregnancy (Raphael-Leff, 2005). Some hold back, minimising or denying the pregnancy for as long as possible, while others are highly invested in the unborn baby from the beginning. While Raphael-Leff linked this orientation to early childhood experiences, she acknowledged current contextual influences. In this chapter we consider the impact of *medical risk* on the woman's orientation to pregnancy, her psychological engagement with a maternal identity, and her developing relationship with the unborn baby. The focus is on women, as is most of the research evidence, but the experience of a tentative pregnancy is likely to be shared with partners. First, the common medical risks of pregnancy are briefly described, followed by a more detailed exploration of research on the experience of pregnancy in different risk contexts, and after pregnancy loss. The chapter concludes with two personal stories of perinatal loss, grief, and adaptation.

Medical Risk in Pregnancy

The medical classification of a pregnancy as 'high risk' can derive from the woman's own medical history (for example diabetes, essential hypertension), her reproductive history (age, infertility, previous miscarriages, or stillbirth), anomalies in blood test results or foetal development that are revealed through antenatal screening or tests, and complications that develop later in the pregnancy, for example, onset of pre-term labour, placental failure. All are more common in older pregnant women, but the associations between maternal age and reproductive complications are complex. Chronological age is not necessarily correlated with biological age or health, and the great majority of pregnancies in older women are relatively uncomplicated with positive outcomes (Cohen, 2014). Nonetheless, as Cohen points out, compared with a group of younger women, a group of older pregnant women will include more individuals with chronic health problems like diabetes, hypertension, or renal disease. Women pregnant at an older age are also more likely to develop complications during the pregnancy, including miscarriage, placenta praevia, and premature labour. The baby is more likely to be small for gestational age and to be delivered by caesarean section. While absolute risk is low, the relative risk of perinatal death is also higher, particularly for women over the age of forty (Vaughan et al., 2014).

Other medical events that can contribute to anxiety about the pregnancy outcome include bleeding during pregnancy (with the threat of miscarriage), and growth problems in the developing foetus (either too small or too large, relative to a normal distribution). Reduced foetal movements or failure to grow later in pregnancy may indicate that the baby's wellbeing is compromised, necessitating regular monitoring. Twin pregnancies are generally viewed as more medically risky.

Coping will depend on how risks are anticipated, perceived, organised, and understood. Risk perceptions will be influenced by personal and family history (attachment in family of origin), prior reproductive experiences (infertility, pregnancy loss), current context (support, stress) and the nature of the medical risk (timing, severity, and significance). The 'controllability' of the problem is important – a medical complication that is predictable, modifiable, and treatable will have a lesser impact on pregnancy adjustment than one that is completely unexpected, and not modifiable. In the next section specific pregnancy risk contexts are discussed and research evidence about how couples adapt is reviewed. The tentative pregnancy construct provides a unifying theme. Many of the risks overlap: older mothers are more likely to conceive through ART, be pregnant with twins, and have a history of pregnancy loss.

Twin Pregnancies

Multiple births have always been considered special and a source of fascination (Holditch-Davis et al., 1999). There are two types of twin pregnancies: monozygotic (one fertilised egg splits), in which case there is one placenta, and the twins are genetically identical; and dizygotic, where there are two different placentas, and the twins are non-identical (fraternal) due to two eggs being fertilised. The latter is more common (Greer et al., 2003). Twin rates vary, but there is relative uniformity about the community incidence of monozygotic twins, about 3 in every 1,000 births. Dizygotic twin rates are influenced by many factors, the most significant being fertility drugs and multiple embryo transfer during IVF treatment, as discussed in Chapter 2.

Twin pregnancies make greater physiological demands on the woman's body, have higher morbidity and mortality rates, and they can be more complicated psychologically (Holditch-Davis et al., 1999). In some cases, one foetus is miscarried, which can complicate grieving and antenatal attachment. Monitoring and conducting diagnostic tests in twin pregnancies can be more complicated: nuchal screening may be preferred to blood tests, and amniocentesis is very challenging – two procedures need to be performed and there needs to be certainty regarding from which sac the sample has been sampled. As a result, some women pregnant with twins may opt not to have tests, so they are not able to be reassured by positive results. Women pregnant with twins are more at risk of premature birth, low birth weight, failure to thrive in one of the twins, and they are more likely to have a caesarean birth (Greer et al., 2003). While some feel joyful and 'blessed' when twins are diagnosed during pregnancy, others have mixed emotions due to concerns about perinatal complications, particularly prematurity, and worry about how they will manage two babies after birth. The process of forming a relationship with the unborn twins may be more complicated: the mother may feel the need to project different fantasies onto each and exaggerate the perceived differences between them, or she may attach to them as a set, de-emphasising individuality (Gowling et al., 2020). Annie, at the end of this chapter describes some of these experiences.

Pregnancy after Infertility and ART Conception

Pregnancies after conception using ARTs challenge theorised normative models of adaptation to pregnancy: the developmental tasks of taking on a maternal identity and developing a relationship with the unborn baby unfold in a different way. All of the vulnerabilities contributing to a 'tentative pregnancy' mindset may be present: difficulty conceiving, the possibility that that this may be the only opportunity to have a child, grief about prior treatment failures and miscarriages, the higher risk (often age-related) of medical complications, perhaps twins. Unique opportunities to see images of the embryo(s) (through early and frequent monitoring and screening) even before implantation, mean that the pregnancy experience is different to pregnancy after natural conception from the outset.

Women respond differently to these challenges. Studies using validated measures in large samples can illustrate overall patterns of adjustment, and in-depth interviews taking account of life history, provide insight into individual experiences.

Replacing an Infertile Identity with a Maternal Identity

The formation of a maternal identity is interwoven with the process of developing an emotional tie to the infant and is an important predictor of adaptation to motherhood (Camberis et al., 2014; Shereshefsky & Yarrow, 1973). As discussed in Chapter 3, the process involves both internal re-organisation of the sense of self and external acknowledgment of the changing role. Due to the protracted period trying to conceive, women with a history of infertility may have idealised motherhood over a long period, while at the same time distancing themselves from a role that they feared they would never achieve (Burns, 2007). As a result, they may have internalised a stigmatised 'infertile identity' such that when they finally achieve their goal of pregnancy, they deny and detach in order to protect themselves from disappointment.

Contrary to theory and expectation, McMahon and colleagues (1999) found that despite intense anxiety about the pregnancy outcome, a large sample of women conceiving through ART did not differ from spontaneously conceiving women from a similar demographic background on their responses to validated questionnaire measures of identification with pregnancy, body image in pregnancy, and self-confidence about mothering. In fact, open-ended responses showed an enthusiastic embracing of the pregnant identity. These findings are consistent with others that illustrate that high pregnancy-focused anxiety can and does co-exist with idealised attitudes to motherhood (Klock & Greenfield, 2000). As 'Janice' explained when asked about how mode of conception and infertility influenced her pregnancy experience: 'If there are any differences, it's that it's better for us. The mode of conception has enhanced the experience of pregnancy, and we expect it to enhance the experience of parenthood as well' (McMahon et al., 1999, p. 353). 'Judy', another study participant, enthusiastically embraced a maternal identity; and a tendency to idealise pregnancy was apparent: 'I love it! I love everything about it. I like the look, I like the feelings inside, I'll put up with the worries. Before I was searching for what was wrong with me, but now everything seems sort of perfect' (p 352).

In a more recent study with a larger sample, Camberis et al. (2014) replicated these findings. Compared with spontaneously conceiving women, those conceiving through ART reported more intense attachment to the foetus, and an enthusiastic identification with motherhood, evident in higher scores for confidence about mothering, more positive attitudes to being pregnant, and more positive feelings about young children. This effect was moderated by maternal age, with older women less likely to endorse these highly positive views, as discussed in Chapter 3.

Pregnancy-Focused Anxiety and Foetal Attachment

There is scant evidence that women conceiving through ART struggle to integrate a maternal identity, nonetheless, for many, the experience of pregnancy maps closely onto Rothman's notion of a tentative pregnancy. 'Jenny' describes a pervasive sense of trepidation after conceiving her first pregnancy through IVF:

> After the scan, I relaxed a little, maybe at about 14 weeks, but in the back of my mind I worry even now at 30 weeks, that something is going to happen. I think until I can actually see the baby, I won't believe it. You just sort of wait for the next disappointment to come along. (McMahon, 1997, p. 150)

'Sue' also experienced significant anxiety about the pregnancy outcome, that persisted until the third trimester:

I'm very nervous about things going wrong. I knew someone who had a baby who was in hospital for nine months when he was first born, and a girlfriend had a Down's Syndrome baby a couple of month ago, so I'm very panicky about things not being right. Not nice thoughts to have to carry all the time. (McMahon, 1997, p. 150)

There is abundant and consistent evidence that compared to women conceiving spontaneously, women conceiving through ART report higher levels of pregnancy-focused anxiety on questionnaire measures (see Hammarberg et al., 2008 for a systematic review). Intriguingly, Hammarberg and colleagues also noted that most studies have found *lower* rates of *generalised* anxiety and depression alongside this pregnancy-focused concern. In contrast, García-Blanco and colleagues (2018) provide the first evidence of higher levels of general state anxiety and stress bio-markers in women conceiving through ART compared with spontaneously conceiving women, but, paradoxically, lower depression symptoms in the third trimester of pregnancy. Pregnancy-focused anxiety was not measured in this more recent study.

Difficulty forming an attachment to the unborn baby is a core feature of 'tentative pregnancies', but studies of women conceiving through ART consistently report more intense and more positive foetal attachment (e.g., Fisher et al., 2008; McMahon et al., 2011). These findings are consistent with Leifer's (1977) contention that temporary anxiety that is specific to the pregnancy can be complementary to the attachment process – women with a strong emotional attachment may be more likely to express anxiety about potential threats to the unborn baby. (Similar associations have also been reported in men during pregnancy, as discussed in Chapter 4.) Findings of intense and positive attachment to the foetus are corroborated in studies using in-depth interviews. Women pregnant in the context of medical risk express an intense sense of protectiveness and sacrifice – a willingness to do whatever is in the best interests of the developing baby – that shapes their emerging maternal identity (Curran et al., 2017). Most of the women in the study by Curran and colleagues thought a great deal about the foetus, and they reported a 'special' emotional connection. Feelings of nurture and protectiveness were intensified due to medical risk, and there was an early personification of the foetus. Concerns about the marginal status of their pregnancy can co-exist with these protective feelings, evident in a tendency to avoid *public* displays of commitment to the baby, such as setting up a nursery, naming the baby, and talking to the baby in utero (McMahon et al., 1999). There are sustained and competing struggles to hold back and to attach, to dream and to keep a lid on things.

The process of adapting to pregnancy is more ambiguous, more intense, generally more positive, and certainly more complicated.

Hassles and Uplifts of Pregnancy

Pregnancy demands unique psychological adaptations – there are 'hassles' and there are joys or 'uplifts' (DiPietro et al., 2004). The struggle to achieve a pregnancy can intensify the appreciation of the joys and confer a greater tolerance for the difficulties. Hassles can be reframed as positives, and this may be particularly the case for women pregnant after conception through ART. As a group, mothers conceiving through ARTs have been shown to be more likely to make light of the significance of discomforts like nausea, heartburn, even anxiety, viewing them as reassuring confirmation of the pregnancy, and secondary to the joy of having achieved a long-awaited goal. In their longitudinal study, McMahon and colleagues found that the greater the struggle to conceive, the more positively (overall group findings) women reported on the pregnancy experience (McMahon et al., 1997a, 1999).

Hammarberg and colleagues (2013) calculated the ratio of reported hassles to uplifts at thirty weeks of pregnancy in a large sample of women, half of whom had conceived through ART. They also found that older maternal age and conceiving through ART were associated with a more optimal experience of pregnancy (reports of fewer hassles, more uplifts). In contrast, Ulrich and colleagues (2004) did not find more positive adjustment in the context of risk, nor was it more negative. Rather, they were surprised by the striking similarities between responses of the women conceiving through IVF, compared with responses of spontaneously conceiving couples: overall, a high degree of relationship satisfaction, satisfaction with the progress of pregnancy, and few complaints, despite more medical complications, and known medical risks. Interestingly, they noted wariness among the women pregnant after IVF conception, when it came to talking about feelings, particularly negative ones. This is consistent with a coping strategy of defensive denial or emotional cushioning, and also with evidence from several studies that women conceiving through ART are more likely to keep any negative feelings to themselves (McMahon, 1997), a coping strategy that may have been acquired during the treatment phase. As 'Melanie' explained: 'Through all this IVF stuff, I learnt to switch off, and G [my partner] was the same. I really learned how not to let myself get overwhelmed by what I was feeling. You learn to hold on to things, and to contain your emotions' (p. 152).

Pregnancy after Pre-implantation Genetic Diagnosis

As discussed in Chapter 2, some couples undergo IVF treatment so that they can have a diagnostic test before a fertilised embryo is implanted. Although they may not have a history of infertility, these women share all of the stresses associated with a pregnancy after ART, as well as additional challenges related to their reproductive and genetic history. Couples eligible for the test are often known carriers of genetic conditions. They may have a lengthy and complicated history of reproductive trauma and loss: including termination due to discovery of a genetic or chromosomal disorder in the second trimester, multiple miscarriages, or perhaps the death of a neonate born with severe abnormalities. While there is a sense of relief and a sense of empowerment that the early test can prevent a recurrence of some of these events, the process itself can re-activate these past traumatic experiences (Karatas et al., 2010b).

It's not surprising, then, that pregnancy is approached extremely tentatively in this context. Passing the gestational milestones when previous pregnancies were lost is experienced as a milestone, albeit one in which they still feel the need to 'keep a lid' on their positive feelings. Despite this stressful context, a prospective study has shown comparable scores to community samples on validated measures of maternal foetal attachment (Karatas et al., 2010b), alongside acknowledgement of hesitancy and tentativeness, as found in other studies of women conceiving through IVF after infertility. As one participant in the longitudinal study by Karatas and colleagues explains:

> I felt sometimes I didn't want to get too close, in case there was something wrong and knowing how distressing it is to lose a pregnancy. And I felt my husband didn't get very close for the same reasons … But I mean I guess I bonded more in terms that I knew when it was kicking and [I would] feel it more then … But I didn't talk or play music to it or anything like that. (p. 775)

'Normal' and 'Special' Pregnancies

Taken together, this body of evidence suggests that the pregnancy experience after conception through ART is qualitatively different, but not necessarily more negative. While infertility and its treatment play a large part, adjustment is also influenced by past life experiences, psychosocial circumstances, a personal world view, and individual life goals (Karatas et al., 2010b). Women who have struggled to achieve a viable pregnancy want to be seen as both 'normal' and 'special' (Sandelowski et al., 1992); they view their pregnancies as equal to, more complicated than, and superior to spontaneously conceived pregnancies. The highly positive identification with pregnancy and motherhood despite intense anxiety about the outcome reflects an adaptive tolerance for mixed feelings most likely acquired through the struggle to conceive. Contradictory negative and positive emotions can and do co-exist – and this has also been noted in the treatment phase (Boivin & Lancastle, 2010).

Traditional theoretical models regarding 'normative' adaptation and coping may not apply; while the struggles and anxieties may be real, the consequences may be different, and not necessarily problematic (McMahon et al., 1999; Sandelowski, 1987). Women with high-risk pregnancies face enough challenges without needing to worry about worrying (Oates, 2002). Being anxious about anxiety and fearful about fear is an additional burden (Gorman, 2005, 2006).

What are the implications of these intense and complex experiences of pregnancy for the developing child and the mother's capacity to take on the maternal role? In Chapter 3, we discussed a growing body of evidence that pregnancy anxiety (particularly pregnancy-focused anxiety) can have a negative impact on the developing foetus and be a precursor for regulatory and behaviour problems in infancy and childhood (Korja et al., 2017). It is worth asking, therefore, given the intense pregnancy-focused anxiety experienced by many women conceiving after IVF, whether there is evidence of regulatory problems in the children conceived in this way? In relation to longer-term developmental outcomes, to date, the answer seems to be a clear 'no'. More than thirty years of research has yielded no evidence of an increased incidence of behaviour problems in children conceived through ART (Golombok, 2019). In the context of tentative pregnancies, however, it is pertinent to focus more closely on infant bio-behavioural regulation during the early months of parenting, and how parents respond and relate to their young infants.

One study has directly addressed this question exploring links between anxiety (general, and pregnancy-focused) during pregnancy and infant temperamental difficulty at four months after birth. McMahon and colleagues (2013) found no evidence of associations between pregnancy-focused anxiety and child temperamental reactivity, frequently noted in community samples, in a large sample of infants conceived through ART. Indeed, mothers conceiving through ART reported significantly *easier* temperament in their young infants. In an earlier study with a smaller sample, an observational laboratory paradigm was used to assess individual differences in infant responses to interactive stress. In that study, while mothers conceiving through ART reported their infants to be more 'difficult', trained coders blind to mode of conception reported no differences in observed infant fussiness and negative affect in response to the stress procedure (McMahon et al., 1997b). Few studies have directly addressed the impact of pregnancy-focused anxiety on the developing infant in the ART context and more research is needed. Nonetheless it is intriguing that the evidence to date does not support the theorised negative consequences of intense pregnancy anxiety. It is possible that pregnancy-focused anxiety that is grounded in realistic pregnancy risk appraisals may play out differently, especially in the context of a very much wanted child.

Despite the more complex process of maternal identity formation (including a tendency to idealisation) and the higher intensity of foetal attachment in the context of a fear of losing the baby, mothers conceiving through ART do not differ in vulnerability to postnatal depression and anxiety, at four months after the birth (McMahon et al., 2011) and up to two years postpartum (McMahon et al., 2015). While mothers conceiving through ART may worry whilst pregnant that their infants will be difficult (McMahon et al., 1999), and subjectively experience them as difficult in the early months after birth (Fisher et al., 2012; McMahon et al., 1997a) evidence to date shows that they do not differ from spontaneously conceiving mothers in parenting behaviour. A study using gold standard observational assessments found no differences in mothers' sensitive responding to infant cues during infancy (McMahon et al., 1997b) or toddlerhood (Gibson et al., 2000), and that they were just as likely as spontaneously conceiving mothers to develop secure attachment relationships with their infants (Gibson et al., 2000). All in all, then, the evidence to date suggests that women conceiving through ART show an impressive adaptive resilience during the transition to parenthood.

Becoming a Parent after Pregnancy or Perinatal Loss

The loss of an anticipated and wanted baby whether through miscarriage, termination due to an adverse test finding, or still-birth, is a devastating experience. The emotional impact can be exacerbated or ameliorated by biological factors (including parental age, fertility issues), the investment of the parents in the pregnancy, previous reproductive struggles and losses, and the intensity of attachment to the unborn infant (Harris & Daniluk, 2010). This section begins by considering the profound impact of stillbirth or death in the early perinatal period, and how this affects adjustment in subsequent pregnancies, then discusses the unique psychological challenges related to termination in the second trimester due to abnormal test results, and the more common experience of miscarriage.

Losing a Baby at Birth

Losing a baby around the time of birth is a loss unlike any other; biologically bewildering, psychologically complex, and socially taboo. Intense and complex grief reactions are common, often complicated by a well-intended conspiracy of silence from those close to the bereaved parents. Fathers and mothers may respond differently, posing significant challenges to the couple relationship, just when they most need each other (Wing et al., 2005). Family and extended social networks often flounder, unsure how to provide much needed support. In this section we consider the unique biological, psychological, and social challenges that follow from stillbirth, debates about how best to support parents through this process, and how a prior stillbirth can influence a subsequent transition to parenthood.

Biological Challenges: 'My Body Has Failed'

Death at the time of birth is a contradiction, profoundly at odds with the natural order of life. Further complicating matters, the cause of the baby's death is often unclear, and may remain unresolved even after parents endure the trauma of a post-mortem. Perinatal death can violate a woman's trust in pregnancy and childbirth as a safe, predictable life transition (Jaffe & Diamond, 2011). She may experience self-blame, as her body has failed in achieving its most fundamental biological function – the safe delivery of a healthy child (Gorman, 2005, 2006). If the loss remains unexplained, what is to stop it happening again?

The baby has died during a biologically volatile period where mother–child bonds that serve to support the survival of the species are heightened (Robinson et al., 1999). The grieving mother is also recovering from the physical exhaustion of labour, without the reward. She is then confronted with the hormonal surges of the early perinatal period, and the onset of lactation, with no baby to feed. These biological challenges may contribute to asynchronous responses to grief for men and women, discussed in more detail later.

Psychological Challenges

Couples face enormous psychological hurdles as they struggle to come to terms with what is, rather than what might have been. Grieving will take time.

Violated Expectations. There is arguable no greater violation of life-cycle expectations than a death that occurs at the beginning of life. The unexpected loss is all the more salient, coming as it does after a long lead-time for a highly anticipated, positive event (Goldberg, 2014; Rubin & Malkinson, 2001). As discussed in Chapter 2, vivid ultra-sound images have given dynamic form and shape to the imagined baby throughout the pregnancy. Foetal movements have settled into a pre-dictable daily routine, suggestive of the baby's individual personality. The imagined child incorporates fantasies that may have been present since the mother was a child herself; an idealised infant preserved as per-fect in the mind of the parents. There are no real-life parenting experi-ences to provide reality checks. This baby never cries, never keeps them awake through the night.

Identity Challenges. Bereaved parents have lost more than a baby, they've also lost an imagined self – their new life role and anticipated identity. They have failed to achieve an expected life task. The death of a child requires a letting go, at least temporarily, of one imagined future and a re-organisation of life (goals and activities) based on a new reality. In Chapter 3, the process of taking on a maternal identity was discussed as a key adap-tive task of pregnancy; earlier in this chapter we considered how this pro-cess can be enriched, intensified, perhaps idealised, when pregnancies have been difficult to achieve. A great deal has been invested: eating the right diet, going to classes, building the nest, fitting out the nursery, reading the 'how to' books, and perhaps leaving a job that has previously been central to one's identity and meaning in life. For those who have enthusiastically embraced this preparation, returning home to the empty nest is particu-larly poignant. In her moving documentary film *Losing Layla,* Vanessa Gorman describes visiting Layla's special place in the house, all the bunny rugs and baby clothes ready for her, and how she goes there when she wants to feel near to her (Gorman, 2005).

Grief and Complicated Mourning. Many of the most intense human emotions arise during the formation and disruption of attachment relationships (Bowlby, 1982) and the loss of a newborn baby juxta-poses these experiences. Classic theories have sought to describe the journey through stages of grief and generally agree that there is initial shock and protest, then a period of sadness, followed by resolution or restitution (Bowlby, 1982; Kubler-Ross, 1997). More recently the prescriptive notion of a normatively sequenced journey through the grief process has been criticised, with recognition that grief involves a complex interplay of ever-changing emotions that can be strikingly individualised and unpredictable (Corr, 2019). A dual process model suggests individuals grapple with the simultaneous challenges to orient to the loss itself (grief work) and to restore some semblance of normal functioning (Rubin & Malkinson, 2001). In this regard, the adaptive value of denial, distraction, and moving on to new things is recognised (Stroebe et al., 2006).

After stillbirth, acute grief symptoms gradually diminish over the next year, and intense grief extending beyond six months is viewed by mental health professionals as problematic (McSpedden et al., 2017). Individual responses and vulnerability to sustained or complicated grief vary; they are influenced by the current context, the intensity of the initial grief, available supports, prior experiences of loss or trauma, and coping and attachment styles acquired over a lifetime (Stroebe et al., 2006). The loss of a baby can be particularly challenging for women who have experienced complicated pathways to pregnancy and/or prior reproductive losses.

The Partner Relationship: Asynchronous Grieving. For most bereaved parents, the partner is the primary support, and the grief is shared. The couple relationship may be challenged, however, by incongruent grief reactions – gender differences in expression, coping, and duration of grief (Doka & Martin, 2011). Prior stillbirth has been associated with a three-fold increase in subsequent relationship breakdown in some studies (Turton et al., 2009). Grief can be a lonely and alienating experience; even when there is support and love from extended family, it can feel like a very solitary journey (Gorman, 2005, 2006).

While both parents may have similar grief reactions early on, research indicates that mothers' grief reactions are generally more intense and last longer (Robinson et al., 1999). Women are more likely to externalise and express their grief (Kersting & Wagner, 2012). They are also more likely to experience guilt and self-blame, as the primary responsibility of carrying and delivering the baby rests with them. The secondary support roles typically assigned to fathers can constrain their expression of grief – they are acutely aware that they are not 'centre stage'. Men may struggle to reconcile their own sadness with social expectations, real or imagined, that they should remain strong for the family. Research shows that many men cope by internalising or repressing their grief reactions, immersing themselves in work, as a distraction (Bonette & Broom, 2012).

Women may find it hard to understand why their partner seems to be doing fine, and they may misinterpret avoidant coping strategies as indicators of not caring. They may feel hurt by an apparent readiness to move on that feels premature to them. Men, on the other hand, may be baffled and overwhelmed by the intensity of their partner's reactions, and hesitate to express their own grief in the belief that it will further upset her. These disparities in how men and women journey through the grief process can create further distress and emotional misunderstandings for both (Wing et al., 2005), as Vanessa and Michael describe at the end of this chapter. Talking about these gender differences with bereaved couples can facilitate tolerance and sensitivity to each other's needs, and they can help to correct misunderstandings and misattributions about different coping styles that can lead to blame and conflict.

Social Challenges
The extended family may also struggle, unsure how to respond and provide support. While the death of a grandparent is a sad event, it is often expected, and families have clear rituals that can make such losses easier to share easier to manage. After the death of a baby, close family and friends may avoid contact as a way of dealing with their own uncertainty about what to do. While it is a searing and intense experience for the parents, a perinatal loss is largely invisible to others, and they may struggle to understand why parents would grieve the loss of a baby that was not fully formed and is physically and psychologically absent. The intensity of the parents' grief may be viewed as out of proportion with the time spent with the child.

A Western cultural taboo against the public recognition and expression of perinatal grief may leave grieving parents isolated and unable to talk about their loss in public (Leon, 2008), often contributing to grief that is severe and long-lasting (Markin & Zilcha-Mano, 2018). This lack of public acknowledgement can feel like a conspiracy of silence and may deflect pain into a rage that nobody can see the wounds, and the suffering. It can feel as though the grief is invisible (Gorman, 2005, 2006).

Individualised Support for Parents after Perinatal Death
There has been debate for many decades about how best to support parents who lose a baby. Health professionals may struggle with their own grief, feeling awkward and uncertain how to engage with bereaved parents. Different practices have dominated at different times and in different settings, and different cultures take different approaches. In the mid-twentieth century, well-intentioned, but paternalistic care practices of whisking away the dead baby were a misguided attempt to protect parents from distress. This approach is symptomatic of a (Western) socio-cultural inclination to invalidate perinatal loss and deny opportunities to grieve properly (Markin

& Zilcha-Mano, 2018). It was assumed the mother would recover best if she could put this negative experience behind her, preferably by moving on to have a replacement baby, as soon as possible. 'Cheering' phrases – the bereaved parent almost certainly does not feel it was a 'blessing in disguise' – and premature advice regarding a replacement baby invalidate the couple's experience (Raphael-Leff, 2005). The suggestion that one baby can simply replace another undermines the intensity of their loss, and their identity as grieving parents (Leon, 2008).

Heartrending stories from scores of women, often decades after a still-birth, bear witness to the negative consequences of secrecy and denial. Indeed, there is abundant evidence that when grief for a lost baby is invisible and invalidated, an intense and complicated grief may follow (Badenhorst & Hughes, 2007). When grieving parents and their surrounding networks can accept perinatal grief as valid, they are better able to deal with it patiently and proactively. In order to mourn the loss of an essentially unknown baby, she or he must be brought to life in the mother's mind. The mother needs something tangible to grieve, so mementos and opportunities to be with the baby are crucial (Leon, 2008), as are opportunities to reflect on the meaning of the loss (Markin, 2018).

How best to achieve this, remains controversial. There are strikingly different opinions on best practice, and conflicting research findings. One thing that is clear is the need to tailor practices to individual coping styles and preferences. In recent decades parents have been encouraged to hold and spend time with the dead baby, and sometimes to invite extended family in. This was exactly what documentary director and writer Vanessa Gorman and her partner Michael wanted and needed to do. After their daughter Layla died in a small rural hospital, they negotiated with the hospital and funeral directors to be able to take the baby home with them for several days. This was very important for Vanessa: 'I needed so desperately to nurture Layla in whatever way I could. I needed a chance to be her mother' (Gorman, 2005, 2006, p. 146).

While several qualitative studies suggest fewer emotional problems for mothers who have this contact, this is not always the case, and contact after still-birth remains a controversial aspect of care (Hennegan et al., 2018). Research suggests that most parents are satisfied with their own decision to hold the stillborn baby, and that those who don't do so, often regret it later. On the other hand, there is evidence that holding the still-born baby is associated with later post-traumatic stress disorder and depression symptoms for some mothers (Redshaw et al., 2016) and some fathers (Hennegan et al., 2018), with the suggestion that there may be more problematic outcomes after holding, but not after simply seeing the baby. Redshaw and colleagues (2016) speculate that tactile experiential memories of holding and caregiving might have a more profound and lasting traumatic impact. Reviews of care practices suggest that it is *how* the contact is implemented, particularly, whether there is respect for the parents' judgement and choice regarding the amount of time spent with the child that is important.

The matter remains unresolved, and it is difficult to come to a consensus from a body of research that is methodologically limited with markedly different samples, flawed study designs, and poorly described methodologies that are difficult to replicate (Redshaw et al., 2014). Hospital guidelines in the United Kingdom recommend individualised care, that should include a discussion about seeing and holding the baby, but one that respects personal choice (National Institute for Clinical Excellence [NICE], 2021a). Raphael-Leff's (2005) model of individual differences in orientation to motherhood, with its focus on different defensive strategies, may be useful here. Different women will be vulnerable in different ways; for some contact (perhaps even taking the baby home) will be helpful, while for others this may add to the trauma. What parents need is validation, autonomy to make decisions that work for their individual circumstances, respect, and empathy.

The Subsequent Pregnancy after Stillbirth

Well-meaning friends and family will often suggest a 'replacement' baby and men and women may feel differently about this. Research shows that having another baby too soon after such a loss can be associated with complex psychological adjustment in the subsequent pregnancy including depression, anxiety, post-traumatic stress, and difficulties in attaching to the subsequent child (Leon, 2008). Depression and anxiety symptoms are higher in parents who conceive shortly after their perinatal loss, and it is generally recommended that women delay conception for at least a year to allow time to process their grief (Badenhorst & Hughes, 2007). However optimal timing for a subsequent pregnancy can be complicated by individual differences in emotional responses and biological risks, related to parental age, fertility, and history of childbearing complications. Eighty-six per cent of women who have suffered perinatal loss become pregnant again within eighteen months, and a small proportion of these continue to experience high levels of distress (unresolved grief, pregnancy-specific anxiety, depression, stress, PTSD) that persist through this pregnancy, at levels that compromise functioning and adaptation (Lee et al., 2016).

The experience of stillbirth is an intense manifestation of reproductive trauma (loss, violated life goals, feelings of inadequacy, loss of control) and therefore the subsequent pregnancy is likely to be 'a perfect storm' – the stakes are even higher, and the couple is back on the emotional rollercoaster again. A recent meta-analysis of nineteen studies showed an increased incidence of anxiety and depression, but not stress in subsequent pregnancies. Pregnancy-focused anxiety was particularly salient (Hunter et al., 2017). Vanessa Gorman describes her experience of a subsequent pregnancy after losing her daughter, Layla:

> Now I know too well that being pregnant does not necessarily end with a new life. I have read too much. I am a walking encyclopedia about what can go wrong ... the entire sorry landscape of fertility loss is branded on the part of my brain marked 'fear'. Still, the last few days I have walked around with a quiet hopeful joy starting to fill me ... but I am holding my breath. It will be a long forty weeks. (Gorman, 2005, 2006, p. 260)

She coped by taking a proactive approach: booking into a hospital with a neonatal intensive care nursery, and by requesting the most experienced obstetrician they had on staff. After a 'natural' pregnancy with Layla, she willingly agreed to all available screening and diagnostic tests. After the amniocentesis, as the weeks passed without mishap, she tentatively began to let herself attach to the developing baby, talking herself into it as the risk receded over time. She found it best to acknowledge, rather than deny her anxiety, accepting that she would need to learn to live with it.

There is limited research on the impact of the previous loss on foetal attachment in the subsequent pregnancy. The expectant mother is challenged to manage the simultaneous activation of the attachment and bereavement systems. While prior attachment bonds cannot be relinquished, they can be reworked to leave room for a new relationship (O'Leary, 2004). The challenge is to make room in her mind for two babies and reconcile the contradictory feelings of sadness over the lost baby and excitement about the one she is yet to meet, whilst somehow not confusing the two (Markin, 2018). It is hardly surprising, then, that some parents struggle with their attachment relationship with subsequent children. Follow-up studies have yielded mixed findings. Many are methodologically flawed. Attachment problems are not inevitable, but they are apparent in some studies. In a well-designed case-control study Turton and colleagues (2009) found that while the next born children after a still-birth were not clinically at risk on developmental and health assessments at six years of age, there was evidence of a less harmonious emotional atmosphere and more controlling behaviour from their mothers. Contributing factors to longer-term adjustment problems included Post Traumatic Distress Syndrome after seeing and holding the earlier baby who had died, the extent of the psychological distress during the subsequent pregnancy, and family breakdown during the child's lifetime.

Terminations for Foetal Abnormality

The loss of a baby earlier in pregnancy may be somewhat less devastating, but nonetheless presents many similar challenges, as well as others uniquely related to the diagnosis, individual circumstances, and timing. In the next sections pregnancy loss in the second trimester (generally related to adverse results from amniocentesis) and the more common experience of loss in the first trimester through miscarriage are discussed with a focus on the implications of these experiences for adjustment during a subsequent pregnancy.

Adverse Findings after Amniocentesis

Waiting for medical test results is invariably stressful – and the stress increases as a function of the waiting time. This is especially the case for tests during pregnancy. All pregnancy screening carries with it the possibility of a negative outcome with profound consequences – the results really matter, and the couple has little or no control. All couples can do while waiting is to try to contain the anxiety and survive in a period of 'suspended animation'. They can deny or distract, they can rationalise and positively reframe, or they can simply accept that their own anxiety is inevitable and unavoidable (Boivin & Lancastle, 2010).

Rothman (1986/1993) argued that 'conditionality in mother love' was implicit in the decision to undertake any antenatal test; there was a need to acknowledge and incorporate an acceptance of termination (and loss) if the result was problematic, or even uncertain. The women in her study described pregnancies characterised by distance or disengagement from the expected baby maintained until they received results of the test. In almost all cases, abortion is the only available 'treatment' when the test result indicates a problem, although this is changing with advances in foetal intervention surgery, possible for some conditions, such as neural tube defects. The decision to abort a child considered likely to have significant disability presents profound ethical and emotional challenges.

Recent advances in non-invasive first trimester screening mean many fewer women now need to undergo amniocentesis (Chapter 2), however those with negative or equivocal early screening results will have to endure a series of stressful tests and waiting periods, over a protracted period. Clearly the later the test in pregnancy, the greater the difficulty – there has been more time to attach to the foetus, the body is visibly changing, the pregnancy is public, and any procedures to end a wanted pregnancy will be painful and traumatic: a birth without a baby. As one of the women in Rothman's study expressed it: 'To abort an accident is one thing. To abort your baby, even your very imperfect baby is something else again' (Rothman, 1986/1993, p. 6). Perhaps hardest of all, the timing of amniocentesis often coincides with the first awareness of foetal movements, intensifying the emotional conflict as the baby is beginning to feel like a person: 'By the time the results came, the baby had been leaping in my womb for a month' (p. 7).

The Termination and Birth Process
Late-term abortions are rare, and terminations after twenty-two weeks, rarer still. In many jurisdictions they exist in a medico-legal grey area. The decision generally arises from an extremely complex and distressing medical situation: the mother's life is considered at risk, or there is a diagnosis of devastating foetal abnormalities that are incompatible with sustained life or quality of life after birth. There is emotional anguish compounding the physical discomfort of the termination, and no reward. The mother (and her partner) will need to make a series of difficult decisions, often in a short timeframe: the type of abortion procedure, whether she wishes to see the foetus, what kind of disposal of the body she prefers (Royal College of Obstetricians and Gynaecologists, 2010).

Many of the emotional consequences of termination after adverse amniocentesis findings are directly comparable to those after stillbirth – a sense of injustice, the loss of a wanted baby, and the loss of an expected future as a parent. One key difference is the presence of control and choice, rather than an unexpected event, but as Rothman (1986/1993) puts it: 'It is a lesser of two evils choice; a devil and the deep blue sea choice, a no-choice choice' (p. 179). Indeed, the moral complexity of the decision complicates the heartbreak – adding guilt and shame to loss, grief, and shattered hopes. Almost all the women in Rothman's study were glad that they had the test, and felt they had good reasons for choosing to terminate the pregnancy, but this didn't diminish the tragedy or the trauma. The loss unfolds in stages. 'Anna', a participant in Rothman's (1986/1993) study described her experience:

> Initially, incredible sadness – I immediately identified with the baby inside me and thought poor thing, you'll not make it – then I recoiled from that knowledge. But my feelings toward the pregnancy and the baby were immediately altered. I spent the next day crying and grieving over what I hadn't lost yet, and what I had already lost at that point – a normal pregnancy and the expectation of a healthy baby. (p. 190)

The parents are faced with an induced miscarriage, a labour, and giving birth to a stillborn infant. There are no clear protocols, rituals, and practices to guide them. Couples will vary in their desire to see, name, or bury the baby.

As in the case of stillbirth, the women in Rothman's study described a complex grief – one that others in their close networks struggled to understand and acknowledge. Indeed, there may be even less recognition of the baby and the loss in these circumstances. Others typically don't want to hear about the pain; rather, they may expect gratitude and relief, and make well-intentioned, but hurtful comments that the couple are 'lucky' to have found out, that they have 'dodged a bullet', and they can move on and have another baby. Women in Rothman's study wanted others to understand that expressing the pain of terminating didn't mean they regretted terminating, nor did it mean they wouldn't experience ongoing ambivalence about the decision. They felt they shouldn't have to deny the grief of the tragedy they were experiencing, because of the tragedy avoided.

There is often a failure to recognise the reality of the loss and pain of late termination for men, and even less research. While undeniably more difficult for the woman, who must undergo the procedures and the birth, men share the distress and loss and are often expected to cope with little or no attention to their needs; they may not feel equipped to support a partner whose grief is overwhelming to them, and they may feel they have no-one to turn to.

Miscarriage

While stillbirth and late terminations after abnormal test results in pregnancy are fortunately rare, miscarriage is the most common adverse outcome of pregnancy. The term is applied to spontaneous pregnancy losses up to twenty weeks; most occur in the first trimester. Estimates of incidence vary, but between one in four and one in six confirmed pregnancies end in miscarriage, and the risk increases with maternal age (Bailey et al., 2019). Some miscarriages are sudden, leaving the woman bewildered; others are more gradual and prolonged, following spotting and cramps. In some cases, early scans suggest problems with the growth of the embryo, but the consequences can take weeks to unfold. Like other perinatal losses, the emotional consequences for an individual woman are influenced by her circumstances, her investment in the role of mother, her previous reproductive difficulties and losses, and her potential to fall pregnant again (O'Leary, 2004). A meta-analysis has shown that approximately 27 per cent of women experience significant depressive symptoms after miscarriage (Adolfsson, 2011).

As in the case of stillbirth, women generally want to know the cause, but are rarely able to find out. They are eager to differentiate a 'random' event from one with a cause that might be able to be cured or prevented in the future (Raphael-Leff, 2005). The loss is more 'invisible' and more private than stillbirth: a lonely, painful experience with little or no social acknowledgement. Even an early miscarriage involves a woman relinquishing her hope for a baby and compromises her trust in the reliability of her body. Miscarriage can also be devastating for an expectant father: writer and psychology researcher, Charles Fernyhough, describes his experience:

> I take the call one grey afternoon in October ... I hear Lizzie's voice, almost unrecognizable with grief. I can hardly understand what she is saying, but I know that we have lost the baby. .... I feel the old sick turmoil, the chatter and glow of low-level hallucinations, the shivery phantasmagoria of grief. This time I can't stop the tape. There is nothing I can do but cry. How can you mourn a child you have never seen? We tried to love an idea into existence and now that love had lost its target. ... Dying made our baby substantial. (Fernyhough, 2008, p. 229)

Recurrent Miscarriages

While one miscarriage can be devastating, a small proportion (about 6 per cent) of women experience recurrent miscarriages, losing two or more pregnancies (Zegers-Hochschild et al., 2009). It is hardly surprising that psychological distress and depression are significantly more common for these women. The experience of each pregnancy is characterised by extreme pregnancy-focused anxiety, with the intensity strongly related to the number of previous miscarriages (Ockhuijsen et al., 2014). Bailey and colleagues (2019) conducted in-depth interviews with fourteen women who had experienced recurrent pregnancy loss. Their responses align closely with the psychological profile of the tentative pregnancy: tumultuous competing and intense emotions in the first trimester – excitement tempered by intense anxiety, compounded by worry about worrying. Anxiety in the first trimester manifests as hypervigilance: repeated checking for bleeding or spotting, and women report craving symptoms (tender breasts, nausea) that confirm the pregnancy. One woman who had experienced six prior miscarriages described her experience:

> You are constantly monitoring your pregnancy symptoms, constantly. Do I feel the same as I did yesterday, are my 'boobs' still sore, do I need to go to the toilet more often … And you are constantly questioning every single twinge you feel, and you are dying to get morning sickness, so you know you are pregnant – it's all consuming. (Bailey et al., 2019, p. 6)

Avoidant coping strategies ('don't count your chickens') described earlier in this chapter can be helpful: emotional detachment from the pregnancy ('bracing for the worst'); holding back from disclosing the pregnancy to others; reigning in reverie about a future with the child; using distraction techniques to try and keep busy (McMahon et al., 1999; Ockhuijsen et al., 2014). Passing the gestational age when previous losses have occurred may be cautiously interpreted as a positive milestone. Frequent scans provide much needed reassurance. A strong theme is the need for professional affirmation and support, not typically provided during the early stages of pregnancy. Ockhuijsen and colleagues note that women who become pregnant after miscarriage have to deal with three different waiting periods, each of which can be experienced as stressful because the outcome is unpredictable and uncontrollable: the time from the pregnancy loss until the woman tries to conceive again, the time from trying to achieve a pregnancy to receiving a positive pregnancy test, and the period between the positive test and confirmation that the pregnancy is viable. All of these can be even more complicated for women with a history of infertility, and so we return to where this chapter began.

Miscarriage after Infertility and Conception through ART

Women conceiving through ART are more likely to miscarry and to have a history of pregnancy loss. Even if they haven't previously miscarried, unique features of ART conception can intensify negative emotional responses. As discussed earlier in this chapter, the extent of prior treatment failure, seeing the embryo prior to implantation or in very early ultrasound scans, and unresolved grief regarding infertility can compound the experience of miscarriage. For some, it is a final breaking point leading them to stop treatment (Harris & Daniluk, 2010). Harris and Daniluk concluded from their research that women with a history of infertility, who miscarried in the first trimester, reported similarly intense grief emotions to other women with second and third trimester losses (discussed earlier). They noted that most women referred to the loss of a 'baby', rather than a 'foetus', suggesting that despite defensive attempts to hold back from attachment, they were highly invested in the pregnancy and the potential baby. They also commented on additional pain if the significance of this loss was minimised – they wanted the loss to be named and validated, and they emphasised the importance of including fathers in this process.

Summary Comments

Any pregnancy loss can be experienced as a personal tragedy. The reactions to pregnancy loss are unique to each woman's circumstances and reproductive history, and they are as diverse as the women who experience them. Grief in the context of perinatal loss is too often trivialised (others minimise the significance, talk prematurely about replacement babies), medicalised, or pathologised. Those close to the couple may feel better when the woman is pregnant again, but it is more complicated for the woman herself and for her partner. Real grief for the loss of a child never goes away, rather it is accepted, and incorporated into who the parent is (O'Leary, 2004; Rubin & Malkinson, 2001).

Another baby is a comfort, but not a cure. A new pregnancy is a success, a reaffirmation of a woman's body, a source of joy and pleasure, but it does not replace the lost baby. The loss of a baby is what it is. It is not a detour on the route to a healthy baby; rather, it is a tragedy in its own right. The grief must be acknowledged and respected (Gorman, 2005, 2006; Rothman, 1986/1993). All grieving parents want recognition that they are in pain and respect for what they have lost.

There are also rewards. The experience of loss can fuel appreciation of parenthood when it is finally achieved and inspire a deep connection with a treasured and wanted child (Markin, 2018). It is an ongoing challenge to hold in mind the depth of grief and loss alongside feelings of excitement for the future, and an evolving attachment to a new baby. There may be marked asynchronies in the process for mothers and fathers, as Vanessa and Michael describe. An earlier miscarriage tempers expectations in subsequent pregnancies, but Annie responds by embracing a subsequent pregnancy with twins, irrespective of awareness of risk. She emphasises the importance of social connection and empathic professional support.

Vanessa's and Michael's Story: Asymmetrical Journeys through Perinatal Grief

Soulmates in a passionate and loving relationship, Vanessa and Michael were fundamentally at odds about babies. Vanessa, a writer and documentary director, has memories from when she was just eight years old of wanting to be a mother. Nurturing others was second nature to her. In her mid-thirties, with a well-established career, her longing for a child became urgent, intense, and all consuming. The prospect of arriving in her forties without a child was unthinkable. Her partner, Michael, was equally certain that the unconditional commitment and sheer hard work a baby required was not for him. He wanted to postpone parenthood indefinitely, or better still avoid it altogether.

It was a difficult time. Vanessa decided to film their struggles to resolve their competing and incompatible needs. Ultimately, she took matters into her own hands – stopped contraception and began monitoring her cycle. A few months later she was ecstatic to discover she was pregnant. Telling Michael was even tougher than she had feared. He felt shocked, ambushed, angry, and their relationship was shaken to its core. Vanessa revelled in every aspect of the pregnancy – embracing her changing body shape, preparing her nest, overjoyed to have joined the ranks of pregnant women. Michael's pathway to parenthood was complicated; he continued to feel wounded and betrayed, and with a persistent sense of dread about the impending birth.

While he wanted to support Vanessa, and he did so, he just couldn't shake his ambivalence about the forthcoming baby. When the time came, the labour was long, painful, and difficult. About twelve hours in, Vanessa knew that she needed to go to hospital. After seventeen hours, she was desperate for an epidural, and her plans for a natural birth were abandoned. At twenty hours, with the cervix almost fully dilated, there were signs of foetal distress. Vanessa was rushed to the operating theatre. Layla was delivered after a few minutes by caesarean section and presented to her parents. There were clearly problems. Layla was pale and struggling to breathe. The medical staff worked anxiously to assist her. While Vanessa recovered from surgery, Michael was with Layla as the seriousness of her condition became apparent:

> I came down and Layla was just basically doing these huge gulps for breath … And she had tubes all coming out … And it was like I thought she was going to die any breath. I felt, because I hadn't loved her in the womb, that she was dying through lack of love. So I just needed to tell her that I loved her and that I wanted her, and it was very real for me in that moment, that that was true, which was a big surprise, to have that rush of emotion, to feel so much love for her. And I felt like my love could keep her alive … (Gorman, 2005, 21:11)

Layla was transferred by helicopter to an intensive care unit in the nearest large city. Michael drove two hours to be with her, and when he arrived, the doctors broke the news that she wasn't going to make it. He was able to hold Layla in his arms as she died, and then he drove through the night to bring her back to Vanessa. His grief was devastating, complicated, and confusing. He was afraid that through his ambivalence, he had wished her away.

In the months after Layla died, Michael often felt isolated and unsupported. As he explained to Vanessa:

> I feel like often, my feelings were overlooked, because they weren't as large as yours and they were more complicated than yours. I'd had a more complicated journey. It wasn't longing, longing, longing, loss … It was sort of ambivalence, shock, loss, shame … And I just noticed that people didn't really know how to contact me … and some of that probably made me feel like there was something wrong with what I felt … People didn't want to know about the subtleties of my experience. I would imagine men, in general, probably get missed in these experiences because their relationship with the baby is so different. And their relationship to the events can be very different. (Gorman, 2005, 43:18)

Vanessa's pathway was more straightforward, from intense longing to deep joy to profound loss. She grieved for her lost opportunity to be a mother, but also for her daughter: 'I can speak of my empty arms and aching breasts, my sadness of a future without her in it, but I also grieved so terribly for Layla losing her chance to experience life' (Gorman, 2005, 2006, p. 158).

It was very hard to re-engage with the outside world – the streets seemed full of pregnant women and young babies, and her despair and loss felt invisible. Going out in the small town where they lived, Vanessa often felt infuriated that people looked at her, and interacted with her, as though nothing had happened. She wanted to cry out and tell them about the intensity of her pain. More than anything, Vanessa and Michael wanted their grief to be named and acknowledged.

Now the mother of two thriving children, Vanessa has the last word regarding the loss of her first-born daughter Layla:

> I still feel the sadness of losing her every day, … And I feel like there's a part of me that will never get over it … there's a part of me that will always feel sad to have lost her, even when I'm not feeling the intense rollercoaster of grief. And I don't even want to stop feeling that … That's when I feel the love for her. (Gorman, 2005, 48:49)

(Vanessa Gorman was interviewed for this book, and she gave permission to use these quotations from the film, *Losing Layla*.)

Annie's* Story: A Miscarriage, IVF, and Baby Twins

During her early twenties Annie, an early childhood educator, moved from Australia to South Africa to work in inner-city Johannesburg, where she met her husband, T. Annie had wanted to be a mother for as long as she could remember; a few years after they married, she and T felt ready and eager to become parents. They were surprised when it didn't happen straight away. It was nine months before they received a positive pregnancy test result, and their delight was short-lived. Annie noticed some bleeding, and a scan a few days later confirmed her worst fears – a miscarriage. To make matters worse, the scan also showed a cyst on her ovary. Follow-up investigations showed that the cyst was an endometrioma, the most common form of endometriosis. The diagnosis, completely unexpected, posed a serious threat to her reproductive potential. The next twelve months were harrowing and stressful. Annie had to contend with severe pain, four separate and invasive laparoscopic surgeries, and the derailing of her goal to become pregnant. After the third surgical intervention, her gynaecologist referred her to an infertility specialist.

Following a fourth laparoscopic surgery, A and T were offered the option to start IVF treatment straight away. They knew it was their best chance of achieving a pregnancy – but it was a difficult decision. Annie was acutely aware that it was her longing for a baby that was the driving force, and that she was the one with the medical problem. T was already committed to a plan to study in Europe, and had partially relocated there, which made things more complicated. On top of that, they both had concerns about the ethical complexity of engaging with IVF treatment, particularly in a poor country like South Africa. As Annie explains:

> Spending a substantial amount of money to try and have a child of our own didn't feel 100 per cent right. Not only were there countless individuals and causes more deserving of the money, and there was also no shortage of orphaned children who needed parents. I don't think either of these questions was fully re-solved for us when we decided to go ahead ... Rather, I think we decided to live with the discomfort of these unresolved questions, while giving this option a try.

Annie found it difficult to relinquish the romantic ideal of becoming preg-nant spontaneously as a natural consequence of an act of love. The contrast with conceiving through IVF treatment was stark; such an intimate process, but so clinical, so invasive, and so impersonal. And yet, there was an upside:

> There was something amazing, even magical, about being so in touch with every tiny step in a process that normally happens without awareness: seeing the eggs during the stimulation phase; watching them develop on the scans; seeing the em-bryos before they were transferred. It was remarkable to be witnessing that process and working with such skilful people.

Like most couples undergoing IVF treatment, she and T had to weather the ups and downs, the miscommunications, and the misunderstandings that were part and parcel of the process. Nonetheless, Annie was optimistic. The first treatment resulted in seven eggs, and by the day of transfer, just three embryos were considered viable. Annie and T decided to transfer all three (common practice at that time), notwithstanding the possibility of triplets. After the early morning transfer, Annie was determined to do everything within her power to keep those babies inside.

The next two weeks were nerve-wracking, but the blood test was positive, and the hormone levels suggested a multiple pregnancy. Triplets were now a real possibility. If moving countries with one or two babies was daunting, surely three would be impossible! The first scan, confirming just two heartbeats, was both joyous and a tremendous relief. With memories of her earlier miscarriage still fresh, the early days of the pregnancy were inevitably anxious. There was some spotting, which was terrifying, but it resolved. Passing incremental milestones gradually built confidence. She was reassured by seeing the two heartbeats on the scan, and by the onset of morning sickness. Although aware of the increased risks associated with a twin pregnancy, Annie managed to avoid ruminating and she embraced the pregnancy:

> There was an awareness of fragility, vulnerability, that things could go wrong, definitely. But it didn't make me hold back from connecting with the babies, or from committing wholeheartedly to the pregnancy. The intensity of my grief after my previous miscarriage, so soon after I knew I was pregnant, made me realise how much I had connected even just with the idea of a baby, a potential baby. I think it would have been impossible for me to not connect with these two little lives that were actually growing inside me, however fragile their situation. The anxiety and concern were always there, but they never felt unmanageable.

The birth (a caesarean section) went smoothly, and two healthy baby girls were born. The early days were intense and exhausting. Feeding both was a challenge and initially painful, as one of the babies struggled to latch on. When the time came to leave the hospital, Annie was fortunate to be surrounded by family and friends. Her mother (an experienced midwife) had flown in from Australia and was able to stay for the first few months. Her South-African in-laws were available to help at any time. A roster system meant that Annie, T, and her mother somehow all managed enough sleep to get by:

> It was crazy, full-on, all consuming, but do-able, enjoyable. Feeding those little babies, looking at their little faces, was so precious, and was exactly what I wanted to be doing – times two! There were difficult times, of course, when both were inconsolable. I had to face the fact that I couldn't soothe them both, but I felt comforted that each had someone to hold her. Joy, gratitude, and delight were my dominant emotions during this period.

Despite the considerable logistical challenges, the newly formed family managed to relocate to Switzerland and set up a new life when the babies were just three months old. Annie emphasises the importance of the 'village' for new mothers. She felt sustained by the warmth and generosity of others and encouraged and gratified by their delight:

It was the support that made all the difference: professionals through the IVF process, the pregnancy, the birth, family, friends ... You become public property when you're pregnant, and when you're pushing a baby in a pram, especially two babies, and I loved that too. I loved the delight of others, their desire to see the twins, to ask about them, to engage and tell me about their own children, their grandchildren. It was a wonderful way of connecting in a foreign country where I barely spoke the language. There was a sense of being embraced and connected with others by these two beautiful little girls who engaged everyone. The help and support were priceless.

---

*Names have been changed.

CHAPTER 6

Alternative Pathways
Becoming a Parent through Reproductive Donation or Adoption

While procreation is a biological function, parenthood is a social construct (Leon, 2002). In Western and non-Western cultures, parenting, inheritance, and traditional definitions of the family are grounded in 'bloodlines' and there is a strong drive toward biogenetic parenthood – having a child of one's own (Freeman, 2014). There is growing diversity, however, in those seeking to become parents and the ways in which they can do so (Golombok, 2020; Patterson, 2019). Adoption and medical treatments for infertility have provided alternative pathways to becoming a parent for those unable or disinclined to have children through heterosexual sex (Guzzo & Hayford, 2020). More liberal social attitudes accompanied by legal reforms in many Western countries have enabled same-sex couples to marry, to adopt or foster children, and to participate in medically assisted conception (using donated sperm, eggs, embryos, and in some cases, surrogate gestational mothers). Nonetheless, social acceptance of these pathways to parenthood remains patchy (Dempsey et al., 2021). Becoming a parent is more complex when there are donors involved – conceptually, legally, and biologically. Extensive planning and negotiation are required including some or all of the following: potential donors themselves, sperm and egg banks, ART clinics, surrogacy brokers, adoption agencies. There may be extensive screening protocols (both medical and psychosocial) and there are generally high financial costs. No-one embarks lightly on these pathways to parenthood.

This chapter examines the process of becoming a parent when one or both parents are not genetically related to the child. We begin by reviewing the developmental processes of adapting to pregnancy discussed in earlier chapters on becoming a mother (Chapter 3), becoming a father (Chapter 4), and conception through ART (Chapter 5), in order to explore the additional challenges when reproductive donation is involved.

To recap briefly: theories propose that the first 'developmental challenge' in becoming a parent is to come to terms with the biological reality of the pregnancy, or, as discussed in this chapter, the implications of *not* being genetically (and in some cases gestationally) related to the expected child; the second is the psychological challenge of taking on an identity as a parent and developing a relationship with the anticipated child. Third, expectant parents need to renegotiate their partner relationship and restructure their broader social networks in preparation for parenthood. Pathways to parenthood involving reproductive donation or adoption often follow infertility and prior experiences of reproductive loss, although this is not always the case. Uncertainty regarding the likelihood of achieving the goal of parenthood can add a further layer of complexity.

The chapter then examines research evidence on the transition to parenthood for heterosexual couples who conceive with donated eggs, sperm, or embryos, and the pathways to parenthood for lesbian and gay couples. Finally becoming a parent through adoption is considered.

Biological Connections: Genetics and Gestation

Couples who decide to embark on parenthood when one or both will not be genetically related to the child assign different meanings to the importance of genetic, gestational, and social connectedness, depending on their own context (Almeling, 2015).

Genetic Relatedness: Meanings and Alternatives

Genetics has long been reified as the essence of identity and family relationships; a prerequisite for 'natural' love between offspring and progenitors (Freeman, 2014; Kirkman, 2008). Adults seek to recreate themselves by passing on genes to their offspring, and heterosexual couples seek to consolidate their relationship by bringing their sperm and eggs together. A belief that it is best for children to live with their biological parents is both implicit and explicit in contemporary adoption and fostering systems and underpins policies and practices that aim to reunite children with biological parents or kin.

If medical advice suggests it is even remotely possible, most couples will leave no stone unturned, in their efforts to conceive a child who is genetically related to at least one of them, often at great personal and financial cost. The fact that the woman can experience pregnancy and childbirth is seen as an added benefit (Inhorn, 2020). Non-genetic parenthood is often viewed as a last resort (Leon, 2002). The infertile couple may undergo a period of mourning the inability to conceive a genetically related child with a loved life partner before considering the involvement of a donor. There may also be insecurity about the third party involved, and envy about the gestational experience in the case of surrogacy (Glazer, 2014).

Despite significant advances in ART, discussed in detail in Chapter 2, some heterosexual couples are unable to conceive with sex cells from both parents; if the male partner has a very low sperm count or poor sperm motility, if the woman has stopped producing eggs, or her eggs are not able to be fertilised (generally due to older maternal age), or when the cause of the infertility is not known. When two men or two women are in a relationship, the child conceived can be genetically related to only one of them. There are various combinations in relation to genetic and gestational connectedness: a heterosexual couple can conceive with donated sperm, a donated egg, or a donated embryo. Single women can conceive using donated sperm. A gay male couple can conceive with the sperm of one male and a donated egg (the embryo is transferred to a surrogate). A lesbian couple can conceive using donated sperm; the woman whose egg is fertilised may carry the pregnancy, or the fertilised egg may be transferred to her female partner. When couples conceive with a donated embryo, neither is genetically related to the child, but the woman is gestationally related – she carries the foetus from the time of implantation, and she gives birth to the child. In some cases, heterosexual couples may require a surrogate to 'carry' the pregnancy for medical reasons that preclude the woman being pregnant (prior hysterectomy, uterine problems, recurrent miscarriages). In these cases, both parents are genetically related to the child, but the woman is not gestationally related.

The significance of genetic and gestational relatedness can be downplayed or emphasised. Even when downplayed, for many intending parents selection of phenotypic characteristics in the donor is a conscious and carefully planned process. Following a long-established tradition in domestic adoption, couples conceiving with donated sperm or eggs frequently try to select donors who share characteristics with the parent who will not be genetically related to the child (Murphy, 2013; Wojnar & Katzenmeyer, 2014). Commercial egg and sperm banks advertise for donors based on their phenotypic characteristics, and some even adjust payment rates for characteristics perceived as desirable in a particular culture (for example, height, hair colour, skin colour, ethnicity).

Gestational Relatedness

Recent scientific advances in understanding the neurological and hormonal underpinnings of caregiving draw attention to the biological underpinnings of the caregiving system, emphasised by advocates of natural childbirth, early contact with the infant, and breastfeeding. When conception is achieved with the use of donated sperm, eggs, or embryos, the woman (gestational mother) is able to experience pregnancy, give birth, and breastfeed the child. During pregnancy she experiences changes to her body shape, breasts, sleep patterns, energy, and feels the baby's movements in the womb, discussed in detail in Chapter 3. Hormonal changes driven by the placenta (surges in oxytocin, oestrogen, progestogen) will influence her emotional state and activate her caregiving system. Her partner will have the opportunity to observe the pregnancy at close range, to attend the birth, and perhaps cut the umbilical cord. When heterosexual couples engage a surrogate, they may both be genetically related to the child, but the commissioning mother does not experience the hormonal and physical changes of pregnancy, childbirth, and lactation. In the case of lesbian couples, only one of the women has these biological experiences. For gay couples, one of the men is likely to be the genetic father of the baby, and there is generally an egg donor and a surrogate (discussed later in this chapter).

Adoptive parents do not experience pregnancy, childbirth, or breastfeeding. They may not see their child as a young infant, and the infant is likely to have had prior experiences with different caregivers. Adoptive parents may or may not have access to information about the birth mother's identity, her health and circumstances during pregnancy and childbirth, paternity, and the baby's health and development in early infancy.

Psychological Challenges: Integrating a Parental Identity

It is more challenging for parents who are not genetically or gestationally related to their infant to reconfigure their sense of self, and some struggle to feel like a 'real' parent, doubting their entitlement to parent a genetically unrelated child (Kirkman, 2008; Sandelowski et al., 1993). Assuming a parental identity is grounded in intellectual and emotional work, rather than tangible biological experiences (Hill, 1991). The bureaucratic (often intrusive) screening procedures that have to be negotiated in order to adopt or foster, and, in some settings, to commission a surrogate, require an explicit articulation of motivations. Intending parents are repeatedly asked to demonstrate their capacity to provide a loving nurturing environment for a child, in a way that naturally conceiving parents never have to. Requirements regarding psychological screening and counselling vary for those conceiving with donated gametes, but even in unregulated 'direct contact' environments, intending parents will need to convince potential donors that they have what it takes to provide a positive parenting environment for any child conceived (Jacob, 2017), a process that has been likened to online dating (Golombok, 2020). This is likely to provoke reflection about the meaning of parenthood, the emotional needs of infants and young children, and one's capacity to meet them. Memories of early childhood experiences in the family of origin may surface. Non-heteronormative individuals may revisit memories of coming out, including rejection from parents and extended family, in some cases. Developmental struggles with gender identity may have limited early fantasies about making families and imagining a future as a parent (Glazer, 2014; Murphy, 2013; Wojnar & Katzenmeyer, 2014).

In the case of lesbian couples, only the gestational mother will have the gestational experiences that elicit public validation of impending parenthood. For those conceiving through surrogacy or adopting a child, external validation of their new life roles is delayed. If the baby is from a different racial background, even strangers may publicly and frequently question their parental status.

Developing a Relationship with the Expected Child

The process of forming an attachment may be more complicated when the child is not genetically related, and even more so if the child is from a different cultural or racial background. For gestational mothers, the experience of pregnancy (including quickening, ultrasound images, hearing the baby's heartbeat, diurnal rhythms in the baby's activity levels) is likely to help them accept the viability and individuality of the expected child, and to activate protective feelings and a commitment to caregiving. Those becoming a parent through surrogacy or adoption do not experience these tangible physical confirmations of the baby's development. Foetal attachment, discussed in detail in Chapters 3 and 5, is largely a projection of maternal and paternal fantasies, however (Raphael-Leff, 2005), and one that is enhanced by 'nesting' activities: planning a nursery, selecting a name for the baby. It is not necessary to be genetically related or to experience pregnancy to engage in fantasies and prepare a nest for the baby, as discussed later in this chapter.

Social Challenges

Social constructions of parenthood and families are being challenged by contemporary parents. Mothers are resisting the pressure of gendered and idealised expectations of selfless devotion to infant care, and fathers complain that a tendency to marginalise or exclude them from the process reveals a dismissively low regard for their capacity for nurturing. Those taking alternative pathways to parenthood face additional social challenges.

Judgement and Stigma

There is debate about the universality and legitimacy of the 'right' to parent. Frame (2008) asserts that the right of a child to know, and be genetically related to, its parents is fundamental, and he opposes the deliberate creation of a child involving an egg or sperm donor, or a surrogate, who will be intentionally alienated. Agnes Bowlby (2013) points to the large numbers of children in need of care, and she suggests that the child's need to be cared for should be placed ahead of the adult's need to become a genetic parent.

Same-sex couples, having already grappled with discrimination and a lack of social affirmation of their sexuality, are likely to face additional scrutiny and stigma from extended family and the broader community when they announce their intention to have a child (Glazer, 2014). Stigma is more notable when surrogacy is involved due to opposition from those espousing traditional family values, and from some feminists who argue that surrogacy is inherently exploitative of women, based on the widespread perception that women who agree to be surrogates are poverty stricken, socially disadvantaged, and/or vulnerable (Golombok, 2020).

Secrecy and Disclosure

While there has always been diversity in family forms, for most of the twentieth century, only heterosexual couples could become parents through adoption and with the assistance of ART clinics offering treatment involving donated sperm and eggs. The process was shrouded in secrecy to shield both intending parents and donors from stigma, retribution, and accountability. Over the last two decades, changes to legislation and more tolerant social values in most high-income countries have made it possible for non-married and non-heterosexual couples and single women to adopt and to access donated sperm, eggs, and embryos. At the same time, in response to decades of vehement advocacy from donor offspring, legal reforms in many jurisdictions have enshrined the child's right to know the identity of genetic parents. Nonetheless, non-disclosure remains widespread among heterosexual couples conceiving using donated sperm, eggs, or embryos (Daniels, 2020). Same-sex couples are generally unable to hide the use of donated sperm or eggs, but disclosure of the identity of genetic parents remains optional, at least until the child is eighteen years old. While disclosure is becoming more commonplace (Lampic et al., 2021), when families are formed through non-regulated commercial and informal arrangements, it is at the discretion of participants (Dempsey et al., 2021). The complexities of trans-national surrogacy may make it difficult or impossible for the child conceived through these arrangements to explore their genetic and gestational heritage. Adults intending to become parents with the involvement of third parties will need to grapple with these issues from the outset, and plan for how they will be managed in the longer term.

Couple Relationships and Third-Party Donors and Surrogates

Creating a safe and accepting 'social' space for the baby is a key task of pregnancy. Complex arrangements with outside parties (potentially involving birth mothers, donors, surrogates, and their own families) can be disruptive and threatening. The infertile partner in a heterosexual couple may struggle with feelings of blame and shame, as he or she confronts the fact that the fertile partner could conceive a child with someone else (Burns, 2007). The decision to use donated gametes requires agreement about how the relationship with the donor (if they are known), and disclosure to the child will be managed. These discussions may activate sensitivities that can destabilise the couple dynamic: the non-genetic parent may fear that disclosure will disrupt their relationship with the child, and may envy the child's resemblance to the genetic parent (Dempsey et al., 2021; Imrie et al., 2020).

There is also asymmetry for couples in same-sex relationships. Only one can be genetically related to the baby; and in the case of lesbian couples, only one can be gestationally related. The couple will need to agree about how the sperm or egg donor, or surrogate (if known) is integrated into the family system, and about the extent of involvement of the donor with the child. Like all couples becoming parents, it is challenging to re-orient as two become three, with inevitable changes in attention, emotional availability, and the sexual relationship, which can leave the partner less involved in primary caregiving feeling excluded (Wojmar & Katzenmeyer, 2014).

Relationships with Extended Family

Grandparents are key stakeholders in their children's reproductive choices. Pregnancies are generally proudly shared with grandparents and extended families, particularly in collectivist cultures. The process of conception is private, however. Some heterosexual couples may choose to keep the use of donated gametes secret, due to family, religious, or cultural beliefs. This can lead to conflicting and competing needs for privacy and family support, as the intending parents navigate invasive and emotionally taxing screening and medical procedures (Nordqvist & Smart, 2014). Same-sex couples face additional challenges as they explain their plans to have a baby, and the complex procedures required. They may encounter disapproval and worry that their child will be rejected by extended family and experience stigma in the future (Golombok et al., 2004).

Relationships with Donors, Surrogates, Birth Parents

How is the prospective donor or surrogate to be selected? Should there be contact prior to the birth? After the birth? What form will the relationship take? Sometimes the egg or embryo donor or surrogate is a family member, sometimes a close friend. A new (or different) relationship will need to be negotiated. In cases of open adoption or fostering, the adoptive parents will need to work with the birth mother and the agency to arrive at a level of social connection that is comfortable for all of them.

The above discussion has reviewed the psycho-social adaptations common to all prospective parents during the transition to parenthood. Some of the additional challenges faced by those who take alternative pathways have been outlined in broad terms. In the next section, we turn to the research on adjustment during the transition to parenthood for those becoming a parent using donated sperm, egg, or embryo, or through surrogacy. The chapter concludes with stories of complex alternative pathways to parenthood: two women who adopt and two men who become parents with the assistance of ART and surrogacy.

Conception using Donated Sperm, Eggs, or Embryos

Conception through sperm donation can be arranged with or without medical involvement. The process for the donor (ejaculation through intercourse or masturbation) is straightforward. Freezing and storage of sperm has been a widespread medical practice since the middle of the twentieth century, and there are numerous commercial sperm banks, as well as those attached to ART clinics. Egg storage and donation is more medically complicated. The age-related decline in female fertility is primarily related to ovarian function, due to progressive loss from a finite pool of primordial egg follicles, ultimately culminating in menopause (Stoop et al., 2014). Egg donors are required to undergo hormonal stimulation to increase egg production on any given cycle, and surgical retrieval of eggs is performed under sedation. Recent advances in capacity to successfully freeze and thaw eggs have enabled egg banks (Golombok, 2020). Embryo donation is made possible by the common practice during ART treatment of creating more embryos than individual couples wish to use, and then freezing the surplus embryos.

In recent decades the profile of recipients and donors has changed; advances in treatment of male infertility have meant that fewer heterosexual couples use donated sperm to conceive, while social and legal reforms have opened this pathway to parenting to single women and lesbian couples (Patterson, 2019). A well-established trend to postpone childbearing in high-income countries has led to increased demand for donated eggs and embryos (Human Fertilisation and Embryology Authority, (HFEA, 2020). The desire of single women and gay couples to 'have their own child' with genetic or 'blood ties' and to have a child through means that appear conventional or 'natural' has expanded the clientele engaged with the ART industry and commercial markets for donated gametes (Graham, 2014). There has been a parallel trend for intending parents to make their arrangements directly with potential donors, either through within-family arrangements or through advertisements on contact websites and social media. These unregulated arrangements can lead to medical and legal risks and result in less clear boundaries between donors and recipients (Jacob, 2017).

The most substantial body of research on parenting after conception involving third party donation has come from the UK Longitudinal Study of Children Conceived through ART, led by Susan Golombok in Cambridge, in the United Kingdom. Parent wellbeing, adjustment to parenting, and child developmental outcomes have been examined in samples of parents conceiving through egg, sperm, embryo donation, conventional IVF, surrogacy, and adoption. Mixed methods (quantitative methodologies, in-depth narrative interviews, observations of parent–child relationships, teacher reports, reports from offspring) have offset the influence of socially desirable responding. Results indicate overall positive functioning for parents and their children throughout childhood, irrespective of mode of conception and genetic relatedness (see Golombok, 2019, for a comprehensive review). The researchers acknowledge various limitations of this body of research: relatively low response rates, the use of convenience samples possibly biased towards those experiencing positive adjustment, the possibility of socially desirable responding in those likely to be sensitive to scrutiny and stigma (although study instruments [described earlier] are robust to this), and unanswered questions related to the impact of secrecy and disclosure, particularly for families conceiving through egg and embryo donation (Golombok et al., 2017; MacCallum & Golombok, 2007). Studies typically focus on childhood and adolescence, with very little research on adjustment during the transition to parenthood.

Becoming a Parent through Donor Insemination (DI)

When conception through sperm donation is managed in an ART clinic, medical screening of sperm is mandatory. Many ART clinics collaborate with overseas sperm banks, and require that the legislative requirements in the recipient's home country be met before they accept exported sperm. Women can, however, independently purchase sperm online from commercial sperm banks (often in a different country, with the United States a major supplier), and use 'direct insemination' at home. Conceiving with donated sperm is part of a mercantile process: there are detailed catalogues (displaying photographs, hobbies, religion, academic achievements of donors). The sperm from the selected donor is mailed, frozen in a cannister, to the purchaser. Sperm donation has always provoked social anxiety, with images of adultery and incest and worry about bloodlines, and inheritance. Psychotherapist Joan Raphael-Leff (2005) describes intra-psychic challenges a woman may experience when pregnant with donated sperm; the sense of a 'foreign body' (p. 97) within her, anxiety about who the baby will look like, and fantasies about the donor.

Heterosexual Couples

Donor insemination has been available to heterosexual couples through ART clinics for many decades. Concerns have focused on the potential psychological impact on the parent–child relationship and the family dynamic when one parent (the person the child knows as father) is not genetically related, and the impact on the child of disclosure of that information. Golombok (2019) summarises results from studies across childhood. Findings indicate that heterosexual couples who have conceived through DI generally show effective parenting and positive parent–child relationships, irrespective of genetic relatedness and disclosure. One study found evidence of higher emotional distress in middle childhood for those mothers who kept mode of conception secret (Golombok et al., 2011). While causal links between disclosure and more positive functioning have not been established, there is a broad consensus among social scientists that disclosure in the preschool years is likely to be optimal for the wellbeing of offspring (Golombok, 2020).

Single Mothers by Choice
As legislation has enabled equitable access to ART Clinics, there has been a growing trend for single women to become parents through donor insemination (Golombok, 2020; Guzzo &Hayford, 2020). Nonetheless, they remain vulnerable to stigma and criticism. Media representations reflect disapproval of intentionally creating a child who will not have a father, a view that conception using donor sperm is unnatural, that it represents a concerning consumerist attitude to parenthood, and one that can make men redundant (Zadeh & Foster, 2016). In Chapter 3, discussion about becoming a single mother focused on the challenges for young women who become parents on their own, after unintended pregnancies, often in socio-economically deprived circumstances. In contrast, women who make an active choice to be a single parent through sperm donation, tend to be older, well educated, and financially independent. They have typically spent many years thinking about becoming a parent, and DI is rarely their first choice; rather it is often a decision based on concern about age-related declines in fertility (Golombok et al., 2005; Golombok., 2020).

Playwright Alexandra Collier (2020) describes her decision in her late thirties to take this path to parenthood when her romantic life was out of synchrony with her 'baby hunger' and her reproductive timeline. It was not an easy decision; she worried about judgement from her family and friends (the word 'selfish' was frequently used); she worried it would imply she had failed at finding a partner, and she worried about how she would cope with raising a child alone. The conception was organised through an ART Clinic. She had rejected the option of using a friend's sperm, concerned that it would feel like a pseudo-marriage with complex legal and emotional consequences. The autonomy afforded by using donor sperm seemed preferable. Collier was fortunate; after deliberating for several months about which donor to choose from a database, and injecting herself with hormones to promote ovulation, she conceived with the first insemination procedure; chose a professional support person (doula) to support her during the birth, and subsequently gave birth to a healthy son.

Her parents, initially wary about her decision, became enthusiastic and supportive once the baby was born, and her brother and her father have become important men in her child's life.

There is limited empirical research on adjustment during pregnancy and early parenthood for single women who conceive through DI; most is based on in-depth interviews with socially advantaged samples. The cohort of single women in the United Kingdom longitudinal study have shown positive psychological adjustment during infancy with comparable warmth, joy, and bonding with the infant, and psychological wellbeing, when compared with naturally conceiving couples and heterosexual couples conceiving through DI. The single difference identified was that the single mothers reported less interaction with their young infants and showed less sensitivity during observed interaction, perhaps due to not having a partner to assist during the exhausting early months of parenthood (Murray & Golombok, 2005a). A follow-up at two years, showed, however, that compared with the married mothers, the single mothers reported greater joy and less anger towards their children (Murray & Golombok, 2005b), and these positive findings were sustained when the children were pre-schoolers (Golombok et al., 2016) and in middle childhood (Golombok, 2020). A growing body of research on child and family outcomes in planned lesbian families where women conceive using DI reports similarly positive findings, discussed later in this chapter.

Becoming a Parent through Egg Donation

When a couple conceives using egg donation, the father may be genetically related, but the mother is not. As discussed earlier, the expectant mother experiences pregnancy, birth, and breastfeeding and all the hormonal and neurological changes that go along with that. There is limited empirical evidence on adjustment during the transition to parenthood, with some studies retrospectively exploring the experience of pregnancy.

Golombok and colleagues (2004) found no differences in mood or relationship satisfaction comparing fifty-one parents conceiving through egg donation with eighty naturally conceiving parents when their infants were aged between nine and twelve months, however there was some concern about potential stigma in the egg-donation group. More recently, Imrie and colleagues (2019) explored psychological health and the couple relationship during early parenthood (infants aged between six and eighteen months) in fifty-seven heterosexual couples conceiving through egg donation compared with fifty-six couples conceiving through IVF, where both parents were genetically related to the child. There were more similarities than differences on questionnaire measures of mood, relationship satisfaction, and parenting stress. Scores were generally within the normal range, with some increased vulnerability related to older parental age. Older mothers conceiving through egg donation reported less social support from family, but adequate support from friendship groups and older fathers whose partner had conceived through egg donation reported poorer psychological health.

Developing a Maternal Identity and Relationship with the Unborn Baby
In retrospective surveys, women conceiving through egg donation have indicated that while they thought about not being genetically related to the foetus during pregnancy, most felt this did not influence their developing relationship with the child (Hertz & Nelson, 2016). Conceiving through egg donation may make the process of adapting during the transition to parenthood more complex, however. Maggie Kirkman (2008) conducted in-depth interviews with twenty-one women who had conceived through egg donation. They downplayed the role of genetics and emphasised the importance of gestation, pointing out that they had fed the baby through the umbilical cord for nine months. Nonetheless, the lack of a genetic connection was experienced as a meaningful absence for some of them, who described feeling 'inauthentic' and like an 'imposter' during pregnancy and early parenthood. Future disclosure was also on their minds, as some of the respondents were worried that the child might reject them, or that disclosure would expose that they were not the 'real' mother. Some women worried that inability to conceive with their own eggs, might also compromise their capacity to give birth normally or breastfeed.

Imrie and colleagues (2020) have confirmed with a larger sample that the process of establishing a maternal identity and a relationship with the baby is complex and individualised after conception through egg donation. Their study is the most methodologically sophisticated to date, using an attachment theory informed narrative interview to access unconscious caregiving representations in ninety-nine women conceiving through egg donation. Most did not know the identity of the donor. Thematic analysis of interview transcripts showed that the lack of genetic relatedness raised concerns about bonding with the baby and about who the baby would look like. New mothers described a variety of cognitive strategies to make the baby feel like their own. These included downplaying the donor's contribution, for example likening egg donation to blood or tissue donation, and also emphasising the importance of gestation and their physical contribution through a shared blood supply to the baby's growth and development, also noted in Kirkman's study, discussed earlier. Experiencing pregnancy was important. Some women described how having the baby inside them (feeling movements and kicking) enabled them to develop a representation of the baby as a person. After birth, experiences developing a relationship with the baby varied: some expressed sadness that the baby did not look like them, while others felt the baby was their own from the very beginning. Most highlighted the contribution of consistent, responsive, parenting behaviour, rather than genetics, in shaping the baby's personality, and felt secure and confident as a mother by the end of the first postnatal year. A minority were still struggling at that stage to feel that the baby was really theirs. Clearly many new mothers have struggles of this kind, however the women conceiving through egg donation were inclined to attribute their difficulties integrating a maternal identity to the fact that they were not genetically related to the child.

Becoming a Parent through Embryo Donation

Embryo donation is like adoption in that neither parent is genetically related to the child. There are marked differences, however. The rigorous screening protocols that are typically prerequisites for adoption generally don't apply. Embryo recipients, like donor egg recipients, see the gestational connection during pregnancy and childbirth as significant for developing an attachment relationship to the unborn baby and they value the opportunity to exercise control over the antenatal environment (Goedeke & Daniels, 2017). As is the case for egg and sperm donation, recipient parents need to accept the lack of a genetic link with their child, and consider if, when, and how, they will tell the child of its origins. MacCallum and Keeley (2012) found that many couples conceiving through 'closed' embryo donation do not intend to tell the child, and even when they do have such plans, they often don't enact them. Recent practice changes that support early and ongoing contact between donors and recipients have reduced the potential for secrecy in Australia (Jacob, 2017) and in the United Kingdom (Golombok, 2020), with implications for how communication and contact with the donor couple and their children will be managed.

Becoming a Parent through Surrogacy

Secrecy is not an option for parents having a baby with the assistance of a surrogate. They will need to explain to everyone how they became parents, and they are likely to experience disapproval and stigma (Golombok, 2020). When surrogates are known, the intending parents will need to negotiate with them regarding the degree of contact and their own involvement in the pregnancy and birth. When they are unknown, intending parents may feel excluded or remote from the gestational process, with potential concerns about the surrogate's feelings about relinquishing the child, and the potential for commercial exploitation, discussed in more detail later in this chapter.

Despite the complexity and controversy associated with this path to parenthood, available research suggests positive parenting outcomes. Heterosexual couples conceiving with the involvement of a surrogate who participated in the UK longitudinal study have been compared with parents conceiving through egg donation, and with naturally conceiving parents across childhood, from one year after birth through to adolescence. Estimated to represent about 60 per cent of the eligible families, 70 per cent of the study participants had used an unknown surrogate. Results indicated that those becoming parents with the involvement of a surrogate reported more positively than the naturally conceiving parents on most study measures (parenting stress, depression, enjoyment of parenting, warmth, and attachment behaviours directed to the child) at each of the early study follow-ups (Golombok et al., 2004, 2006). Outcomes were not related to whether the surrogate parents were genetically related to the child, however parent adjustment was more positive in cases where the surrogate was a relative or friend (Golombok et al., 2004). The small numbers and significant attrition limit generalisability, and there is a clear need for more research. There is no published evidence to date on adjustment during pregnancy; a time when managing the relationship with the surrogate may be particularly challenging. There is, however, emerging research on relations between intending gay fathers and surrogates (perhaps the largest group becoming parents via surrogacy) discussed later in this chapter.

Donor/Recipient Relationships: Indebtedness and the 'Gift Dynamic'

Demand for donated sperm, eggs, and embryos greatly exceeds supply, and this has the potential to contribute to a complex 'gift dynamic' whereby recipients feel profoundly indebted to donors (Kirkman, 2008). One approach to boosting the number of donors has been the practice of conditional donation, which allows donors to specify who will receive their embryos (or eggs) (McMahon & Saunders, 2009). This can lead to discriminatory decisions, however. For example, donors may choose to exclude single women or lesbian couples, or couples from specific religious, cultural, or ethnic groups (MacCallum & Keeley, 2012). Despite altruistic motives, complicated and ambivalent power relationships can emerge, particularly when there is direct negotiation between donors and potential recipients on 'contact websites'. In a small Australian study, one embryo donor explained how she arrived at her decision about who would receive her embryos: it was based on her perception of the 'worthiness' of potential recipients: 'I chose her, she didn't choose me. I feel really comfortable; in that I know how hard they've tried, so I know they will be appreciative of the donation' (Jacob, 2017, p. 31).

Study participants reported a range of views regarding contact. Some donors wanted detailed progress reports at every stage of the pregnancy, while others felt a tension between their desire for contact and the need to respect recipient privacy and freedom from scrutiny: 'We want to know, but we also don't want to know ... we would only keep in contact for the children, because they're full-blooded siblings' (Jacob, 2017, p. 33). Another donor was wary, and preferred minimal contact: ' if you know too much you can start to get concerned' (p. 34). There are different views on the appropriateness of an 'open adoption' model for embryo donation. Millbank and colleagues (2017) recommend flexible, elective approaches that reflect different donor and recipient preferences and needs. Currently, there is no clear evidence regarding which practices are in the best interests of donors, recipients, and offspring, but there is consensus that early disclosure is generally best for children and families (Golombok, 2020).

Increasingly, sperm, egg, and embryo donation arrangements are organised by potential donors and recipients through online communities via social media. It can be challenging for couples to manage early and regular contact in a fully open environment without professional support and oversight (Goedeke & Daniels, 2017; Jacob, 2017; van den Akker, 2017). While Millbank and colleagues (2017) argue that mandatory counselling can be an obstacle to donation, Jacob takes the view that counselling is a duty of care for clinics as part of their contribution to the conception of the child. Open donation is increasingly the preferred practice, however there is very little evidence regarding how couples manage the process, which can be particularly complex when it is other family members who donate.

In a more open environment, there is the potential for difficult relational dynamics with sperm donors as well. In one landmark legal case in

Australia, a sperm donor who was a close friend of the mother (a woman in a lesbian relationship), was involved in the life of the baby from the outset. He was present for the pregnancy scans; he cut the cord at the birth; he regularly visited the family afterwards; and often did childcare, preschool, and school pick-ups. When the two mothers decided to relocate to New Zealand, he objected, took his fight for paternity rights through the court system, ultimately to the High Court, and won the case, setting a legal precedent (Callaghan, 2019).

The gift dynamic is most complex in the case of surrogacy. The surrogate's contribution is more substantial, intimate, and personal, as she carries and gives birth to the infant (Golombok, 2020). Reviews to date suggest surrogates generally adjust well to relinquishing the baby and that they are able to maintain satisfying ongoing relations with intending parents and offspring (Söderström-Anttila et al., 2016; van den Akker, 2007, 2017), however there are few studies, and they have significant limitations, most notably in the representativeness of samples (Söderström-Anttila et al., 2016). Van den Akker (2007, 2017) points out that both surrogate and intending mothers (and fathers) use cognitive restructuring to reconcile their unusual path to parenthood. For example, surrogate mothers are trained and encouraged to view the foetus as 'not theirs', and to view themselves as not the 'real mother'. One surrogate mother interviewed by Golombok and colleagues (2006) describes how she intentionally avoided activities that might promote attachment to the foetus. She refrained from speculating about what the baby would look like, buying clothes, and preparing a nursery, arguing that these were the prerogative of the intending parents. Many surrogates report moderate short-term distress after birth, and that they particularly miss the close and regular contact with intending parents during pregnancy (Golombok, 2020; van den Akker, 2017).

When the surrogacy process is highly regulated, there are few reports of emotional distress. There are more concerns about surrogate wellbeing when arrangements are trans-national, as there can be marked socio-economic inequities between intending parents and surrogates, and different cultural expectations and legal guidelines around contact and procedures (Golombok, 2020; van den Akker, 2007). A study of 50 Indian surrogates recruited between 2015 and 2017 found that the surrogates had more depressed mood than a comparison group of pregnant Indian women during pregnancy and postnatally, that most were unable to meet with intending parents, and many were not allowed to see the baby or even keep a photograph, leading to considerable distress after birth (Lamba et al., 2018). More positive relationships between intending parents and surrogates have been reported for Italian gay fathers whose surrogates were pregnant and gave birth in North America (Carone et al., 2017), discussed in more detail later in this chapter.

LGBTQ Parents

There are several pathways to parenthood for gender diverse adults. While some same-sex, transgender, and gender non-binary couples may have become parents with prior heterosexual partners, the next section focuses on a growing body of research evidence regarding the processes of adaptation when lesbian or gay couples choose to embark on parenthood together, using donated sperm, eggs, or surrogates (and ART), or adopting a child. The section concludes with an overview of emerging research on options for bisexual, queer, transgender, and gender non-binary adults who want to become parents.

Two Mothers: Becoming Parents as a Lesbian Couple

While women have raised children together over many generations, families initiated by openly identified lesbian couples deciding to become parents together are a relatively recent phenomenon. There is limited research on the decision-making process, and their experience of pregnancy and the transition to parenthood. Some lesbian couples will choose to foster or adopt a child (discussed later in this chapter). The choice to conceive using insemination with donor sperm (DI) is increasingly the preferred pathway (Patterson, 2019). In common with all women becoming pregnant through DI, there are practical decisions to be made regarding the method of conception (home or clinic), and the involvement of the sperm donor in the child's life. There may be additional challenges: reconciling a maternal with a lesbian identity, confronting the potentially divisive relational dynamics of choosing which of the women will become pregnant and be genetically related to the child, and, in some cases, hostility and opposition from extended family (Wojnar & Katzenmeyer, 2014).

Birth Mothers and Co-Mothers: Complexities of Maternal Identity
Which of the women will become pregnant? There are practical considerations: age, health, individual differences in the desire to be pregnant, and in capacity to conceive. Some couples plan more than one child and

intend to alternate (Wojnar & Katzenmeyer, 2014); some opt for a more complex approach, whereby one woman will donate her egg, while the other will be the gestational mother; after embryo transfer, she will carry the pregnancy and give birth. This approach requires ART (Golombok, 2019; Patterson, 2019). Hayman and colleagues (2015) interviewed 30 Australian lesbian women (15 couples) about the decision-making process. The decision related to a 'butch–femme' dynamic (Rosario et al., 2009) where the 'femme-identified' woman was considered the obvious choice for childbearing in some cases. Couples who did not identify butch–femme roles based their decision on age and health, generally choosing the younger partner. If more than one child was planned, the older partner was chosen for the first pregnancy, in case her time for childbearing was limited.

The 'Co-Mother'.   Navigating the transition to co-parenthood can be challenging. First, the terminology can be confusing and problematic. The woman who does not give birth is generally referred to as the co-mother (or non-birth mother). In some cases, as noted earlier, the co-mother is the genetic mother of the child. The perspective of the non-birth (non-gestational) co-mother has been largely absent in research. Two studies (McKelvey, 2014; Wojnar & Katzenmeyer, 2014) have conducted in-depth interviews to explore the experiences of the transition to parenthood of co-mothers who do not give birth . Feeling like an outsider was a pervasive theme in both, accompanied by a sense of unreality about the pregnancy in the absence of physical symptoms (although this was mitigated by seeing ultrasound images of the baby moving). Non-birth mothers reported taking on a protective role towards their partner and the baby during the pregnancy, doing most of the physical housework and preparing healthy meals (McKelvey, 2014). In both studies, non-birth mothers reported feeling jealous and excluded, at least some of the time, when they were confronted with the intimate connection between their partner and the infant, particularly in relation to breastfeeding. Like most new parents in the early weeks and months, they struggled with changes to their relationship, whereby they received far less attention from their partner, and they felt guilty about feeling this way (Wojnar & Katzenmeyer, 2014). Similar feelings are frequently reported by fathers in heterosexual couples (Chapter 4).

In terms of relations with the baby, non-birth mothers were conscious of the potential role of biology in attachment and caregiving. Several feared that the baby would not bond with them, and that they would never achieve the deep connection to the infant that their partner had, even if they took on the role of primary caregiver. As one woman explains:

> I was the one who stayed behind and changed the diapers and fed him. But when she came home from work, he would instantly squeal in joy. Sometimes I felt there were just the two of them in the entire universe. He loves me too, there's no question about it, but when it comes to choosing between the two of us, he knows who his real mother is. I guess the biology always prevails when it comes to mothers and babies. (Wojnar & Katzenmeyer, 2014, p. 57)

Choices regarding sperm donors and method of conception are often aimed at ensuring the non-birth mother feels included (Hayman et al., 2015; Wojnar & Katzenmeyer, 2014). Some couples explained that they had chosen an anonymous donor to protect the parenting status of the non-birth mother, as it avoids a complex dynamic where the sperm donor (biological father) may want an active parenting role and/or feels that he could stake a claim to the child. In both studies, women reported trying to match physical characteristics of the non-birth mother with those of the sperm donor. When a known donor was chosen, the goal was to facilitate the child's ease of contact with their genetic father, whilst ensuring that the non-birth mother didn't feel marginalised. Some chose a brother of the non-birth mother, so they could achieve a genetic link, and several gave the infant the last name of the non-birth mother to formalise and legitimise her connection.

A lack of external recognition and validation as a mother was also challenging and distressing. In the hospital, non-birth mothers reported feeling ignored, misunderstood, or judged by nursing staff. Defined by 'who I am not', they felt they had to repeatedly come out as a lesbian and explain themselves and their family to relative strangers (McKelvey, 2014, p. 108). While some of these feelings (being ignored, treated as marginal), have been described by heterosexual fathers in healthcare settings, the experience was further compounded due to a lack of legal and semantic recognition of non-birth mothers as parents, leaving them to feel that their very legitimacy was questioned.

There is some evidence that non-birth co-mothers are more involved in childcare than is typical for fathers (Patterson et al., 2014), and that they may be more vulnerable to post-partum depression than the birth mother (Wojnar & Katzenmeyer, 2014). This may be due to stigma, and to the absence of scripts, role models, and guidance, as parenting literature is targeted almost exclusively at birthmothers (McKelvey, 2014).

Psychological and Social Adjustment
The national longitudinal lesbian family study in the United States is one of the most comprehensive sources of research data (see Gartrell 2020; Patterson, 2019 for reviews). The study commenced before birth and continued across childhood into adolescence with exceptional retention of participants. Experiences of lesbian mothers were compared with US normative data. Findings to date indicate overall positive outcomes; a greater likelihood of two actively engaged parents, and equitable sharing of childcare and housework achieved through mutual agreement. There are many similarities with the well-documented experiences of heterosexual couples during the transition to parenthood: concerns about the decline in available time and energy for partners, more relationship conflict, and less sexual engagement. Lesbian women generally reported enhanced relationships with their families of origin, including a more explicit acceptance of their own couple relationship, and changes in their social network, with declines in socialising with childless lesbian friends.

Two Fathers: Becoming Parents as a Gay Couple

The numbers of gay men expressing a desire to become parents together is growing (Guzzo & Hayford, 2020). It is not an easy path, however, as the gap between desire and intention to parent is larger for gay men than for lesbian women (Patterson, 2019). Social barriers are similar: there may be a lack of support from the family of origin for some, as well as social stigma and a questioning of entitlement to parent (Murphy, 2013). These barriers can be even more daunting for men, as they need to engage with complex and costly arrangements involving Assisted Reproductive Technology (including surrogacy), or adoption (Patterson, 2019). The pathway chosen is likely to be influenced by financial, medical, and legal considerations (see Josh's story at the end of this chapter).

Taking on a Paternal Identity
Like lesbian mothers, gay fathers may struggle to reconcile seemingly contradictory identities as members of the gay community and parents (Bergman et al., 2010). The decision to become a parent runs counter to both heteronormative definitions of masculinity and paternity, and the dominant gender and sexual norms of gay culture. Many gay men have assumed that coming out as gay means that parenthood is not an option for them (Berkowitz & Marsiglio, 2007; Murphy, 2013). Earlier developmental conflicts and social stigma about gender identity can be reactivated

when gay men contemplate parenthood (Glazer, 2014). For some, coming out as gay activates and intensifies their procreation and caregiving desires (Berkowitz & Marsiglio, 2007). There are also social motivations. Gay men participating in a study by Blake and colleagues (2017) described the importance of intergenerational transmission of the family line and the family name (Blake et al., 2017). Dean Murphy (2013) interviewed thirty Australian gay men who became parents through surrogacy (arranged in the United States). Several described a powerful, innate desire to reproduce, to the extent that they had prioritised finding a partner interested in having children, and they had raised the issue early in the relationship. More liberal social attitudes and public discourse were also influential – the growing representation of gay parents in the media, and web-based promotional materials published by commercial surrogacy agencies. Men in this study were well informed about the practical challenges and the costs and benefits of surrogacy (not legal in Australia) compared with adoption. The opportunity to have genetically related children (at least for one member of the couple), was a powerful motivator:

> I guess a lot of parents probably would probably deny this, but I think that for a lot of people there's a biological imperative to reproduce and I don't know if it's to do with ego or what, but to almost … see themselves in children … I think with an adoptive child, maybe, of course you'd love them, but maybe there's not that actual, it's an animal kind of thing, that animal connectedness with them. (Murphy, 2013; Andrew, p. 1116)

Becoming Gay Fathers through Surrogacy

Surrogacy is the most controversial application of ART; it is not legal in many jurisdictions, frequently involves international arrangements and brokers, and is extremely costly, with estimates of a minimum of US$100,000 in the United States (Golombok, 2020). Golombok points out that gay father families formed through surrogacy are a minority group, even among other non-traditional family forms. They defy both personal and social conventions and deviate most from the traditional nuclear family, as there are two fathers and two mothers, a genetic (egg donor) and gestational mother, but no mother in the family home.

Available evidence about the quality of parenting, wellbeing of the children, and life satisfaction for the men concerned is generally positive (see Carneiro et al., 2017 for a systematic review). This may be due, in part, to the fact that men who achieve parenthood through ART and surrogacy are a highly selected and well-resourced group. Maturity, resolute motivation, and financial security are required to negotiate the daunting social, structural, legal, and institutional barriers. Gay couples are required to meet stringent mental health criteria for acceptance into some, but not all, surrogacy programs (Greenfeld & Seli, 2011). There is currently scant research focusing on the transition to parenthood for gay fathers, however a few qualitative studies have explored the decision-making processes, the desire for children, and relations with the surrogate.

Compared with adoption, surrogacy allows gay parents to have knowledge of both progenitors and provides the opportunity to acquire the baby very soon after birth, so the child will not have had previous separation or abandonment experiences. Genetic relatedness is not important to all gay fathers (Blake et al., 2017; Goldberg et al., 2012; Murphy, 2013). Those who assign less importance, are more likely to adopt, discussed later.

Which Father will be Genetically Related? Gay couples face similar dilemmas to those described above for lesbian mothers. Men in Murphy's (2013) study described several strategies to address the fact that the baby could only be genetically related to one of them. Some planned two children, preferably using eggs from the same donor, fertilised with sperm from each father, either consecutively (taking turns to provide sperm) or with the goal of a twin pregnancy. Others sought to achieve a similar phenotype to the father who was not genetically related, through their choice of egg donor. For example, one couple used sperm from one of the men and an egg donated by his partner's sister; for one mixed race couple, it was important to choose a Eurasian egg donor, to ensure the baby looked similar to the father whose sperm were not involved. Still others went to considerable lengths to obscure the genetic connection, mixing sperm for 'intentional unknowing' (which has implications for the child, later); others were committed to secrecy, and chose not to tell others which father was the biological parent: 'So we don't want people thinking "oh right, your're the real father, and no, you're not". We're both equal fathers, we want to be recognized that way ....' (Murphy, 2013, p. 1118).

Contact with the Surrogate. During pregnancy, physical distance from the surrogate mother and the foetus growing inside her can be a source of anxiety for gay intending fathers, leading to a sense of alienation and detachment from the pregnancy (Ziv & Freund-Eschar, 2015). This is particularly the case for international arrangements. One Israeli father whose surrogate was brokered and managed through an agency in India described his experience as follows:

> ... pregnancy is this folder ... my pregnancy is fed on emails, reports and Excel tables. This binder is full of formal documents but has no emotionality ... You do not see anything or know anything ... You travel to India and you come back with a child in your hands. (Roy, p. 161)

Six of the eight men interviewed in this study described their experience of pregnancy as unreal, 'theoretical'. While all men are one step removed from the biological experience of pregnancy, these gay fathers regretted that they couldn't accompany the woman for scans, see her growing belly, and feel and observe the baby's movements. They struggled to imagine the foetus and described feelings of powerlessness – that they had no capacity to protect the wellbeing of the surrogate or the future child. In contrast, the fathers in the study who had a surrogate in the United States or Canada (a significantly more costly arrangement), had regular contact in an open arrangement with the surrogate, including the option to visit her in her home, observe her way of life, and talk with her about her interactions with the developing foetus.

Fathers in an Italian study (also involving international surrogacy arrangements) emphasised the importance of the surrogate helping them to feel emotionally connected with the developing child, however they were keen to clarify that her role was temporary:

> I could trust her, for me the pregnancy meant only that something which was mine was growing somewhere else, in someone else's house ... she was amazing in involving us ... she wrote down every aspect of the pregnancy. (Carone et al., 2017; p. 185)

Another highlighted the importance of the surrogate's language: 'She always said "your child". In doing so, all was defined ... we were the parents, she was the surrogate' (p. 185). Most were profoundly grateful to the surrogate and determined she would always be a part of their child's life as an 'auntie' or 'tummy-mummy'.

Enthusiastically embracing practical preparations (the complexities of surrogacy-related travel, taking legal steps to formalise parental status, reading parenting books, preparing a nursery) provided compensation when there was physical distance. Nonetheless, all men interviewed were acutely conscious of a missing an emotional layer during pregnancy and hoped this would be overcome once they had a physical connection with the child.

Psychological and Social Adjustment

Bergman and colleagues (2010) conducted an in-depth study of the transition to parenthood for forty gay American fathers who became parents through surrogacy. Interviews indicated very similar experiences to those described for heterosexual couples and lesbian women: marked changes to lifestyle and work patterns, and declines in romance, personal intimacy, and sexual relations, alongside an improved self-esteem and sense of meaning in life. While changes to social networks are typical during the transition to parenthood, the gay men reported a notable shift, socialising more with heterosexual parents, with whom they had more in common, and many found they had less contact with their gay childless friends. In this study, all but two of the forty participants were pleasantly surprised by the support from grandparents and extended family, which led to more frequent contact and explicit endorsement of their relationship with their partner and their new family unit, also noted by lesbian mothers (as discussed earlier). The complexity and the costs of the surrogacy pathway to parenthood are prohibitive, and this pathway to parenthood is not an option for many gay men, who may need to explore options to become parents through adoption, discussed later in this chapter (Goldberg et al., 2012).

Transgender and Gender Non-Binary Parents

Sex and gender are in alignment for some individuals and not for others. A growing number of adolescents and adults are identifying as transgender or gender non-binary (TGNB) (Tornello et al., 2019). Research is only beginning to emerge on their pathways to parenthood, their experiences of pregnancy and early parenthood, and family wellbeing. In the most substantial study to date, Tornello and colleagues reviewed pathways to parenthood for 311 TGNB parents from diverse geographical locations in the United States. Most became parents through biological means rather than adoption or fostering. Those with a partner assigned a different sex at birth generally did so through sexual intercourse, and those whose partner was assigned the same sex at birth conceived using an egg or sperm donor, generally with ART). Transgender women (assigned male at birth) were likely to become parents before their gender transition, while transgender men (assigned female at birth) and gender nonbinary adults were more likely to become parents after gender transition. Tornello and colleagues point out that this can present significant emotional and biological challenges due to the need to stop hormone therapy and deal with the physical changes of pregnancy. The younger participants in this large study were more likely to become parents *after* their gender transition, likely due to changing social norms, however many reported difficulties finding health providers who would work with them in culturally sensitive ways tailored to their individual needs.

Similar challenges were reported in a smaller British Study, where researchers interviewed eleven transgender parents about their experiences. Respondents found the transition to parenthood to be a very stressful time, as they negotiated non-supportive and judgmental attitudes in IVF and adoption services (Bower-Brown & Zadeh, 2021). Riggs and Bartholomaeus (2020) discuss the need for trans-inclusive fertility education that allows adolescents who intend transition to make informed decisions regarding fertility preservation options at the time when decisions are being made about puberty suppression, so that the option of biological parenthood remains open in the future. Riggs and Bartholomaeus caution that education programs need to ensure informed choice, whilst avoiding pronatalist pressure. We return to these issues in Chapter 9.

An exploratory study by Imrie and colleagues (2020) examined family functioning and parent–child relationships in thirty-five families with transgender parents, using the multi-informant, multi-method approach employed in the UK longitudinal study of non-traditional families. Results indicated generally good quality relationships and positive child adjustment (compared with normative British data) during middle childhood, however the researchers acknowledged the small sample size, which is problematic given the heterogeneity of the sample – there were diverse family structures, a broad age range of children and parents, and many different methods of achieving parenthood. Child wellbeing was related to relationships within the family, and to parent stress, depression, and social support, rather than parent sexuality, gender identity, or family type.

The Transition to Parenthood for Adoptive Parents

Much of the above discussion has focused on genetic and gestational relatedness. Adoptive parents have neither. The adoption process is bureaucratically onerous, costly, and lengthy. It can take anything from nine months to nine years (Skandrani et al., 2019). Widespread access to contraception and termination of pregnancy has led to a situation where there are dramatically fewer healthy newborns available for adoption in Western countries, compared to the middle and latter decades of the twentieth century. There was a surge in intercountry adoptions during the 1990s, due to global health problems, political instability, and Government policies in China that mandated one child families. These numbers have also significantly declined in recent decades, due to changes in China's population policy, concerns about child trafficking and commodification, debate about cross-ethnic and cross-racial adoptions, cross-cultural sensitivities, and increased regulation of intercountry adoption (Guzzo & Hayford, 2020).

The children available through intercountry adoption tend to be older, and come from countries struggling with internal conflict, poverty, and war. There are many challenges establishing a relationship with an older child who may be from a different racial, language, and cultural background. The child's pre-adoption history is likely to be complex; there may be pre-existing health, developmental, or emotional problems related to a history of trauma or abuse, and multiple separation experiences. Information may not be available about birth parents and early health history. When adoption processes are open, adopting parents will need to support the adopted child's contact with birth parents, on a regular basis (Skandrani et al., 2019).

Skandrani and colleagues note that on a day-to-day basis, parents adopting older children may be faced with a child who has under-developed or disrupted attachment capacity, unresolved grief, organic learning or behaviour problems, and cultural disorientation. The parents will need to manage naïve, sometimes idealised expectations about the extent to which parental love and good intentions can heal past trauma. Parents adopting older children need professional support to relinquish idealised expectations, develop the skills required to support a child with complex needs, and embrace and accept the long-term nature of the process they have embarked upon.

In some Western countries, there is a growing trend to facilitate early adoption of children removed from their birth families and placed in temporary foster care in the child protection system (e.g., Australian Institute of Health and Welfare, 2021b). These children, who have experienced several separations, are likely to present similar challenges to those adopted through intercountry arrangements discussed above. The goal is to provide a safe-haven and secure base for the child by avoiding the trauma and instability of multiple placements and separation experiences when the preferred option of reunification with birth parents is not possible. Meg and Kym describe their experiences of adopting a daughter through the welfare system later in this chapter.

Adoptive parents face many challenges. Well-meaning friends tell stories of adoptions gone wrong, and adoptive parents and children may experience stigma and discrimination. There is an extensive literature on developmental outcomes for adopted children and family dynamics in adopted families, and a broad consensus that adoption is a social intervention that generally leads to long-term positive outcomes for the child (Palacios & Brodzinsky, 2010). There has been scant research, however, regarding the experience of the transition to parenthood for adopting parents.

Who Adopts?

The profile of adopting parents is changing. More lesbian, gay, trans and gender non-binary couples, and professional single women are now able to adopt as social attitudes have become more inclusive and liberal (Guzzo & Hayford, 2020). The capacity of adoptive parents to adapt to the stress of the transition to parenthood is influenced by characteristics of the adoptive context (the child's age, trauma, and placement history, whether the adoption is intercountry or domestic, whether it is an open or closed adoption), and their own psycho-social resources and vulnerabilities (Belsky, 1984). Adoptive parents are generally older, well educated, financially well-resourced, and have been in a couple relationship for some time (Palacios & Brodzinsky, 2010). Perhaps due to extensive screening and scrutiny of their suitability, they are typically high-functioning adults with excellent potential and high motivation to parent. Research shows that both heterosexual (Calvo et al., 2015) and gay adoptive parents (Goldberg et al., 2012) are likely to have positive recall of their own parents, secure attachment styles, positive relationships with partners, and healthy psychological functioning. They are, therefore, well placed to negotiate stressful life transitions and to provide the corrective attachment experiences that children need after trauma, abandonment, and institutionalised care.

The two partners are more equal travellers during the transition to parenthood than is the case for heterosexual couples conceiving spontaneously, or for same-sex couples conceiving through sperm and egg donation (as discussed previously). The lengthy screening process and intensive planning also make it more likely that any differences in expectations and potential conflicts will be identified and dealt with before the child arrives.

The Process of Becoming a Parent through Adoption: Women's Experiences

In their quantitative study with a large, randomly selected, and nationally representative US population sample, Ceballo and colleagues (2004) found more similarities than differences during the transition to parenthood for adoptive compared with biological parents. Where there were differences, they were in the direction of more favourable adjustment for the adoptive parents, who reported less marital strain and higher satisfaction with becoming a parent. The researchers acknowledged that the children in this study were adopted during infancy, did not have special needs, and that the study relied only on self-report data.

Two in-depth qualitative studies shed some light on how adoptive mothers adapt as they prepare for their child and cope with the challenges of early encounters. Sandelowski and colleagues (1993) interviewed thirty-five infertile American women waiting to adopt domestically. Almost ten years later, Solchany (2000) interviewed twenty-one American women after they had adopted a child from China. Women in both studies described a lengthy period of 'hoping to be parents' with no clear starting point, no guaranteed due date, no pregnancy landmarks, no public signs to show others they were expecting a child, and no cultural rituals or scripts. Several used the term 'disembodied', describing an acute sense that there was a child somewhere, out there, but not inside. Nonetheless, it was a rich period of anticipation: 'a dynamic interlude in which they actively worked to ... transform disadvantage into advantage' (Sandelowski et al., 1993; p. 482). Like women pregnant after egg or embryo donation, adoptive parents downplayed the importance of genetics, pointing out that there was no guarantee that a genetically related child would be a good temperamental fit for parents, and that love was not contingent on a biological connection, as evident in their love for their partners.

The parents-in-waiting constructed fantasies about the child, the birth, and the birth parents. Sometimes a photograph offered a material reality. The pregnancy was experienced cautiously – in the earlier study, all participants had prior experiences of reproductive loss, and they were careful to limit their emotional investment: As one woman put it, 'I put a shield up over my heart' (Sandelowski et al., 1993; p. 473). There was a poignant awareness that their gain represented a loss for the relinquishing mother. In cases where there were 'matching criteria', some of the women invoked fate, and magical thinking. They felt it was worth waiting for the *right child*: 'when all the elements come together at the proper time, when we get her, we'll be able to say, "She's the one".' (p. 477). There were dilemmas, too, about the difficult choices adoptive parents are asked to make. One of the women, who had indicated that she would not accept a handicapped child, felt uncomfortable and guilty about the 'commodification' implicit in setting criteria that were acceptable to her (p. 479).

In Solchany's (2000) study of international adoption, intending mothers were troubled by the ethics of taking a child from one country to another. When they finally met the baby, many didn't feel entitled to call her their own. Conscious of the intimate pre-birth connections the baby had experienced with another woman, they worried that they would be rejected. Several described the challenge of having their first contact with the child in a public setting, dealing with the 'curt' business-like manner of the officials, and feeling like they were on trial or probation. One mother, who was suddenly presented with an older baby in a crowded waiting room in a foreign country, was unable to settle her, no matter what she tried:

> So her caretakers gave her to me. She … cried and cried and I cried, and she kicked, and she screamed, she tried to fight herself out of my arms … She looked up at me and sobbed big huge tears … Oh it was just awful, it was awful. It was awful. And I worried that they would take her away from me … nothing I did would comfort her. I just felt badly for her. Really overwhelming. (p. 49)

Adoptive parents need to reconcile the actual baby with the imagined baby, as all parents must do. This can be complicated by the need to come to terms with the child's history. When the baby's history was not available, imagined histories and birth mothers often loomed large for adoptive parents. They created elaborate reconstructions of the background to the adoption, attributing altruistic motives to the birth mother regarding the child's abandonment or relinquishment, but this in turn made them feel more guilt and empathy for her loss.

Adoptive mothers work through the challenges of forming a relationship with their baby in their own way, in their own time, and in the context of their own attachment history (Sandelowski et al., 1993; Solchany, 2000). Like all new parents, the baby's behaviour can be baffling at first, but gradually rendered understandable through observation, and ascribing meaning to the child's cues and signals. New parents may seek to 'normalise' challenging behaviour, for example interpreting crying and unsettled behaviour as evidence that the child had been securely attached prior to adoption. Some cope by minimising the significance of the child's pre-adoption trauma, and try to avoid thinking about it (Skandrani et al., 2019). Others may positively reframe, believing that due to their complex history, adopted babies have a deeper understanding of the world – a deeper awareness, attunement to joy, and capacity for happiness. (Solchany, 2000). As noted earlier, these idealised expectations may make it more difficult for adoptive parents to acknowledge and accept the protracted timeframe for establishing a relationship with the child and the inevitable hurdles they are likely to face.

Same-Sex Parents Adopting: Adoptive Fathers' Perspectives

There has been very little research attention directed to fathers' experiences of adoption, and most of the existing work focuses on gay fathers. Same-sex couples are more likely than heterosexual couples to adopt children (Gates, 2015) and gay men are more likely to pursue adoption than are lesbian women (Golombok, 2020). The willingness to adopt may be related to a greater valuing of relational than genetic ties in sexual minorities (Goldberg et al., 2012) and the fact that biological parenthood via surrogacy is so complex and inaccessible to many, due to extremely high costs. Goldberg and colleagues studied motivations for parenthood among seventy men (thirty-five gay male couples) who were planning to adopt, and they found a high concordance with the motivations described for heterosexual couples: they were strongly influenced by their partner's desire for a child and expressed altruistic motives to share their considerable financial resources and give a child in need a better chance in life.

The limited empirical research has studied fathers from middle- to upper-middle class backgrounds, typical of those who adopt. Few studies have included comparison groups of heterosexual fathers or lesbian mothers (Carneiro et al., 2017). Some have suggested that men in same-sex couples may experience a more stressful pathway through adoptive parenthood than do heterosexual and lesbian couples due to stigma, discriminatory attitudes, and questioning of their entitlement to parent (Golombok et al., 2014). The few available studies, however, report comparable parenting stress to heterosexual fathers and other adoptive parents (Farr, 2016; Golombok et al., 2014) and comparable warmth and sensitivity as a basis for secure attachment with their children (Carneiro et al., 2017). One study with a francophone Canadian sample of ninety-two gay adoptive fathers (forty-six couples) reported a more egalitarian division of tasks and high levels of involvement in childcare compared with community normative data (Feugé et al., 2019).

Summary Comments

The desire to have children is innate and universal, and one that crosses the lines of gender and sexual orientation (Goldberg et al., 2012). Research evidence challenges assumptions that genetic parents have instinctive advantages or that coping with infertility or social obstacles to parenting impedes parenting capacity. Adoptive parents (Palacios & Brodzinsky, 2010), and those who become parents through sperm, egg, or embryo donation are generally competent and loving parents, irrespective of gender or sexual orientation (Golombok et al., 2014) supporting the axiom that family processes, rather than family structure determines child wellbeing (Goldberg et al., 2012; Golombok, 2019; Lamb, 2012).

Psychological motivations to parent inform normative adult life-course decision making for heterosexual and same-sex couples, alike. Nonetheless, sexual minority status and genetic relatedness are likely to shape representations and experiences. By the time they overcome all the hurdles, couples opting for alternative, non-traditional pathways to parenthood tend to be cognitively comfortable with their unusual method of forming a family (van den Akker, 2007). This chapter concludes with two accounts of the transition to parenthood: Meg and Kym, a lesbian couple who adopted their daughter through the welfare system and Josh and Sean, a gay couple who became parents of twins with the assistance of a surrogate.

Meg and Kym's Story: Adopting a Baby Girl

Meg,* a mental health professional, had been with her partner Kym,* who worked in the creative arts, for twenty years. As a lesbian couple, they had always assumed they wouldn't have children; it simply would not be part of their lives. Their lives changed completely, however, when Tina* came into their home – initially as a foster baby, and they began proceedings to adopt her two years later. From the outset, it was clear to Meg that becoming a parent didn't need to involve a genetic child:

> Well, I ... didn't want children for a long, long time. I'd had a very difficult childhood and I felt that having children would be incredibly stressful. So I didn't have a craving. I just never felt a need to have my own child. And I say that because I know that a lot of people do ... I just never had that need, that, it had to come from me.

In their late thirties, Meg and Kym both started to question their longstanding assumption that they wouldn't have a child. For most of her adult life, Meg had assumed that she wouldn't cope well with the stress of mothering: and then at some point it dawned on her that she *could* care for a child; what's more, she wanted to do it. She was about to embark on a Masters' degree, and she and Kym were both working full-time, so the timing was not ideal, but they were aware that if they were to become parents, time was running out.

Significant policy and practice reforms that facilitated earlier placement of children in the child protection system provided the impetus. Meg, who had worked for many years with foster parents, felt the system was changing for the better, and that both children and their carers would benefit. She had always felt strongly that 'she didn't want to add more children to the planet' and the idea of fostering suddenly felt right to her: 'The first hurdle was me thinking, can I do it? And the answer was yes, of course I can. And then it seemed to be the most amazing and wonderful idea, and it's been amazing ever since.'

The process was lengthy and thorough: assessments, panel interviews, home visits, training courses. Meg didn't find it intrusive. In her view, it was just as it should be: 'It's what kids like Tina deserve. It's their job to get it right. It was exciting for me to do the training and I went into it whole-heartedly. I wasn't going in as a professional. I was going in as a parent to be.'

The first proposed placement didn't eventuate, but some months later, Meg and Kym were invited to meet a baby girl. Tina had been removed from her mother's care at birth, and placed with foster-carer, Jane. Meg's eyes fill with tears and her voice is choked with emotion as she describes their first encounter with Tina. It was filled with wonder and joy, but tempered by sadness and empathy for Jane, her foster mother:

> Oh, I remember it so clearly. We had to go down to a dingy office. We walked down these stairs, we kept walking down and down, and there was a big meeting

table in the office. There was a woman at one end of the table. It was Jane, the foster mum, and she had a little baby sitting on the table – she was just sitting there. She was a very chubby little girl, and she had her hair up in this topknot, and these amazing blue eyes. She was extraordinarily beautiful, just so beautiful. But I could also tell quickly that Jane [foster mother] was upset. Then, about half-way through the meeting, they asked If we wanted to hold her, and she came and sat on Kym's lap. After a while, it was my turn. I was trying not to cuddle her, because I felt, well poor Jane; this was a very serious thing to be handing over a child, but I was completely overcome with emotion. I thought she was just the most beautiful baby. It was astonishing!

Over the next month there was a gradual transition to Meg and Kym's care: brief visits to Jane, the foster mother's home, short outings, a day visit to their home for a nap. Meg reflects on those early days:

There are so many kids in need. And you've got the chance to love one; just one! You simply need to love that one child and love her completely. It's her mum's loss, which is terrible. But for us, it was amazing. Soon the little thumper was part of our lives, forever. I was tired. It was all consuming, but in a really good way.

Like all new parents, Meg and Kim had to adjust to huge changes in their relationship and lifestyle. They didn't designate a primary caregiver, juggling Tina's care and household tasks based on their different skill sets and diurnal rhythms. Meg felt fortunate to have a supportive network of gay couples; women they had been friends with over many years who also now had young children of their own, mostly through IVF and sperm donation. She reflected on the highly positive social change that had made this possible:

When I came out, I was nineteen, and that was really, really hard. There weren't same-sex parents. There just weren't any … as gay people we never expected to have this in our life, and nor did our friends. It's no mistake we're all in our forties before becoming parents. It's more culturally available now. The changing social influences have enabled it to happen. It's been a dramatic and welcome change.

---

*Names have been changed.

Josh and Sean: Two Fathers, Two Babies

Broadcaster Josh Szeps and his partner, Sean, had been together for seven years (married for three) when they became parents. Before the twins, life had felt like one long honeymoon: footloose, and fancy-free, with all the excitement and opportunities New York City had to offer. They had no commitments, no mortgage, no obligations. During his twenties, Josh had engaged in an ongoing debate with himself, weighing up the pros and cons of becoming a parent. There was no sense of urgency, and certainly no pressing visceral longing for a newborn infant:

> To be honest, I never felt drawn to having kids on a raw emotional level. I don't like babies. I like children who can talk and play with you, but I feel no affection towards the little lizard creatures, who are covered in goo and poo and wail all the time.

Ultimately, his motivation was intellectual and philosophical: 'If I died never having been a father, I might feel I had missed out on something fundamental to the human experience.' Sometimes Josh wanted kids, and Sean didn't; then Sean did, and Josh didn't. When their respective desires to become parents finally synchronised, there were two pathways open to them as a gay couple. Both were complicated: adoption and surrogacy.

They considered adoption, but 'the adoption process seemed fraught with delays, uncertainty, and risk. Surrogacy offered more confidence about the outcome, provided you had the large amounts of money required for legal and medical (IVF) fees.' Josh and Sean sought a premium quality agency – one that would take every care to minimise exploitation of the women working as surrogates. The agency they chose accepted only married women who already had at least one child, and positive experiences of pregnancy and childbirth. Sara, the surrogate had three children of her own. There was mutual and amicable agreement about the desirability of close contact during the pregnancy and ongoing contact after the birth. The egg donor had altruistic motives for donating. The extended family were enthusiastic, excited, and supportive. Everything was in place.

Sara lived in the mid-west and the IVF procedure took place in California, so there were a lot of cross-country flights and skype calls during the pregnancy. Josh and Sean had hoped to be present for the birth, but as things turned out, they narrowly missed it. When they heard that Sara was about to go into labour, earlier than expected, they jumped on a plane, landing in the middle of the night. It felt like a scene from a movie – they were speeding in their rental car from the airport to the hospital when they received the call. The babies had been born. As he pressed the after-hours buzzer, Josh found himself uncharacteristically lost for words: 'Baby, baby, we're having a baby', he mumbled. The security guard buzzed them in, and they dashed up a flight of stairs. They were able to see the babies within half an hour of birth. Josh describes this first contact as 'terrifying, surreal, and extraordinary. I didn't know what to make of it. I was full of emotion, but also fear. What to do with these helpless, slimy little things?'

And two of them! They had decided that two embryos would be implanted, hoping to maximise the likelihood of a pregnancy. Twins were always a possibility, and while not explicitly planned, seemed like a good option. Josh had no illusions about becoming a parent. He knew that having kids was going to be hard – he was aware that he might not love it. So, the idea of having a complete family and not having to repeat the costly processes of IVF and surrogacy, and the exhaustion of parenting a young infant was appealing. Despite these longer-term advantages, early parenting is extremely arduous with twins. Initially, the strain was cushioned by generous and sensitive support from Sean's mother. Never overbearing, she allowed them to make their own mistakes, and was always there for them. This got them through the first two months.

When the babies were eight weeks old, the family flew to Australia where Josh was starting a new job. It was a formidable undertaking. They both had to be full on parents, all the time. Josh describes this two-month window before his own parents (who were overseas) were available to help: 'It was a mayhem of mutual depression, antagonism, sleeplessness, and anxiety. It was really, really hard; by far the most emotionally gruelling thing either of us had ever lived through.'

He found himself temperamentally quite unsuited to the parenting role, at least when it came to very young infants:

> One misconception that I had; I knew it was going to be stressful, but I'm good at handling stressful situations. I'm a good ring-master and a multi-tasker. I thought – I'll be able to keep tap-dancing, whilst keeping all those balls in the air. What I didn't realise is that while multi-tasking skills might be useful when the kids are about five years old, when they're just a few months old, it's not complicated at all, and being a multi-tasking tap-dancer is completely useless. You need to be resilient, enormously patient, and not easily bored. It is relent-less: the drudgery of sleep, feed, change, cry, sleep, feed, change nappy. I did not love it, at all.

From time to time, Josh found himself wondering if the process of becoming a parent might be easier for women. Perhaps the gradual nine-month period of discomfort, during which a woman can gradually adjust to disturbed sleep and physiological changes in her body eases the transition:

> For us, a switch was flicked, and we went from normal life to suddenly having a baby. So I do think perhaps nature has a clever way of gradually acclimatising you, over the course of a pregnancy, and we missed out on that.

Relationships change when adults become parents. Both Josh and Sean found themselves much more forgiving of their own parents' shortcomings. Josh delighted in watching his own parents as they stepped into the roles of grandparents 'with enormous grace, tenderness, and joy'. As for their own relationship with each other, it became more about coping than celebrating life. Both felt warmly supported by extended family and close friends. Many gay parents report stigma, but it wasn't a big issue for Josh. Like many gay fathers, he was subject to frequent assumptions that there must be a mother in the picture, and 'Where's Mummy?' questions when out on his own with the babies. He took the pragmatic view that those asking were just playing the statistical odds, and nothing untoward was intended:

> I think generally the culture has done a great job of moving very quickly to accept something that was really, really, weird, until very recently. I'm impressed that everyone's doing a bang-up job of trying to be OK with it.

Nonetheless, he appreciates some progress towards inclusiveness, for example, official forms that now say 'Parent 1 and Parent 2' rather than mother and father. Asked whether he'd recommend parenthood to other couples, Josh is disarmingly frank:

> Not necessarily. In the long arc of my life, I'm delighted that I did it, but there are huge opportunity costs. As long as you're cool with that, then do it. But I don't think people should be cajoled into having kids, or shamed for not having them.

CHAPTER 7

Childbirth

Childbirth is a momentous event: creative, powerful, and deeply personal. Surrendering to the primordial processes of her body can be an exhilarating and life affirming experience for a woman. From the earliest times, however, childbirth has been accompanied by profound cultural echoes of danger and fear. Labour pain is legendary, and when labour fails to progress smoothly, the consequences can be devastating. For most of history and in most cultures, birth has been exclusively the domain of women, taking place in the home, assisted by midwives, with folklore and knowledge passed down informally from one generation to the next. In the late sixteenth and seventeenth centuries male physicians first became involved in delivering babies and by the late nineteenth and early twentieth century, medical doctors (exclusively male at the time) had established themselves as the unquestioned authority on birth (Michaels, 2014). Gendered turf wars about the management of childbirth, in particular the need for medical interventions, have played out ever since.

This chapter begins with a brief historical overview of medical interventions and the natural childbirth movement. Next, the biology of childbirth and common medical interventions are described, before focusing on the psychology of childbirth, psychological strategies for managing labour pain, and the impact of the social context in which birth takes place. Research evidence on early contact with the infant is analysed, and the chapter concludes by discussing the experience of premature birth. Grace tells her birth story – having a premature baby during the first wave of the COVID-19 Pandemic, and Kate describes a vaginal birth that didn't run according to plan.

Medical Intervention and the Natural Childbirth Movement

Practices around childbirth have been fiercely contested for generations. They are closely intertwined with social attitudes towards women and the professionalisation of healthcare in high-income societies. In an often-quoted anecdote, Queen Victoria began the trend for pain relief during childbirth in 1853, after inhaling chloroform during the birth of her seventh child. This radical act, in opposition to patriarchal, clerical, and medical traditions of the day (Eley et al., 2015), opened the way for anaesthesia as part of obstetric practice, however it was generally only upper-class women who had access. Over time, medical intervention became the norm. By the mid-twentieth century women giving birth in hospitals in high-income countries were close to unconscious after taking a combination of sedatives, tranquilisers, and anaesthetics, and most had little or no memory of the event. While access to pain-free childbirth was an early feminist cause, the widespread experience of 'twilight sleep' where women were 'knocked out' with a general anaesthetic prompted a new wave of feminist action to reclaim the birth experience from male doctors – women objected to waking up after such a momentous event, feeling powerless, groggy, and disoriented (Rich, 1979/1986).

The 1970s and 1980s saw a backlash against the practice of sedating women during labour. Earlier in the twentieth century, Obstetricians Grantley Dick-Read (2004) and Fernand Lamaze (1972), had pointed out the associations among fear, tension, and pain, arguing that it was beneficial for women to understand the physiology of labour, and how training in breathing and relaxation could be used to manage pain. The Lamaze approach, based on structured breathing techniques, dominated childbirth preparation for decades and remains influential today.

Anthropologist and childbirth educator, Sheila Kitzinger (1980) and physician Michel Odent (1984/1994) advocated a psychosexual model of childbirth that encouraged women to trust their bodies and their instincts so that they could fully co-operate with the powerful physiological processes and involuntary reflexes that drive labour. As part of this movement Janet Balaskas (1983) coined the phrase 'active birth' emphasising the distinction between *giving birth* through your own will and determination ... [and] a vaginal extraction or *passive delivery*' (p. 1, italics added). Women were encouraged to embrace labour pain as a fulfilling, natural (even sexual) experience, best appreciated without the filter of drugs or anaesthesia.

These approaches sought to empower women to take back the control of childbirth from male physicians. Some feminist writers, however, have been sceptical about the natural childbirth movement. Early feminist Shulamith Firestone (2003) took the view that pregnancy and childbirth were barbaric, and recommended women pragmatically embrace technology if it saved them from pain. Subsequently some feminist writers have argued that extreme adherence to natural childbirth is based on an idealisation of the experience and a denial of the reality of pain, leading to pressure on women to conform to a pernicious norm, and feelings of guilt and inadequacy if they opt for pain relief (Jones, 2012; Wolf, 2003). As writer Rachel Cusk (2008) wryly observes, feeling outraged at the patriarchal medicalisation of childbirth may not be sufficient to get through labour, and natural instincts may be hard to find.

In summary, there have been two opposing strands of feminist analysis of childbirth: those who see medical interventions as appropriating women's reproductive potency and forcing them to submit to male control; and those concerned that romanticising natural childbirth and advocating birth without medical pain relief has led to inflated and unrealistic expectations of control, and a sense of disappointment and failure for many (Jones, 2012). Contemporary women approach childbirth in their own way; some view birth as a defining female experience and they are strongly committed to avoiding any medical interventions; others are more pragmatic, and keen to welcome standard birth practice as defined by medical practitioners, provided there is a live baby as the end result.

An exploration of how biological, psychological, and social influences interact to influence the experience of becoming a parent provides the thematic structure for this book. Nowhere are these influences more intertwined than in relation to childbirth. While labour is a visceral bodily process, it is also a profound psychological experience, and one that is strongly socially and culturally determined.

The Biology of Childbirth

Pregnancy typically lasts forty weeks after a woman's last menstrual period prior to conception, with babies born prior to thirty-seven weeks considered premature. Labour is a physiological and mechanical event; it is involuntary, largely governed by hormones and autonomic reflexes. Common medical interventions include synthetic hormones to stimulate contractions (and initiate or accelerate labour), opiates and anaesthesia to manage pain, instrumental deliveries that may involve cutting the perineum, and surgical delivery (caesarean section).

The Three Stages of Labour

In the first stage of labour, the muscles of the walls of the uterus contract at regular intervals and with increasing intensity. As a result, the cervix (at the entry to the uterus) shortens and dilates from a closed seal to 10 centimetres open. This stage lasts between one hour and several days, and it is generally the longest stage of labour. At the end of the first stage there is a brief, intense 'transition' phase. In the second stage of labour (which usually lasts between half an hour and two hours), the mother experiences an intense urge to push the baby down the vagina (birth canal). The third stage of labour involves the delivery of the placenta after the baby is born.

Subjective experiences vary, and it is difficult to capture the primal intensity in words. Birth remains essentially unknowable and mysterious until it is experienced. Describing the challenges of negotiating the first stage of labour as analogous to a body surfer negotiating waves in the ocean is a common metaphor. Anthropologist and pioneering Childbirth Educator, Sheila Kitzinger, describes it as follows:

> Uterine contractions are felt by many women to sweep towards them, rise in crescendo and then fade away like the waves of the sea ... A woman must 'swim' over the wave and not allow it to envelope her, and to do this she must go forward to meet it with her breathing, rather than waiting until it is already on her. If she retreats from it, it will almost certainly sweep over her. (Kitzinger, 1978, p. i)

Classical pianist and writer, Anna Goldsworthy decided that her task in labour was simply to endure it. She extends the waves metaphor:

> The next wave is symphonic, arriving from all directions at once. It takes me out of my body – *out out out* – or so far into it that I no longer know myself – until I see the fissures in the air and feel the lurch of nausea and realise I am returning to the room. Then it vanishes, leaving no residue except a glaze of perspiration on my skin. (Goldsworthy, 2014, p. 64)

Hormones drive the initiation, pace, and progression of labour, and also influence responses to pain. Oxytocin stimulates contractions of the uterus and the opening of the cervix during the first stage. The body produces natural opioids (endorphins) which can mitigate pain. The second stage of labour can be experienced as overwhelming or exhilarating, often both. The baby is expelled from the woman's body with a surge of energy that is largely outside her voluntary control. The third stage of labour, after the baby is born, is instigated through oxytocin or its synthetic derivatives, and involves the expulsion of the placenta and the cutting of the umbilical cord.

Common Complications and Medical Interventions during Childbirth

While labour is always challenging, most births can proceed without complications or need for intervention. Nonetheless, for a sizable minority, problems arise during the birth process and medical intervention is needed to safeguard the mother or the baby. Medical complications of late pregnancy such as pre-eclampsia (high blood pressure, fluid retention, protein in urine) and placenta praevia (when the placenta descends in the uterus and blocks the baby's passage through the cervix to the birth canal) are life-threatening and require an emergency caesarean section. Monitoring during labour includes physical examination, listening to foetal heart rate and the use of electronic foetal monitors which yield a consistent tracing of the foetal heart rate, but may limit the mother's mobility.

The most common complication during the first stage of labour is failure to progress. A prolonged first stage can lead to maternal exhaustion, and foetal distress, evident if the baby's heartbeat slows, or the baby passes meconium (faeces). Augmentation (using a synthetic oxytocin derivative administered through an intravenous drip) may be implemented to speed up the labour. If there is consistent evidence of foetal distress, a decision may be made to deliver the baby by caesarean section.

Complications can arise during the second stage of labour if the baby has the umbilical cord around its neck, or the mother has trouble pushing the baby out. Both can cause foetal distress. Difficulties pushing may be due to the side-effects of an epidural anaesthetic (which reduces the mother's capacity to voluntarily push), the size of the baby's head and shoulders relative to the mother's pelvis, or to the position of the baby. For example, if the baby is facing forwards (referred to as a posterior presentation, or 'sunny side up') delivery is more difficult. Medical responses to complications in the second stage of labour include instrumental delivery (forceps or vacuum suction extraction), and an episiotomy (or cut) to the perineum. Alternatively, the perineum may spontaneously tear as the baby's head is born. Either way, stitches are required. In some cases, if there is slow progress and foetal distress, an emergency caesarean section may be needed.

A synthetic oxytocin injection is often given to speed up the third stage of labour. Bleeding may occur if the placenta is difficult to detach from the uterine wall. When fragments of placenta are retained, the woman will experience bleeding, pain, and, in some cases, infection. Postpartum haemorrhage is a more severe complication that can accompany a retained placenta. Should this occur, the mother may need a blood transfusion.

While some medical interventions are a response to problems detected through monitoring during labour, others (such as inducing labour) are planned prior to the birth, or they are implemented as routine practice.

Intervention rates vary markedly in different birth settings, as do opportunities for input and decision making from the mother and her partner. Eley and colleagues (2015) describe a cascade effect where one intervention is reciprocally related to another: epidural anaesthesia slows labour and this is then countered by oxytocin to speed it up; oxytocin leads to more painful contractions and a greater likelihood of epidural anaesthesia; epidural anaesthesia reduces the mother's capacity to push and increases the likelihood of forceps; forceps require anaesthesia and episiotomy, and so on.

Elective Induction
Synthetic oxytocin can be delivered via intravenous drip, or prostaglandin gel may be used to initiate labour, or to 'augment' a labour that is not progressing. Some inductions are medically indicated, for example when there are complications of pregnancy such as pre-eclampsia, low amniotic fluid levels, or concerns about placental functioning after forty-two weeks' gestation, but many are 'elective' (Oster, 2019). Reasons for inductions vary in different health systems. The rate is higher for first births. A marked increase in induced labours in recent decades in the United States has been attributed to social (not medical) preferences of the doctor and/or the mother; the rate of inductions in 2012 was 23.3 per cent of births, more than doubling in the twenty years between 1990 and 2010 and inductions are much more prevalent in women with private health insurance (Osterman & Martin, 2014). Australian figures indicate 32% of births involved induction in 2018 and 43% of first births (Australian Institute of Health and Welfare, 2021a). In the United Kingdom where there is a universal free healthcare system, around 30 per cent of births are induced (36 per cent of first-time mothers). In contrast to the United States and Australia, women with lower education and those living in disadvantaged environments are more likely to be induced (Carter et al., 2020).

There are disadvantages of induction. Contractions last longer and are stronger so women are more likely to need pain relief (typically an epidural). A randomised controlled trial has shown that women whose labours are induced are significantly more likely to require a caesarean section (Miller et al., 2015), and babies may be compromised if they are delivered before they are fully mature and ready. While there are alternative 'natural' techniques (herbal teas, primrose oil), sexual intercourse, and nipple stimulation to try and initiate labour, there is limited evidence of their effectiveness (Oster, 2019).

Caesarean Section

Some caesarean births are planned (elective) and some are unplanned and implemented as an 'emergency' in response to complications causing foetal distress in late pregnancy or during labour, as discussed earlier. Reasons for elective caesarean section include breech presentations (baby presents feet rather than head-first), known maternal medical or physical problems that may complicate vaginal delivery, multiple pregnancy, a cautious approach based on perceptions of elevated birth risk related to older maternal age and ART conception (Fisher et al., 2013), physician concerns about exposure to litigation in the event of adverse outcomes, and, in a small number of cases, maternal preference. There has been a striking increase in caesarean births in recent decades, with an average caesarean section rate across high-income countries of about one in three births, and particular concern about the rise in caesarean deliveries that have no medical indication (Keag et al., 2018; National Institute for Clinical Excellence [NICE], 2021b). Caesarean birth may be associated with postpartum health problems for the mother (pain, limited mobility, fatigue, longer recovery period) and less baby-friendly hospital practices immediately after birth that may impact negatively on establishing breastfeeding and early parenting (Fisher et al., 2013). There are also greater relative risks (although absolute risks are small) of placenta problems in subsequent pregnancies and a significantly increased likelihood of a caesarean delivery for subsequent births. On the other hand, risks related to perineal tears and episiotomies, and later vaginal prolapse and urinary incontinence are reduced (Keag et al., 2018). There has been significant progress in minimising short-term maternal morbidity after caesarean section (NICE, 2021b).

Contemporary practice means most women have epidural anaesthesia, so they are awake for the caesarean birth. It is helpful if they are aware in advance that there will be several people present, with the father generally seated at the mother's head. A screen blocks the view of the body from the waist down. There is a buzz of activity as the mother is prepared for surgery and the epidural is administered. The lights are bright. The mother may feel cold, and shivery. She can hear the clatter of metal tools, and she will inhale the antiseptic theatre smell. Once the effectiveness of the anaesthetic is confirmed, the delivery of the baby may be surprisingly quick. Mothers can generally feel tugging and pulling, but not pain. There may be the sound of suctioning fluids, and then the surprising sound of the baby's cry. Generally, the doctor will hold the baby up so the mother can see her immediately. The baby's breathing is checked before allowing the parents to have physical contact and a closer look. The father may be able to accompany the baby after the operation as the mother will need to spend time in recovery.

In summary, recent medical evidence suggests that induction of labour at term is safe and that caesarean sections are generally as safe as vaginal deliveries. Nonetheless rising rates of medical interventions are concerning. It is important that women are given evidence-based information and support to make informed choices about their birth. When interventions, such as caesarean sections are indicated, it is important to accommodate, whenever possible, the woman's preferences about how the procedure is conducted, and early contact with the infant (NICE, 2021b). See birth stories from Grace (caesarean section due to pre-partum haemorrhage) and Kate (induction, due to low amniotic fluid) at the end of this chapter.

Pain in Childbirth: Medical Approaches
It is generally agreed that labour pain is one of life's most intense pain experiences: stronger than toothache, backache, or cancer pain. The experience of pain is subjective. It is influenced by a woman's own history, by memory, and by anticipation (Rich, 1986). The fact that it is 'normal' and leads to a positive result is a redeeming feature, differentiating labour pain from most other pain that indicates something is wrong. The use of non-medical techniques including breathing, massage, movement, mindfulness, and cognitive reframing is generally a first response to labour pain, however most women now use some form of anaesthesia during labour as well (Declerq et al., 2013; Oster, 2019), with a widespread view amongst medical staff and the general public that access to analgesia during childbirth is a woman's right (Eley et al., 2015).

Medical approaches include inhaled nitrous oxide gas, opioids (narcotics), and neuraxial analgesia (also referred to as epidural or spinal block). All have some side-effects and contribute to immobility and passivity in the labouring woman. Opioids can have undesirable effects on the child, compromising breathing after birth, so they are generally limited to the early stages of labour. In recent decades they have been largely superseded by nitrous oxide gas and by epidural (spinal block) anaesthesia (Oster, 2019). Epidural anaesthesia is administered under local anaesthetic into the lower region of the back and blocks the nerves that transmit pain, as well as limiting the woman's capacity to move around and to push the baby out. A recent Cochrane review concludes that epidurals provide effective pain relief. Negative consequences (longer labour and greater likelihood of instrumental delivery) have been offset in the last twenty years by improved techniques including lower concentrations of anaesthetic, and patient-controlled administration so that women can be mobile (Anim-Somuah et al., 2018; Bamber et al., 2020). Epidural use varies greatly in different settings. Recent national figures indicate that about two-thirds of women use an epidural anaesthetic during labour in the United States with rates varying between 40 and 80 per cent in different states (Butwick et al., 2018). Much lower rates (around 21 per cent) are reported in the United Kingdom (Bamber et al., 2020), with figures of around 30 per cent in Australia. While epidural anaesthesia is by far the most common method of pain relief in high income countries (WHO, 2018a), rates vary within populations in relation to socio-economic status, country of birth, ethnicity, and are highest in well-off women with higher health literacy and private health insurance (AIHW, 2021a; Eley et al., 2015;).

The Psychology of Childbirth

Birth is an intensely engaging moment for a couple, the realisation of a shared and profoundly meaningful project. For some the experience is a very positive one; for others, while the ultimate outcome is pleasing, the journey through labour or a caesarean birth is difficult and frightening. A small minority of women experience birth as traumatic, in the clinical sense of the term, with lasting negative effects including disturbing flashbacks and nightmares (Muzik & Rosenblum, 2018). Psychological considerations during childbirth include the influence of early life experiences, expectations (including fear) about the birth process, anxiety arising from unanticipated complications, strategies for dealing with pain, and the effectiveness of professional and personal support.

There is necessarily a focus on the gestational mother's experiences when discussing pregnancy and childbirth, however the perspective of the supporting partner also needs to be considered. Some of the psychological challenges relate to the physical intensity of the experience; some to unanticipated and worrying medical complications; some to the vulnerabilities that can arise from adverse life events. Women who have had early childhood experiences of harsh caregiving or prior experiences of interpersonal, and particularly sexual violence (including childhood maltreatment and partner violence) and those who have had prior traumatic experiences in health care settings are most vulnerable to birth trauma (Fisher et al., 2018).

While non-medical strategies to manage pain in labour draw on psychological principles, few have been developed and evaluated by psychologists

(Saxbe, 2017). Most include some or all of the following: addressing pregnancy and childbirth focused fear and anxiety; cognitive reframing to change thinking about labour pain; an emphasis on the importance of a sense of control and agency compared with learned helplessness; and dissociation and distraction strategies, including relaxation training, breathing techniques, mindfulness, and body awareness. Individual differences in relational styles are also pertinent to understanding the effectiveness of support people during childbirth.

Psychological Approaches to Managing Fear and Pain

Childbirth is the penultimate mind–body experience. Some have likened it to running a marathon. Hormones released in response to stress, anxiety, and fear can negatively influence progress (Wadwa et al., 2001). On the other hand, if a woman can achieve a relaxed state of mind, her body will be more likely to release natural opiates (endorphins). Awareness of these mind–body connections can be helpful and empowering, or it can engender more anxiety – worry about worrying, and stress about not being able to relax and regulate one's breathing, for example.

Fear of Childbirth

There are many reasons women may approach childbirth with fear, not least the graphic 'battle' stories that are part of childbirth folklore. There are plenty of things to be fearful about – legendary pain, losing control in front of others; having medical interventions; not having medical interventions. There may also be concern for the baby's wellbeing, or fear of judgement for 'failing as a woman' to achieve a planned, natural childbirth (Jones, 2012; Kukla, 2008).

A prospective study by Duncan and colleagues (2017) found that anticipatory fear of labour pain during pregnancy negatively influenced the perception of pain in labour. Fear of childbirth also predicted low self-efficacy during labour, a prolonged first stage of labour, a greater use of pain medication, and more unwanted obstetric interventions, including caesarean sections. While pain perception is subjective and therefore theoretically amenable to cognitive restructuring (Saxbe, 2017), the reality is that labour pain is objectively severe, and euphemisms like 'discomfort' can be dishonest and counter-productive (Kitzinger, 1978; Kukla, 2008). Women appreciate and benefit from candid, but non-sadistic descriptions of labour that help them to prepare realistically (Raphael-Leff, 2005).

Psychoprophylactic Approaches: 'Doing the Breathing'

As noted earlier, the earliest 'natural' (psychoprophylactic) approaches to managing pain in labour (Dick-Read, 2004; Lamaze, 1972) shared a focus on breathing training, relaxation, and visualisation. These approaches draw on classical and operant conditioning techniques, and rely on dissociation and distraction, with the aim of controlling the mind, and inhibiting awareness of what is going on in the uterus. They include structured breathing, chanting, and singing to 'block' or over-ride pain cues. These techniques are widely taught in antenatal classes and effective for some, but they have been criticised for intentionally creating a gap between the mind and the body. As well as blocking pain, they consume energy and Kitzinger (1978) argues that they can block important cues that will enable the woman to work effectively with her body. Clearly, different strategies suit different people. Some women will benefit from dissociation, particularly those for whom pain cues may have associations with prior traumatic experiences, while others do better when structured breathing is used in conjunction with tuning in to body sensations.

Mindfulness Approaches.   More recent iterations of breathing-based approaches have much in common with yoga, and mindfulness and meditation, contemporary psychological therapies that aim to achieve harmony between mind and body. Mindfulness has been defined as the process of accepting things as they are. Approaching labour with an open, accepting state of mind is believed to reduce tension, fear, and physiological reactivity, and promote positivity and stability (Dhillon et al., 2017). Mindfulness shares features with other psychoprophylactic approaches – namely a focus on breathing, body awareness, relaxation, and also incorporates aspects of cognitive reframing, for example neutral low-key descriptors of labour pain as 'unpleasant physical sensations that come and go moment by moment' (Duncan et al., 2017, p. 4). While extensively implemented and evaluated in the treatment of anxiety and chronic pain, mindfulness has only recently been studied as a technique for managing labour pain. A recent meta-analysis showed limited, but promising, evidence of effectiveness in reducing pregnancy anxiety and depression (Dhillon et al., 2017). One randomised trial of a 'mindfulness in labour' intervention found improvements in sense of self-efficacy during labour and lower depression symptoms after birth, but no differences in perceptions of pain or use of analgesia, compared with women receiving conventional childbirth education. The sample was small, so the study was underpowered to detect many of these differences (Duncan et al., 2017). Further, studies of psychoprophylactic approaches may be fundamentally confounded by selection bias, as women who invest in learning them may be particularly committed to natural childbirth (Oster, 2019).

A Sense of Control?

There is debate about 'control' in labour. In general, women want some predictability and a clear strategy to help them manage labour pain, and structured breathing techniques can help them to achieve this. On the other hand, proponents of a psychosexual approach, have argued that the process of giving birth is all about *relinquishing control* (Kitzinger, 1978; Odent, 1994), particularly in the second stage of labour when the body makes the decisions. The woman's task is to just let it happen. A law of reversed effort is invoked with analogies to falling asleep, or having an orgasm (Noble, 1983). Giving in to involuntary bodily responses and allowing oneself to 'go with the flow' may be a good deal easier said than done, however (Cusk, 2008). Kukla (2008) has argued that inflated expectations of the control that can and should be exercised over the birth process can set women up for failure and a profound sense of shame.

Green and Baston (2003) describe three distinct types of control relevant to childbirth – feeling in control of contractions and pain, feeling in control of one's own behaviour during labour, for example making animalistic noises or using disinhibited language, choosing activities and positions, and feeling in control of decision-making and the actions of support staff. They surveyed a large sample of more than a thousand women one month before and six weeks after birth. Results indicated that fear of labour pain in late pregnancy was a strong predictor of a low sense of control about dealing with pain during labour (as assessed retrospectively), while freedom to choose positions that gave relief and comfort during labour enhanced perceived control. Active birth approaches teach women strategies to control pain and progress in labour through freely choosing changes in posture, mobility, and the use of gravity assistance in upright delivery positions. While control over pain is important, results of this large survey showed that a woman's perception that she had some influence over staff behaviour towards her was the strongest indicator of satisfaction with the birth experience. Green and Baston (2003) concluded that the women wanted to 'feel cared *about*, rather than experiencing "care" as something that is done to them' (p. 247).

Psychoeducation: Feeling Prepared. The pathway to perceived control for most women is preparation and clear information. Most couples in high-income countries participate in some form of formal childbirth education. Classes generally aim to increase factual knowledge about the process of labour and birth, various strategies to manage pain, the common problems faced in labour and delivery, medical interventions that are available to address these problems, and the risks and benefits associated with them. The key premise of psychoeducation is that information is empowering (Fenwick et al., 2015). Although they vary in philosophy, emphasis, and approach, childbirth classes are grounded in an underlying assumption that when women have evidence-based information they can make informed choices that fit with their own preferences and priorities. Women need to know the positives and the negatives and be included in decision making (NICE, 2021a). Some childbirth classes focus on the tools and techniques of the midwifery trade (positions, procedures), using a classroom style, while others take a more experiential, philosophical approach aiming to present just a few guiding principles, whilst encouraging a respect for the physiology of labour and the individuality of each woman's birth experience (Noble, 1983). Noble argues that an excessive focus on techniques and control can result in couples losing sight of the fact that the experience of birth is highly individual and larger than the sum of its parts.

Birth Plans. Many childbirth educators recommend that couples develop a birth plan. Ranging from a list of demands to idiosyncratic preferences, the plan is helpful in decision making and communication with hospital staff. Ideally birth plans will be flexible; perhaps an optimistic 'best-case scenario' as the leading plan and a 'plan B' if unexpected complications occur. Birth plans could include preferences to avoid induction if possible; the setting for the birth (some hospitals have birth centres, which provide a more low technology home-like environment; some women will choose a homebirth); whether the couple wants to be accompanied by a doula (a paid support person who understands labour and childbirth and is able to remain a calm and relaxed advocate); a preference for intermittent mobile monitoring rather than continuous; a position against routine episiotomy; attitudes to hormone injections to stimulate the third stage of labour; who will cut the cord, and so on. A stated preference to avoid an epidural anaesthetic (with an explicit prerogative to change one's mind) may influence the extent to which non-medical pain relief strategies are offered.

While the focus is on vaginal births, a birth plan for caesarean births can also enable a sense of control, despite the surgical context. In many cases, the negative psychological consequences that can follow from caesarean birth are due to a sense of disappointment and failure in the context of a cultural discourse that reifies the ideal of natural childbirth (Jones, 2012). These feelings may be difficult to avoid after an emergency (unplanned caesarean), but a birth plan that incorporates the possibility of a caesarean birth, with explicit preferences for how it would be managed, may offset some of these negative consequences.

Women can plan who will accompany them (usually just one person); and state their preferences for contact with the baby after delivery (e.g., partner accompanies baby to the nursery), and timing of their own contact after – it is often possible for the baby to be brought to the mother sooner and left with the mother longer than is typical of routine practice.

Perhaps the most contentious aspect of birth plans in recent times, has been the issue of whether women can and should choose an elective caesarean delivery, when there are no medical indicators.

Caesarean Birth on Maternal Request. The notable increase in rates of caesarean births in high-income countries is predominantly doctor initiated, but there is also a growing trend for women to request a caesarean birth (Oster, 2019). After extensive research exploring the advantages and disadvantages, journalist Jane Gardner (2019) requested a caesarean section for her first birth, although there were no medical indications for it. She believed that women should have access to accurate information and autonomy over individual birth choices, including surgical delivery, free of judgement and shame. Her doctor agreed. In contrast to accounts from women disappointed by a caesarean birth after a long and difficult labour (e.g., Cusk, 2008; Wolf, 2003), Gardner reports very positively about her birth: 'The operation was a surreal and incredible experience. Within half an hour of the spinal block, I had a tiny snuffling baby on my chest. My greatest love and my everything.' She acknowledges the post-operative pain and lengthy recovery, but it was the judgement she encountered when she disclosed her decision to others that posed the greatest challenge. 'In online support groups, I would sometimes be made to feel like because I didn't labour, I didn't really deserve to join the motherhood club. Once, someone actually told me I was "too posh to push"' (Gardner, 2019). Gardner began telling people the caesarean was due to the baby being in breech position to avoid disapproval, particularly prevalent in online forums.

While autonomy and informed choice are compelling arguments, and a woman will only have an elective caesarean for non-medical reasons if her doctor agrees, there are legitimate concerns about choosing significant abdominal surgery when it is not medically indicated, and philosophical concerns about depriving women of meaningful engagement with the natural process of childbearing (Jones, 2012). Informed medical opinion recommends counselling women against caesarean birth on maternal request (D'Souza, 2013), but also notes the need for caution, sensitivity, and respect for the legitimacy of individual perspectives and choice (NICE, 2021b). In some cases, psychological motivations related to previous birth trauma or sexual violence could be considered valid medical (mental health) grounds.

Individual Differences in Orientation to Childbirth

Childbirth has different meanings for different women. These may evolve from their individual attachment and trauma history, but may also be a response to current contexts, circumstances, peer networks, and dominant social discourses about birth. Raphael-Leff's Facilitator-Regulator model (2005), discussed in relation to adjustment to pregnancy in Chapter 3, can be helpful in understanding different psychological orientations and vulnerabilities in the context of childbirth. At one end of the spectrum, a strong 'facilitator' orientation is associated with idealisation of childbirth as the ultimate expression of female power and creativity. Women who endorse this orientation may feel passionately committed to a natural intervention-free labour, anticipate a rewarding psychosexual experience, trust that their bodies will instinctively 'know' what to do, and fear any interruption to natural processes precipitated by pharmacological intervention. Women with a 'regulator' orientation, on the other hand, may adopt a pragmatic and planful approach to childbirth, in order to avoid being overwhelmed by the primitive nature of the experience. Prioritising a sense of control and dignity, they may prefer a planned induction, or even a planned caesarean section. Medical interventions are viewed positively for their potential to speed up the process, make it more predictable, and guarantee relief from pain. Minimum discomfort and maximum control are the goals.

Women wedded to either of these positions are vulnerable if the birth experience doesn't conform to their expectations. The woman who plans a birth at home or in a birth-centre may be very distressed if unexpected medical complications arise and she needs to transfer to a hospital. She may feel a sense of shame and failure as a woman if she succumbs to an epidural anaesthetic, and these feelings can be intensified if the medical emergency requires a caesarean section and subsequent separation from the baby, which in her mind may threaten the natural flow of bonding and establishment of breastfeeding. A woman who is hoping for a controlled birth experience, on the other hand, may be traumatised if she finds herself going into an unexpected, perhaps precipitate, labour without enough time for a planned epidural anaesthetic, let alone a caesarean delivery. Consistent with the applications of the model to pregnancy adjustment, Raphael-Leff argues that a flexible intermediate orientation is most adaptive: the preference for a 'natural' or a 'planned' delivery is accompanied by a reality-based acknowledgement that other outcomes are possible, and that they are not necessarily catastrophic or shameful. Kate's story at the end of this chapter is illustrative.

The Social Context for Childbirth

Unlike many animals and other mammals who give birth alone, human mothers need assistance – there is almost always someone with them (Declerq et al., 2013; Hrdy, 1999). As well as an attending midwife or doctor, the woman is typically accompanied by a partner, and some may be accompanied by a doula who has professional training and understanding about the process of labour. In his social ecological model of human development, Bronfenbrenner described the complex multi-layered influence of context (Bronfenbrenner & Morris, 2006). When the model is applied to childbirth, close relationships (the partner or support person) provide the proximal emotional context. The effectiveness of the support partners can provide is influenced by the attitudes and communication styles of attending health professionals (midwives, doctors) and hospital practices and environments, which, in turn, are influenced by prevailing cultural, economic, and political beliefs (regarding birth, women, gender relations, and babies).

Men and Childbirth: The Experience and Contribution of the Father

Although they are invited to be present, and they want to be authentically engaged, many men in labour wards feel powerless, out of place, vulnerable, and marginalised on the periphery – an intruder on a quintessentially female experience (Deave & Johnson, 2008; Draper, 2003). One of the men in Draper's qualitative study likened his experience of childbirth to that of a 'hitch-hiker', he felt like a passenger on a journey of some sort, clearly not in charge and not even sure of his destination.

Howarth and colleagues (2019) surveyed 155 first-time New Zealand fathers about their experience of childbirth. Overall, the fathers reported a high level of satisfaction, a desire to be involved, and a need to feel included. Their greatest concern was for the health and safety of their partner and the baby. When professional staff effectively facilitated their involvement and supported them in supporting their partners, the men in this study felt part of the team, and that they had made a genuine contribution in assisting the mother to give birth. On the other hand, poor communication from staff resulted in low satisfaction and feelings of marginalisation. Situations requiring medical interventions including caesarean deliveries can be experienced as positive (or at least not negative), if the escalation to a surgical delivery is well managed with respectful communication, inclusion in decision-making, and reassurance.

Some men find it difficult to be present for internal examinations, and medical procedures such as episiotomies of epidurals. Like women, they vary in their preference for a controlled or a natural and spontaneous experience, and their emotional investment in a particular outcome. For many men, the effective pain relief provided by an epidural anaesthetic makes their support role easier to manage. Others, however, assume the role of highly involved labour 'coaches' and advocates, and conflicts can arise if they seek to restrict the woman's autonomy if she changes her mind and asks for pain relief, despite a planned 'natural birth' (Raphael-Leff, 2005). Most (with the support of midwives and staff) will be a loving presence, doing the best they can in a highly arousing and stressful situation. There is evidence that women who receive continuous labour support from a birth professional or doula require less pain medication and have better outcomes in relation to pain medication, length of labour, and satisfaction with birth (see Hodnett et al., 2013 for a Cochrane review), however few studies have focused on the nature and impact of partner support on the woman's subjective birth experience (Saxbe, 2017).

Setting and Cultural Context for Childbirth

Bronfenbrenner's ecological model also provides a framework for understanding changes in the experience of childbirth across broad time intervals and cultures, taking account of changing expectations and events in the larger society (Bronfenbrenner & Morris, 2006). In Western cultures, as discussed earlier in this chapter, there have been fluctuations in birth ideologies over time: from home-based midwife deliveries to medicalisation of childbirth in hospital settings presided over by predominantly male physicians. This is changing, however. Growing gender equity has led to many women doctors specialising in managing pregnancy and childbirth, and also to changing beliefs and practices about the role of the father, infant needs, and the importance of early contact and breastfeeding.

There has been a growing recognition that giving birth in hospital settings is associated with higher intervention rates, particularly when women have private health insurance (Oster, 2019). The interventions justify the costly institutions in which they are implemented and the premiums that are paid. Hospital settings and procedures may be incompatible with the psychological wellbeing of the woman and her partner, and with early contact with the baby, and there has been a push in recent decades to provide a more supportive, home-like atmosphere.

Feminist positions on childbirth have largely focused on empowering women – expressed through the psychosexual and active birth philosophies that sought to reclaim a conscious experience of childbirth in the 1970s and 1980s, and a shift in recent times to a view that women should be supported to give birth as they choose, with or without medical intervention (Wolf, 2003; Kukla, 2008). An autonomous and satisfying experience of childbirth is possible if the birth takes place in a setting with helpers committed to supporting the woman to experience her birth in her own preferred way.

Respectful, individualised care is fundamental. For some this may be a home birth, while others feel safer and more confident in a hospital where there is emergency medical back-up if needed. Overall, challenging the hyper-medicalisation and pathologising of childbirth over many decades has led to many useful insights, practices, and reforms. Many birth settings now offer labour lounges, birth pools and baths, family-friendly environments, and routine support of mothers rooming-in with the baby after the birth (Jones, 2012). If a caesarean birth is required, involving the parents in the decision, providing a clear rationale, and giving input into how the procedure and recovery phase are managed, can make it an autonomous and satisfying experience (Raphael-Leff, 2005). Afterwards, each woman needs an honest acknowledgement, without platitudes, of the birth she had, including any disappointments she may feel, and a validation that the experience is her own, and one that does not need to be compared with others'. Childbirth is not a simple binary, natural vs medicated – rather there is a broad spectrum of individual preferences and experiences (Raphael-Leff, 2005).

Early Contact with the Baby: 'Doing the Bonding'

> There is a bawling baby on my stomach, furious at being born. Around
> me, other people are weeping too, but more recreationally. Mine are
> the only dry eyes here. I know certain responses are expected, certain
> lines required from the overjoyed mother, but I cannot find my way
> to them. Instead, I am stuck on this non-sequitur: the violence, and
> now this stranger in the room. The nurse wraps the baby in a blanket
> and places him on my chest, and I give him a polite pat. He might
> not yet belong to me, but it is important to make him welcome.
> (Goldsworthy, 2014, p. 71)

Many women will relate to Goldsworthy's sentiments. She is exhausted by
the labour and delivery. When asked if she would like to learn to suckle
the baby, her first thought is that she is exhausted, and she would like to
retire from all future human endeavour. After a sleep, she is much more
ready to engage: 'When I wake up, I have a baby. And not just any baby,
this baby. You' (p. 72).

It can take weeks, even months, for parents to feel that a newborn really
belongs to them. In the period immediately after birth, they need to reconcile their fantasy baby with the real baby they encounter, a baby who
may have a moulded head, squashed features, marks and bruises from
delivery with forceps. Classic studies conducted by Klaus and Kennel in
the 1970s brought the study of early contact between human mothers
and infants into public focus for the first time. Their work was in part a
response to routine practices of childbirth in the United States and other
Western high-income countries during the 1960s that separated mothers and infants, after extreme sedation of mothers during labour. Infants
were cared for in rows of cribs in a nursery remote from their parents.

These practices were in stark contrast with proximity-oriented Eastern
and indigenous childbirth practices that emphasised extended early contact between mother and infant, and with ethological observations that
showed that maternal licking and tactile contact supported early regulation in mammal infants in the sensitive period after birth. Klaus and
Kennell (1976) observed and described an orderly predictable pattern
of maternal touching, that seemed to be instinctive and species specific,
when human mothers were allowed uninterrupted skin-to-skin contact with the baby immediately after birth. They also noted that newborn infants were briefly alert and wide eyed immediately after birth.
Subsequent research has shown this to be an important transitional
time for the onset of lactation (Jaafar et al., 2016), and confirmed that

maternal touch in the early hours after birth can ameliorate stress reactivity in human infants in the same way that has been demonstrated in rodents (Abraham et al., 2016).

Klaus and Kennel's work on bonding was influential, and it contributed to many positive changes in perinatal care practices, notably allowing the infant to 'room in' with the mother and encouragement of early skin-to-skin contact, with benefits for establishing the early relationship and for breastfeeding. There is a solid biological basis for recommending contact between mother and infant immediately after birth. Infant suckling stimulates oxytocin release in the mother, which can assist with the third stage of labour, reduce bleeding, and stimulate prolactin for breastfeeding (Raphael-Leff, 2005). With well supported early contact, human mothers and infants can achieve an unconscious entrainment of body movements and circadian rhythms (Murray & Trevarthen, 1986). A large body of work has confirmed there are benefits of sustained skin-to-skin contact for full-term infants with respect to infant biological regulation, establishment of breastfeeding, contingent maternal responsiveness, and mother–child interactions (see Norholt, 2020 for a comprehensive review).

Although there has been scant research, similar patterns of early touching behaviours have been observed in fathers who have contact with the baby after caesarean sections, with similar benefits for their caretaking relationship. Erlandsson et al. (2007) report that while they are highly motivated to bond with the baby, fathers generally need to navigate the bonding process alone, and they often feel overlooked in the period immediately after birth (Scism & Cobb, 2017). Scism and Cobb note many opportunities for physical contact for fathers include umbilical cord cutting, performing newborn massage, and facilitating skin-to-skin contact with fathers when newborns are born after caesareans or when the mother is unwell.

There are important caveats, however, regarding extrapolation from animal to human research, the over-simplification of complex attachment processes, and over-estimating the duration of any putative effects of early contact. The body of research evidence on benefits has led the World Health Organisation (WHO) to recommend perinatal services facilitate early and extended contact with the baby after birth whenever possible (WHO, 2018b), and encouraged hospitals to provide family-friendly care environments immediately after childbirth. Hrdy (1999) notes, however, that in the 1990s the pendulum had swung so far that in some hospitals mothers were being rated in medical files as 'bonded' or 'not bonded'. While changes in care practices are to be applauded and encouraged, mothers who cannot have early contact with the infant for medical reasons, for example premature birth, a sick baby, an emergency caesarean section, post-partum haemorrhage, can be further burdened with guilt and anxiety about their capacity to develop a relationship with their child, on top of the disappointment and trauma of a medically risky birth. There are also cautionary tales about the consequences of idealising early contact. Many women don't enjoy the first contact due to shock, exhaustion, over-arousal, tearing, and pain. Many fathers feel excluded from it. Both parents may need a supportive person to guide them through the process, to encourage their nascent intuitive responses, and to model and guide them in how to read these early infant cues (Hrdy, 1999; Raphael-Leff, 2005).

In summary, the biological synchrony of the mother and infant around the time of birth is special and important and it can be the basis for a positive developmental trajectory for the new family. Clinical practices and birth settings should support this whenever possible. However, human relationships are complex, and human infants are resilient. Early contact with the infant is neither necessary nor sufficient for parents to form a secure attachment relationship. Raphael-Leff (2005) points out that generations of parents have formed secure loving relationships with their offspring despite enforced early separations. Adoptive parents and parents of premature infants can and do form secure attachments, attesting to the complexity, resilience, and adaptability of human relational systems. The earliest encounter with the baby for adoptive parents and those who are not able to be present for the birth is discussed in more detail in Chapter 6.

Having a Premature Baby

Premature birth (before thirty-seven weeks) presents a sudden and unexpected end to the pregnancy that catches expectant parents completely off their guard. The psychological process of taking on an identity as a parent is interrupted. It is also a frightening and sometimes traumatic event, one that may involve an emergency caesarean section, realistic concerns about the survival of the baby, and the bewildering and alienating experience of a highly technological crisis-oriented care setting. Approximately one in ten infants worldwide is born prematurely – with subcategories based on gestational age: 'extreme' prematurity for infants born less than twenty-eight weeks' gestation, 'very' premature infants born between twenty-eight and thirty-two weeks and 'moderate' prematurity thirty-two to thirty-seven weeks (WHO, 2018a).

From a biological perspective, mothers may feel that their body has failed to sustain and support the baby, and that their nurturing role has been superseded by machines. They may feel guilty, wondering if it was something they did – or something they should have done, but didn't do (similar to reactions described in Chapter 5 in response to perinatal loss). Psychologically, all parental expectations are upended. Rather than the plump, cuddly baby that was anticipated, the scrawny, immature, premature infant attached to wires and alarms may seem alien and frightening. Many parents will experience grief at not having the normal birth experience they anticipated (Kassa et al., 2019). The baby may be 'whisked away' straight after the birth, making it difficult for the parents to process what has happened, and leading to separation distress, and concerns about bonding with the baby.

The shock of the birth and early separation can challenge the parents' ability to develop an emotional connection with the baby. Will the baby survive? Will it develop normally? When the medical outcome is uncertain, the parents may withdraw and hold back their feelings toward the baby to protect themselves from possible loss (Chapman & Paul, 2014), as parents sometimes do in medically at risk 'tentative' pregnancies (Rothman, 1986/1993), discussed in more depth in Chapter 5. If the baby has a significant medical condition, parents need to come to terms with the implications, and may have to make difficult decisions about complex medical interventions with uncertain outcomes.

The first encounter with the baby, when it does happen, will occur in the presence of a professional mediator; the new parents do not have the opportunity to freely handle and interact with their baby in private. This may make it difficult for the woman to 'feel like a mother'. In fact, it is often the father who has the first contact, thrust into the spotlight, while the mother recovers from surgery, (see Christopher's story in Chapter 4). A premature or medically unwell baby may not display the interactive cues that draw parents to them, their high-pitched cry patterns may be distressing and aversive; and they are likely to have reduced capacity for self-regulation and adaptive behavioural responses, which can make parents feel incompetent and inept (Kassa et al., 2019).

The neonatal intensive care environment may feel surreal and frightening – tubes, alarms, monitors, ventilators, and a tiny baby in a little glass box (humidicrib) which serves as a physical barrier. In this highly technical environment 'expert' nurses and doctors are the primary caretakers – effectively usurping the parental role. The constant presence of doctors and nurses may make parents feel powerless and de-legitimised. Parents have described a feeling of temporal suspension as the timetables of their daily life are defined by the institution. Many parents of premature infants have commented that it feels as if the baby belongs to someone else (Padovani et al., 2009).

The experience of ongoing neonatal intensive care can be frightening and traumatic – a prolonged state of crisis (Raphael-Leff, 2005). It is hardly surprising, then, that parents of infants born prematurely are significantly more at risk of anxiety and depression. A premature birth may be experienced as a psychological trauma – acutely at the time, and for some the trauma will persist with flashbacks up to a year later (Chapman, 2020). For many parents, however, the experience is an acute crisis that diminishes after the baby is discharged from hospital. Premature infants place greater demands on caregivers than full-term infants and parents need skilled help to adapt to their infant during the hospital phase so that they can form a loving relationship with their baby, and gain confidence that they can care for her. In the last thirty years, neonatal intensive care nurseries have followed protocols for individualised developmental care (Als et al., 1994) that aim to support shell-shocked parents to touch, fondle, and cuddle their premature infants. See Grace and Edward's account of the premature birth of their son at the end of this chapter.

Emotional and Physical Health around Childbirth

Childbirth is generally a normal event, which, while intensely painful at the time, is quickly forgotten, as parents engage in the challenges of new parenthood. For a significant minority of women, however, childbirth is associated with lasting physical health problems and/or psychological difficulties that have the potential to compromise early caregiving capacities, relationships, and change future reproductive goals (Fisher et al., 2018). Psychological reactions to childbirth need to be understood in context; they are influenced by life history, lifetime emotional wellbeing, and pregnancy mood, as well as the events that occur during or immediately after the birth. As noted earlier, birth can reactivate past hurts, worries, and feelings of vulnerability. Pregnancy stress can influence fear of childbirth, gestation, length of labour, and the likelihood of obstetric complications and caesarean section (Wadwa et al., 2001). Pregnancy mood problems are among the strongest predictors of post-traumatic stress reactions to childbirth and postnatal mood problems and complicated difficult births can influence immediate recovery, bonding with the baby, and establishment of breastfeeding (Fisher et al., 2018).

Difficult and complicated deliveries can result in lasting physical problems including a fractured coccyx (tailbone), pain related to abdominal surgery, or to a severe episiotomy or tear, and damage to the vaginal wall or bladder leading to sexual dysfunction. Mental health can be further complicated by these physical health problems. Some women experience birth as traumatic, and those with prior experiences of trauma or abuse may be particularly vulnerable (Muzic & Rosenblum, 2018).

In a meta-analysis, Ayres and colleagues (2016) found that approximately 3 per cent of women met criteria for Post-Traumatic Stress Disorder (PTSD) after childbirth. Vulnerability factors included depression in pregnancy, fear of childbirth, prior PTSD, complications in pregnancy, and negative birth experiences. Birth experiences that can contribute to childbirth as a traumatic event include real or perceived risks to the life of the mother or the baby (for example a pre-term birth), perceiving the birth experience as dehumanising, a long labour with severe pain and inadequate support, and caesarean sections or difficult forceps deliveries without adequate analgesia.

Clinicians need to be sensitive to individual perceptions of the birth experience. A key determinant of a positive response is whether parents feel respected, cared for and informed during labour and delivery, irrespective of complications and interventions (Green & Baston, 2003), as illustrated by Kate's story at the end of this chapter. Birth trauma can have lasting negative impacts on breastfeeding and relations with the infant, but post-traumatic growth is reported by some women – coping can make them feel stronger, enable them to communicate more openly with partners, and help them to acknowledge their vulnerabilities and ask for help when needed (Beck & Watson, 2016). Beck and Watson's research emphasised the importance of acknowledging birth trauma, and not 'glossing over' it because of the positive outcome of a child. There are many windows of opportunity to intervene and prevent traumatic reactions to childbirth becoming a slippery slope to ongoing postnatal difficulties. While most births are straightforward and uncomplicated, the stories below provide a perspective on becoming a parent when things don't proceed according to plan.

Grace's Story: An Early Baby during a Pandemic

Grace* was already feeling anxious about her first pregnancy, when the extent of the threat posed by the COVID-19 pandemic gradually began to dawn on people. Working in a corporate environment in London was stimulating, but also challenging. A snap 'work from home' decision was greeted with relief. It meant Grace no longer had to deal with crowded public transport. Still, the day-to-day encounters with crowds while competing for scant supplies of life essentials had to be negotiated:

> London is always busy, but I felt so anxious about the crowds and the pushy behaviour – I was pregnant ... the only way for us to get food was if I went with my 'pregnant badge' prominent during the early morning hour set aside for vulnerable people.

Across the country people were dealing with confusing messages, and rapidly changing public health guidelines. Antenatal care was no exception. Grace's pregnancy unfolded in a context of isolation and anxiety. As the seriousness of the Pandemic became more apparent, the hospital began cancelling appointments, and then they moved exclusively to tele-health with no face-to-face visits. While Grace appreciated the social distancing benefits, the telephone consultations felt like a cursory routine: 'They'd call up – "so how do you feel?" And I would respond, "I don't know." And then they'd ask – "what about the baby's movements, are they normal?" And I'd say, "I don't know, I think so."' As Grace explains, it was her first baby, and she simply didn't know what 'normal' felt like. She'd had a few bleeds early in the pregnancy, so she craved the reassurance of face-to-face, hands-on care. She wanted someone to examine her, listen to the baby's heartbeat, put their hands on her growing abdomen.

When face-to-face consultations resumed later in the pregnancy, Grace was relieved, but apprehensive about being out in public. She took a very long walk (about an hour) to the hospital to avoid public transport and taxis, but then there was the crowded waiting room. With typical wait times of forty-five minutes, Grace didn't want to touch anything; she was afraid to use the bathroom, and she tried to sit as far from others as possible.

One morning, when she was thirty-five weeks pregnant, Grace had a dramatic bleed in the shower. The volume of blood was terrifying. She called the doctor, and they were advised to go straight to hospital for monitoring and steroid injections. COVID-19 restrictions meant Edward* was not allowed to accompany her. He stood outside; alone, bewildered, afraid, holding the blood-soaked towels, and relying on Grace's text updates. After a few hours he was advised to go home, and then the hospital called him back almost straight away. Grace was to have a caesarean section, and she was relieved that Edward was allowed to be in the operating theatre with her.

More than a year later, Grace is overcome with emotion as she recalls the birth, particularly her distress when her baby was taken straight to the Neonatal Intensive Care Nursery (NICU), due to breathing problems: 'The thing that really upset me was them taking him away. I was pregnant. Then I was not pregnant. I hadn't seen him. I hadn't held him. It was really, really hard to process. There was no baby.' With her mobility limited after surgery, it was difficult getting herself to the NICU, which was two floors down. Once there, being with her newborn son was a surreal and very lonely experience:

> I felt socially awkward with my own baby ... I just felt, what should I do? Should I keep talking to him? What should I say? It was just hard; really, really, hard ... You couldn't just go down to see him when you wanted to, and Edward and I weren't ever able to be there at the same time. We had to visit separately. Edward wasn't permitted to come and see me at all.

Breastfeeding a premature baby was very challenging. Before she could take baby Harry home, Grace had to convince the nurses that feeding was successfully established: 'It was miserable. There was a heatwave. It was a baking hot room. I wasn't allowed to leave the room for two days, and Edward wasn't allowed in. It was just awful.' It wasn't easy for Edward either. As Grace explains:

> It's really hard on mothers, of course, but I think fathers get ignored. The way he described it to me was 'My whole world is in that hospital, and I'm not allowed in.' He was really worried about me, and he couldn't see me. He was trying to bond with a baby he didn't know, a baby he wasn't allowed to pick up, and he didn't have the biological cues, or the purposeful act of feeding. And half the time he wasn't even allowed in the building. I think it was very scary and isolating for him. At the same time, he felt like he couldn't complain ... It's supposed to be all about the mother. In a normal world, with a normal baby, you expect to be able to go about your normal day-to-day business, and Edward couldn't do any of that. He was supporting me, while I was supporting Harry. Afterwards, it was just us in our house. He was part of it, but at the periphery. So that was really challenging too. The thing was, I just didn't have any bandwidth to support him, to look after him. I was barely keeping it together. It wasn't fair on him. He also needed people around him to nurture him.

Getting home and being able to be together was a great relief, but like most new parents, Grace and Edward 'had no idea what they were doing'. Comprehensive and co-ordinated postnatal support was greatly appreciated. Calls from health visitors, lactation experts, all the relevant experts, came in straight away. But it still wasn't plain sailing. After three weeks, Grace noticed baby Harry was drawing his chest in as he breathed. They weren't sure how serious it was, but she followed her instincts and took him to the emergency department at the hospital. He was admitted and seven days later, after a full barrage of tests, and with no clear explanation of what had happened, he was discharged. For Grace, it felt like a replay of the traumatic period after the birth: a screaming, unhappy baby; staying with him in the hospital, without her partner, Edward, who was not able to be with them at all – not even to visit. While it was a difficult time, there was incremental progress. Grace felt reassured that she had read Harry's cues correctly, that she had made the right decision, in going to hospital. For the first time since his birth, she began to feel like a mother; more importantly, like Harry's mother. She was beginning to understand her own baby, his individual needs, and his patterns throughout the day.

Parents of premature babies are propelled abruptly into parenthood. Edward and Grace had enjoyed their online childbirth classes and the opportunity they provided to meet local couples, but they felt completely unprepared for an emergency caesarean section and their premature baby who was 'scrawny and thin, not ready to be in the world'. They took six weeks to name him, in part due to a lack of confidence that he would survive – and then there were the practical challenges. While Grace was trying to learn to feed the baby in hospital, Edward was frantically assembling the cot and trying to get the house set up. The Pandemic made even routine tasks difficult. Tiny (pre-term) baby clothes were in short supply. The social isolation required during the Pandemic meant no visitors in the house, no childcare, no practical support, no-one else to hold the baby. Finally reunited with their own families later in the year, with Harry robust and thriving, life slowly began to feel normal again: 'Just being able to have people around that we trusted to share our baby with them … It was heaven on earth. I can't explain. It was just joy.'

---

*Names have been changed.

Kate's Birth Story: Calling on Plan B

Kate's* career was taking off; she had just moved from Australia to the United States with her husband, Pete* to take up a fellowship:

> I was bursting to work; I was doing so many cool, creative projects; it was a very engaging and fun time. Unique in our lives. I felt I had a magic touch; Everything I did just worked. I felt success. I had momentum. It was also a great time in my relationship with Pete.

Progress toward their shared life goal of becoming parents was more challenging, however. When Kate received a positive pregnancy test result, her excitement was tempered by the three miscarriages she had experienced the previous year:

> Being pregnant was not for me. I just worried all the time. I hadn't felt that at all in my first pregnancy; I was over the moon, full of boundless hope and optimism. The miscarriages changed things … The first was devastating; the second disappointing; the third frustrating. So then when I was pregnant again with Tara, I was just waiting to miscarry – that was how I felt for much of the early pregnancy. I didn't get excited until the end of the first trimester when we had our thirteen-week scan. I remember the scan took a long time, so we got to watch her on the ultrasound for a while. And I thought – that is a little person growing inside me – that is bloody amazing!

Kate and Pete named their baby that night. Her eyes fill with tears as she recalls: 'I was bursting with joy. It was the most amazing feeling.' The second trimester was uneventful: 'I essentially forgot I was pregnant: I worked a lot; I was still running [for exercise]; my life didn't change much.' They moved back to Australia at thirty weeks and Kate started a new job. She was pleased to be busy: 'I didn't want to open myself to the underlying vulnerability. Because of the losses that came before, I was too scared. If I let myself have the joy; the pain would somehow be bigger. So, overall, I didn't enjoy being pregnant.'

Although Kate and Pete attended a natural birthing course at the local hospital, Kate didn't prepare in the way that she normally would for a big event:

> Maybe I was avoiding it, still worried about all the things that could go wrong. I didn't put a lot of thought and energy into preparing for a baby. A friend asked whether I had bought a cot, enrolled her in day-care? And I said why would I do that? I don't have a baby yet … I didn't understand the question. I wasn't in that space at all of thinking ahead to the next stage.

She wrote a birth-plan based on natural birth ideas:

> I had just assumed a natural birth would happen. I never felt scorn or judgement towards medical intervention like you sometimes hear. It was more that I was afraid of it. I was very afraid of having a caesarean section. That was major

surgery, and I felt I would do whatever it took to avoid it, so I didn't want any interventions.

The intention was to stay at home for the first twenty hours, and use the bath for pain relief, but things didn't go to plan. At forty weeks, Kate presented for her routine check at the clinic. The midwives had a minimal intervention philosophy, but Kate felt a compelling need for a scan to confirm that everything was OK. Her instincts served her well. The scan revealed that the baby was very small, and her amniotic fluid levels were worryingly low. She was told she needed an induction – and right away. Things moved quickly from there. There was no time to go home, or to rewrite the birth plan:

> Telling the story – it's clear it didn't go very well. But my experience of the birth was fine. A lot of my positive experience was thanks to the lead midwife, who was there with me for the bulk of my labour. She made me feel heard, respected, and supported. So, I never felt helpless or out of control during the labour, which meant a lot to me. BUT – it didn't go all that smoothly. My body was nowhere near ready. I had a balloon catheter, and prostaglandin gel, overnight; then they ruptured my membranes in the morning. There was frequent speculation about a C-Section – and I was very keen to avoid that. At each decision point, they would talk me through what was happening, and would take my requests and preferences into account, which was really appreciated. They were willing to wait and give me a chance at the natural birth I was expecting. After waiting an hour to see if I went into labour, they started the Syntocinin. Tara was showing signs of distress, so the dose was rapidly increased, and that was horrible.

There was little progress during the first four hours. Kate felt like she'd be in labour forever. The pain was intense, relentless. She tried gas, but it didn't help. She hopped in the bath – which felt wonderful – at first. Soon, however, the pain became overwhelming, with contractions coming every minute. Kate decided she wanted an epidural, and she wanted it right away. The midwife, respectful of her clearly stated preference to avoid one, was hesitant, but Kate was emphatic. She was astonished to learn after the epidural was in place that she was already fully dilated. There was a brief nap, followed immediately by an intense second stage of labour. Kate pushed for all she was worth, but the baby had a large head, and the cord was around her neck. Given signs of foetal distress, forceps and episiotomy were required. There was no time to wait.

Kate smiles wryly as she recalls the moments straight after birth:

> I might not be the right person for you to speak to. I remember one of my first thoughts being: 'I've made a really big mistake' (laughs). Because I had always said to Pete – If anything goes wrong at the time of birth, I want you to go with the baby. But then – he actually went with her! And I thought - 'Wait a minute. I'm the one who was just torn open!' I remember a very acute realisation that this was a huge shift in what our relationship would be. It felt like from that moment –

it's not just us anymore. There's someone else in our relationship now that we will both probably put before each other. Of course, Tara is not a mistake. She's an incredible little gift in our lives. But I remember, at first, not feeling the maternal love and joy that I was promised.

While the birth clearly didn't go to plan, Kate didn't experience any trauma reactions afterwards:

I think it was OK because I always felt calm. Even when my vision blacked out during the contractions, and during the surreal feeling in the breaks between contractions, I felt 'I'm just me'; everything is fine. Then twenty seconds later, another contraction came around. But I never felt scared or helpless. I didn't feel traumatised.

The main challenge was feeling disconnected:

At first, I definitely felt very different from what I was expecting to feel. It felt different from depression … it was more like an identity crisis. I didn't know who I was supposed to be; or how to fulfil this role of being a mum. I found it really hard, in part because so much of my identity at that time was wrapped up in my work, and then I wasn't working. All of a sudden, instead of being an independent, successful, creative person, I had this little gremlin who needed me around the clock and cried all the time; it drained me in a way that was not what I expected.

Kate returned to work when Tara was three months old and found the balance of parenting and working helped her to feel like a better parent: 'I felt more like myself and that made me feel less helpless and disconnected. It helped me enjoy my time parenting a lot more.' She was fortunate to have wonderful support. Pete was flexible (studying part-time), and they were living with her parents. As Kate explains:

We were both committed to fighting against the gendered expectations of how things are done. In fact, Pete is much more parental than I am – it was like he was born to be a dad. He is amazing. He just took to it, and it's such a core piece of his identity now. And we've both faced prejudice and judgement about that decision; me for going back to work after three months, and Pete for being a primary carer. We're trying to consciously choose the roles we want. I'm not a certain type of parent just because I'm a woman; and he's not a certain type of parent just because he's a man. Our shared parenting approach has worked really well for us, and it's benefited our baby enormously to have two happy parents who support each other.

---

*Names have been changed.

CHAPTER 8

The Fourth Trimester

How best to help new parents to cope with the challenges of early parenting? There are countless 'how to' manuals with practical tips and detailed instructions about caring for young infants. Some are evidence-based and grounded in years of professional experience with new parents. Many are personal and anecdotal. There are a multitude of motherhood blogs, and 'survival guides' written by media personalities, influencers, stand-up comics, 'sleep whisperers'. Literary motherhood memoirs (and a handful of fatherhood memoirs) document the profound personal dislocation of the new lifestyle and seek to make the work of mothering visible – the feeding, the changing, the endless washing.

Yet what's written never seems to be enough, and can be readily criticised – as too positive, too negative, too baby-focused, too prescriptive, too dogmatic, too judgemental. Despite unprecedented public discourse on the subject, new parents frequently ask why nobody told them what the early weeks of parenthood would be like. Writer Rachel Cusk (2008) describes a 'tone-deafness' of non-parents to parents. Early parenthood makes no sense until it is experienced: the experience is *always* different from the imagined version. The intensity, the bewilderment, the wonder, the sleeplessness is difficult, if not impossible to communicate. In any case, it may be futile to try. As childbirth educators will attest, with labour and delivery looming so large, expectant parents struggle to process any information about life after the birth.

The transition to parenthood is a nexus of biological, psychological, and social transformations. This chapter begins with a discussion of the embodied aspects of early mothering, the developmental capacities and vulnerabilities of young infants, and evidence-based approaches that support parents as they learn to care for their infants. Next, key psychological challenges related to profound changes to identity are discussed – for mothers, for fathers, and for the couple relationship. The social and cultural context of parenting provides a framework for examining the importance of social support and different cultural practices in the early months after birth. The chapter concludes with an overview of research on postnatal wellbeing and mood problems. For the most part, the experiences of mothers and fathers are integrated. It is acknowledged, however, that mothers are uniquely challenged to adapt to physical recovery from childbirth; that it is mothers who breast-feed, and typically bear the largest responsibility for childcare, and that they experience a more radical change to lifestyle and identity.

Biological Challenges

The early months after birth are a time of biological upheaval. The woman's body is recovering from pregnancy and childbirth, she is learning to breastfeed, and she may be experiencing sharp swings in hormone levels. She is also very likely to be sleep deprived.

Recovery from Childbirth

For some women, physical recovery from childbirth is straightforward and uneventful. Those who have had a difficult second stage of labour or an instrumental delivery may experience significant pain due to vaginal tearing, the bristle and prickle of perineal stitches, and the sting of urine passing over them. Some will have a caesarean section scar, and possible side-effects from epidural anaesthesia. There may be haemorrhoids, incontinence of urine, constipation. All will have to contend with vaginal bleeding over several weeks and the challenges of establishing breastfeeding.

Early Breastfeeding

Breast milk, designed to meet the newborn's digestive capacity and immunological needs, has sustained human infants for thousands of years. There is consistent evidence that breastfeeding is best from a health perspective, so it is actively promoted in most obstetric settings (WHO, 2018b). Research supports the benefits of breastfeeding for infants in the short-term, particularly in boosting immunity to diarrhoea and respiratory infections. Longer-term benefits have also been identified including a reduced risk of obesity, as well as more optimal child intellectual and educational outcomes. The higher-education and socio-economic status of breastfeeding mothers in Western high-income countries need to be taken into consideration when interpreting these research findings (Horta, 2019). There are also physiological benefits for the mother; the accompanying hormones, prolactin and oxytocin, help to regulate stress and increase protective behaviours and attentiveness to infant needs. Breastfeeding helps the uterus to shrink back to its normal size and delays the return of menstruation (Hrdy, 1999). Long-term health benefits include a reduced relative risk for breast and ovarian cancer (Chowdury et al., 2015).

Once established, breastfeeding can be a straightforward, natural process that is sensual and pleasurable for the mother and extraordinarily convenient (Barker, 2014). The close skin-to-skin contact, mutual gaze, and rhythmical suck/pause pattern can help new mothers to synchronise their tactile and vocal behaviour with their infant. Writer Naomi Wolf (2003) described her early breastfeeding as a 'rough-and-tumble' animal experience – the baby's approach was intense, frenzied, and vigorous – the connection between the baby's mouth and her nipple had an electric force. She relished the mutual satisfaction and wondered if there were any other times in life where it was possible to make someone so completely happy.

Evidence from experimental studies shows that skin-to-skin contact soon after birth and proximal care practices in the early weeks are associated with longer maintenance of breastfeeding and a more positive breastfeeding experience (Norholt, 2020), as discussed in Chapter 7. In agrarian cultures, feeding is integrated with daily work and lifestyle. The baby is carried close to the mother's body, and can suckle as needed throughout the day. Breastfeeding is viewed as mundane, practical, and routine, rather than transcendent. (LeVine & LeVine, 2017). In high-income countries, the duration of breastfeeding tends to be shorter than the six months recommended by the WHO (2018b). Not having access to paid maternity leave is a major contributing factor to early weaning, and the pragmatic necessity of pumping breast milk to enable a return to work is a far cry from the mutually satisfying and sensual experience of feeding described by Wolf or the ease of feeding for mothers who carry their babies on their bodies as they work.

It is not uncommon for women to experience difficulties with breastfeeding in the early weeks. Babies need to learn to suck, especially if born prematurely. Some have difficulties latching on, others suck voraciously. Pain from cracked nipples can be excruciating; some women struggle with blocked milk ducts which may progress to infection and systemic illness (mastitis). Lactating breasts leak, become hard, engorged, heavy, lopsided. The often-surprising intensity of the let-down reflex can be experienced as painful. Because of the intimately intertwined supply and demand systems, the lactating mother needs to be available at least intermittently twenty-four hours a day. Demand-fed babies who are given free access may want to feed every two hours. This can lead to physical and emotional exhaustion. Breastfeeding can also bring psychological and relational challenges related to sexuality, intimacy, commitment (the infant's need for a constant physical presence). A woman's anxiety about her capacity to provide adequate sustenance may activate a sense of feminine inadequacy and body concerns (Raphael-Leff, 2005.

Most of these difficulties can be overcome with individualised support in the early postnatal weeks. The clear benefits to mother and infant (maternal and child health, cost, ease of delivery) justify social and health policies encouraging breastfeeding, however the enthusiastic promotion of breastfeeding for valid health reasons can become a zealous and inflexible imperative, leading to unrealistic expectations, and distress and guilt if breastfeeding problems are insurmountable. While health evidence on benefits of breastfeeding is compelling at a population level, and particularly so in low-income countries, Barker (2014) has cautioned against extrapolating from these data in relation to outcomes for otherwise well cared for infants, when breastfeeding is not possible. Breastfeeding can certainly promote bonding between mother and infant in the early weeks (Horta, 2019), but there is no compelling evidence that the mother–child attachment relationship differs based on whether the baby is breast of bottle fed (see Jansen et al., 2008 for a review), Healthy, loved babies can also thrive on formula or a combination of breast and formula feeding (Barker, 2014).

Barker observes that few women choose not to breastfeed and when breastfeeding is abandoned, it is usually because circumstances make it impossible to continue. Her twenty-five years of professional experience supporting new mothers have convinced her that while many breastfeeding difficulties can be solved with education and support, some cannot. Psychological difficulties associated with breastfeeding are often due to social pressure (which can be intense), and expectations that it will be easy and pleasurable, which lead to feelings of guilt and failure if breastfeeding is not successful or desired (Raphael-Leff, 2005; Wolf, 2003). Raphael-Leff points out that conflicting advice can be distressing, and interventionist practices of midwives and lactation consultants (helping babies to latch on to breasts) can be experienced as intrusive by some women.

Neurological and Hormonal Changes that Support Caregiving

As you become more human, I become more animal … When you wake at night, my arms register your cry before my ears do. A muscular alarm, an anticipated fatigue … even in your sleep I keep one ear focused on your snuffling breath in the adjoining room. (Goldsworthy, 2014, p. 96)

Maternal physiology is transformed during pregnancy and the early months of parenting as the antenatal endocrine environment sets the stage for the onset of caregiving and attachment in humans and other mammals (Glynn et al., 2018). The volume of grey matter in the hypothalamus, amygdala, and substantia nigra in the mother's brain increases significantly between birth and three to four months postpartum. There is also increased functional connectivity of white matter. Imaging studies have shown that these brain changes are related to positive perceptions of the infant (Hoekzema et al., 2017) and responsive maternal behaviour (Swain et al., 2014). For both mothers and fathers, a down-regulation of testosterone levels is associated with increased responsiveness to infants (Kuo et al., 2018). There is also recent evidence that vasopressin levels may be related to fathers' engagement in stimulatory interaction with their infants (Abraham & Feldman, 2018), and evidence that lesbian co-mothers who do not give birth also experience hormonal changes during the early months of caregiving (Chin et al., 2020).

The hormone oxytocin plays a significant role in sexual reproduction, labour, breastfeeding, and early caretaking. Oxytocin, released in response to stimulation of the nipples, is responsible for contracting breast muscles to release milk (the let-down reflex), and contracting the uterus as it resumes its normal size after birth. Colloquially referred to as the 'love hormone', oxytocin is a natural opiate that contributes to the neurological activation of the caregiving system and promotes affiliative feelings in all mammals (Hrdy, 1999). There is a growing body of evidence that oxytocin levels (which increase across pregnancy and are sustained by breastfeeding) are associated with more positive maternal (Kohlhoff et al., 2017) and paternal (Abraham & Feldman, 2018) bonding to the infant. Intriguingly, however, there is also evidence that lactating women, like their mammalian counterparts, show low levels of stress reactivity, but increased aggression towards others believed to be a protective response of the caregiving system to ensure the survival and wellbeing of their offspring (Hahn-Holbrook et al., 2011). Hahn-Holbrook and colleagues speculate that this may contribute to assertiveness in social exchanges between partners, as the couple adjusts to new relational dynamics as new parents. We return to this idea later in this chapter.

Understanding the Young Infant: A Developmental Perspective

The term 'fourth trimester' (Karp, 2018) captures the dependency of the human newborn in the first three months of life and the corresponding sustained demands on the parent. Compared to other mammals, human neonates are immature at birth, and arguably just as physiologically dependent on their mothers as they were in utero. In good news for mothers, however, and in contrast to pregnancy, the second parent can also meet most infant dependency and contact needs.

Like other baby mammals, the human infant is born with a suite of primitive reflexes – involuntary, stereotyped responses to the environment that underpin a basic drive to survive (Brazelton, 1983). These reflexes (for example, the rooting reflex to find the nipple, the 'grasp' reflex) provide an index of the infant's neurological integrity – they should be present, but not too strong. Over time they are integrated as higher brain regions develop. By the age of three to four months, primitive reflexes have evolved into more flexible, intentional, motor behaviours, and nascent self-regulation capacities are emerging, including a more predictable sleep routine.

Infants are not simply slaves of their reflexes, however. From the moment of birth, they are primed to attend to inanimate objects, interact with people in their environment, and form attachments that ensure their survival. Importantly, newborns are also born with the ability to habituate to (or shut out) repeated stimuli. This enables them to maintain sleep or a calm state, even in a chaotic or noisy environment. Influential developmental paediatrician, T. Berry Brazelton viewed 'infant state' as the key to understanding the newborn: the infant moves rapidly through states of alertness, readiness to play or explore, and phases where they need to shut down and limit incoming stimulation. They need to be supported through these transitions. As the baby develops over the first three months, periods of engaged alertness become more frequent and last longer. The infant becomes a more social being (Brazelton, 1983).

Individual Differences: Infant Temperament

There is no 'ideal baby', no 'typical' 3-month-old. There is *this* baby, at *this* age, in *this* setting, at *this* time of day and with *this* history.'
(Bruner, 1969 in Brazelton, 1983, p. xix, italics added)

Babies are individuals from the outset. And context is always important. While the presence of reflexes and orienting social responses is universal, infants differ in awareness of their environment, in the threshold and intensity of their responses, in their capacity to habituate, and in their background muscle tone and activity level. Some seem inclined to continue to hibernate, while others are alert, volatile, and 'rearing to go'.

Newborn infants differ in their capacity to attend, to transition smoothly from one state to another, to soothe themselves when distressed, and in the regularity of their biological functions (sleeping, eating). Some infants approach new experiences with what seems like adventurous ease, while others withdraw and resist when confronted with different foods, different people, different places to sleep. An infant's default demeanour may be sunny and cheerful or grumpy and irritable. This cluster of behavioural and emotional predispositions is referred to as infant temperament: biologically based individual differences in reactivity and self-regulation that tend to be stable over time and across contexts (Rothbart, 2011).

Temperament is an enduring predisposition influenced by genes; identical twins share more temperament traits than fraternal twins or siblings do. Environment also plays a role, however. Exposure to environmental teratogens (nicotine, recreational drugs, chemicals) or high levels of maternal stress hormones in pregnancy, can lead to a more reactive and unsettled temperament (Korja et al., 2017, and see Chapter 3). The baby who has experienced a prolonged and difficult delivery, may be more unsettled in the immediate postnatal period, and the baby whose mother has taken opioids to manage pain in labour may be more unresponsive in the early hours after birth. Evidence from many large longitudinal studies shows that while temperament is broadly stable over time, it can be modulated by caregiving. Approximately 10–15 per cent of infants are born with a temperament that is challenging or 'difficult' for caregivers (Putnam et al., 2002). These infants are neither regular nor predictable about when they will sleep and feed; they do not settle easily, and they wake frequently. They are keenly sensitive, and likely to react negatively to new environments or unfamiliar caregivers; they protest strongly, and they are not readily soothed. On the other hand, the baby who is classified as 'adaptable' or 'easy' (about 40 per cent of infants) can be fed at predictable times, in different places, by different people, put to sleep anywhere, and left in the care of others. Clearly parents of such infants will experience less disruption when it comes to re-engaging with the outside world, while the baby who is difficult to soothe may leave his parents feeling anxious and incompetent, and disinclined to take the baby out, because it's all just too difficult.

Negative Labels and Self-Fulfilling Prophecies
While temperament is a biological predisposition, there is a large social overlay. Labels are influential, they confer meaning on infant behavioural styles. Cultures differ in their definition of 'the ideal child' and the extent to which different temperament traits are valued, or viewed as

problematic (Keller et al., 2007). Temperament researchers have coined the term 'goodness of fit' to capture the match between the infant's temperament, the parents' expectations and preferences, and the culture and environment into which the child is born (Lerner & Lerner, 1987). A lively, active father may have more difficulty relating to a passive, slow to warm up infant, and feel more affinity with one who is active and alert. Gender stereotypes can influence how parents respond to different temperament traits. There is evidence, for example, of less acceptance of 'difficult' temperament in girls and 'inhibited' temperaments in boys (Putnam et al., 2002).

Fussy, irritable, unpredictable infants (discussed in more detail later in this chapter) may be labelled 'difficult' or 'demanding' by parents and others. These early labels can have long-term influences: by implication, either the baby or the parents are failing. Childrearing experts caution against typecasting young infants, as children can grow into the labels attached to them (Putnam et al., 2002). Parents are encouraged to think about their infant as 'challenging', 'high-need', or 'interested and sensitive' rather than 'difficult' (Brazelton, 1983). Reframing 'demands' as legitimate attachment needs can be transformative in how parents view their child, despite challenging and unsettled behaviour (Powell et al., 2014).

'Orchid Children'. There is intriguing evidence that infants and children with challenging temperaments may be especially susceptible to their caregiving environment: more vulnerable to stressful environments, but also more likely to thrive in enriched and supportive environments (Boyce, 2019). Infants with challenging temperaments need special nurturing; they can bring out the best (and the worst) in their parents. When parents are well supported and resourced, they may be able to respond flexibly and sensitively, but if they are exhausted or depressed, perhaps living in highly stressful circumstances, an infant with a challenging temperament can be the 'straw that breaks the camel's back' in the new family system. We return to these themes later in this chapter.

Getting to Know the Baby

One of the first tasks facing new parents is to get to know and understand their infant as a unique individual. Understanding the infant and how he responds to and manages his environment engenders respect for his competence, as well as appreciation of his quirks and idiosyncrasies, and sensitivity to his vulnerabilities (Brazelton, 1983).

Even for those with no prior exposure, the pitch and cadence of adult communication with young infants suggests there is some hard-wired intuitive understanding of the innate spatial and temporal organisation of infant behaviour. As Hrdy (1999) puts it: 'Anywhere in the world, no matter how aloof … people smile and chat up babies. Normal social rules don't apply' (p. 156). In random encounters (in supermarkets, on the street), adults use stylised voices – a sing-song tone, a wide pitch range, short utterances, long pauses, accompanied by exaggerated facial expressions and body movements. This performance style, referred to as 'motherese', and more recently as 'parentese', characterises the games adults play with young infants (and their pets!) across diverse cultures and languages. Intriguingly, Stephen Malloch and Colwyn Trevarthen (2009) have documented the musical notation of parent–child interactions. Their recordings demonstrate an unconscious communicative musicality characterised by distinct and synchronised melodies, and clear turn-taking. The mutual satisfaction expressed during these interactive moments contributes to the development of a sense of intimacy between parent and infant.

Newborns are social beings, primed to interact. They are born with a repertoire of attachment behaviours that serve the goal of achieving proximity and contact with the parent – they signal (cry, smile, reach), they cling and nestle in to maintain contact, and they are oriented visually to the parent, even when they are not in close proximity to them. From the moment of birth, infants find human faces compelling; they follow with their eyes, and they turn their heads toward voices. These nascent interactive skills seem designed to elicit care. The signals they emit, along with physical characteristics advertising their vulnerability (small size, large eyes, jerky movements), are compelling and irresistible to most adults (Hrdy, 1999). Infant social responsiveness is typically indiscriminate in the early months (true attachment develops in the second half of the first year), but some will already display a preference for the primary caregiver in the first two months after birth showing differential smiling and settling, and separation distress (Brazelton, 1983).

Empathy, Attunement, and Sensitive Parenting
What is going on in the infant's mind? What does she want? Why won't she stop crying? From the earliest days, parents construct and label their infant's world, based in part on objective reality, in part on speculation, and in part on unconscious projections of their own world views and early experiences. They make a best guess about what the infant may be feeling and the meaning of her behaviour. This process confers personhood and agency, forming

the basis of empathy and intimacy (Stern, 2018). An emotional connection including attributions of personhood can begin in pregnancy, as discussed in Chapters 3 and 4, however the concrete basis for building a reciprocal relationship begins after birth. Empathy begins with observation and curiosity – watching the baby, followed by a genuine attempt to see the world from her point of view. The parent's capacity to *notice* infant cues, *interpret* them correctly, and *respond* promptly and appropriately are the crucial foundations for a child's sense of self-worth, and trust in others (Ainsworth et al., 1974). Repeated affirming experiences with a sensitive, responsive caregiver in the early months of life make infants feel understood, accepted, and safe, the foundation for a secure attachment relationship (Bowlby, 1982).

Mutual Regulation: A Relational Perspective. For the infant, the first twelve weeks is all about feelings and raw experiences. Foetal attachment reflects the subjective feelings the parent has about an imagined child. True attachment, which begins to develop after birth, but is not established till later in the first year of life, is a dyadic relational construct and co-regulation of emotion is at its core (Bowlby, 1982). There is a nuanced reciprocal interplay between infant cues and parent responses – the parent's soothing vocalisations, touch, and mirroring of facial expressions help the infant to learn about feelings and to regulate emotional arousal and distress. This early co-regulation helps the infant to organise her level of arousal, her attentional focus, her feelings, her transitions to sleep. Through trial and error, the parent learns how to soothe and calm the infant when she is highly aroused or distressed, and to stimulate, challenge, and encourage her engagement with the outside world when she is calm and alert. Gradually, the parent scaffolds the infant's developing capacities, as she shifts from a complete reliance on external regulation to self-regulation (Papousek & von Hofacker, 1998).

This is not easy! Despite their best intentions, parents don't always get it right. Nor do they need to. Influential psychotherapist and attachment theorist Donald Winnicott (1953) famously coined the phrase 'good enough mothering' to explain that it is neither necessary nor desirable for the mother to be always attuned:

> A mother is neither good nor bad nor the product of illusion, but is a separate and independent entity: The good-enough mother ... starts off with an almost complete adaptation to her infant's needs, and as time proceeds she adapts less and less completely, gradually, according to the infant's growing ability to deal with her failure. Her failure to adapt to every need of the child helps them adapt to external realities. (p. 93)

Although this much-quoted phrase provides some solace to parents struggling to cope with the often baffling and unpredictable nature of their infant's behaviour, Bowlby's work and Bowlby–Ainsworth attachment theory that followed from it have been criticised for placing undue pressure on mothers to meet their infant's every need (Hays, 1998). Based on decades of detailed observations of mothers and infants in different cultures, LeVine and LeVine (2017) conclude that indulgence, warmth, and sensitivity are in the eye of the beholder. Caregiving behaviour is underpinned by different cultural styles of emotional expression and driven by different childrearing goals. Parenting evolves to meet the needs of a particular context.

Crying, Settling, and Sleep

Infant crying, unsettled behaviour, and night-waking are the major challenges of the fourth trimester for new parents. There is endless advice, often unsolicited, from friends, extended family, random strangers in the shopping mall, professionals, social media. The advice is idiosyncratic, often contradictory, and may have no grounding in evidence. A primal battle for survival is invoked: the baby's insatiable needs pitted against the parents' diminishing resources. As writer Rachel Cusk (2008) points out, however, this is not a zero-sum game. The system is necessarily unbalanced, and the mother (or father) simply has to do more. Over the first few months, infants gradually mature, and parents and infants adapt to each other as their diurnal rhythms synchronise. The intensity and duration of crying bouts declines, more predictable sleeping patterns generally emerge by twelve weeks, and the baby begins to acquire the developmental capacities to learn how to fit into the parents' world (Barker, 2014). While things generally get easier, sleep instability may recur during developmental transitions as the infant struggles to integrate new motor competencies, such as rolling (Mindell et al., 2016).

Crying

> My son is crying. Again. The baby books and other mothers assure me that it's 'just a Phase'. That all babies go through a period of refusing to play on their own. Of crying when they aren't being cuddled. Of constantly demanding the security of human contact … but in this moment a 'phase' means nothing … This feels like an everlasting cycle of tears and noise; a cycle from which I will never escape. (Rizvi, 2015, n.p.)

The young infant's cry is piercing, elemental, heart-rending – it activates a visceral response in all who hear it. Crying is a powerful and effective signal. Designed to achieve contact and elicit care, when infant crying is too intense, or too prolonged, it can be distressing and aversive for parents. Why do some babies cry more than others? It has long been believed, based on a classic study by Bell & Ainsworth (1972), that prompt parental responding reduces the amount of infant crying, but more recent observational studies have shown that it's not that simple. Several studies report no differences in maternal sensitivity and responsiveness comparing parents of infants who cry a great deal with those who cry less (Giesbrecht et al., 2020; Hubbard & van Ijzendoorn, 1991; St James-Roberts, et al., 1998). Ian St James-Roberts (2007) conducted a comprehensive review of research on associations between caregiving and infant crying and sleeping, and he concluded that Western babies who cry a lot seem to do so despite care that is adequate for most other babies. In other words, there seems to be an objective effect of infant characteristics on parent behaviour, rather than the other way around (Giesbrecht et al., 2020).

Different cultural contexts and practices need to be considered. Traditionally, Western parents have put babies in prams, strapped them in baby seats or bouncers, and put them to sleep in a separate bed in a separate room, with the goal of promoting autonomy and independence (Maute & Perren, 2018). In agrarian and non-Western cultures, however, carrying the baby on the parent's (generally mother's) body most of the day is common practice, as is co-sleeping (Norholt, 2020). St James-Roberts and colleagues (2006) studied infant crying in relation to these different cultural caregiving practices. Results showed that 'proximal parenting' (a lot of holding and body contact) was associated with less *overall* crying, indeed up to 50 per cent less! Interestingly, however, proximal parenting did not influence *inconsolable* crying (noted in 5–13 per cent of infants). This supports the view that the intractable crying observed in a minority of infants is likely due to neuro-developmental immaturity, and not much influenced by what parents do. In this study, infants of parents who engaged in proximal caretaking woke and fed more often during the night, however their parents (who generally co-slept with their babies) did not consider this a problem, as their own sleep was less disrupted.

Understanding the developmental trajectory of infant crying and sleep patterns is helpful (Doi et al., 2020; Hiscock et al., 2014). Fussing and crying durations are highest in the first six weeks of life, and they reduce significantly between six and twelve weeks. Just knowing that the crying won't last forever can be very reassuring. Parental concerns about crying typically peak around five to six weeks after birth in Western cultures (St James-Roberts, 2007). For the most part, infant crying reflects a physical (hunger, tiredness, discomfort) or emotional (lonely, overstimulated) need, and the baby is soothed by prompt parent responses and comforting. Some crying has no obvious explanation, however, and parent interventions have little effect, as noted earlier. Despite a large body of theory and research over the last century, leading to a series of new 'cures' or strategies, each superseding the one before it, there has been little progress in stopping otherwise healthy babies crying (Barker, 2014). As Barker points out, a certain amount of crying is normal for young infants; some babies simply cry a lot, and there is no clear explanation or solution.

Persistent Inconsolable Crying. Most babies between two and eight weeks of age have a period of wakeful distress each day. Often referred to as the 'witching' or 'arsenic' hour, the crying may last for two or three hours, generally in the late afternoon and early evening. Vexingly, the crying persists despite the parents' full repertoire of soothing attempts. Often labelled infant 'colic', it has little to do with gut function. An official 'diagnosis' of colic has long been defined by the 'rule of threes': crying for at least three hours, at least three days a week, for at least three weeks (Wessell et al., 1954). Studies vary depending on the criteria applied, however a recent review reported that 17–25 per cent of infants in Western settings have colic, higher than the prevalence of 5–15 per cent in non-Western cultures. Colic usually resolves by two to three months of age, as the infant's repertoire of behaviour and emotional expression expands, and they achieve a new level of self-regulatory competence (see Wolke et al., 2017 for a review). Parents of infants who are frequently inconsolable are likely to feel distressed, incompetent, and helpless. The presence of someone (partner, extended family) who can provide support, reassurance, and some respite is crucial.

Night Waking and Broken Sleep

Crying and sleep are intertwined. When inconsolable crying occurs in the middle of the night, it is even more challenging. There are many myths about infant sleep and the extent to which it can be controlled or managed. Healthy newborns spend approximately eighteen of each twenty-four hours asleep, with short periods of wakefulness every three to four hours, both night and day. Sleep patterns mature slowly, and in stages. A day/night diurnal pattern (circadian rhythm) emerges gradually, beginning by the end of the first month, with a more distinct twelve-hour-day pattern generally established by three to four months. As with adults, exposure to natural daylight, avoiding bright and blue lights at night, and a predictable, consistent bedtime routine can support infant sleep. Infants need to integrate cycles of active or rapid eye-movement (REM) with quiet (non-REM sleep) sleep, and the transitions between cycles can be challenging. For newborns these cycles alternate in periods lasting forty-five to sixty minutes, with a high proportion of REM sleep. The infant needs to mature and develop some capacity for self-comforting in order to achieve longer periods of deep sleep, typically four hours (Tresillian, 2018). Nocturnal video observations confirm that many infants can self-settle and sleep for longer periods by three to four months of age (St James Roberts et al., 2015).

Mothers and infants are biologically synchronised through breastfeeding and this bio-behavioural co-regulation is enhanced through close ventral body contact (Norholt, 2020). In the early weeks, when breastfeeding is being established, regular feeds through the night are necessary, due to the small capacity of the infant's stomach. They are also important for establishing milk supply. Night-time breast milk is rich in melatonin which supports sleep. While many new parents focus on the baby acquiring the capacity to 'sleep through the night', this can be misguided and unrealistic in the early weeks, and can cause unnecessary angst (Barker, 2014; Tresillian, 2018). In fact, most infants wake at least once during the night throughout the first postnatal year. During the first three months, 95 per cent will cry and need parental help to resettle; by twelve months around 70 per cent are able to self-settle. There is substantial variability in how often infants wake at night, how long they take to settle, in family sleep arrangements, and in parent capacity to cope with disrupted sleep.

Strategies to Manage Crying, Settling, and Sleep Problems
Concerns about sleep and crying are the most common reason that new parents present to health services (St James-Roberts, 2007; Wolke, 2019). They have given rise to a new profession of 'sleep consultants' and 'sleep whisperers'. Negative feedback loops are all too easily established when parents are exhausted and vulnerable during the early phase of postnatal adaptation. These can contribute to persistent dysregulated infant behaviour, which in turn engenders feelings of failure as a parent, relationship strain, and an increased likelihood of anxiety and depression (Papousek & von Hofacker, 1998; Wolke, 2019). This is particularly the case for parents whose socio-economic, interpersonal, or emotional resources are

compromised, and it is doubly difficult for single parents, or parents of twins (Barker, 2014). While parents may *understand* that crying is normal and necessary, and that all infants wake at night, they may *feel* that their baby is trying to make their lives difficult. This is particularly the case for young mothers, who may take the crying personally (Doi et al., 2020). Persistent inconsolable crying can make parents feel angry, helpless, and frustrated, and is a risk factor for child abuse, particularly shaken baby syndrome (Wolke, 2019).

Conflicting Advice.   The public discourse around infant crying and sleep can easily become a contested battleground reflecting different childrearing ideologies and beliefs; a perfect storm of anecdote, strongly held opinion, and 'expert' advice. Contradictory advice is confusing; uncertainty makes parents vulnerable (Senior, 2015). Rigidly held views and edicts are not helpful. Parents need flexible, individualised support that takes account of the infant's evolving attachment and developmental needs. At the same time, professionals need to be mindful of the parenting context (particularly availability of support), what the parents can realistically cope with, and the importance of parent mental health.

Advocates of infant-led parenting view sleep and crying problems from a relational perspective. Drawing on attachment theory principals, they advocate consistent, prompt, and empathic responses to infant distress, particularly at night (Higley & Dozier, 2009). A recent randomised trial showed that an attachment-theory-informed intervention teaching parents to tune in, understand, and respond promptly to infant cues throughout the day, particularly during the transition to sleep, can be effective in increasing total sleep time in infants between four and ten months of age (Middlemiss et al., 2017). Attachment theory also emphasises, however, that parents need to provide developmentally graded support for the infant's emerging autonomy and self-regulation (Bowlby, 1982; Gradisar et al., 2016; Winnicott, 1960). Approaches to sleep and settling that are informed by learning theory and behavioural protocols emphasise the latter. Proponents argue that parents need to be educated about how to support their infant's developing capacity to resettle and self-regulate; that this is determined by how the parent responds during normal sleep–wake transitions; and that external regulation can begin between two and three months of age (Wolke, 2019).

Parents need individually tailored support and reassurance that is respectful of their childrearing philosophy and cultural background; they will differ in their thresholds for sleep deprivation, their tolerance for infant distress, and their beliefs about 'good' parenting (Middlemiss et al., 2017). In the first three months, parents can be gently supported to provide developmentally 'scaffolded' care. Through trial and error, they will gradually learn when to soothe the baby, and when to step back and wait, allowing him or her to self-settle (Papousek & von Hofacker, 1998; Wolke, 2019).

Management of parent stress levels and exhaustion is as important as managing infant crying, however. Extreme tiredness resulting from fragmented sleep can impair parent capacity to read infant cues and provide responsive support. The exhausted parent is emotionally aroused, irritable, and their thinking can become confused. They may lose their belief in their capacity to care for their infant, lose confidence in their own judgement, and feel frustrated and angry that they are being robbed of their own time. Exhausted parents who feel they are failing to manage their infant are more at risk for postnatal depression and anxiety, especially if they are in an unsupported environment (St James-Roberts, 2007; Wilson et al., 2019). Chronic sleep deprivation and depression share many symptoms (teariness, irritability, lack of pleasure), and it can be difficult to differentiate between the two. Some parents respond by over-regulating, providing hyper-responsive interventions that deprive infants of the opportunity to learn to settle themselves; others under-regulate, failing to provide adequate regulatory support, with the result that the infant's distress escalates to an intensity where soothing is very difficult (Papousek & von Hofacker, 1998). The 'sweet-spot' between fussing (which can be a path to self-settling), and all-out crying is a fine judgement call.

Soothing Techniques.   Most soothing and settling techniques draw on animal models and ancient wisdom: they include swaddling (to contain flailing body movements and startle responses) movement (particularly rhythmic rocking to provide vestibular stimulation), music or white noise (believed to emulate womb sounds), and sucking, using a pacifier or the breast. Some combination of these time-worn strategies is employed by most parents, and there is recent evidence from observations and heart-rate data that they are modestly effective in reducing fussing in infants under three months of age (Möller et al., 2019). Specially designed cradles and wraps that use artificial intelligence to adjust rocking to infant cues are anecdotally helpful. While there are many parent testimonials and consumer reviews on parent websites, there are no published quality trials at time of writing to support their effectiveness. When soothing strategies are not effective, and parents are exhausted, parent training programmes based on limiting parental presence and response to infant signals, (referred to as graduated extinction, or also 'controlled crying'), may be a next step.

Sleep and Crying Training Programmes.   Paediatrician Ian St-James Roberts has studied infant sleep, settling, and crying over many decades and in different cultural groups. He contends that while not appropriate during the first six weeks after birth when infant behaviour is largely reflexive, structured parenting that supports sleep–wake organisation during transitions to sleep may begin to be effective after six weeks of age (St James-Robert, 2007). There is some empirical support for parent training programmes to manage infant crying in older infants, but scant research on infants under three months of age. A recent systematic review of trials including 1187 infants and parents found only weak evidence, with a reduction in overall infant crying time in three of the seven studies included. Most studies had significant methodological limitations (Gordon et al., 2019).

Two recent well-designed studies with follow-up including observational measures in the second year of life suggest that graduated extinction (or delayed responding to crying) is effective in reducing nocturnal wakefulness when implemented in three-month-old (Giesbrecht et al., 2020) and six-month old infants (Gradisar et al., 2016). Importantly, results of these studies indicate that this approach does not lead to problems in infant social-emotional development, or quality of parent–child attachment in the second year of life. Giesbrecht and colleagues observed parent–child interactions, and they found no differences in sensitive responsiveness when they compared parents who used graduated extinction of responses to infant crying and those who didn't. Their findings are consistent with Winnicott's (1951) 'good-enough' parenting notion, and previous research suggesting that sensitivity may be optimal when there is *moderate* rather than complete contingency between infant distress and parental responsiveness (Bornstein & Manian, 2013; Hubbard & van IJzendoorn, 1991).

Co-Sleeping.   In many cultures, co-sleeping is the norm, and often necessary due to the realities of space and housing. Bed-sharing happens by default. Parents who share a bed with their infant report fewer sleep problems, but also that their infants wake and feed more frequently at night, as noted earlier (LeVine & LeVine, 2017; St James-Roberts, 2007). Contemporary public health advice in Western countries urges caution regarding co-sleeping, due to evidence from large population studies of increased relative risk of Sudden Unexpected Death in Infancy (SUDI) which includes Sudden Infant Death Syndrome (SIDS) (Marinelli et al.,

2019). Parents who choose to co-sleep need to carefully follow health guidelines regarding risky co-sleeping – when the parent is affected by alcohol, recreational drugs, or medications that cause drowsiness, and in relation to sleeping on sofas, couches, or hammocks (Tresillian, 2018).

Summary Comments. Parents of babies who cry inconsolably may feel desperate. They are particularly vulnerable to unsolicited advice – glib 'solutions' that are difficult to implement –potentially distressing regimes involving limiting parent responses to infant distress on the one hand, and on the other, recommendations of highly proximal 'intensive' parenting, with a relentless and demanding regime of constant rocking, patting, breastfeeding, and carrying the baby in a sling (Barker, 2014). Either strategy, if applied too rigidly, is likely to lack the flexibility required to adapt to evolving infant developmental needs and both may make unrealistic demands on the caregiver.

For most infants, crying will run its developmental course, however inconsolable infant crying in the early months requires careful and timely attention from health professionals to prevent negative 'vicious cycles' of arousal and distress in both parents and infants (Papousek & von Hofacker, 1998; St James-Roberts, 2007). A recent study of Japanese mothers has shown that early education about infant crying is particularly effective in preventing depressive symptoms in young mothers aged under twenty-five years (Doi et al., 2020). Interaction guidance that promotes mutually rewarding feedback when the infant is in a state of active alertness can be a buffer against negative feedback cycles in parent–infant interaction, allowing parents to feel effective and to experience delight in their infant (Papousek & von Hofacker, 1998).

From an attachment-theory perspective, providing comfort and pro-tection to an intensely distressed infant is fundamental. Recent evidence, however, supports the pragmatic view that occasionally allowing a healthy well-fed baby to cry is a realistic and safe option for exhausted parents (Giesbrecht et al., 2020; Gradisar et al., 2016), and one that provides an opportunity for the infant to exercise her emerging capacities to regulate negative emotions (Barker, 2014). The 'goodness of fit' between childrear-ing beliefs, approaches to managing infant crying, parent resources, and individual infant characteristics is crucial. Parents need to be supported and empowered to make caregiving choices that are consistent with their individual context, cultural orientation, and values (LeVine & LeVine, 2017; Raphael-Leff, 2005; St James-Roberts, 2007), but all may be relieved to know they don't need to be 100 per cent responsive all the time.

Psychological Challenges: A New Identity

Everything changes once the baby is born. New parents need to come to terms with the baby they have, rather than the one they may have fantasised about. At the same time, they must reconcile their imagined self as a parent and their expectations of life after birth with their day-to day reality. Adapting to a radically different lifestyle, and renegotiating their relationships with one another, with extended family, and with the outside world, is not achieved without substantial psychological upheaval. Identity challenges are generally greater for women who are more likely to take on the primary caregiver role, and, at least temporarily, leave the workforce.

The Maternal Identity: Fusion or Autonomy?

Despite psychological preparation for a new identity during pregnancy (discussed in Chapter 3), in the fourth trimester expectations rub up against reality, as women find themselves at home in a new and unfamiliar role. Feelings of loss about a past lifestyle are inevitable, alongside tentativeness about managing the caregiving demands in the present, and uncertainty about what is to come.

Paediatrician and psychoanalyst, Donald Winnicott, (1960) described early motherhood as a symbiotic state of dual unity, coining the phrase 'primary maternal pre-occupation'. He saw this symbiotic state as a crucial, but temporary, phase of complete identification with the infant, beginning in the third trimester of pregnancy and gradually diminishing over the early postnatal weeks. The mother's fundamental purpose during this phase of parenthood was to act as a 'container': to absorb and process the infant's primitive emotions. These views of early mothering are fundamental to psychoanalysis and attachment theory. Feminist scholars have criticised a failure to acknowledge maternal subjectivity and ambivalence that permeates these influential theories; so that mothers are not adequately recognised as desiring and deserving subjects in their own right (Baraitser, 2009).

During the early weeks of parenting, a unified sense of self may be elusive; the two selves (mother and infant) can feel fused, yet also split in two. As discussed earlier in this chapter, the emerging relationship is necessarily skewed toward the needs of a fragile young infant during these early weeks. Establishing feeding and settling cycles requires a bio-behavioural synchrony driven by infant needs that can feel intense and insatiable. It may be only when the baby sleeps, that the mother can reconnect, albeit briefly, with herself. Writer Rachel Cusk (2008) describes the guilty pleasure of her daughter's daytime nap as she savours the prospect of reconnecting with her former self for an hour or two.

Laney and colleagues (2015) conducted in-depth interviews with thirty women at different stages of motherhood. All were acutely conscious of their changing identity in the initial months after birth. There were striking differences among them, however: some craved fusion with the infant – they felt completely defined by the infant's experiences, and willingly so. Others did not experience this symbiotic unity. Rather, they reported (and appreciated) an emotional distance from the infant and were committed to ensuring that their identity was not significantly changed – describing conscious efforts to reconnect with their pre-maternal identity. These different responses align with the facilitator/regulator orientations described by Raphael-Leff (2005), discussed in Chapter 3. In keeping with Raphael-Leff's notion of an adaptive middle position, Laney and colleagues found that women who engaged in self-reflection, and who were able to articulate flexible views about the ups and downs of their evolving relationship with their infant were most able to balance intense connection with an acknowledgement of the infant's separateness. Rachel Cusk (2008) eloquently describes parallel formative journeys during the early months of parenting. She gradually came to appreciate that the harrowing weeks of colic and crying represented her daughter's path to becoming a person, and that her own capacity to be fully present during these struggles (even though she felt helpless and couldn't fix them) was what consolidated her identity as a mother. Being there for the baby, however, meant she could not be anywhere else.

Adopting a maternal identity is a nuanced and complex process, and it takes time. The new mother is challenged to integrate pervasive idealised cultural representations of what a mother *should* be with the reality of her individual experience, and her own personal goals as a woman. There are losses and gains as she moves from an autonomous, unified sense of self as non-mother to a more interconnected, less defined motherhood self (Arnold-Baker, 2019; Laney et al., 2015; Wolf, 2003). In the study by Laney and colleagues, some of the women interviewed managed to maintain a sense of continuity by adapting their existing identity to incorporate the new experiences, describing feeling utterly changed, yet essentially the same: 'I still think I'm me. I can easily switch off the mum [identity] – well I don't ever switch off being a mum. But you know, when he's in bed ... it's as if he's not here' (Laney et al., 2015, p. 268). These women felt that motherhood had expanded, enhanced, and intensified their core identity. The transition to parenthood had provided a pivot point that provoked them to reflect on and renew their own personal narrative, with a new sense of social and inter-generational connectedness and a feeling that they were making a meaningful contribution to the life cycle of the species. Other women described a much more difficult and protracted process. It was an ongoing struggle to come to terms with what they had lost and accept that the social label of mother applied to them (Arnold-Baker, 2019; Laney et al., 2015).

Reconciling the Losses
The losses outweigh the gains for many women, especially in the early months, as their identity feels fractured, and they feel cut off from the rest of the world (Cusk, 2008). They mourn the loss of their former self as a competent career woman, and the dynamic, spontaneous, and connected lifestyle they had grown accustomed to (Rizvi, 2018, and see Jamila's story, Chapter 3). While taking care of the infant is a loving, worthwhile, and intimate activity, it can also be repetitive, dreary, and boring (Wolf, 2003; Senior, 2015). Wolf describes the grief she felt for her former life, as her world contracted to breastfeeding her infant on the couch. She felt chained to the home and exhausted. To top it off, she had moved to the suburbs.

Baraitser (2009) argues that the mother's subjective experience is an acutely sensitised state, at times so encumbered, by the 'stuff' of caregiving that it feels like she is 'wading through treacle' (p. 67). There may be breakdowns of the new self and breakthroughs of the old self; the transformed self that ultimately emerges can feel in turn messy, broken, enriched, attuned, and incompetent (Bueskens, 2018). Social expectations of intensive infant-focused parenting have increased at the same time as women are expected to successfully and simultaneously manage ever more challenging workplace demands (Hays, 1998). This provides a string of potential opportunities to fail (Faircloth & Gürtin, 2018). A tolerance for ambivalence and imperfection (just being a 'good-enough' mother) is adaptive, while idealisation and derogation of mothering are both problematic (Raphael-Leff, 2005). Tensions between maternal and professional identity, and some potential strategies to address these are discussed in more depth in Chapter 9.

Integrating a Paternal Identity

Despite the growing recognition of fathers' rights and obligations to be more involved, the gendered burden of early parenting is still mostly borne by women. Fathers remain marginalised in the parenting literature, dated stereotypes persist, few theories of adaptation to fatherhood have been developed and tested – and they generally fail to account for how changing gender roles are influencing the transition to fatherhood (Mickelson & Biehle, 2017) and the ways that fathers form attachment relationships with their infants (Roggman, 2004). Role expectations remain ill defined. Widely accepted social expectations of female care in the early months of parenting are generally rationalised through a naturalising logic that invokes biological truths: women carry and nurture the baby through pregnancy, they give birth, and only they can breastfeed (Faircloth & Gürtin, 2018). From this evolutionary and historical perspective, men are generally expected to assume the gendered role of provider or breadwinner and to embrace their role as secondary caregiver, protecting and nurturing the mother–baby unit first, before the twosome becomes a threesome, as discussed in Chapter 4.

Role and identity change are less dramatic for men. Their bodies are not transformed, and they are likely to remain in the workforce. Nonetheless, like women, they may grieve the loss of a carefree and independent lifestyle. Mastering new skills and caregiving responsibilities is challenging, as they try to develop their own relationship with the baby, and, at the same time, re-organise their sense of self in order to integrate multiple roles (Habib & Lancaster, 2006). Like mothers, fathers evaluate themselves against socially prescribed roles and internalised standards of performance (Palkowitz, 2002), however social banter and media representations generally set a 'low bar' with respect to their day-to-day involvement with their baby. Even minimal caretaking can elicit fulsome praise. A longstanding gendered model of parenting dichotomises 'complementary' paternal and maternal functions. 'Play' is central for fathers and 'nurturing' for mothers (Paquette, 2004). Fathers often feel able (and entitled) to focus their undivided attention and energy on fun activities and physical play – they stimulate and activate the child. This is enabled by their partners taking on the primary carer role, including all the tedious and repetitive tasks involved (Roggman, 2004). While most contemporary fathers willingly accept a secondary caregiving role and conform to traditional parenting prototypes, both men and women are pushing for change (Fletcher & StGeorge, 2011; Sturrock, 2020), as discussed in more detail later, and in Chapter 9.

Significant personal and institutional barriers remain. Bracks-Zelloua and colleagues (2011) interviewed a small sample of fathers about their involvement with their babies in the first two years. With few exceptions, the men viewed the newborn infant as a passive being with primordial needs that only the mother could meet. A sense of alienation and disconnection from day-to-day childcare was common. This view is being challenged. Advocates for greater father involvement point out that men can provide all of the necessary physical and emotional nourishment for a young infant, except breastmilk, and further, that women can be equal or more effective breadwinners (Sturrock, 2020). Indeed, a recent trend for gay men to become parents together has provided evidence that this is so, as discussed in Chapter 6. The primary caretaker role is still undertaken by mothers in most contemporary families, but a growing number of fathers want more involvement in parenting from the outset. Like mothers, they are struggling to combine the roles of breadwinner, nurturer, and support person at a time when social and workplace systems generally don't support this.

Sometimes maternal gatekeeping (which may be unconscious or inadvertent) limits father involvement. Fathers' beliefs that they lack the skills to care for their infant may be confirmed by partner criticism, as Matt explains: 'She's right, I'm too much of a pushover ... He needs routine. It's a very structured world and she walks him through that world ... I haven't got a clue ... I'm just hopeless at that kind of thing, so she's the one that makes things work.' (Bracks-Zelloua et al., 2011, p. 5). To facilitate more equal father involvement, mothers may need to relinquish their expert role, and allow fathers the space to participate freely, make mistakes, and learn about parenting in their own way. More flexible work arrangements are needed to enable this process, as discussed in Chapter 9.

It may be stating the obvious to point out that fathers generally receive less formal preparation and informal socialisation for parenthood (Gross & Marcussen, 2017). Rob Sturrock (2020) argues that learning by doing is the path to constructing an identity and sense of competence as a father. He urges fathers to 'get stuck in' – to engage fully in the nitty-gritty of infant care, as well as domestic tasks. This level of immersion remains the exception rather than the rule. And when men do engage at this level, they often receive disproportionate praise and accolades for performing basic care activities (feeding, nappy changing), or for just being around. While irksome to their partners, this gratuitous praise may support greater father contributions to infant care as research shows that feeling incompetent limits paternal involvement and predicts postnatal depression symptoms for men in the early months after birth (Gross & Marcussen, 2017).

Parental Identity: Summary Comments

To summarise, the transition to a new identity as a parent can be positive and life affirming: an opportunity for personal growth, and an expanded sense of self. It can also present significant challenges that outstrip existing resources and trigger or amplify existing vulnerabilities. There are high costs *and* high rewards. Feelings of loss and grief regarding a previous lifestyle and identity need to be validated and supported. The emotional returns – a more connected life, a new sense of purpose, and delight in infant developmental achievements take longer to accrue. Costs will generally be higher for mothers. Existing gendered social expectations of mothers and fathers need to be revised to better accommodate more equitable co-parenting relationships that will benefit women, men, and their infants. When it comes to developing a relationship with the child, there is abundant research evidence that the same relational dynamics apply to father–child and mother–child relationships.

The Social and Cultural Context for Early Parenting

Becoming a parent generally unfolds in the context of a couple relationship, embedded in relationships with extended family and the broader community. Single parenthood presents additional challenges, and the role of extended family and friends is even more important, as discussed in Chapters 3 and 6. Feminist scholars have emphasised how powerful culturally endorsed ideals of what a mother should be can shape the experience of becoming a mother, and the extent to which fathers are engaged parents (Hays, 1998). Hollway (2016) discusses inevitable tensions for feminists in the context of reproduction: the need to downplay, even deny biology in the pursuit of equality is pitched against a desire to fully appreciate the harmony of a woman's reproductive body and life-giving capacities during the transition to parenthood.

This section focuses on changes to the couple relationship, and relations with extended family after becoming a parent. Community resources and access to paid help and support networks are also important. Relationships with external support networks vary in relation to cultural beliefs about childbearing, extended family structures, and geographical proximity. Family-friendly policies in the workplace can make a crucial difference to how men and women negotiate the transition to parenthood, and these are discussed in more detail in Chapter 9.

The Couple Relationship

New parents are intensely reliant on each other. The transition to parenthood typically increases stress, and amplifies any existing relationship vulnerabilities (Figureido et al., 2018). The strongest predictor of relationship satisfaction after becoming a parent is the quality of the relationship prior to becoming a parent. As relationship expectations and dynamics change, there is the potential for enhancement, but also for conflict, as couples become acutely aware of each other's shortcomings (Murray et al., 2019). An extensive body of research confirms a significant, but modest decline in relationship satisfaction for both partners (see Mitnick et al., 2009 for a meta-analysis). The decline has been attributed to caring demands (physical and emotional), less time for companionate activities, changing financial responsibilities, and inequality regarding the burden of caregiving and changes to lifestyle. Most couples revert to more traditional gender roles, at least in the short-term and satisfaction (or dissatisfaction!) with the 'who does what' of day-to-day life is consistently related to individual and couple adaptation. A backdrop of fatigue can lead to irritability, and undermine co-operative problem-solving, as writer and musician Anna Goldsworthy (2014) explains:

> After several weeks of sleeplessness, Nicholas and I are no longer comrades-in-arms. We have reached the limits of our generosity towards each other ... If Nicholas takes an unauthorized nap during the day, my housework becomes loud and punitive. (p. 100)

Although it is a shared destination, men and women arrive at parenthood on different trains, taking different routes, and there are different trajectories of psychological distress for mothers and fathers (Cowan & Cowan, 1992). The mother's transition is radical and immediate. She may feel she has had to give up everything: her lifestyle, her career, her social connections (as discussed earlier), while men get to keep those things, and just add the fun parts of being a parent (Arnold-Baker, 2019). For writer and editor of 'The Motherhood' Jamila Rizvi (2018), this inequality was acutely felt after the birth of her son:

> My husband is at work and in a few hours' time I will start texting him incessantly, berating him for leaving me alone so long. I'm burning mad at him. He has the privilege of being able to leave each weekday, whereas I am a caged animal. I live in captivity. I am wild and scared. (p. 1)

While it is generally the case that marital satisfaction decreases in the short-term, and more so for women, not all couples show a decline. The transition to parenthood is a catalyst for change – a significant proportion show an improvement in relationship satisfaction and greater marital stability (Cowan & Cowan, 1992; Rholes & Paetzold, 2019). Some studies report paradoxical declines in personal happiness juxtaposed with increases in relationship satisfaction (Doss et al., 2009). In their meta-analytic review, Mitnick and colleagues (2009) found that declines in relationship satisfaction were most marked when new parents were young, when the pregnancy was unplanned, and when there had been problematic relationships in their family of origin. Couples whose relationships were of shorter duration before pregnancy were at the highest risk. Relationship dissatisfaction was attenuated by attending childbirth preparation classes, suggesting that realistic expectations and skills training may help couples to negotiate the transition with less conflict.

Interpreting research on relationships has been limited by the failure to include control groups of childless couples. Longitudinal studies that do so show a similar (although less sharp) decline in relationship satisfaction for childless couples over time (Keizer & Schenk, 2012). Another limitation has been the failure to adequately consider the interdependence of the couple. Keizer and Schenk point out that many studies show that partners share more similarities with each other than with other individuals, and relationship satisfaction tends to change in tandem. For the most part, men and women react similarly to becoming a parent: 'Although there are his and her starting points, the transition into parenthood is *theirs*' (p. 771). The extent to which parents work together in a supportive parenting partnership is crucial: shared and equitable division of duties, shared philosophies and practices regarding childrearing (for example how to manage sleep, feeding, soothing and crying, views on childcare) are important to relationship satisfaction and provide a sense of psychological safety for both mothers and fathers (Mickelson & Biehle, 2017). Supportive co-parenting relationships are particularly important predictors of fathers' long-term engagement in parenting.

The 'Baby' in the Room: Two Become Three
When new parents are asked to 'carve up' pie pieces to illustrate how they feel about their various roles and identities across the transition to parenthood, the salience of the 'parent' component of identity typically increases, while the sense of self as 'partner' or 'lover' decreases (Cowan & Cowan, 1985). These changes are generally more striking for women. The sexual relationship changes due to the presence of the baby, lactation, and recovery from the physical consequences of childbirth. The infant dominates the emotional aspects of the couple's life, and limits the time, space,

and energy for intimate and companionate activities. There is a tendency to blame the baby for any difficulties being experienced, however both parents tend to report that the relationship with the baby as the most satisfying aspect of their lives. They are excited by and invested in the baby, but at the same time, weighed down with the new sense of responsibility (Murray et al., 2019). Evidence suggests very similar patterns of change in relational dynamics for lesbian and gay couples during the transition to parenthood. Unique aspects are discussed in detail in Chapter 6.

Social Connection and Support

While partners are generally identified as the primary source of support, paternity leave is generally brief, and new parents can benefit from sharing experiences with other parents, and with their local health providers (general practitioners, early childhood services). Community groups (face-to-face, or through social media) can help parents to feel less alone, bearing in mind that many have lost the social connection they experienced in the workplace. These networks can be a rich source of practical tips and local information about resources and venues that are family friendly. Practical help at home with baby care or household chores can enable exhausted new parents to rest, catch up on sleep, or do something positive in relation to self-care. While these forms of support were traditionally informal – provided by extended family (as discussed below), many contemporary parents live a long way from where they grew up, and more formal community support structures and paid services may be needed (discussed further later in this chapter and in Chapter 9).

A Cross-Cultural Perspective: The First 100 Days

This chapter focuses on the fourth trimester – the first three months of parenthood when infant needs are primal and require intensive parental involvement. The perspective on childrearing practices that has been presented has been drawn largely from contemporary Western cultures. Gottlieb and DeLoache (2017) point out the strikingly different views between cultures and across generations – about what babies are like, where they should sleep, how they should be fed, what roles mothers, fathers (and grandparents) should play, and how children should be raised. In all cultures, a baby acts as a centripetal force that brings the nuclear and extended family closer together. Traditional practices, rituals, and wisdom bind social systems, families, and communities and bring much shared joy.

Traditional folk wisdom from grandparents and extended family about how to care for babies can be a double-edged sword, however, leaving new parents feeling overwhelmed by unsolicited and unwanted advice. In diverse multicultural communities, contemporary parents may be in transition from traditional beliefs, and keen to stretch the boundaries of traditional views of family (as discussed in Chapter 6). At the same time, they may be eager to recreate their own childhood experiences and seek proximity to their own parents, as they become parents themselves. Opportunities to observe and learn traditional caregiving practices and receive support from extended family are diminishing due to global occupational mobility – many new parents live a long way from grandparents. In the context of reduced access to family support, expectations of women's participation in the workforce and the demands of modern workplaces (discussed in Chapter 9) can be difficult to reconcile with traditional practices.

Despite the differences, there are common threads across cultures. In most cultures, successfully negotiating the first few months after birth is viewed as a significant milestone, and one worth celebrating. The 'first 100 days' are considered a period of vulnerability, due to a history of high infant mortality rates. Many cultures (Chinese, Japanese, Korean, Middle Eastern, Eastern European) maintain a practice of mothers and infants staying inside the home ('lying in') during this period to avoid contracting diseases. In its purest form, this practice requires mothers to stay warm, wear shoes, avoid open windows, and water (even bathing and showering). The new mother and her infant are under the jurisdiction and care of the grandmother (see Daisy's story, Chapter 3, and Aisha's story, this chapter). Cultural ceremonies, often focused on the communal joys of food, are a public acknowledgement of survival during the transition from newborn infant to healthy baby. Magic rituals and symbols are invoked as harbingers of longevity and health, and the baby is formally welcomed into the social world. Practices are evolving. In contemporary Japan, for example, cultural traditions are maintained in modified ways; mothers are no longer expected to stay inside for 100 days, and traditional and modern practices co-exist side by side (Kishi et al., 2010).

Becoming a Parent in the Context of Disability

Women with a disability may welcome pregnancy as affirmation of their identity as a woman, however they are likely to experience stigmatised perceptions that they are not capable of mothering, negative comments about passing their disability to their child, and structural barriers, including lack of access to appropriate services and facilities during the transition to parenthood. In depth interviews with twenty-five Australian (Hull, 2022) and seventeen Irish (Walsh-Gallagher et al., 2012) women with a range of sensory, cognitive, and physical disabilities reveal consistent themes. Irrespective of the nature of their disability, disabled women were keen to affirm the 'normality' of their experience; they experienced the same joys and challenges as any other mother, and generally defied expectations of 'difference' (their own and others') engendered by the disability label. Nonetheless, there were significant obstacles – and the greatest was the attitudes of other people. Disabled women report that they always feel under professional and community surveillance regarding their competence to give birth and care for their baby and that they encounter discriminatory practices, communication difficulties, and a lack of access to tailored information specific to their circumstances and needs. Katrina, a Deaf woman interviewed for this book, tells her story of becoming a mother at the end of this chapter.

When an infant has complex medical needs or disabilities, parents are faced with additional challenges. They are embedded from the outset in a complex professional network of carers, and acutely conscious of their additional role as advocates and case-managers of their infant's development, whilst trying to avoid being labelled pushy or intrusive (Todd & Jones, 2003) Parents of developmentally atypical infants may also feel a responsibility to manage the discomfort of others who don't understand how to respond to their infant – 'translating' their child to the world, and the world to their child (see Katrina's story).

Psychological Wellbeing in the Fourth Trimester

The emotional and social upheaval of the transition to parenthood means a substantial number of new parents experience moderate to severe distress. There is broad consensus about the need to challenge idealised stereotypes (particularly of motherhood), and to forewarn expectant parents with honest information about the downside of life with a young baby. There is also an upside, however. Journalist and expectant mother Amelia Lester (2018) found herself searching for the positive aspects when she was expecting her first child. Instead, she encountered mostly dire warnings and schadenfreude: contemporary popular discourse frequently focused on the drudgery, and painted a bleak, dismal, and daunting picture of new parenthood. Lester argues that expectant parents deserve the full story, 'even, and especially the good stuff'. Primal feelings of fear, pride, joy, moments of fleeting bliss, and a new sense of meaning and purpose in life receive scant attention. Let's begin with the positives.

Positive Emotional Responses to Becoming a Parent

Emotional responses to new parenthood are complex, multidimensional, and they fluctuate from day to day. While low mood is easily described and measured, positive feelings in response to becoming a parent are more global, nuanced, and 'existential', and therefore more difficult to capture empirically. Brandel and colleagues (2018) conducted a study that aimed to explore the rewards as well as the costs associated with becoming a parent. They examined two dimensions of wellbeing: hedonic or subjective wellbeing, which refers to positive and negative affect (mood), and eudaimonic wellbeing, defined as a sense of purpose, self-growth, and meaning in life, including pride and social integration (McAdams, 2013) In their prospective study of fifty mothers and fifty fathers, Brandel and colleagues found that depression symptoms increased modestly over the transition to parenthood, consistent with a large body of research, but there was also a significant increase in eudaimonic wellbeing for both women and men, with the positive change larger for men.

Several other studies report similar findings. An Israeli study compared individually matched father and non-father (but partnered) gay men. The gay men who were fathers were happier than gay non-parents on measures of both hedonic and eudaimonic wellbeing (Shenkman & Shmotkin, 2014). Nelson and colleagues (2014) compared parents and non-parents from a nationally representative sample in the United States. They wanted to explore the so-called 'parenthood paradox' of co-occurring and contradictory emotional states. While parents in their study indicated that the early weeks were certainly challenging, they also reported feeling happier, more satisfied, and thinking more frequently about meaning in life than the non-parents. Study results were qualified, however, by the social context: young parents and those with fewer economic resources were more vulnerable and reported lower wellbeing.

In an in-depth qualitative study, Cox and colleagues (2021) invited 179 urban-dwelling, African American women to describe how becoming a parent had changed their lives. The young women, teenagers at the time they gave birth, reported many more positives than negatives. They acknowledged stresses around caregiving responsibilities, disrupted sleep, and limited social life, but many viewed becoming a parent as a positive turning point, one that prompted them to redirect their focus to education and employment. They found new meaning and commitment through placing their babies' needs ahead of their own. (See also Chapter 3 for a detailed discussion of becoming a parent at different ages).

Context is always relevant. Ceballo and colleagues (2004) found more positive emotional wellbeing during the transition to parenthood for adoptive, compared with biological parents. Similar trends have been reported for those who become a parent after infertility and assisted reproduction (Golombok, 2020). Parents conceiving with medical assistance have explained that the heightened meaning the child holds, after a long struggle to achieve parenthood, can be a buffer that offsets the day-to-day stress and drudgery of parenting (McMahon et al., 2003b). These different contexts for becoming a parent are discussed in detail in Chapters 5 and 6.

Postnatal Distress: Depression, Anxiety, and Parenting Stress

Most women (and men) experience some emotional adjustment difficulties after having a baby. These include mood fluctuations, many of which are intermittent, and transient (perhaps related to sleep deprivation) that will pass in time. For a smaller, but significant number (figures vary between 7–20 per cent depending on population risk factors and whether validated diagnostic interviews or screening questionnaires are used to identify the mood problem) the distress is more severe. When symptoms are persistent most of the day, most days, for at least two weeks, and they interfere significantly with daily functioning and relationships, they meet criteria for classification as a mental health problem: Postnatal Depression and/or Postnatal Anxiety. Recent Australian figures indicate that about one in seven women (15 per cent) experience clinically significant depression and about one in five experience anxiety (20 per cent) in the first year after birth (Austin et al., 2017). Comparable figures have been reported in the United Kingdom (NICE, 2014b), and the United States (American Psychological Association, 2017). Depression and anxiety occur together (are comorbid) in about 50 per cent of cases (Austin et al., 2017).

A small percentage of women experience severe mental illness that includes psychotic symptoms in the postpartum period. Approximately 1 in 100 experience bipolar disorder and approximately 1–2 per 1,000 experience postpartum psychosis, sometimes referred to as puerperal psychosis (Osborne., 2018). Postpartum psychosis is a medical emergency. Both mother's and baby's safety can be at risk, so immediate hospitalisation and treatment is indicated. Generally occurring in the first two postnatal weeks, the onset is sudden, and characterised by insomnia, severe mood fluctuations, and psychotic symptoms.

When mood problems are pervasive, and functionally debilitating, they generally do not resolve without treatment. Mood problems in the early months of parenting are symptomatically comparable with mood problems at any other time in life, but they are uniquely challenging due to the concurrent requirement to care for a totally dependent infant, the disruptions to sleep that are involved, and the social isolation that is typical for new parents. While negative consequences for the developing child are not inevitable, a large body of work confirms there are negative impacts on the child when mood problems are persistent or severe (Austin et al., 2017), highlighting the need for early detection and treatment.

Under-Recognition or Over-Pathologising Motherhood?

For generations, perinatal mood disorders have been under-recognised and under-treated. They are now recognised as a major public health priority (Austin et al., 2017; NICE, 2014b). Nonetheless, it is still the case that many new mothers (Austin et al., 2017; McCarthy & McMahon, 2008) and fathers (Fletcher & StGeorge,2011) who are suffering from mood disorders in the early months of parenthood don't receive the professional support they need, and many don't seek help from friends and family either. The stigma associated with admitting to negative feelings at a time when one is supposed to be blissfully happy and fulfilled is a significant barrier, and recognition among primary care practitioners has traditionally been poor.

McCarthy and McMahon (2008) interviewed mothers in rural New Zealand who had been hospitalised with severe postpartum depression to explore their individual pathways to diagnosis and care. Many found their way into a treatment facility only after they had reached a crisis point, and completely fallen apart. While they were aware from early on that there was something wrong, they didn't realise that what they were feeling was postnatal depression. It can be difficult to distinguish depressed mood from the symptoms and distress (irritability, teariness, loss of pleasure) that might be expected due to sleep disruption and the twenty-four-hour demands of caring for a new baby. As one woman explained: '[I was] very tired all the time, which everybody says, "Oh that's normal. You've got a new baby," but it seemed to be extreme. I was really desperate, and I knew something was not quite right' (p. 624). For the women themselves, and those in their network, it was all too easy to 'normalise' such feelings and explain them away. This was a key barrier to seeking help, and one that led to significant delays in onset of treatment. Another woman described reaching breaking point. When the midwife visited her at home and asked what was wrong, it all poured out: 'Nothing. I just want to have my own life and I don't know if I want to keep this baby as my own, because I don't love it, I can't look after her, and I can't look after myself, and so I started crying and crying and crying' (p. 626).

It is easy to see how the stigma of deviating from the social norm of fulfilled and blissful motherhood can make it difficult to admit to such negative feelings. Women feel afraid, not just that they are mentally ill, but that they are bad mothers. For some, receiving a diagnosis of postnatal depression (PND) was a relief. It provided a legitimate explanation for their feelings – what they were experiencing had a name. Others rejected the label. They had read or seen sensational stories in the media, which typically focused on 'mentally ill' mothers who harmed their children. They worried that they would be stigmatised: I was afraid I would be seen as 'one of those mothers who just abused her children ... and that I was going to lose them. That was my biggest fear' (p. 628). Another woman found it comforting to know that others had been through a similar experience, however her own stigmatised representations of women with mental health problems remained a barrier to receiving care herself: 'I wasn't a weirdo, I wasn't a nutter. I wasn't a freak, I was just a normal person suffering what mums, some mums, suffer' (p. 630).

Clearly identification of postnatal depression is a prerequisite for appropriate and timely treatment and support. It is also important to educate the general public and destigmatise postnatal depression, and mental health services. There is a tension, however, between normalising the expected and understandable emotional upheaval of new parenthood and thereby failing to identify significant mental health problems, and over-pathologising the commonplace adjustments and ups and downs experienced by all new parents (Matthey, 2010). This can be a delicate balance. Matthey argues it is important to differentiate between transient and more persistent distress, and he recommends that commonly used screening questionnaires need to be supplemented with validated clinical interviews. Depression and anxiety 'symptoms' can certainly be normal responses to the unsettling demands of being a parent. As Barker (2014) points out, a feeling of slight worry all the time is common and normal. These feelings require acknowledgement, empathy, and social support, but not necessarily diagnostic labels and medical intervention. Matthey calls for prudent and evidence-based assessment to give parents and professionals alike a more accurate picture of perinatal distress that will enable the most appropriate allocation of resources to the women and men most in need.

Postnatal Mood Problems in Fathers

It is generally accepted that the emotional and physical challenges during pregnancy and the first months of parenthood are greater for women. Fathers have been part of the discussion in relation to the important role they can play in detecting mood problems in their partner in their capacity to support their partner through this difficult time in both practical and emotional ways, and also their contribution in providing an alternate positive caregiving experience for the infant if the mother is unable to do so (Fletcher et al., 2020). In the study by McCarthy and McMahon (2008), fathers were often the first to 'name' the postnatal depression in their partners and they were generally the ones who initiated bids to seek help. This confirms the importance of including partners in antenatal education, childbirth, and postnatal health visits.

The emotional wellbeing and mental health of fathers warrants attention in its own right. While the 'support act' role is certainly important, fathers, like mothers, experience unprecedented demands on their physical resources, time, and emotional reserves during the transition to parenthood. They, too, are vulnerable to postnatal depression and anxiety, but they are significantly less likely to engage with health services where their difficulties could be identified and treated (Fletcher & StGeorge, 2011). A recent meta-analysis and systematic review of forty-five studies (Chhabra et al., 2020) showed a prevalence rate in fathers of about 10 per cent (with a broad range between 2 and 18 per cent), for both anxiety and depression in the postnatal period. Chhabra and colleagues suggest this may be an under-estimate, as under-reporting and under-diagnosis are even more likely for men than for women, due to less contact with the health system. The presentation of depression may be gendered; it is sometimes masked in men through externalising behaviours such as substance abuse, anger, and avoidance (Boyce et al., 2007). Limited awareness and understanding of paternal depression and anxiety during early parenthood present barriers to fathers seeking the help and support they need – a theme that we return to in Chapter 9.

Who is Vulnerable?

While any new parent can experience postnatal anxiety and depression, and most experience parenting stress as they learn to care for the baby and adapt to role changes and a new lifestyle, some are more vulnerable than others. Numerous prospective studies have examined predictors of postnatal mood problems, and the key predictors are similar for men and women. The most important is depression or anxiety prior to birth. Most new parents who experience postnatal depression and/or anxiety have had mood problems in the past – only 20 per cent of postnatal mood problems in women are new presentations. Indeed, many cases of postnatal depression follow depression in pregnancy, so a great deal of public health attention in recent years has been directed to identifying mood problems in pregnancy (Austin et al., 2017), more prevalent in women than in men (Chhabra et al., 2020). Other risk factors are similar for men and women: a family history of mental health problems (including genetic risk); a developmental history of adverse early caretaking experiences in the family of origin; an unsupportive, critical partner relationship, particularly exposure to intimate partner violence; and stressful life events during the pregnancy. Contemporaneous social factors, including young parental age, low income, low social support; coming from a culturally and linguistically diverse background, and baby factors including twins, inconsolable crying, premature birth, or other medical problems in the child (Austin et al., 2017; American Psychological Association, 2017).

While all the above are also significant risk factors for men, the three strongest risks identified in a recent meta-analysis were depression in the partner (which doubled the risk), marital conflict, and concurrent parenting stress (related to the combination of work, financial, and caregiving demands in the context of disturbed sleep). Chhabra and colleagues (2020) point out that these are closely interconnected: when a partner is depressed, the father will need to contribute more to infant care, adding to perceived stress, especially if combined with earning responsibilities, and these together will contribute to partner conflict, which in turn, leads to further stress.

The Importance of Context and Social Capital

While prior family and life history are important, living in socially disadvantaged circumstances predicts onset, severity, and likelihood of relapse of mood problems. Women and men living in circumstances with low support, social isolation, cultural disadvantage, and family violence are most vulnerable, particularly migrant and Indigenous women (Austin et al., 2017). Socio-cultural barriers, including language, traditional and restrictive gender norms, and structural barriers (culturally insensitive service models, a lack of knowledge of available services or problems with access) need to be addressed (see Chapter 9).

Women who reject traditional gender stereotypes regarding maternal roles and mothering may also be more vulnerable (Hogan, 2017) and for men, perceptions of subordination to women, intellectual inferiority, and performance failure are unique risk factors (Chhabra et al., 2020). Men who cling to traditional gender roles may also be more likely to avoid help seeking or have negative attitudes to help seeking.

Adverse Childhood Experiences.   Adverse childhood experiences (parental abuse or neglect, exposure during childhood to intimate partner violence, protracted marital conflict and/or divorce, parent substance abuse or incarceration) can confer life-long vulnerability to mental health problems. There is a growing body of evidence that early life trauma operates via neurophysiological and epigenetic pathways to prime physiological stress responses in offspring, with implications for stress reactivity and emotion regulation across the lifespan. Women who have had adverse childhood experiences involving maltreatment are more vulnerable to Post Traumatic Stress Disorder (PTSD) and depression during the transition to parenthood (Grasso et al., 2020; Muzik & Rosenblum, 2018; Souch et al., 2022). Souch and colleagues systematically reviewed forty-nine studies and concluded that childhood maltreatment, especially sexual and emotional abuse, were consistently associated with maternal and infant difficulties with emotion regulation. Impacts on infants were mediated by disruptions to maternal emotional functioning. Perinatal psychiatrist Anne Buist (2020) describes the triggering impact of infant distress and crying for women who have a childhood history dominated by memories of fear: 'Without supportive intervention, they are at risk of reacting through the lens of their attachment trauma and re-creating the same problems for their children'. She emphasises the importance of clinicians understanding the ambivalence, anger, and fear that may underlie postnatal depression and anxiety. They need to 'help and support rather than stigmatise and demonise a mother who is struggling to love and protect her child'.

Summary Comments

The fourth trimester is an extremely challenging time, as the new family system is necessarily skewed toward the needs of the infant, and new parents are doing their best to meet these needs against a backdrop of fatigue, in what can be a very opinionated and judgmental world. By the time infants are twelve weeks old, there is a significant bio-behavioural transition, as they gradually evolve into little people who are more able to self-regulate, play with objects, and engage with the world around them. Parents are beginning to emerge from the emotional fugue of broken sleep;

they are developing an understanding of their own unique baby, who by now provides them with more interactive rewards. They are renegotiating and restructuring their relationship with each other and their lifestyle. They are ready to engage more fully with the extended family and the wider community, and they will be getting to know a new community of parents. Those who have not already needed to return to work will be starting to plan for it and facing the daunting challenge of finding appropriate childcare (considered in Chapter 9).

This chapter concludes with the stories of two women, members of minority groups, describing their experience of becoming a parent. Katrina, who is profoundly Deaf, describes her experiences of pregnancy, childbirth, and early parenting and the access and communication barriers she encountered. Aisha, a mother at twenty, and a grandmother at forty, provides an intergenerational perspective on becoming a parent, and then watching her young daughter become a mother.

Katrina's Story: A Deaf Woman's Experience of Becoming a Mother

Katrina, a team leader with a non-government organisation, and her husband, Charles, have two children. She and Charles are both Deaf, as is their first-born child, Riley. Their second daughter, Paige, is a hearing child. I asked Katrina to reflect on her experiences of becoming a parent for the first time.

Diagnosed with Polycystic Ovary Syndrome in her teens, Katrina had resigned herself to the fact that it would be difficult, perhaps impossible, to have children. She was focused on other life goals, her education, and developing a career, so when she fell pregnant it was a complete shock. Katrina had only been with Charles for a few months, and she had just moved to a new city. The idea of becoming a parent at that point seemed impossible. She and Charles took some days to even feel they could talk about it, let alone begin to process it. Gradually, they came to appreciate that this was, in fact, 'really, really, good news!'

The pregnancy was challenging, and Katrina was repeatedly frustrated by not having access to interpreters for her routine medical visits:

> The hospital would forget to book the interpreter; I would have to advocate for myself and explain that I would need an interpreter for each appointment; I had to do it every single time. It needed to be a qualified person, not just anybody. It needed to be somebody who could understand how to communicate with me, convey information appropriately. I was always worried. What if they don't understand me? What if I don't understand them? I had to be an advocate with the hospital, with the agency, and that was ongoing throughout the pregnancy.

Katrina and Charles were able to attend one or two antenatal classes (having advocated for an interpreter), but many of the services for pregnant couples were not available to them. Katrina was used to having to work hard to get her needs met. She was determined to ensure the support she would need for the birth, and was able to arrange for her sister, Kylie, a professional interpreter, to be there with her. Kylie represented a 'two-in-one package': someone who really understood Katrina, and could communicate with hospital staff, as well as supporting her through labour, 'at least when she and Charles weren't lying back, watching the cricket!'. It was a long labour, thirty-six hours from start to finish. By the time the baby was born, Katrina was exhausted.

The postnatal care in hospital was sensitive and supportive with one notable exception: communicating the results of the newborn screening hearing test. As Katrina explains:

> Riley (first-born baby) is Deaf as well. So, the nurses, were really, really upset to discover this. From their perspective, Riley had failed the test, and they found it so hard to tell me. I had to put my foot down and say: 'This is not a bad thing for me. I am a profoundly Deaf person, I have access to community, I have access to language, I have pride in my Deafness. I am fine.' It felt like I had to step into the carer role for them ... It felt like, this is not about me, it's about them.

Managing baby distress and unsettled behaviour are fundamental parenting challenges in the early weeks. Katrina explains the additional challenges for Deaf parents:

> Often people tell me how lucky I am, as I can't hear the screaming and the crying. But I still feel it. I can see the crying. And when I'm holding the baby, I can feel the stress. When I'm sleeping, it can be a constant worry. What if they wake up? What if they're crying? What if I miss something? Like any parent, you just have to work it out: What do they need? Do they need to be changed? Do they need some stimulation? Do they need food? I went through the same process, but for me the audio aspect was missing.

In the early weeks, Katrina spent a lot of time rocking Riley and 'babywearing', because touch was so important to him, and to her. She always had him in the same room, where she could see him, and describes frequently wetting her finger and putting it under his nose: 'That new parent thing – is he breathing? I didn't want to touch him to wake him up, and I couldn't hear him breathing.'

The first few months after birth are a challenging time for couples. This was certainly the case for Katrina, as the pregnancy was unexpected and happened so early in her relationship with Charles: 'We skipped the honeymoon phase, and it was straight into real life'. She adopted her usual coping style: taking control, with everything very structured, and she found herself putting pressure on Charles to follow her routine and do things in her way. The days were long; Charles was away for twelve hours at a time. When he finally came home, she felt he couldn't understand and appreciate how stressful a day spent enduring hours of infant crying could be.

New to the city, she had few supports, and no established social networks. There was no interpreter funding available for the local community parenting and mothers' groups, so they were not an option. She felt very isolated. Katrina had always found it difficult to ask for help: 'I really missed the support of other mothers who were going through the same things as I was. But even if I had been able to go to the mothers' groups, socialising would have been difficult for me.'

When asked to describe the biggest challenge in becoming a parent, Katrina doesn't hesitate:

> Access and the attitudes of other people. Other parents assume you can't communicate, they don't approach you, they are most likely afraid and unsure how to communicate with you. As well as the social barriers, she experienced judgmental attitudes, particularly from older adults. 'Is that your baby? How can you hear if he wakes up at night? How do you know what he wants?' I got the impression that they thought I wasn't fit to be a parent. I always had to explain things to them, I was frustrated that these attitudes persist. Advocacy took a lot of emotional effort, and it still does.

There were a lot of negatives during the early months of parenthood, but there was more to it than that:

I felt like I'd lost my career plans, I felt isolated, I didn't feel like I had any support. But then, that all washed away when I looked at my baby. I'd forget about all those other things, and just focus on that. The wonder of just saying to myself, over and over 'I made that. I made him. I grew him.' Now I look at my children and I'm incredibly proud of who they are. They're strong, they're confident, they're assertive. And I made them.

Katrina reflects on how becoming a parent has changed her:

Before, I was very much focused on myself. My career, my job, everything was about me. How can I change things to achieve more? The focus on me has shifted down in the priority list. And I'm fine with that. Now that my children are a little older, I'm able to make more time for me, for my goals. But my priority is their happiness, and their access. Overall, I'm better with organising my priorities since becoming a parent. I don't waste time on things that are not important. I feel I've become 'soft', as a person. I know that sounds a bit contradictory, but that's it.

Aisha's Story: A Young Mother and a Young Grandmother

Aisha* became a mother aged twenty, and a grandmother, aged forty. While raising four young children, she embarked on a lengthy and staged journey to a career of her own. After many years, she achieved another key life goal: becoming a Social Worker and Counsellor. She now works supporting women who are struggling during the transition to parenthood, particularly those from ethnic and cultural minorities. Her story is embedded in the cultural practices of the Lebanese migrant community.

Aisha married straight after finishing school, and soon after she became pregnant with her first child:

> It was just what you did. For a Lebanese woman, there was an expectation that you have a baby, fulfil your duties as a Lebanese wife, and as a daughter-in-law. Also, I felt I was ready. I was a mature twenty-year-old.

She didn't engage in any formal preparation for childbirth. It was all provided, by exposure and osmosis, spending time with older women in her community:

> I'd sit amongst these mature women, all at home, looking after their children. And I was just waiting for my baby to be born. And I got my knowledge from them – what it's like to be a Mum ... When I sat with them, I heard their stories about being a Mum, attending to your children, attending to the house. These things were important to them. It reflected on their reputation as a woman. It was very important, that reputation, and you had to maintain it at all costs.

She had no knowledge about childbirth:

> When I sat with the ladies we talked about birth, but none of them would tell me how difficult it was. My mother never told me anything, because you just didn't speak to your mother about these things. Being a Lebanese woman, you never spoke to your mum about intimacy because it's rude – you just don't do that. As a result, I just didn't know anything.

When the time came, Aisha had a difficult delivery. She went to the hospital when her waters broke. Her memory is hazy; the labour was long, she had an epidural at some point, and slept fitfully from time to time. After about seventeen hours, she noticed that the atmosphere had changed. The nurses were rushing around:

> I didn't know what was going on. I didn't ask anything, but they seemed worried. The next thing, I see this thing – this big metal thing – it was forceps, and they pulled my son out. I saw him, but I was so tired, that when they put him on my chest, I didn't say anything to him. The doctor told me to hold him, and I just said: 'I'm so tired'. He said again – 'hold him', and so I held him. The poor baby was battered and bruised.

Aisha was also battered and bruised, and she had a difficult physical recovery. Sitting down was excruciatingly painful for quite some time. It wasn't until she went for her six-week check-up that she learned what had actually happened during the birth: 'They finally explained. I was torn, inside and out; they'd had great difficulty getting the baby out with forceps.'

What Aisha recalls most vividly was the strain of meeting local social and cultural expectations during those fragile early weeks at home. As she explains, the Lebanese community feel a duty, after a child is born, to visit as soon as possible, with a gift, and congratulate the new parents. At home with a newborn, recovering from stitches and a very traumatic birth, barely able to sit down, it was Aisha's job to entertain her visitors:

> You could have five or six families all at the one time, visiting. You had to serve them drinks, nibbles, coffee, sweets, and then the baby would be crying, and you'd have to leave them briefly and go to the baby, and then go back and be the hostess again. It was awful! There was no consideration for the mother to have private time with her family or with her child. Just to allow things to settle. It was all about duty, image, ticking the boxes.

Traditional practices remain important, but they are evolving. Aisha describes how they differ for migrant Lebanese communities, compared with traditional practices in the home country, and how they are changing across generations. When her own daughter became pregnant, also aged twenty, Aisha made sure that things were done differently. In contrast to her own experience, she talked with her daughter about the pregnancy, about childbirth, and about what to expect. There was happiness and joy in sharing these experiences. Aisha's eyes fill with tears as she recalls her daughter giving birth:

> When the birth came around, I was there with her in the room with her husband. I was assisting and guiding her, telling her to push – giving her that strength. When the baby was born, the staff quickly shifted their attention to the baby. And I felt 'what about *my* baby?' I saw the blood between my daughter's legs and automatically, I started to wipe her, and to care for her. She was my baby, and she needed looking after. I remember thinking at the time – her baby is fine, and well cared for. I need to look after *my* baby. And then, I saw that she was shivering, and I made sure she was OK and I wrapped her, so she was warm. When they brought her baby back to her, my daughter (my baby) was settled.

There were other welcome changes. While the community was still very connected, there was more understanding of pressure on the new mother and fathers were more involved: 'Her husband was more hands on than mine was. And I was there for her – whatever she needed, whatever the baby needed, I was by her side.' When the visitors came, Aisha was determined to protect her daughter, and assist.

She reflects on the ways in which becoming a parent and then a grandparent have changed her:

> Being a very young mum, I had nothing to compare to. No life experience, no expectation. I just did what I could. I just did my best. Now looking back, I

think I did have a hard time. But then, I just managed. I made do with what I had, and I hoped for the best. That was just how it was then.

Becoming a parent heightened Aisha's awareness of her relationship with her own mother. As a young woman, she had struggled with her own mother's inability to be close with her. Becoming a grandparent has helped her to see things from her mother's perspective; to understand, and to forgive:

> Being a parent has changed me. I learnt to understand my mother. I had relationships with my children that I had never had with my Mum. That's what I grieved – my mother wasn't emotionally there for me, when I had my children. She didn't have it in her own life, so there was no way she could be close with me. It wasn't until I was older that I could understand my mother. I can now give her my knowledge, and she enjoys and appreciates that. I've learnt to understand her and accept her limitations, why she couldn't give that closeness to me. I don't blame her; I learn from her. I learnt from her how I could have a better relationship with my daughter, and with my daughter-in-law.

Aisha also has special relationships with her grandchildren. As 'Tayta', she is a source of wisdom, but also fun:

> It comes with the territory of being a Lebanese woman; that they would respect you – you have the Title; you have the respect. But I also wanted the relationship. That was important to me. I wanted to be able to have fun with them.

In her work in a parentcraft hospital, Aisha frequently finds herself explaining the importance of community and connection to staff from Anglo-Celtic backgrounds.

> Lebanese families, and others from traditional cultures, are very connected. Whether it's the mother-in-law or the maternal mother, they are very, very involved; the mother-in-law may be ringing constantly wanting to know exactly what's happening with the mother – staff may see it as intrusive, but we see at it as connection.

*Names have been changed.

CHAPTER 9

The Way Forward
Research, Clinical, and Policy Directions to Support Families during the Transition to Parenthood

Decades of research confirm the importance of early life experiences for physical and mental health, and the negative long-term consequences when young children don't receive the predictable, emotionally responsive caregiving they need (Moore et al., 2017). The developmental needs of infants are clear, and essentially immutable (Hrdy, 1999). Like infants, new parents are vulnerable and needy; those who didn't receive dependable loving caregiving in their families of origin and those who don't have a safe home and financial security are especially so. Parenting is a uniquely demanding occupation. Knowledge is necessary, but not sufficient. Parents need to be nurtured and supported if they are to nurture effectively. Becoming a parent is an exciting life transition that brings enhanced social connectedness and meaning in life, but it is also a time of predictable and well-documented disruption and stress. Helping parents to successfully navigate this key life transition can benefit the couple relationship, the relationship parents develop with their child, and the child's long-term development (Cowan & Cowan, 1995; Keizer & Schenk, 2012).

Most adults want to become parents, and in the modern world, they also want (or need) to work. Indeed, two incomes are essential for most couples, as the costs of housing and raising children increase. Following the feminist lessons learned from their own mothers, many contemporary women believe that aspiring to the rewards of motherhood, need not be at the expense of their personal and career aspirations (Cannold, 2005). As one young woman explains:

> I didn't really challenge the idea in my own head about whether or not I would have children. But I certainly did challenge the idea that you had to choose one or the other [children or career] and I always felt I was going to do both. (Maher & Saugeres, 2007, p. 16)

Combining work and parenting is challenging, particularly when infants are young. Glass and colleagues (2016) point out that throughout the developed world, the stressors are increasing, the social and economic rewards are declining, and parents are left to shoulder significant burdens as they try to resolve the tensions between family and work demands. There is a compelling social imperative to forge innovative compromises that can accommodate infant needs, parent wellbeing, and the demands of modern workplaces. While parenting has become a gender-neutral verb, becoming a parent remains a gendered experience; the caregiving burden falls disproportionately on women, who make more career sacrifices, a situation that is neither fair, nor sustainable. Meanwhile, a growing number of men would like to become more involved in caregiving, but current social policies and workplaces don't adequately support this (Crabb, 2019). Structural social change is necessary so that both fathers and mothers can balance their need for career success and autonomy with their desire to be actively engaged in caring for their children.

All parents can benefit from educational input about the practical aspects of infant developmental needs, parent–child relationships, and early parenting. Universal programmes that provide evidence-based information and the opportunity to share experiences with others can promote parenting efficacy, adaptive self-care and coping strategies, and healthy social engagement. More targeted therapeutic interventions that offer individualised support and sustained nurturant contact are needed for those identified as vulnerable, due to mental and or physical health problems or adverse social circumstances. To begin at the beginning, however, there is a need for less gendered, more inclusive, and more timely fertility education.

Fertility Education

The demographic changes that have given rise to delayed childbearing are entrenched in high-income countries. As discussed in Chapter 1, committed long-term relationships are in decline, and they tend to begin later, if at all. Birth-rates are falling, and age at first birth is rising. Among those who want to be parents, the number of couples needing the assistance of ART to conceive is growing; many will have fewer children than desired; and some will face unintended childlessness. While becoming a parent at an older age may confer advantages in terms of emotional maturity and financial capacity (Camberis et al., 2014), there are significant implications for fertility, particularly for women. Social expectations have changed, but biology has not. Women's fertility declines significantly in a linear fashion from age thirty-five and men's fertility declines from age forty (Evans et al., 2019). As consequential as this is, there is a striking gap in knowledge about age-related fertility decline (Evans et al., 2019; Prior et al., 2019). Decisions about whether to become a parent, and when, are matters of individual choice, of course, but informed choice depends on adequate and accurate information. Unintended childlessness can lead to intense and prolonged grief (Gameiro & Finnigan, 2017).

The Imperative to Include Men

Although there are many factors contributing to the trend for women to postpone childbearing, finding a male partner willing to commit to parenthood is the most common explanation offered (Hammarberg et al., 2017a; Koert & Daniluk, 2017). This reinforces the need to include men in public discourse and medical consultations about fertility and family planning. Men have poor knowledge of factors influencing fertility (see Hammarberg et al., 2017c for a systematic review). The perception that fertility planning is a women's issue limits their engagement with decision making (da Silva et al., 2018), but the default assumption that men are not interested can become a self-fulfilling prophecy (Grace et al., 2019), leading them to think (inaccurately), that the biological clock does not apply to them. Grace and colleagues emphasise the importance of male-friendly educational materials, and fertility services. Men participating in their UK study expressed a preference for online resources and telephone consultations which enabled a degree of anonymity when exploring a 'taboo' and 'private' topic (p. 5). Websites, mobile applications, and virtual agents can provide scalable low-cost options for fertility and pre-conception health education.

Age-appropriate educational programmes about fertility and reproductive health need to begin early in adulthood. Studies have found that young men and women in Australia (Hammarberg et al., 2020), the United Kingdom (Grace et al., 2019), Japan (Maeda et al., 2020), and the United States (Guzzo & Hayford, 2020) are open to discussions with primary healthcare practitioners about fertility intentions and pre-conception health. Providing accurate, accessible information about the probability of conception at various ages, and the limits of what can be achieved through ART and egg freezing can significantly increase fertility knowledge and influence decision making (Maeda et al., 2020).

Population-based statistics and public health initiatives may not be enough – they can be too readily dismissed as 'not applicable to me'. Broadly based educational campaigns need to be reinforced by personalised interactions with health professionals. Family doctors, for example, can start the conversation by asking young adults, irrespective of their current relationship status, about their intentions to have a child. Such conversations with young men and women can open a pathway to contraceptive, pre-conception health, or fertility advice, as appropriate. Evans and colleagues (2019) proposed a controversial approach to improving 'reproductive awareness' of age-related fertility limits, by routinely offering an 'egg-timer test' to young women. The test screens serum hormones to assess ovarian reserve. Reproductive health and infertility specialists have been critical of this approach due to the potential that it may offer false reassurance. There are also concerns that the test could generate anxiety, resulting in young women outlaying a lot of money for expensive egg freezing procedures, despite limited evidence that they are beneficial in the long term (Salleh, 2019). The controversy about fertility preservation through egg freezing is discussed further later in this chapter.

The Need for Accurate Information about ART Success Rates

Decisions to postpone childbearing are frequently influenced by the assumption that ART can guarantee a child in the future (Maeda et al., 2015; Miron-Shatz et al., 2020). Couples consistently overestimate the likelihood of successful conception and these optimistic expectations persist, despite a low likelihood of conception after repeated treatment failure (da Silva et al., 2018). Miron-Shatz and colleagues (2020) found that women in their early forties maintained unrealistic expectations about the likelihood of conceiving with their own eggs, even when accurate information on probabilities was provided to them. These studies demonstrate the limitations of generic fertility education and the need for personalised counselling tailored to individual circumstances, age, and gender. Decision-making tools can help couples to consider trying to fall pregnant at an age when success is more likely, and they can also assist couples to make the difficult decision to stop ART treatment when continuing is to the detriment of their psychological health (da Silva et al., 2018).

Fertility Preservation: Egg Freezing

The number of women undergoing the elective procedure of oocyte cryopreservation (colloquially referred to as egg freezing) is growing rapidly, despite the significant financial, emotional, and physical costs, and equivocal evidence of effectiveness. The procedure is actively promoted to women in corporate employment (for example, large companies may offer to pay the costs as part of a wage package) and aggressively marketed by ART clinics as an 'insurance policy' to extend the reproductive window. However, as discussed in Chapter 2, encouraging women to rely on egg freezing may falsely reassure them that they can put off childbearing without compromising their chances of having a child. The benefits of 'egg timer' tests of ovarian reserve, ART, and egg freezing are frequently oversold: advertising about egg freezing on fertility clinic websites is frequently biased and/or inaccurate, and there is a lack of transparency about success rates, risks, and costs (Beilby et al., 2020; Hammarberg et al., 2017b). Clear regulatory guidelines are needed to make sure commercial interests do not compromise women's long-term reproductive wellbeing. Another concern is the fact that relatively few women ultimately return to use their eggs. Polyakov and Rozen (2021) propose a model whereby clinics could link those who have frozen oocytes and no longer need them with those seeking donated eggs. This could be one way of addressing the increasing gap between demand and supply of donated oocytes, however appropriate compensation for the significant procedural and storage costs incurred, and counselling around the long-term implications of donation would be essential.

A new direction in fertility education is the growing recognition of the importance of discussing childbearing desires and fertility preservation with young adults considering medical intervention to achieve gender transition. Recent research has found that comprehensive fertility counselling for young adults with gender dysphoria who are planning to transition is associated with high fertility preservation rates; significantly higher among transgender women (35 per cent) than transgender men (6.25 per cent) (Amir et al., 2020).

Equity of Access to Fertility Treatments

The high cost of ART treatments raises ethical and moral concerns regarding equity of access, exploitation, and commodification. More liberal social attitudes, and rejection of discriminatory practices regarding access to ART have made becoming a parent possible for single women, and LGBTI adults. This has contributed to the growth of a multi-billion-dollar trans-national market in donated eggs, sperm, embryos, and surrogates run by private equity companies with international subsidiaries. Access is very unequal, both within and between countries (Inhorn, 2020). As Schurr (2018) points out, the same technologies and services have vastly different costs in different countries; some are legal only in certain places; others restrict access based on sexuality and marital status. There is the potential for commodification of reproductive capacities: body tissues (eggs, sperm) and babies, including racialisation, as race becomes a commodity that is selected, and White(r) sex cells draw a higher market value (Schurr, 2018), and exploitation of donors, individuals wanting a child, and surrogates.

Extremely high costs (as most ART is provided in private clinics) mean access is limited to those who are very well-off. At a population level, less than 2 per cent of births in the United States are conceived through ART (Guzzo & Hayford, 2020), a significantly lower proportion than in other high-income countries, and ART is available only through private health clinics. Infertility is more likely to affect African American women than white women, however, and there are profound racial inequalities in access to fertility treatment and antenatal care (Almeling, 2015; Guzzo & Hayford, 2020). There is a public contribution to the costs of ART in the United Kingdom, Europe, Australia, and New Zealand, with variations in conditions, eligibility, and access from one country to another. There are also concerns about financially exploitative practices such as add-on treatments that have a limited evidence base (Ledger, 2019). Human rights and anti-discrimination principals are frequently invoked in calls for more access to affordable ARTs in low-resource settings (Inhorn, 2020). The reality is that globalisation of the highly profitable reproductive technology industry reflects traditional power and economic inequalities.

Educational and Therapeutic Interventions to Support New Parents

Becoming a parent is a time of vulnerability, and risk, but also openness to change (Rowe et al., 2017; Saxbe et al., 2018). The transition can be viewed as a developmental crisis, or, more positively, as a 'critical window' of opportunity (Saxbe et al., 2018, p. 1192). Normative stress can engender growth and positive adaptive responses. When couples are living with chronic stress, however, becoming a parent can exacerbate pre-existing vulnerabilities, adding to the cumulative toll on physical and mental health, and compromising their capacity to meet the challenges of parenting. Parent education can help equip parents to respond adaptively. Parent wellbeing, grounded in positive self-esteem and self-efficacy, is the foundation for future family functioning.

Childbirth and parenting education need to be inclusive and sensitive to diverse parent needs. Traditionally, 'preparation for childbirth' classes have reified a white, middle-class model of intensive parenting (always putting infant needs first, for example), which can alienate men, younger parents, poor women, women of colour, non-binary individuals and those from marginalised communities (Deeb-Sossa & Kane, 2017; Faircloth & Gürtin, 2018). Deeb-Sossa and Kane conducted an ethnographic observation of childbirth classes in the United States and noted a tendency to undermine young women, with explicit or implicit 'mother-blaming' messages. They recommended that childbirth and parenting classes take more account of the diversity of parent backgrounds, if they are to empower young parents and those from marginalised communities to recognise and articulate their own needs. The needs of pregnant women with disabilities, for example, are rarely considered in antenatal education, and they need to be integrated into a holistic model of care (Walsh-Gallagher et al., 2012). Bower-Brown and Zadeh (2021) interviewed trans and non-binary parents, and they identified a need for more education on inclusive practice for staff in child and family health and adoptive services to enable institutional support for parents living in diverse family structures. A tendency to exclude men from childbirth and parenting education, discussed at length in Chapter 4, is considered further later in the chapter.

Supporting Parent Mental Health

Mood disorders are common during pregnancy and after childbirth, affecting 10–20 per cent of women and 5–10 per cent of men in high-income countries. Prevalence is higher for those from culturally and linguistically diverse communities (Arifin et al., 2018). Those with histories of adverse childhood experiences, those living in poverty, and those exposed to intimate partner violence are most vulnerable. In poor and marginalised communities, these risks cluster together (American Psychological Association, 2017; Austin et al., 2017). Untreated perinatal mood disorders can persist, with significant and lasting costs to the parents, the developing child, and the broader community, so timely psychological interventions are strongly recommended (American Psychological Association, 2017; Austin et al., 2017; NICE, 2014b). Interventions have traditionally focused on mothers, and on depression after birth. With recognition that mood problems often begin in pregnancy, there has been a shift in recent decades towards public health initiatives that enable identification and treatment of mood problems during pregnancy (NICE, 2014b). There is also a growing recognition of the importance that screening and treatment for mood problems should include fathers (Fletcher et al., 2019; Rowe et al., 2017; Shorey et al., 2019). While they share many experiences with mothers, fathers may respond differently to the challenges of becoming a parent (Parke & Cookston, 2019) and express their psychological distress in different ways (Boyce et al., 2007).

Initiatives aimed at promoting mental health in the perinatal period are a sound public health investment, and one that provides significant long-term public health benefits for the community at large (Organisation for Economic Co-operation and Development, (OECD) 2019; Shonkoff & Fisher, 2013). Screening is a first step, with the proviso that adequate systems need to be in place to ensure accurate diagnosis, as well as accessible pathways to effective treatment and follow-up. There are moves to extend screening to include fathers. The UK National Health Service has announced that mental health checks and treatment for new and expectant fathers will be implemented as part of a long-term mental health plan by 2023 (Darwin et al., 2021).

A large Australian population study shows that universal screening for perinatal depression is cost-effective, with increases in hospital admissions prior to birth (suggesting early detection and treatment), greater uptake of mental health services from general practitioners and mental health professionals (Chambers et al., 2016), and reductions in hospital admissions for mental health problems after birth (Wang-Shee Lee et al., 2019). A recent systematic review and meta-analysis confirmed good sensitivity and specificity for the most widely used screening tool in pregnancy and postnatally (the Edinburgh Postnatal Depression Scale), but they concluded that more trials are needed to determine if screening actually improves mental health outcomes (Levis et al., 2020).

Once mood problems are identified, a broad range of interventions is needed, ideally with a stepped-care approach, and flexible modes of delivery. Universal interventions that educate new parents about infant needs and self-care can assist all new parents in meeting early parenting and relationship challenges, whether or not they meet diagnostic thresholds for depression or anxiety. Low-resource population-based interventions have shown clear benefits for those with subclinical levels of postnatal distress (Khanlari et al., 2019). Results from randomised trials support the effectiveness of telephone-based peer support (Dennis et al., 2009) and web-based, brief, cognitive behavioural therapy (Loughnan et al., 2019). Individualised and intensive psychological treatments (alongside pharmacological interventions) are needed for moderate to severe mood problems, and in-patient care may be indicated for severely ill mothers, or extremely unsettled infants. There is a growing body of evidence that cognitive behavioural therapy (CBT) and interpersonal psychotherapy (IPT) reduce the prevalence of mild-moderate perinatal depression and the risk of remission (see O'Connor et al., 2016 for a meta-analysis). While reducing depression and anxiety symptoms is important, research shows that alleviating symptoms doesn't necessarily have flow-through benefits for the parent–child relationship and the child's development. A parenting component is also recommended in interventions for mothers experiencing postnatal depression (Forman et al., 2007; Murray et al., 2015).

Enhancing Parenting and Relationship Capacity

There is no shortage of advice about parenting. The commercialised world of entrepreneurial parenthood, with its saturation of social media feeds and 'expert' and commercially fuelled blogs can be bewildering and overwhelming for new parents (Nelson & Robertson, 2018). Parents need consistent information from a trusted evidence-based source, and contact with others in the same life stage (Rowe et al., 2017). Rowe and colleagues recommend that interventions in the early months after birth should focus on the two key risks to parental mental health and wellbeing: unsettled infant behaviour (including guidance regarding individual differences in infant temperament, and skills training in sustainable settling strategies) and challenges to the intimate partner relationship (including couple skills for renegotiating the unpaid work of infant care and household tasks). As infants mature and become more regulated, support and enhancement of parent–child relationship skills can have profound long-term benefits for the child, the parents, and the couple relationship (Cowan & Cowan, 1995; Powell et al., 2014).

Accessibility and Scalability

Broadly targeted parenting interventions need to be scalable, flexible, engaging, and accessible. They can be delivered face-to-face by primary health care workers (child and family health nurses, general practitioners, social workers, psychologists), by telephone, through various online modalities, or a combination of these. Flexibility is important: content needs to be adapted to suit the developmental stage of the infant, the level of parental impairment or distress, and parent characteristics and context, including age (Deeb-Sossa & Kane, 2017; Doi et al., 2020), disability (Walsh-Gallagher et al., 2012), and cultural background (Rowe et al., 2017).

Digital educational resources are effective, accessible, and appealing to millennial parents. As discussed in Chapter 8, parents appreciate information that helps them to understand their infant's behaviour in a broader developmental context. Books explaining developmental milestones have a long tradition. In the 1940s, Gesell & Ilg (1943/1974) provided a detailed map of the organised sequence of infant behaviour maturation. Importantly, they integrated developmental milestones with a 'big picture' overview of the cyclic phases of disequilibrium, as infants transition to new skills not yet mastered, followed by stability and equilibrium, as new capacities are consolidated, and enjoyed. Interactive and engaging platforms delivered through smartphone applications (apps) provide this content to contemporary parents, helping them to understand their infant's world by providing a developmental framework in simple lay terms, enhanced through engaging graphics and interactive videos. These applications have the flexibility to provide age-specific, targeted, real time information to parents about their own baby, in the moment, as well as a broader sense of what lies ahead in the coming weeks and months.

Different parents in different circumstances have different needs, and flexible, tailored delivery is important. Young parents may benefit most from educational video-clips. Doi and colleagues (2020) conducted a cluster randomised trial in Japan that examined the effectiveness of an educational video about infant crying, viewed during the hospital stay, in reducing subsequent depression symptoms in mothers. While there was no effect of the video exposure on older mothers, the mothers under the age of twenty-five who received the intervention had a marked reduction in depression symptoms. Digital applications also show promise in engaging fathers, as discussed later.

Encouraging Fathers to Participate.   Despite the growing expectation that men will take some responsibility for infant care (Fletcher et al., 2019), they frequently remain marginalised and excluded from parenting support services (Ruffell et al., 2019). Programmes during pregnancy that are specifically focused on fathers can lead to higher involvement with the baby, facilitate the adaptation of the new family, and provide new mothers with more effective support, which, in turn, may buffer against postpartum depression (Brandel et al., 2018). Barriers to father participation include personal avoidance of help-seeking behaviour, interventions being offered inflexibly during work hours (Rowe et al., 2017), and a non-inclusive mother-focused atmosphere in child and family health settings (Fletcher et al., 2019; Ruffell et al., 2019). Proactive approaches that are more likely to engage fathers include directly inviting them, rather than recruiting them via mothers (Brandel et al., 2018), offering classes on weekends, or in the evening, and including content on co-parenting and the couple relationship (Rowe et al., 2017; Shorey et al., 2019). Classes run just for fathers that focus on the father–child relationship (Fletcher et al., 2019) have been shown to be effective in engaging fathers and enhancing their self-efficacy about parenting.

Innovative Modes of Delivery. Innovative technology-based interventions have made information about parenting more accessible to both mothers and fathers and can be offered alongside more conventional postnatal supports. As discussed earlier, technology-based parenting programmes can be readily integrated with telephone support, hands-on infant care classes (Shorey et al., 2019), or face-to-face workshops (Rowe et al., 2017). These approaches can be particularly effective in overcoming participation barriers for fathers (Fletcher et al., 2019), but also mothers, who are increasingly time-poor (Rowe et al., 2017). Two studies provide emerging evidence of the potential of these approaches for fathers. SMS4Dads is a text-based intervention comprising 184 brief text messages (each 160 characters or less) that contain information tailored to a father's perspective on the transition to parenthood including information about mental health, self-care, relationships with partner and baby, and links to supportive resources. The texts are sent out intermittently from sixteen weeks pregnancy until the baby is four months old, and content is synchronised with the gestational stage of pregnancy and the baby's age. A process evaluation indicates that fathers appreciate the content, and the mode and timing of delivery (Fletcher et al., 2019). Flexible prompts that encourage fathers to interact and reflect are uniquely possible with digital delivery. Fathers also appreciated feeling connected to 'a sort of mate tapping you on the shoulder' (p. 8) and coming to realise that many other men shared their experiences.

Shorey and colleagues (2019) conducted a randomised trial in Singapore to evaluate the effectiveness of a mixed modality parenting intervention compared with routine perinatal care. The intervention comprised two telephone consultations (one antenatal, one postnatal) and a mobile phone app that was available for four weeks after birth. The phone app included daily push notifications on parenting and infant milestones, as well as an interactive discussion forum with daily expert input and peer interaction. Mothers and fathers participated, and assessments were conducted in pregnancy and on three occasions after birth, with the last at three months postpartum. The content was theoretically grounded, including information about breastfeeding, self-care, infant care, and strategies to enhance parent self-efficacy and bonding with the infant. The intervention group showed significantly better scores than the control group for self-efficacy, bonding, perceived social support, parenting satisfaction, and lower depression symptoms across the transition to parenthood.

Digital applications need to be evaluated in a timely manner, as they are rapidly superseded by new offerings. There is a responsibility to ensure that the easy access provided by web-based digital resources does not increase the risk of new parents being exposed to false or unreliable information. Battineni et al. (2020) point to the need for professional guidance in the choice of online resources, and a system of accessible, reliable, quality-control ratings.

Relationship-Focused Interventions
Relationship-focused interventions that explain the dynamics of the parent–child attachment relationship can enhance self-efficacy, encourage new parents to think more positively about their infant, and reduce depression symptoms (Maxwell et al., 2021a; Shorey et al., 2019). In the early weeks, a simple focus on soothing skills, and the importance of face-to-face interaction can help parents to experience delight in their infant (Powell et al., 2014). As the infant develops, parents can learn to reframe 'demanding behaviours' as legitimate attachment needs, and to understand how to support the infant's complementary needs for closeness and comfort and autonomous exploration. As discussed previously, parent–child relationship principles can be effectively communicated through innovative online applications and web-based programmes accessible to all parents. Face-to-face delivery in groups can provide additional benefits. The group process and sharing of experiences and perspectives helps new parents to feel supported, and that their feelings and struggles are valid, and shared by others. While contemporary parents can find peer support through social media and online activities, the presence of a skilled facilitator can ensure a safe and trusting environment, and guide and extend reflection and discussion (Maxwell et al., 2021b). Parenting groups need to be inclusive and sensitive regarding diverse family forms, and different cultural beliefs about how infant behaviour should be managed, and how emotion is expressed.

Meeting Diverse Parent Needs
As noted in Chapter 8, there may be significant barriers to access and participation in for families from culturally and linguistically diverse backgrounds, due to lack of information and culturally insensitive or inappropriate content.

Indigenous and Minority Cultures. Appropriately tailored approaches grounded in a deep cultural understanding, and with a focus on self-determination are crucial to empower parents from indigenous or minority cultures (Equity Economics, 2020). Some parents will need specialised, trauma-informed approaches. Sustained home visiting programmes can be the most effective approach way to reach families experiencing high levels of adversity. Short-term benefits to parents and offspring can translate into longer term gains for the family and the community (Olds, 2016).

Evidence for effectiveness of broadly based home-visiting programmes is mixed, however. Many studies have methodological limitations, and effect sizes are generally modest (US Department of Health and Human Services, 2021). There is evidence that the Nurse Family Partnership in the United Kingdom is effective in improving birth, health, and child developmental outcomes, specifically for young first-time mothers (Avellar & Supplee, 2013). A recent randomised controlled trial in Australia shows promising benefits of a nurse home-visiting program in promoting child safety practices in the home, more parental warmth, lower hostility, and a more stimulating home learning environment (Goldfeld et al., 2019), with sustained mental health and self-efficacy benefits for participating parents at three years (Goldfeld et al., 2021). Further research is required to corroborate these findings (based on parent report) with observational measures of parenting.

Adoptive Parents. Becoming a parent through adoption or fostering presents unique challenges, including long wait periods with uncertain timing, no pregnancy period of preparation, and the fact that children are often older and have complex needs due to difficult pre-adoption experiences. Pre-adoptive preparation could help parents to establish realistic expectations and build awareness of available resources. Interviews and focus groups have identified a clear need for better communication between adoption services and intending parents including support to overcome cultural and legal barriers, and tailored parent training, education, and support (Barnett et al., 2018).

Parents with Disability. As noted in Chapter 3, approximately 9 per cent of adults of childbearing age have a disability (ABS, 2018) and they are a heterogeneous group. Challenges for women with disability during pregnancy include physical barriers, lack of specialised services, information barriers, and problems with communication and attitudes of health service providers, most notably a lack of respectful care (Malouf et al., 2017; Walsh-Gallagher et al., 2012).

A recent review found strong evidence that support from healthcare providers has a positive impact on the birth experience of women with disabilities (Heideveld-Gerritsen et al., 2021). The findings are encouraging. For example, a US population-based study of 645 Deaf women found no evidence of an increased likelihood of adverse pregnancy outcomes, other than a small increased likelihood of caesarean section. Despite some communication difficulties, they experienced comparable outcomes to hearing women, and they rated their birth and the care they received positively. Postnatally, however, it is very important that mothers' and fathers' groups and early childhood services be adequately resourced to allow inclusive educational and social engagement. Significant problems with communication and lack of interpreters have been highlighted as barriers for Deaf parents (as discussed in Chapter 8 in Katrina's story). A survey of women with disability regarding their experiences of postnatal services in England (Malouf et al., 2017) identified a need for more guidance and training of healthcare professionals, particularly in relation to communication barriers, the need to focus on abilities rather than disabilities, and the need for integrated care between different services (for example, mental health, disability, and obstetric services).

Parents with Complex Needs: Intensive Individualised Support

New parents who have longstanding emotional problems and/or severe depression may benefit from brief psycho-educational approaches, but they are likely to also need more intensive, sustained, and individualised therapy from highly trained practitioners if they are to thrive emotionally themselves, and forge secure attachments with their infants (Forman et al., 2007). Intensive therapeutic interventions require long-term parental engagement, service commitment, highly trained staff, and adequate clinical supervision. They are costly to implement, but parenting programmes are only cost-effective if they achieve the desired outcomes, and if the outcomes are sustained. Vulnerabilities acquired over a lifetime of adversity will not be 'fixed' overnight. Guild and colleagues (2021) provide longitudinal evidence that child–parent psychotherapy, delivered one-to-one, and sustained over a twelve-month period, increases the likelihood of secure mother–child attachment in mothers with significant depression and a history of abuse during childhood. Follow-up during middle childhood demonstrated sustained benefits – a secure parent–child attachment relationship was protective for the child's social and emotional development. More evidence is needed to enable informed and tailored allocation of appropriate interventions and programmes, given scarce public health resources and constraints on funding.

Work and Family: Structural Change to Support Families More Effectively

Social institutions in high-income societies need to reduce stressors on families and create more positive work and neighbourhood environments. Workplaces need to be restructured to create the structural conditions that foster sustained patterns of healthy relationships and healthy lifestyles (Kukla, 2008). New parents need time, financial security, and a supportive environment to enable the self-care necessary for mental health and the sensitive parenting that sets the family on a positive life trajectory (Saxbe et al., 2018). Parents with young infants also need clean environments, community spaces (playgrounds, toy libraries), and walkable suburbs that support life with a young child and welcome and encourage social engagement (Wolf, 2003). Social investment in families during this time of transformation and fragility can have positive impacts that will reverberate through communities and workplaces and resonate across generations. Family leave policies and family-friendly workplaces that are responsive to parental wellbeing are fundamental to achieving these long-term positive outcomes (Saxbe et al., 2018).

Most women want to return to paid work after having a child, and even if they would like to stay at home, they may not be able to afford to do so. Neoliberal economic systems are increasingly reliant on the participation of women in the workforce, with an expectation of only a brief time out of the workforce immediately after birth (Manne, 2018). Family-friendly policies (including affordable childcare) are frequently framed in terms of productivity benefits, rather than benefits to women and families. Meanwhile, the social expectation that women will also provide the care that older family members need has not changed. As a result, most women work a 'double shift', leading to chronic exhaustion (Crabb, 2015, 2019; Manne, 2018). Devaluing caregiving by prioritising the rewards of workplace success is not the answer, nor is ignoring or minimising the fundamental needs of infants (Manne, 2018; Petre2016; van der Gaag et al., 2019; Wolf, 2003).

Expectations of father involvement in caregiving *are* changing, albeit slowly. Many fathers feel a desire and a duty to be deeply involved at home, not just with chores, but with the emotional development of the baby as well (Birkett & Forbes, 2019; Sturrock, 2020), but most are still 'chafing at the strait jacket of gendered expectations at work' (Crabb, 2019, p. 35), as workplace expectations remain strikingly different for men and women. Systemic structural barriers commonly prevent men from being primary carers, or even taking their fair share of caregiving responsibility. There is evidence that men who take parental leave early in the child's life have a deeper engagement with the child later in life (Patnaik, 2019), and that employers benefit from happy, fulfilled employees with families, and that flexible work can lead to greater productivity (Petre, 2016). As entrepreneur Daniel Petre (2016) observes with frustration, despite all we know about the importance of parent–child relationships, many work practices still seem to be specifically designed to undermine or destroy them.

Socio-economically advantaged 'successful' parents attract the most media and research attention when it comes to work–family conflict, however they are more likely to be able to access quality (expensive) childcare options and paid help with housework. It is disadvantaged parents who are exposed to the greatest parenting stress in trying to reconcile competing demands of work and family (Saxbe et al., 2018). As well as juggling the demands of a workplace without family-friendly policies, they are likely to live in under-resourced communities that may struggle to provide the foundations of parenting and family life including safe housing, and affordable childcare (Manne, 2018). Choosing work over family leads to anguish as parents have to prioritise one part of the self at the expense of the other. Workplaces need to be flexible enough to support workers, irrespective of gender, in giving priority to family when they need to. Sadly, this is not yet the norm. In a large study of 3,500 Australian fathers, most reported long work hours, work–family conflict, poor mental health, and little or no flexibility in the workplace (Hokke et al., 2020).

The real revolution will occur when women demand that the world conform to their needs as mothers, and when all humans have the opportunity to engage in paid work, and to devote a portion of their lives to the 'humanising and essential' work of care (Manne, 2018, p. 30). Manne argues that if caregiving was a universal expectation, and caregiving experience was viewed as a valuable addition to any curriculum vitae, the current gender disadvantage would end, and the needs of the vulnerable and the dependent would be better met.

Paid Parental Leave

Saxbe and colleagues (2018) make a passionate case for paid parental leave as a fundamental reform to promote a healthy transition to parenthood. Paid maternity leave for women can enhance postnatal health, lead to more positive child outcomes, reduce financial strain during the vulnerable postnatal period, and improve labour-market opportunities for women (Bilgrami et al., 2020). Glass and colleagues (2016) conducted a sophisticated cross-national analysis of the relations between parent happiness and family-friendly social policies and practices in English-speaking countries (United States, United Kingdom, Canada, Australia, New Zealand) and Europe. Controlling for income and socio-economic status, they found that more generous family policies, particularly paid parental leave and child-care subsidies, were associated with smaller disparities in happiness between parents and nonparents, and there were no detrimental impacts of these policies on non-parents.

There is a growing body of research evidence confirming the positive impact of parental leave on psychological wellbeing, including a reduced vulnerability to depression after childbirth in Australia (Bilgrami et al., 2020), in the United Kingdom (Birkett & Forbes, 2019), and in California, one of just four American states with a paid parental leave scheme (Doran et al., 2020). In the latter study, the benefits were most substantial for socially disadvantaged mothers (younger and single mothers, and non-white mothers), and those with mild, rather than moderate postpartum distress. Paid parental leave is also associated with longer breastfeeding duration, and improved infant and child health outcomes. Importantly, from a broader social perspective, paid parental leave has economic and labour market benefits (see Nandi et al., 2018, for a systematic review).

Scandinavian countries have been the European leaders in work and family policies that promote gender equity and support parents in the first postnatal year. Japan and South Korea are also moving towards more generous paid parental leave polices (van der Gaag et al., 2019). The duration of leave is important; with limited benefits when leave is less than twelve weeks, and greater mental health benefits for mothers when leave is longer than six months, and when fathers also take some paid leave around the time of birth (Bilgrami et al., 2020).

Recent British research shows that extending parental leave opportunities to men can benefit the men themselves, their partners, and their children (Birkett & Forbes, 2019; van der Gaag et al., 2019), however significant barriers remain. These include gender stereotyped beliefs around caregiving, maternal gatekeeping, and organisational barriers, most notably poor communication about the scheme from employers (Birkett & Forbes, 2019; International Labour Organisation, 2015). There are also social class barriers to men's involvement in caregiving. Those in professional occupations are the most likely to benefit from more generous parental schemes, particularly longer time off work. Those in low paid, casual, or insecure employment still have very limited access to parental leave (Nandi et al., 2018).

Flexible Workplaces

Flexible workplace practices are crucial determinants of women returning to work, and to career advancement during their childbearing years (International Labour Organisation, 2015). The COVID-19 pandemic has accelerated changes that were already beginning to provide better conditions for new parents. Some workplaces are leading the way by providing supportive environments for breastfeeding, health and wellbeing strategies in the workplace, facilitating remote work, welcoming children in offices, and supporting parents to take leave when their children are ill. Progressive family-friendly social policies have the potential to change childbearing behaviour by reducing some of the costs, especially to women, and increasing the benefits (incentives) of having children, with long-term social and economic benefits for the community at large.

Access to High Quality Childcare

A full discussion of return to work after becoming a parent and engagement with formal childcare is beyond the scope of this book which focuses on the transition to parenthood and concludes at the end of the fourth trimester (when the baby is three months old). Nonetheless, even parents who are able to postpone their return to work until after the baby is three months old will be thinking, planning, and perhaps worrying, about childcare.

Community childcare centres are a recent evolutionary phenomenon as economic conditions have made it imperative for parents to work (Hrdy, 1999). They need to be reconciled with the needs of young infants. A large body of theory-driven research has defined the key characteristics of optimal childcare, designed around infant needs. Hrdy points out that all infants need the consistent loving care of a few predictable people. It need not necessarily be the mother, but consistency is crucial. Each infant, irrespective of the care setting, needs to feel that they are important, that they are wanted, that they will not be ignored, that they can elicit delight, and that they will be protected and provided for (Powell et al., 2014).

High-quality childcare provides developmentally appropriate stimulation and opportunities for learning, and the sensitive promotion of individual emotional growth. Meeting these needs, particularly for young infants, is more complex than it sounds. Societies need to recognise that the work that childcare workers do is fundamental social capital; they are currently among the lowest status and lowest paid workers in the community. Childcare and early childhood education provide significant long-term benefits for learning, academic achievement, and behavioural and emotional adjustment, but only when the quality is moderate to high (Vandell et al., 2010). The benefits are particularly strong for children from disadvantaged backgrounds, but high costs are a barrier to participation. Investment in quality childcare and early education can yield large social dividends in terms of emotional health and resilience (Shonkoff & Fisher, 2013) as well as future productivity of children and participation of women in the work force. This requires adequate training and remuneration for childcare workers, and genuine and sustained collaboration between governments, private childcare providers, managers, carers, and parents.

Conclusions

The public discourse on becoming a parent has shifted dramatically in recent decades, as mothers and fathers struggle to reconcile the competing demands of meeting the physical and emotional needs of infants, with a fulfilling life outside the home. Too often, regrettably, the debate becomes polarised. Simplistic false dichotomies abound. As a reaction to a long history of idealising parenthood, and motherhood in particular, parenting is frequently denigrated, with negative scaremongering describing a dismal experience with few redeeming features (Lester, 2018, Senior, 2015).

This book has sought to acknowledge the biological realities of the transition to parenthood, the complex psychological correlates and consequences of becoming a parent, and the powerful influence of social and cultural representations of motherhood, parenting, and socialisation. During pregnancy and in the early months after birth, women (who remain for the most part the primary carers) can find themselves torn between two compelling and incompatible urges – they are forced to make trade-offs between their desire to be fully present with their infant, and their desire to maintain a satisfying career and engagement with the wider world.

Increasingly, men are sharing the same struggles. Parents, irrespective of gender, require flexibility (and flexible workplaces) if they are to reconcile these competing desires and needs.

While infants are a profound source of delight, Hrdy (1999) argues for an honest acknowledgement of their selfish and animalistic needs, and the sound evolutionary reasons for what can seem insatiable demands. Put simply, parents need to make conscious choices that run counter to their self-interest: 'Forging workable compromises between infant needs and maternal and paternal ambition requires considerable ingenuity, self-understanding and common sense' (Hrdy, 1999, p. 112). As Hrdy points out, we are a resourceful and highly innovative species, but not infinitely so. As a community, we continue to struggle with the fundamental challenge of reconciling infant needs with gender equity and balanced fulfilling lifestyles, reflecting a broader social trend to devalue the importance of caregiving (Manne, 2018).

Identifying, articulating, and advocating for infant needs is one thing. Deciding who will provide for them and in what context is another. Collectively, as a society, we need to support and invest in parents so that they can provide the nurturing, encouragement, and love that all young children need, while continuing to lead rich and fulfilling lives themselves. This requires a collective social acknowledgement of the 'inconvenient truth' that infants are entirely dependent on adults for their survival, and they are hardwired for relationship and learning from the beginning of life.

A compelling body of research has demonstrated the impact of early experiences on brain development and the long-term physical and mental health of children. As a community, we need to affirm and celebrate the importance of caregiving and the contribution it makes to our social capital. Hilary Clinton (1996) popularised the African proverb 'it takes a village to raise a child'. Decades of feminist activism and scholarship have pointed out the unfair and unsustainable caregiving burden on women in modern industrialised societies, as they are expected to contribute to productivity while carrying the full burden of childrearing. Innovative policy and cultural change is urgently needed to build sustainable patterns of healthy social and family relationships.

> If a society values its children, it must cherish their parents. (Bowlby, 1951, p. 84).

References

Abraham, E. & Feldman, R. (2018). The neurobiology of human allomaternal care: Implications for fathering, co-parenting, and children's social development. *Physiological Behavior, 193*(Pt A), 25–34. https://doi.org/10.1016/j.physbeh.2017.12.034

Abraham, E., Hendler, T., Zagoory-Sharon, O., & Feldman, R. (2016). Network integrity of the parental brain in infancy supports the development of children's social competencies. *Social Cognitive and Affective Neuroscience, 11*(11), 1707–1718. https://doi.org/10.1093/scan/nsw090

Adolfsson, A. (2011). Meta-analysis to obtain a scale of psychological reaction after perinatal loss: Focus on miscarriage. *Psychology Research and Behavior Management, 4,* 29–39. https://doi.org/10.2147/PRBM. S17330

Ainsworth, M. D. S., Bell, S. M., & Stayton, D. J. (1974). Infant–mother attachment and social development: Socialisation as a product of reciprocal responsiveness to signals. In M. P. M. Richards (Ed.), *The integration of a child into a social world* pp. 99–135. Cambridge University Press.

Akesson, B. (2017). A baby to tie you to place: Childrearing advice from a Palestinian mother living under occupation. In A. Gottlieb & J. DeLoach (Eds), *A world of babies* (2nd ed., pp. 91–122). Cambridge University Press.

Akolekar, R., Beta, J., Picciarelli, G., Ogilvie, C., & D'Antonio, F. (2015). Procedure-related risk of miscarriage following amniocentesis and chorionic villus sampling: A systematic review and meta-analysis. *Ultrasound in Obstetrics & Gynecology, 45,* (1), 16–26. https://doi.org/10.1002/uog.14636

Alhusen, J. L. (2008). A literature update on maternal–fetal attachment. *Journal of Obstetric, Gynecologic, and Neonatal Nursing, 37*(3), 315–328. https://doi.org/10.1111/j.1552-6909.2008.00241.x

Alhusen, J. L., Gross, D., Hayat, M. J., Woods, A. B., & Sharps, P. W. (2012). The influence of maternal–fetal attachment and health practices on neonatal outcomes in low-income, urban women. *Research in Nursing and Health, 35*(2), 112–120. https://doi.org/10.1002/nur.21464

Alhusen, J. L., Hayat, M. J., & Gross, D. (2013). A longitudinal study of maternal attachment and infant outcomes. *Archives of Women's Mental Health, 16*(6), 521–529. https://doi.org/10.1007/s00737-013-0357-8

Ali, M. & Parekh, N. (2020). Male age and andropause. In S. J. Parekattil, S. C. Esteves, & A. Agarwal (Eds), *Male infertility* (pp. 469–477). Springer. https://doi.org/10.1007/978-3-030-32300-4_36

Almeling, R. (2015). Reproduction. *American Review of Psychology, 41*, 423–442. https://doi.org/10.1146/annurev-soc-073014-112258

Almond, B. (2010). *The monster within: The hidden side of motherhood*. University of California Press.

Als, H., Lawhon, G., Duffy, F. H., McAnulty, G. B., Gibes-Grossman, R., & Blickman, J. G. (1994). Individualized developmental care for the very low-birth-weight preterm infant. Medical and neurofunctional effects. *Journal of the American Medical Association, 272* (11):853–858. https://doi.org/10.1001/jama.1994.03520110033025

American Psychological Association. (2017). What is postpartum depression and anxiety? www.apa.org/pi/women/resources/reports/postpartum-depression

Amir, H., Yaish, I., Oren, A., Groutz, A., Greenman, Y., & Azem, F. (2020). Fertility preservation rates among transgender women compared with trans-gender men receiving comprehensive fertility counselling. *Reproductive Biomedicine Online, 41*(3), 546–554. https://doi.org/10.1016/j.rbmo.2020.05.003

Anim-Somuah, M., Smyth, R. M., Cyna, A. M., & Cuthberth, A. (2018). Epidural vs. non-epidural or no analgesia for pain management in labour. *The Cochrane Database of Systematic Reviews*, (5). Art. No. CD000331. https://doi.org/10.1002/14651858.CD000331.pub4

Argyle, C. E., Harper, J. C., & Davies, M. C. (2016). Oocyte cryopreservation: Where are we now? *Human Reproduction Update, 22*(4), 440–449. https://dx.doi.org/10.1093/humupd/dmw007

Arifin, S. R. M., Cheyne, H., & Maxwell, M. (2018). Review of the prevalence of postnatal depression across cultures. *AIMS Public Health, 5*(3), 260–295. https://doi.org/10.3934/publichealth.2018.3.260

Arnold-Baker, C. (2019). The process of becoming: Maternal identity in the transition to motherhood. *Existential Analysis: Journal of the Society for Existential Analysis, 30*(2), 260–274. https://www.existentialanalysis.co.uk/page22.html

Atwood, M. (1985). *The handmaid's tale*. McClelland and Stewart.

Austin, M.-P., Highet, N., & The Expert Working Group. (2017). *Mental health care in the perinatal period: Australian clinical practice guideline*. Centre of Perinatal Excellence. https://www.clinicalguidelines.gov.au/portal/2586/mental-health-care-perinatal-period-australian-clinical-practice-guideline

Australian Bureau of Statistics (ABS) (2018). *Disability, ageing and carers*. Australian Government. https://www.abs.gov.au/statistics/health/disability/disability-ageing-and-carers-australia-summary-findings/latest-release

Australian Institute of Health and Welfare. (2021a). National Core Maternity Indicators, AIHW, Australian Government, https://www.aihw.gov.au/reports/mothers-babies/ncmi-data-visualisations/contents/labour-and-birth-indicators/caesarean-section

Australian Institute of Health and Welfare. (2021b). *Adoptions Australia 2019–2020*. Child welfare series no. 73. Cat. no. CWS 79. AIHW.

Avellar, S. A., & Supplee, L. H. (2013). Effectiveness of home visiting in improving child health and reducing child maltreatment. *Pediatrics, 132* (Suppl 2), S90–S99. https://doi,org/10.1542/peds.2013-1021G

Ayres, S., Bond, R., Bertuillies, S., & Wijma, K. (2016). The aetiology of posttraumatic stress following childbirth: A meta-analysis and theoretical framework. *Psychological Medicine, 46*(6), 1121–1134. https://doi.org/10.1017/S0033291715002706

Badenhorst, W. & Hughes, P. (2007). Psychological aspects of perinatal loss. *Best Practice & Research Clinical Obstetrics & Gynaecology, 21*(2), 249–259. https://doi.org/10.1016/j.bpobgyn.2006.11.004

Bahamondes, L. & Makuch, M. Y. (2014). Infertility care and the introduction of new reproductive technologies in poor resource settings. *Reproductive Medicine and Biological Endocrinology, 12*, 87. https://doi.org/10.1186/1477-7827-12-87

Bailey, S. L., Boivin, J., Cheong, Y. C., Kitson-Reynolds, E., Bailey, C., & Macklon, N. (2019). Hope for the best … but expect the worst: A qualitative study to explore how women with recurrent miscarriage experience the early waiting period in a new pregnancy. *BMJ Open, 9*(5), e029354. https://doi.org/10.1136/bmjopen-2019-029354

Balaskas, J. (1983). *Active birth*. Harper Collins.

Bamber, J. H., Lucas, D. N., Plaat, F., & Russell, R. (2020). Obstetric anaesthetic practice in the UK: A descriptive analysis of the National Obstetric Database 2009–14. *British Journal of Anaesthesia, 125*(4), 580–587. https://doi.org/10.1016/j.bja.2020.06.053

Baraitser, L. (2009). *Maternal encounters: The ethics of interruption*. Routledge.

Barker, R. (1994/2014). *Baby love*. Macmillan. First published in 1994.

Barnett, E. R., Jankowski, M. K., Butcher, R. L., Meister, C., Parton, R. R., & Drake, R. E. (2018). Foster and adoptive parent perspectives on needs and services: A mixed methods study. *Journal of Behavior and Health Services Research, 45*(1), 74–89. https://doi.org/10.1007/s11414-017-9569-4

Battineni, G., Baldoni, S., Chintalapudi, N., Sagaro, G. G., Pallotta, G., Nittari, G., & Amenta, F. (2020). Factors affecting the quality and reliability of online health information. *Digital Health*, Aug 30; 6. https://doi.org/10.1177/2055207620948996

Beck, C., & Watson, S. (2016). Posttraumatic growth after birth trauma: 'I was broken, now I am unbreakable'. *The American Journal of Maternal Child Nursing, 41*(5), 264–271. https://doi.org/10.1097/NMC.0000000000000259

Beilby, K., Dudink, I., Kablar, D., Kaynak, M., Rodrigo, S., & Hammarberg, K. (2020). The quality of information about elective oocyte cryo-preservation (EOC) on Australian fertility clinic websites. *Australian and New Zealand Journal of Obstetrics & Gynaecology, 60*(4), 605–609. https://doi.org/10.1111/ajo.13174

Bell, S. M. & Ainsworth, M. D. (1972). Infant crying and maternal responsiveness. *Child Development, 43*(4), 1171–1190. https://doi.org/10.2307/1127506

Belsky, J. (1984). The determinants of parenting: A process model. *Child Development, 55*, 83–96. https://doi.org/10.2307/1129846

Benedek, T. (1959). Parenthood as a developmental phase. A contribution to the libido theory. *Journal of the American Psychoanalytic Association, 7*(3), 379–417.

Benzies, K. M. & Magill-Evans, J. (2015). Through the eyes of a new dad: Experiences of first-time fathers of late preterm infants. *Infant Mental Health Journal, 36*(1), 78–87. https://doi.org/10.1002/imhj.21489

Berg, A. & Wiseman, R. (2019). On choosing life. *The Point*, 20, September. https://thepointmag.com/letter/on-choosing-life/

Berger, L. M. & Langton, C. E. (2011). Young disadvantaged men as fathers. *The Annals of the American Academy of Political and Social Science, 635*(1), 56–75. https://doi.org/10.1177/0002716210393648

Berger, R. & Paul, M. (2008). Family secrets and family functioning: The case of donor assistance. *Family Process, 47*(4), 553–566. https://doi.org/10.1111/j.1545-5300.2008.00271.x

Bergman, K., Rubio, R., Green, R., & Padron, E. (2010). Gay men who become fathers via surrogacy: The transition to parenthood. *Journal of GLBT Family Studies, 6*(2), 111–141. https://doi.org/10.1080/15504281003704942

Berkowitz, D. & Marsiglio, W. (2007). Gay men: Negotiating procreative, father and family identities. *Journal of Marriage and Family, 69*(2), 366–381. https://doi.org/10.1111/j.1741-3737.2007.00371.x

Bernier, A. & Matte-Gagné, C. (2012). More bridges: Investigating the relevance of self-report and interview measures of adult attachment for marital and caregiving relationships. *The International Journal of Behavioral Development, 35*(4), 307–316. https://doi.org/10.1177/0165025410396766

Bhatia. (2018). *Gender before birth: Sex selection in a transnational context.* University of Washington Press. https://www.jstor.org/stable/j.ctvcwnstn

Bibring, G. (1959). Some considerations of the psychological processes in pregnancy. *Psychoanalytic Study of the Child, 14*(1), 113–121.

Biehle, S. N. & Mickelson, K. D. (2011). Personal and co-parent predictors of parenting efficacy across the transition to parenthood. *Journal of Social and Clinical Psychology, 30*(9), 985–1010. https://doi.org/10.1521/jscp.2011.30.9.985

Bilgrami, A., Sinha, K., & Cutler, H. (2020). The impact of introducing a national scheme for paid parental leave on maternal mental health. *Health Economics, 29*(12), 1657–1681. https://doi.org/10.1002/hec.4164

Billari, F. C., Goisis, A., Liefbroer, A. C., Setterson, R. A., Aassve, A., Hagestad, G., & Speder, Z. (2011). Social age deadlines for the childbearing of women and men. *Human Reproduction, 26*(3), 616–622. https://doi.org/10.1093/humrep/deq360

Birkett & Forbes. (2019). Where's dad? Exploring the low take-up of inclusive parenting policies in the UK. *Policy Studies, 40*(2), 205–224. https://doi.org/10.1080/01442872.2019.1581160

Blackstone, A. & Stewart, M. D. (2016). There's more thinking to decide. *The Family Journal: Counseling and Therapy for Couples and Families, 24*(3), 296–303. https://doi.org/10.1177/1066480716648676

Blake, L., Carone, N., Rafanello, E., Slutsky, J., Ehrhardt, A. A., & Golomok, S. (2017). Gay fathers' motivations for and feelings about surrogacy as a path to parenthood. *Human Reproduction, 32*(4), 860–867. https://doi.org/10.1093/humrep/dex026

Bodin, M., Holmström, C., Plantin, L., Schmidt, L., Ziebe, S., & Elmerstig, E. (2021). Preconditions to parenthood: Changes over time and generations. *Reproductive Biomedicine and Society Online, 13*, 14–23. https://doi.org/10.1016/j.rbms.2021.03.003

Boivin, J. (2019). How does stress, depression and anxiety effect patients undergoing treatment. *Current Opinion in Obstetrics & Gynecology, 31*(3), 195–199. https://doi.org/10.1097/GCO.0000000000000539

Boivin, J., & Lancastle, D. (2010). Medical waiting periods: Imminence, emotions and coping. *Women's Health, 6*(1), 59–69. https://doi.org/10.2217/whe.09.79

Boivin, J., Bunting, L. E, Collins, J. A., & Nygren, J. E. (2007). International estimates of infertility prevalence and treatment-seeking: Potential need and demand for infertility medical care. *Human Reproduction, 22*(6), 1506–1512. https://doi.org/10.1093/humrep/dem299

Bonette, S. & Broom, A. (2012). On grief, fathering and the male role in men's accounts of stillbirth. *Journal of Sociology, 48*(3), 248–265. https://doi.org/10.1177/1440783311413485

Bornstein, M. & Manian, N. (2013). Maternal sensitivity and responsiveness reconsidered: Some is more. *Development and Psychopathology, 25*(4, Pt 1), 957–971. https://doi.org/10.1017/S0954579413000308

Bouchard, G. (2011). The role of psychosocial variables in prenatal attachment: An examination of moderational effects. *Journal of Reproductive and Infant Psychology, 29*(3), 197–207. https://doi.org/10.1080/02646838.2011.592975

Bower-Brown, S., & Zadeh, S. (2021). Binary-trans, non-binary and gender-questioning adolescents' experiences in UK schools, *Journal of LGBT Youth* 2021, 1–19. https://doi.org/10.1080/19361653.2021.1873215"10.1080/19361653.2021.1873215

Bowlby, J. (1951). *Maternal care and mental health*. World Health Organization.

Bowlby, J. (1957). An ethological approach to research in child development. *British Journal of Medical Psychology, 30*, 230–240. https://doi.org/10.1111/j.2044-8341.1957.tb01202.x

Bowlby, J. (1982). *Attachment and loss. Vol. 1: Attachment* (2nd ed.). Basic Books. First published 1969.

Bowlby, R. (2013). *A child of one's own*. Oxford University Press.

Boyce, W. T. (2019). *The orchid and the dandelion: Why some children struggle and how all can thrive*. Alfred A. Knopf.

Boyce, P., Condon, J., Barton, J., & Corkindale, C. (2007). First time fathers' study: Psychological distress in expectant fathers during pregnancy. *Australian and New Zealand Journal of Psychiatry, 41*(9), 718–725. https://doi.org/10.1080/00048670701517959

Bracks-Zelloua, P., McMahon, C., & Gibson, F. (2011). IVF-conceiving fathers' experiences of early parenthood. *Journal of Relationships Research, 2*(1), 1–9. https://doi.org/10.1375/jrr.2.1.1

Brandão, T., Brites, R., Pires, M., Hipólito, J., Nunes, O., & Fiese, B. H. (2019). Anxiety, depression, dyadic adjustment, and attachment to the fetus in pregnancy: Actor–partner interdependence mediation analysis. *Journal of Family Psychology, 33*(3), 294–303. http://dx.doi.org/10.1037/fam0000513

Brandel, M., Melchiorri, E., & Ruini, C. (2018). The dynamics of eudaimonic well-being in the transition to parenthood: Differences between fathers and mothers. *Journal of Family Issues, 39*(9), 2572–2589. https://doi.org/10.1177/0192513X18758344

Branjerdporn, G., Meredith, P., Strong, J., & Garcia, J. (2017). Associations between maternal-foetal attachment and infant developmental outcomes: A systematic review. *Maternal Child Health Journal, 21*(3), 540–553. https://doi.org/10.1007/s10995-016-2138-2

Brase, G. L., & Brase, S. L. (2012). Emotional regulation of fertility decision making: What is the nature and structure of 'Baby Fever'? *Emotion, 12*(5), 1141–1154. http://dx.doi.org/10.1037/a0024954

Brazelton, T. B. (1983). *Infants and mothers.* Dell. First published in 1969.

Bretherton, I. (2010). Fathers in attachment theory and research: A review. *Early Child Development and Care, 180*(1), 9–23 https://doi.org/10.1080/03004430903414661

Brinsden, P. R. (2003). Gestational surrogacy. *Human Reproduction Update, 9*(5), 483–491. https://doi.org/10.1093/humupd/dmg033

Bronfenbrenner, U. & Morris, P. (2006). The bioecological model of human development. In W. Damon & R. M. Lerner (Eds.), *Handbook of child psychology Vol. 1,* (pp. 793–828). John Wiley & Sons.

Bueskens, P. (2018). From containing to creating. In C. Nelson & R. Robertson (Eds.), *Dangerous ideas about mothers* (pp. 197–210). University of Western Australia Publishing.

Buist, A. (2020). *Maternal flame. Weekend Australian, Review,* May 9–10.

Burns, L. H. (2007). Psychiatric aspects of infertility and infertility treatments. *Psychiatric Clinics of North America, 30*(4), 689–716. https://doi.org/10.1016/j.psc.2007.08.001

Buss, D. M. (2015). *Evolutionary psychology: The new science of the mind* (5th ed.). Pearson. First published in 2004.

Butwick, A. J., Bentley, J., Wong, C. A., Snowdon, J. M., Sun, E., & Guo, N. (2018). United States state-level variation in the use of neuraxial analgesia during labor for pregnant women. *Journal of the American Medical Association, Network Open, 1*(8), e186567. https://doi.org/10.1001/jamanetworkopen.2018.6567

Cabrera, N. T., Tamis-LeMonda, C. S., Bradley, R. H., Hofferth, S., & Lamb, M. E. (2000). Fathers in the 21st century. *Child Development, 71*(1), 127–136. https://doi.org/10.1111/1467-8624.00126

Callaghan, G. (2019). 'What makes a father'? The sperm donor who asked the courts to answer this question tells his story. https://www.smh.com.au/national/what-makes-a-father-the-sperm-donor-who-asked-the-courts-to-answer-this-question-tells-his-story-20190722-p529js.html

Calvo, V., Palmieri, A., Codamo, A., Scampoli, M. R., & Bianco, F. (2015). Perceptions of parental bonding, adult attachment, and marital adjustment in prospective adoptive parents. An empirical study in the pre-adoptive period. *Sexual and Relationship Therapy, 30*(4), 419–432. https://doi.org/10.1080/14681 994.2014.1001355

Camberis, A.-L., McMahon, C., Gibson, F., & Boivin, J. (2014). Age, psychological maturity, and the transition to motherhood among English-speaking Australian women in a metropolitan area. *Developmental Psychology, 50*(8), 2154–2164. https://doi.org/10.1037/a0037301

Cameron, E. E., Giesbrecht, G. F., & Tomfohr-Madsen, L. M. (2021). Psychometric properties of the Pregnancy-Related Anxiety Scale for use with fathers during pregnancy. *Psychology of Men & Masculinities, 22*(1), 26–38. https://doi.org/10.1037/men0000260

Cannold, L. (2005). *What, no baby? Why women are losing the freedom to mother and how they can get it back.* Freemantle Arts Centre Press.

Carneiro, F. A., Tasker, F., Salinas-Quiroz, F., Leal, I., & Costa, P. A. (2017). Are the fathers alright? A systematic and critical review of studies on gay and bisexual fatherhood. *Frontiers in Psychology, 8*, Article 1636. https://doi.org/10.3389/fpsyg.2017.01636

Carolan, M. (2005). 'Doing it properly': The experience of first mothering over 35 years. *Health Care for Women International, 26*(9), 764–787. https://doi.org/10.1080/07399330500230987

Carone, N., Baiocco, R., & Lingiardi, V. (2017). Italian gay fathers' experiences of transnational surrogacy and their relationship with the surrogate pre- and post-birth. *Reproductive Biomedicine Online, 34*(2), 181–190. https://doi.org/10.1016/j.rbmo.2016.10.010

Carter, S., Channon, A., & Berrington, A. (2020). Socioeconomic risk factors for labour induction in the United Kingdom. *BMC Pregnancy Childbirth, 20*(146), 146. https://doi.org/10.1186/s12884-020-2840-3

Ceballo, R., Lansford, J. E., Abbey, A., & Stewart, A. (2004). Gaining a child: Comparing the experience of biological parents, adoptive parents and stepparents. *Family Relations, 53*(1), 38–48. https://doi.org/10.1111/j.1741-3729.2004.00007.x

Cenerini, M. V. & Messina, D. (2019). A 'strong enough' father. Observations from groups for expectant and new fathers. *Infant Observation, 22*(2–3), 147–164. https://doi.org/10.1080/13698036.2019.1689839

Chamberlain, D. (2013). *Windows to the womb.* North Atlantic Books.

Chambers, G. M., Randall, S., Hoang, V., Sullivan, E. A., Highet, N., Croft, M., Mihalopoulos, C., Morgan, V. A., Reilly, N., & Austin, M.-P. (2016). The National Perinatal Depression Initiative: An evaluation of access to general practitioners, psychologists and psychiatrists through the Medicare Benefits Schedule. *Australian & New Zealand Journal of Psychiatry, 50*(3), 264–274. https://doi.org/10.1177/0004867415580154

Chapman, M. (2020). Reflecting on babies in the NICU: An exploration of parental reflective functioning in a quaternary neonatal intensive care unit. Doctoral thesis submitted to the University of Melbourne. http://hdl.handle.net/11343/254808

Chapman, M. & Paul, C. (2014). Working in twilight: Infant mental health interventions with babies who may die. In C. Paul & F. Thomson-Salo (Eds), *The baby as subject: Clinical studies in infant-parent therapy*. Karnac.

Chhabra, J., McDermott, B., & Li, W. (2020). Risk factors for perinatal depression and anxiety: A systematic review and meta-analysis. *Psychology of Men and Masculinities, 21*(4), 593–611. https://doi.org/10.1037/men0000259

Chin, K., Chopik, W. J., Wardecker, B. M., LaBelle, O. P., Moors, A. C., & Edelstein, R. S. (2020). Longitudinal associations between prenatal testosterone and postpartum outcomes in a sample of first-time expectant lesbian couples. *Hormones and Behavior, 125*, 104810. https://doi.org/10.1016/j.yhbeh.2020.104810

Chodorow, N. J. (2004). Psychoanalysis and women: A personal thirty-five-year retrospect. *Annual Journal of Psychoanalysis, 32*, 101–129.

Cholodenko, L. (Director). (2010). *The kids are all right*. [Film] Focus Features.

Chowdhury, R., Sinha, B., Sankar, M. J., Taneja, S., Bandhari, N., Rollins, N., Bahl, R., & Martines, J. (2015). Breastfeeding and maternal health outcomes: A systematic review and meta-analysis. *Acta Paediatrica, 104*(467), 96–193. https://doi.org/10.1111/apa.13102

Clark, A., Skouteris, H., Wertheim, E. H., Paxton, S. J., & Milgrom, J. (2009). The relationship between depression and body dissatisfaction across pregnancy and the postpartum: A prospective study. *Journal of Health Psychology, 14*(1), 27–35. https://doi.org/10.1177/1359105308097940

Clinton, H. R. (1996). *It takes a village and other lessons that children teach us*. Simon & Schuster.

Cochrane, L. (2017, June 29). Baby Gammy, now Grammy, starts kindergarten amid tensions over charitable donations. https://www.abc.net.au/news/2017-06-29/baby-gammy-starts-kinder-amid-tensions-over-donations/8585596

Cohen, W. R. (2014). Does maternal age affect pregnancy outcome? *British Journal of Obstetrics & Gynecology, 121*(3), 252–254. https://doi.org/10.1111/1471-0528.12563

Coles, R. (1967). *Children of crisis: A study of courage and fear*. Little, Brown.

Collier, A. (2020). 'Leaving the land of romantic fantasy': Why I chose to be a single mum. 6 November 2020. https://www.smh.com.au/lifestyle/life-and-relationships/leaving-the-land-of-romantic-fantasy-why-i-chose-to-be-a-single-mum-20201007-p562xu.html

Condon, J., Boyce, P., & Corkindale, C. J. (2004). The first-time fathers' study: A prospective study of the mental health and wellbeing of men during the transition to parenthood. *Australian and New Zealand Journal of Psychiatry, 38*(1–2), 56–64. https://doi.org/10.1177/000486740403800102

Condon, J., Corkindale, C. J., & Boyce, P. (2008). Assessment of postnatal paternal-infant attachment: Development of a questionnaire instrument. *Journal of Reproductive and Infant Psychology, 26*(3), 195–210. https://doi.org/10.1080/02646830701691335

Conn, B. M., de Figureido, S., Sherer, S., Mankerian, M., & Iverson, E. (2018). 'Our lives aren't over': A strengths-based perspective on stigma, discrimination, and coping among young parents. *Journal of Adolescence, 66*, 91–100. https://doi.org/10.1016/j.adolescence.2018.05.005

Conti, J., Abraham, S., & Taylor, A. (1998). Eating behaviour and pregnancy outcome. *Journal of Psychosomatic Research, 44*(3–4), 465–477. https://doi .org/10.1016/S0022-3999(97)00271-7

Cooke, A., Mills, T. A., & Lavender, T. (2012). Advanced maternal age: Delayed childbearing is rarely a conscious choice: A qualitative study of women's views and experiences. *International Journal of Nursing Studies, 49*(1), 30–39. https:// doi.org/10.1016/j.ijnurstu.201107.013

Corpuz, R., & Bugental, D. (2020). Life history and individual differences in male testosterone: Mixed evidence for early environmental calibration of testosterone response to first-time fatherhood. *Hormones and Behavior, 120*, 104684. https://doi.org.10.1016/j.yhbeh.2020.104684. Epub 2020 Jan 24.

Corr, C. A. (2019). Should we incorporate the work of Elizabeth Kübler-Ross in our current teaching and practice, and if so, how? *Journal of Death and Dying*, 31 July. https://doi.org/10.1177/0030222819865397

Côte-Arsenault, D., & Donato, K. (2011). Emotional cushioning in pregnancy after perinatal loss. *Journal of Reproductive and Infant Psychology, 29*(1), 81–92. https://doi.org/10.1080/02646838.2010.513115

Cowan, C. P., & Cowan, P. A. (1985). Transitions to parenthood: His, hers, and theirs. *Journal of Family Issues, 6*(4), 451–481. https://doi .org/10.1177/019251385006004004

Cowan, P. A., & Cowan, C. P. (1992). *When partners become parents: The big life change for couples*. Basic Books.

Cowan, C. P., & Cowan, P. A. (1995). Interventions to ease the transition to parenthood: What they are, and what they can do. *Family Relations, 42*(4), 412–423. https://doi.org/10.2307/584997

Cowan, P. A., Cowan, C. P., & Knox, V. (2010). Marriage and fatherhood programs. *The Future of Children, 20*(2), 205–230. https://doi.org/10.1353/ doc.2010.0000

Cox, S. M., Lashley, C. O., Henson, L. G., Medina, N. Y., & Hans, S. L. (2021). Making meaning of motherhood: Self and life transitions among African American adolescent mothers. *American Journal of Orthopsychiatry, 91*(1), 120–131. https://doi.org/10.1037/ort0000521

Crabb, A. (2015). *The wife drought: Why women need wives and men need lives*. Ebury Press. First published in 2014.

Crabb, A. (2019). Men at work. In *Quarterly Essay, Issue 75* (pp. 1–73). Black Inc, Schwartz Books Pty. Ltd.

Cranley, M. S. (1993). The origins of the mother-child relationship: A review. *Physical and Occupational Therapy in Pediatrics, 12*(2–3), 39–51. http://dx.doi .org/10.1080/Joo6v12n02_03

Crawford, G. E., & Ledger, W. L. (2020). In vitro fertilisation/intracytoplasmic sperm injection beyond 2020. *BJOG, 126*(2), 237–243. http://doi .org/10.1111/1471-0528.15526

Crespi, I., & Ruspini, E. (2016). Transition to fatherhood: New perspectives in the global context of changing men's identities. *International Review of Sociology, 25*(3), 353–358. https://doi.org/10.1080/03906701.2015.1078529

Curran, L., McCoyd, J., Munch, S., & Wilkenfeld, B. (2017). Practicing maternal virtues prematurely: The phenomenology of maternal identity in medically high-risk pregnancy. *Healthcare for Women International, 38*(8), 813–832. https://doi.org/10.1080/07399332.2017.1323904

Cusk, R. (2008). *A life's work.* Faber & Faber. First published in 2001.

Daly, I. & Bewley, S. (2013). Reproductive ageing and conflicting clocks: King Midas' touch. *Reproductive Biomedicine Online, 27*(6), 722–732. http://dx.doi.org/10.1016/j.rbmo.2013.09.012

Daniels, K. (2020). The perspective of adult donor conceived persons. In: K. Beier, C. Brugge, P. Thorn, & C. Weisemann (Eds.), *Assistierte Reproduktion mit Hilfe Dritter* (pp. 443–459). Springer. https://doi.org/10.1007/978-3-662-60298-0_29

Darwin, Z., Domoney, J., Iles, J., Bristow, F., McLeish, J., & Sethna, V. (2021). Involving and supporting partners and other family members in specialist perinatal mental health services. *Good practice guide.* NHS England

Darwin, Z., Galdas, P., Hinchliff, S., Littlewood, E., McMillan, P., McGowan, L., & Gilbody, S. on behalf of the Born and Bred in Yorkshire (BaBY) team. (2017). Fathers' views and experiences of their own mental health during pregnancy and the first postnatal year: A qualitative interview study of men participating in the UK Born and Bred in Yorkshire (BaBY) cohort. *BMC Pregnancy Childbirth, 17*(1) 45. https://doi.org/10.1186/s12884-017-1229-4

da Silva, S., Place, J. M., Boivin, J., & Gameiro, S. (2018). Failure after fertility treatment: Regulation strategies when facing a blocked parenthood goal. *Human Fertility, 23*(3), 179–185. https://doi.org/10.1080/14647273.2018.1510186

Davis, G. (2017). 'A tragedy as old as history': Medical responses to infertility and artificial insemination by donor in 1950s Britain. In *The Palgrave Handbook of Infertility in History* (pp. 359–382). Palgrave.

Deater-Deckard, K. & Panneton, R. (Eds) (2017). *Parental stress and early child development: Adaptive and maladaptive outcomes.* Springer Ebooks. https://doi.org/10.1007/978-3-319-55376-4

Deave, T., & Johnson, D. (2008). The transition to fatherhood: What does it mean for fathers? *Journal of Advanced Nursing, 63*(6), 626–633. https://doi.org/10.1111/j.1365-2648.2008.04748.x

Declercq, E. R., Sakala, C., Corry, M. P., Applebaum, S., & Herrlich, A. (2013). *Listening to mothers III: Pregnancy and birth.* Childbirth Connection.

Deeb-Sossa, N. & Kane, H. (2017). Pregnancy without women: Lessons from childbirth classes. *Sexuality Research and Social Policy, 14*(4), 380–392. https://doi.org/10.1007/s13178-016-0265-6

Dempsey, D., Nordqvist, P., & Kelly, F. Beyond secrecy and openness: Telling a relational story about children's best interests in donor-conceived families. *BioSocieties* (2021). https://doi.org/10.1057/s41292-021-00225-9

Dennis, C.-L., Hodnett, E., Kenton, L., Weston, J., Zupancic, J., Stewart, D. E., Love, L., & Kiss, A. (2009). Effect of peer support on prevention of postnatal depression among high risk women: Multisite randomised controlled trial. *BMJ Online, 338*, a3064. https://doi.org/10.1136/bmj.a3064

Deutsch, H. (1945). *The psychology of women.* Grune & Stratton.

Dhillon, A., Sparkes, E., & Duarte, R. V. (2017). Mindfulness-based interventions during pregnancy: A systematic review and meta-analysis. *Mindfulness, 8*(6), 1421–1437. https://doi.org/10.1007/s12671-017-0726-x

Dick-Read, G. (2004). *Childbirth without fear: The principles and practices of natural childbirth.* Pinter & Martin. First published in 1942.

Dimond, R. (2015). Social and ethical issues in mitochondrial donation. *British Medical Bulletin, 115*(1), 173–182. https://doi.org/10.1093/bmb/ldv037

DiPietro, J. A., Ghera, M. M., Costigan, K., & Hawkins, M. (2004). Measuring the ups and downs of pregnancy stress. *Journal of Psychosomatic Obstetrics & Gynecology, 25*(3–4), 189–201. https://doi.org/10.1080/01674820400017830

Doi, S., Fujiwara, T., Isumi, A., & Mitsuda, N. (2020). Preventing postpartum depressive symptoms using an educational video on infant crying: A cluster randomised controlled trial. *Depression and Anxiety, 37,* 449–457. https://doi.org/10.1002/da.23002

Doka, K. J. & Martin, T. L. (2011). *Grieving beyond gender: Understanding the ways that men and women mourn.* Revised ed. Routledge. https://doi.org/10.4324/9780203886069

Doran, E. L., Bartel, A. P., Ruhm, C. J., & Waldfogel, J. (2020). California's paid family leave law improves maternal psychological health. *Social Science & Medicine, 256,* 113003, doi: 10.1016/j.socscimed.2020.113003. Epub 2020 Apr 24.

Doss, B. D., Rhoades, G. K., Stanley, S. M., & Markman, H. J. (2009). The effect of the transition to parenthood on relationship quality: An 8-year prospective study. *Journal of Personality and Social Psychology, 96*(3), 601–619. https://doi.org/10.1037/a0013969

Dowdy, D. (2016). Keepsake ultrasound: Taking another look. *Journal of Radiology Nursing, 35*(2), 119–132. https://doi.org/10.1016/j.jradnu.2016.02.006

Draper, J. (2002). 'It's the first scientific evidence': Men's experience of pregnancy confirmation. *Journal of Advanced Nursing, 39*(6), 563–570. https://doi.org/10.1046/j.1365-2648.2002.02325.x

Draper, J. (2003). Men's passage to fatherhood: An analysis of the contemporary relevance of transition theory. *Nursing Inquiry, 10*(1), 66–78. https://doi.org/10.1046/j.1440-1800.2003.00157.x

Drife, J. (2004). Teenage pregnancy: A problem or what? *British Journal of Obstetrics and Gynaecology, 111*(8), 763–764. https://doi.org/10.1111/j.1471-0528.2004.00187.x

D'Souza, R. (2013). Caesarean section on maternal request for non-medical reasons: Putting the UK National Institute of Health and Clinical Excellence guidelines in perspective. *Best Practice Research in Clinical Obstetrics and Gynaecology, 27*(2), 165–177. https://doi.org/10.1016/j.bpobgyn.2012.09.006

Dubow, S. (2011). *Ourselves unborn: A history of the fetus in modern America.* Oxford University Press.

Duncan, L. G., Cohn, M. A., Chao, M. T., Cook, J. G., Riccobono, J., & Bardacke, D. (2017). Benefits of preparing for childbirth with mindfulness training: A randomized controlled trial with active comparison. *Pregnancy and Childbirth, 17*(40), 1–11. https://doi.org/10.1186/s12884-017-1319-3

Dunkel-Schetter, C. (2011). Psychological science on pregnancy: Stress processes, biopsychosocial models, and emerging research issues. *Annual Review of Psychology, 62*(1), 531–558. https://doi.org/10.1146/annurev.psych.031809.130727

Easterbrooks, M. A., Crossman, M. K., Caruso, A., Raskin, M., & Miranda-Julian, C. (2017). Maternal mind–mindedness and toddler behavior problems: The moderating role of maternal trauma and posttraumatic stress. *Development and Psychopathology, 29*(4), 1431–1442. https://doi.org/10.1017/S0954579417000360

Easterbrooks, M. A., Katz, R. C., & Menon, M. (2019). Adolescent parenting. In M. H. Bornstein (Ed.), *Handbook of parenting, Vol. 3. Being and becoming a parent* (3rd ed., pp. 199–231). Routledge.

Edvardsson, K., Mogren, I., Lalos, A., Persson, M., & Small, R. (2015). A routine tool with far-reaching influence: Australian midwives' views on the use of ultrasound in pregnancy. *BMC Pregnancy and Childbirth, 15*(1), 1–11. https://doi.org/10.1186/s12884-015-0632-y

Eickmeyer, K. J. (2016). *Over twenty-five years of change in men's entry into fatherhood 1987-2013*. National Center for Marriage and Family Research.

Eisert, C. (2012). Imagining a psychology of the pill: Women, experts and contraception in the 1960s. Doctoral Dissertation, Princeton University, New Jersey. http://arks.princeton.edu/ark:/88435/dsp016h440s504

Eley, V. A., Calaway, L., & van Zundert, A. A. (2015). Developments in labour analgesia and their use in Australia. *Anaesthesia Intensive Care.43*(Suppl), 12–21. https://doi.org/10.1177/0310057X150430s104

Ellis, E. (2018). *If at first you don't conceive: Your friendly guide to tackling infertility*. Pan Macmillan.

El-Thouky, T., Bhattacharya, S., & Akande, V. A. on behalf of the Royal College of Obstetricians and Gynaecologists. (2018). Multiple pregnancies following assisted conception. *BCOG An International Journal of Obstetrics and Gynaecology*, Scientific Impact Paper No 22. https://doi.org/10.1111/1471-0528.14974

Emanuel, L. (2008). Father 'there and not there': The concept of a 'united couple' in families with an unstable partnership. In L. Emanuel & E. Bradley (Eds), *What can the matter be? Therapeutic interventions with parents, infants, and young children* (pp. 187–188). Karnac Books.

Equity Economics and Development Partners. (2020). Re-imagining the potential of parents, children and Australia. https://www.theparenthood.org.au/report

Erikson, E. H. (1950). Growth and crises of the healthy personality. In M. J. E. Senn (Ed.), *Symposium on the Healthy Personality* (pp. 91–146). Josiah Macy Jr Foundation.

Erikson, E. H. (1994). *Identity and the life cycle*. W. W. Norton & Co. (This book collects three early papers that – along with *Childhood and society* – many consider the best introduction to Erikson's theories.)

Erlandsson, K., Dsilna, A., Fagerberg, I., & Christensson, K. (2007). Skin to skin care with the father after caesarean birth and its effect on newborn crying and prefeeding behaviour. *Birth, 34*(2), 105–114. https://doi.org/10.1111/j.1523-536X.2007.00162.x

Evans, A., de Lacey, S., & Tremellen, K. (2019). Australians' understanding of the decline in fertility with increasing age and attitudes towards ovarian reserve screening. *Australian Journal of Primary Health, 24*(5), 428–433. https://doi.org/10.1071/PY18040

Faircloth, C. & Gürtin, Z. B. (2018). Fertile connections: Thinking across reproductive technologies and parenting culture studies. *Sociology, 52*(5), 983–910. https://doi.org/10.1177/0038038517696219

Farr, R. H. (2016). Does parental sexual orientation matter? A longitudinal follow-up of adoptive families with school-age children. *Developmental Psychology, 53*(2), 252–264. https://doi.org/10.1037/dev0000228

Feldman, R. (2019). The social neuroendocrinology of human parenting. In M. Bornstein (Ed.), *Handbook of parenting, 3rd Edition, Vol 2 Biology and ecology of parenting* (pp. 220–249). Routledge.

Feng, W. (2017). Policy response to low fertility in China: Too little, too late? *AsiaPacific Issues, 30*(April). https://www.eastwestcenter.org/publications/policy-response-low-fertility-in-china-too-little-too-late

Fenwick, J., Toohill, J., Gamble, J., Creedy, D. K., Buist, A., Turkstra, E., Sneddon, A., Scuffham, P. A., & Ryding, C. L. (2015). Effects of a midwife psycho-education intervention to reduce childbirth fear on women's birth outcomes and postpartum psychological wellbeing. *BMC Pregnancy Childbirth, 15*(1), 284. https://doi.org/10.1186/s12884-015-0721-y

Fernyhough, C. (2008). *The baby in the mirror: A child's world from birth to three.* Granta Books.

Feugé, E. A., Cossette, L., Cyr, C., & Julien, D. (2019). Parental involvement among adoptive gay fathers: Associations with resources, time constraints, gender role and child adjustment. *Psychology of Sexual Orientation and Gender Diversity, 6*(1), 1–10. https://doi.org/10.1037/sgd0000299

Figureido, B., Canário, C., Tendais, I., Pinto, T. M., Kenny, D. A., & Field, T. (2018). Couples' relationship affects mothers' and fathers' anxiety and depression trajectories over the transition to parenthood. *Journal of Affective Disorders, 238*, 204–212. https://doi.org/10.1016/j.jad.2018.05.064

Fillo, J., Simpson, J. A., Rholes, W. S., & Kohn, J. S. (2015). Dads doing diapers: Individual and relational outcomes associated with the division of childcare across the transition to parenthood. *Journal of Personality and Social Psychology, 108*(2), 298–316. https://doi.org/10.1037/a0038572

Finer, L. B. & Zolna, M. R. (2016). Declines in unintended pregnancy in the United States, 2008–2011. *New England Journal of Medicine, 374*(9), 843–852. https://doi.org/10.1056/NEJMsa1506575

Firestone, S. (2003). *The dialectic of sex: The case for feminist revolution.* William Morrow & Company. First published in 1970.

Fishel, S. (2019). *Breakthrough babies: An IVF pioneer's tale of creating life against all odds.* Practical Inspiration Publishing.

Fisher, A. (1989). *IVF: The critical issues.* Collins Dove.

Fisher, J. R. W. & Hammarberg, K. (2012). Psychological and social aspects of infertility in men: An overview of the evidence and implications for psychologically informed clinical care and future research. *Asian Journal of Andrology, 14*(1), 121–129. https://doi.org/10.1038/aja.2011.72

Fisher, J. R. W., Hammarberg, K., & Baker, G. H. W. (2008). Antenatal mood and fetal attachment after assisted conception. *Fertility and Sterility, 89*(5), 1103–1112. https://doi.org/10.1016/j.fertnstert.2007.05.022

Fisher, J. R. W., Rowe, H., & Hammarberg, K. (2012). Admissions for early parenting difficulties among women with infants conceived by assisted reproductive technologies: A prospective cohort study. *Fertility and Sterility, 97*(6), 1410–1416. https://doi.org/10.1016/j.fertnstert.2012.02.050

Fisher, J. R. W., Wynter, K., Hammarberg, K., McBain, J., Gibson, F., Boivin, J., & McMahon, C. (2013). Age, mode of conception, health service use and pregnancy health: A prospective, cohort study of Australian women. *BMC Pregnancy and Childbirth, 13*(1), 1–13. https://doi.org/10.1186/1471-2393-13-88

Fisher, J. R. W., Acton, C., & Rowe, H. (2018). Mental health problems among childbearing women: Historical perspectives and social determinants. In M. Muzik & K.L. Rosenblum (Eds), *Motherhood in the face of trauma: Pathways towards healing and growth* (pp. 3–20). Springer International Publishing.

Fletcher, R. & StGeorge, J. (2011). Heading into fatherhood-nervously: Support for fathering from online dads. *Qualitative Health Research, 21*(8), 1101–1114. https://doi.org/10.1177/1049732311404903

Fletcher, R., Knight, T., Macdonald, J. A., & StGeorge, J. (2019). Process evaluation of text-based support for fathers during the transition to fatherhood (SMS4dads): Mechanisms of impact. *BMC Psychology, 7*(1), 1–11. https://doi.org/10.1186/s40359-019-0338-4

Fletcher, R., StGeorge, J. M., Rawlinson, C., Baldwin, A., Lanning, P., & Hoehn, E., (2020). Supporting partners of mothers with severe mental illness through text – A feasibility study. *Australasian Psychiatry, 28*(5), 548–551. https://doi.org/10.1177/1039856220917073

Forman, D. R., O'Hara, M. W., Stuart, S., Gorman, L. L., Larsen, K. E., & Coy, K. C. (2007). Effective treatment for postpartum depression is not sufficient to improve the developing mother–child relationship. *Development and Psychopathology, 19*(2), 585–602. https://doi.org/10.1017/S0954579407070289

Foster, C. (2000). The limits to low fertility: A biosocial approach. *Population and Development Review, 26*(2), 209–234. https://www.jstor.org/stable/172515

Fraiberg, S., Adelson, E., & Shapiro, V. (1975). Ghosts in the nursery: A psychoanalytic approach to impaired mother-infant relationships. *Journal of American Academy of Child Psychiatry, 14*(3), 387–421. https://doi.org/10.1016/s0002-7138(09)61442-4

Frame, T. (2008). *Children on demand: The ethics of defying nature.* University of New South Wales Press.

Freeman, T. (2014). Introduction. In T. Freeman, S. Graham, F. Ebtehaj, & M. Richards (Eds), *Relatedness in assisted reproduction: Families, origins and identities* (pp. 1–8). Cambridge University Press. http://dx.doi.org/10.1017/CBO9781139814737.001

Freud, S. (1924). The passing of the Oedipus complex. *International Journal of Psychoanalysis, 5*(4), 419–424.

Fuller-Tyszkiewicz, M., Skouteris, H., Watson, B., & Hill, B. (2012). Body image during pregnancy: An evaluation of the suitability of the Body Attitudes Questionnaire. *BMC Pregnancy and Childbirth, 12*(91). https://doi.org/10.1186/1471-2393-12-91

Gabbe, S., Niebyl, J., & Simpson, J. L. (2007). *Obstetrics: Normal and problem pregnancies.* Churchill Livingstone.

Gameiro, S. & Finnigan, A. (2017). Long-term adjustment to unmet parenthood goals following ART: A systematic review and meta-analysis. *Human Reproduction Update, 23*(3), 322–337. https://doi.org/10.1093/humupd/dmx001

Gameiro, S., Boivin, J., Peronace, L., & Verhaak, C. (2012). Why do patients discontinue fertility treatment? A systematic review of reasons and predictors of discontinuation in fertility treatment. *Human Reproduction Update, 18*(6), 652–669. https://doi.org/10.1093/humupd/dms031

García-Blanco, A., Diago, V., Hervás, D., Ghosn, F., Vento, M., & Cháfer-Pericás, C. (2018). Anxiety and depressive symptoms, and stress biomarkers in pregnant women after in vitro fertilization: A prospective cohort study. *Human Reproduction, 33*(7), 1237–1246. https://doi.org/10.1093/humrep/dey109

Gardner, J. (2019, 31 October). Because I chose a caesarean doesn't make me too posh to push. https://www.smh.com.au/lifestyle/life-and-relationships/because-i-chose-a-caesarean-doesn-t-make-me-too-posh-to-push-20191030-p535s6.html

Gartrell, N. (2020). Overview of the 35-year US National Longitudinal Lesbian Family Study and its 92% retention rate. *Journal of GLBT Family Studies, 17*(3), 197–213. https://doi.org/10.1080/1550428X.2020.1861573

Gates, G. J. (2015). Marriage and family: LGBT individuals and same-sex couples. *The Future of Children, 25*(2), 67–87. http://www.jstor.org/stable/43581973

Gerrity, D. (2001). A biopsychosocial theory of infertility. *The Family Journal, 9*(2), 151–158. https://doi.org/10.1177/1066480701092009

Gesell, A. & Ilg, F. L. (1943/1974). *Infant and child in the culture of today.* Lowe & Brydone.

Gibson, F. L., Ungerer, J. A., McMahon, C. A., Leslie, G. I., & Saunders, D. M. (2000). The mother child relationship following in vitro fertilization (IVF): Infant attachment, responsivity and maternal sensitivity. *Journal of Child Psychology and Psychiatry, 41*(8), 1015–1023. https://doi.org/10.1111/1469-7610.00689

Giesbrecht, G. F., Letourneau, N., Campbell, T., Hart, M., Thomas, J. C., Tomfohr-Madson, L., & The APrON Study Team. (2020). Parental use of 'cry-out' in a community sample during the first year of infant life. *Journal of Developmental and Behavioral Pediatrics, 41*(5), 379–387. https://doi.org/10.1097/DBP.0000000000000791

Gillespie, R. (2003). Childfree and feminine: Understanding the gender identity of voluntarily childless women. *Gender & Society, 17*(1), 122–136. https://www.jstor.org/stable/3081818

Glass, J., Simon, R. W., & Andersson, M. A. (2016). Parenthood and happiness: Effects of work-family reconciliation policies in 22 OECD countries. *The American Journal of Sociology, 122*(3), 886–929. https://doi-org.simsrad.net.ocs.mq.edu.au/10.1086/688892

Glazer, D. (2014). LGBT transitions to parenthood. *Journal of Gay & Lesbian Mental Health, 18*(2), 213–221. https://doi.org/10.1080/19359705.2014.883668

Glynn, L. M., Howland, M. A., & Fox, M. (2018). Maternal programming: Application of a development psychopathology perspective. *Development and Psychopathology, 30*(3), 905–919. https://doi.org/10.1017/S0954579418000524

Goedeke, S. & Daniels, K. (2017). We wanted to choose us: How embryo donors choose recipients for their surplus embryos. *Journal of Reproductive and Infant Psychology, 36*(2), 132–143. https://doi.org/10.1080/02646838.2018.1424324

Goldberg, W. (2014). *Father time: The social clock and the timing of parenthood.* Palgrave Macmillan.

Goldberg, A. E., Downing, J. B., & Moyer, A. M. (2012). Why parenthood, and why now? Gay men's motivations for pursuing parenthood. *Family Relations, 61*(1), 157–174. https://doi.org/10.1111/j.1741-3729.2011.00687.x

Goldfeld, S., Price, A., Smith, C., Bruce, T., Byron, H., Mensah, F., Orsini, F., Gold, L., Hiscock, H., Bishop, L., Smith, A., Perlen, S., & Kemp, L. (2019). Nurse home visiting for families experiencing adversity: A randomized trial. *Pediatrics, 143*(1), e20181206.

Goldfeld, S., Bryson, H., Mensah, F., Gold, L., Orsini, F., Perlen, S., Price, A. M., Hiscock, H., Grobler, A., Dakin, P., Bruce, T., Harris, D., & Kemp, L. (2021). Nurse home visiting and maternal mental health. *Pediatrics, 147*(2).

Goldsworthy, A. (2014). *Welcome to your new life.* Black Inc. (Schwartz Publishing)

Golombok, S. (2015). *Modern families: Parents and children in new family forms.* Cambridge University Press.

Golombok, S. (2019). Parenting and contemporary reproductive technologies. In M. H. Bornstein (Ed.), *Handbook of parenting, Vol. 3, Being and becoming a parent* (3rd Ed, pp. 482–512). Routledge.

Golombok, S. (2020). *We are family: What really matters for parents and children.* Scribe Publications.

Golombok, S., Lycett, E., MacCallum, F., Jadva, V., Murray, C., Rust, J., Abdalla, H., Jenkins, J., Margara, R., & Kazak, A. E. (2004). Parenting infants conceived by gamete donation. *Journal of Family Psychology, 18*(3), 443–452. https://doi.org/10.1037/0893-3200.18.3.44

Golombok, S., MacCallum, F., Murray, C., Lycett, E., & Jadva, V. (2005). Families created by gamete donation: Follow-up at age 2. *Human Reproduction, 20*(1), 286–293. https://doi.org/10.1093/humrep/deh585

Golombok, S., Jadva, V., Lycett, E., Murray, C., & MacCallum, F. (2006). Surrogacy families: Parental functioning, parent-child relationships and children's psychological development at age 2. by gamete donation: Follow-up at age 2. *Journal of Child Psychology and Psychiatry, 47*(2), 213–222. https://doi.org/10.1111/j.1469-7610.2005.01453.x

Golombok, S., Readings, J., Blake, L., Casey, P., Mellish, L., Marks, A., & Jadva, V. (2011). Children conceived by gamete donation: Psychological adjustment and mother-child relationships at age 7. *Journal of Family Psychology, 25*(2), 230–239. https://doi.org/10.1037/fam0000188

Golombok, S., Mellish, L., Jennings, L., Tasker, F., Casey, P., & Lamb, M. E. (2014). Adoptive gay father families: Parent-child relationships and children's psychological adjustment. *Child Development, 85*(2), 456–468. https://doi.org/10.1111/cdev.12155

Golombok, S., Zadeh, S., Imrie, S., Smith, V., & Freeman, T. (2016). Single mothers by choice: Mother-child relationships and children's psychological adjustment. *Journal of Family Psychology, 30*(4), 409–418. https://doi.org/10.1037/fam0000188

Golombok, S., Iloi, E., Blake, L., Roman, G., & Jadva, V. (2017). A longitudinal study of families formed through reproductive donation: Parent adolescent relationships and adolescent adjustment at age 14. *Developmental Psychology, 53*(10), 1966–1977. https://doi.org/10.1037/dev0000372

Goodman, S. H. & Gotlib, I. H. (2002). *Children of depressed parents: Mechanisms of risk and implications for treatment.* American Psychological Association.

Gordon, M., Gohil, J., & Banks, S. S. C. (2019). Parent training programs for managing infantile colic. *Cochrane Database of Systematic Reviews, 12*, Art no: CD012459. https://doi.or/10.1002/14651858.CD012459.pub.2

Gorman, V. (Writer and Director). *Losing Layla.* (2005). An ABC/FEC Accord documentary originally produced as an Australian Story episode ABC TV 2002; DVD includes follow-up of Raphael's first three years and the birth of their daughter, Francesca. See www.vanessagorman.com

Gorman, V. (2006). *Layla's story.* Penguin Books. First published in 2005.

Gottlieb, A. & DeLoach, J. (Eds). (2017). *A world of babies*, 2nd ed. Cambridge University Press.

Gowling, S. A., McKenzie-McHarg, K., Gordon, C., & Harrison, L. K. (2020). 'Our relationship is different': Exploring mothers' early experiences of bonding to their twins. *Journal of Reproductive and Infant Psychology, 39*(5), 475–485. https://doi.org/10.1080/02646838.2020.1726307

Grace, B., Shawe, J., Johnson, S., & Stephenson, J. (2019). You did not turn up … I did not realise I was invited … understanding male attitudes towards engagement in fertility and reproductive health discussions. *Human Reproduction Open, 2019*(3), 1–7. https://doi.org/10.1093/hropen/hoz014

Gradisar, M., Jackson, K., Spurrier, N. J., Gibson, J., Whitman, J., Sved Williams, A., Dolby, R., & Kennaway, D. J. (2016). Behavioral interventions for infant sleep problems: A randomized controlled trial. *Pediatrics, 37*(6), 1–16. https://doi.org/10.1542/peds.2015-1486

Graham, S. (2014). Stories of an absent 'father': Single women negotiating relatedness through donor profiles. In T. Freeman, S. Graham, F. Ebtehaj, & M. Richards (Eds), *Relatedness in assisted reproduction: Families, origins, and identities*, (pp. 212–231). Cambridge University Press.

Gramzow, R. H., Sedikides, C., Panter, A., & Insko, C. A. (2000). Aspects of self-regulation and self-structure as predictors of perceived emotional distress. *Personality and Social Psychology Bulletin, 26*(2), 188–205. https://doi.org/10.1177/0146167200264006

Grasso, D. J., Drury, S., Briggs-Gowan, M., Johnson, A., Ford, J., Lapidus, G., Scranton, V., Abreu, C., & Covault, J. (2020). Adverse childhood experiences, posttraumatic stress, and *FKBP5* methylation patterns in postpartum women and their newborn infants. *Psychoneuroendocrinology, 114*, 104604. https://doi.org/10.1016/j.psyneuen.2020.104604

Green, J. M., & Baston, H. A. (2003). Feeling in control during labor: Concepts, correlates, and consequences. *Birth, 30*(4), 235–247. https://doi.org/10.1046/j.1523-536x.2003.00253.x

Greenfeld, D. A. & Seli, E. (2011). Gay men choosing parenthood through assisted reproduction: Medical and psychosocial considerations. *Fertility and Sterility, 95*(1), 225–229. https://doi.org/10.1016/j.fertnstert.2010.05.053

Greer, I. A., Cameron, I. T., Magowan, B., Roberts, R. N., & Walker, J. J. (2003). *Problem-based obstetrics and gynaecology*. Churchill Livingston.

Gross, C. L. & Marcussen, K. (2017). Postpartum depression in mothers and fathers: The role of parenting expectations during the transition to parenthood. *Sex Roles, 76*(5–6), 290–305. https://doi.org/10.1007/s11199-016-0629-7

Guild, D. J., Alto, M., Handley, E., Rogosch, F., Cicchetti, D., & Toth, S. (2021). Attachment and affect between depressed mothers and their children: Longitudinal outcomes of child-parent psychotherapy. *Research on Child and Adolescent Psychopathology, 49*(5), 563–577. https://doi.org/10.1007/s10802-020-00681-0

Guzzo, K. B. & Hayford, S. R. (2020). Pathways to parenthood in social and family contexts: Decade in review, 2020. *Journal of Marriage and Family, 82*(1), 117–144. https://doi.org/10.1111/jomf.12618

Habib, C. & Lancaster, S. (2006). The transition to fatherhood: Identity and bonding in early pregnancy. *Fathering: A Journal of Theory, Research and Practice about Men as Fathers, 4*(3), 235–253. https://doi.org/10.3149/fth.0403.235

Hahn-Holbrook, J., Holt-Lunstad, J., Holbrook, C., Coyne, S. M., & Lawson, E. T. (2011). Maternal defense: Breastfeeding increases aggression by reducing stress. *Psychological Science, 22*(10), 1288–1295. https://doi.org/10.1177/0956797611420729

Hammarberg, K., Astbury, J., & Baker, H. W. G. (2001). Women's experience of IVF: A follow-up study. *Human Reproduction, 16*(2), 374–383. https://doi.org/10.1093/humrep/16.2.374

Hammarberg, K., Fisher, J. R. W., & Wynter, K. H. (2008). Psychological and social aspects of pregnancy, childbirth and early parenting after assisted conception: A systematic review. *Human Reproduction Update, 14*(5), 395–414. https://doi.org/10.1093/humupd/dmn030

Hammarberg, K., Wynter, K. H., Fisher, J. R.W., McBain, J., Gibson, F., Boivin, J., & McMahon, C. (2013). The experience of pregnancy: Does age or mode of conception matter? *Journal of Reproductive and Infant Psychology, 31*(2), 109–120. https://doi.org/10.1080/02646838.2013.782606

Hammarberg, K., Norman, R. J., Robertson, S., McLachlan, R., Michelmore, J., & Johnson, L. (2017a). Development of a health promotion programme to improve awareness of factors that affect fertility, and evaluation of its reach in the first 5 years. *Reproductive Biomedicine & Society Online, 4*, 33–40. https://doi.org/10.1016/j.rbms.2017.06.002

Hammarberg, K., Kirkman, M., Pritchard, N., Hickey, M., Peate, M., McBain, J., Agresta, F., Bayly, C., & Fisher, J. (2017b). Reproductive experiences of women who cryopreserved oocytes for non-medical reasons. *Human Reproduction, 2*(3), 575–581. https://doi.org/10.1093/humrep/dew342

Hammarberg, K., Collins, V., Holden, C., Young, K., & McLachlan, R. (2017c). Men's knowledge, attitudes and behaviours relating to fertility. *Human Reproduction Update, 23*(4), 458–480. https://doi.org/10.1093/humupd/dmx005

Hammarberg, K., Hassard, J., De Silva, R., & Johnson, L. (2020). Acceptability of screening for pregnancy intention in general practice: A population survey of people of reproductive age. *BMC Family Practice, 21*(1), [40]. https://doi.org/10.1186/s12875-020-01110-3

Hammarberg, K., Halliday, J., Kennedy, J., Burgner, D. P., Amor, D. J., Doyle, L. W., Juonala, M., Ranganathan, S., Welsh, L., Cheung, M., McLachlan, R., McBain, J., & Lewis, S. (2022). Does being conceived by assisted reproductive technology influence adult quality of life? *Human Fertility,22*, 1–7. https://doi.org/10.1080/14647273.2022.2042860

Handyside, A. H. (2020). Pre-implantation genetic testing: Thirty years of pre-implantation genetic testing. *Reproduction, 160*(5), E1–E3. https://doi.org/10.1530/REP-20-0412

Handyside, A. H., Pattinson, J. K., Penketh, R. J., Delhanty, J. D., Winston, R. M., & Tuddenham, E. G. (1989). Biopsy of human preimplantation embryos and sexing by DNA amplification. *Lancet, 18*(8634), 347–349. https://doi.org/10.1016/s0140-6736(89)91723-6

Hansen, T. (2012). Parenthood and happiness: A review of folk theories versus empirical evidence. *Social Indicators Research, 108*(1), 1–36. https://doi.org/10.1007/s11205-011-9865-y

Harper, T. S. & Gentry Barras, K. (2018). The impact of ultrasound on prenatal attachment among disembodied and embodied knowers. *Journal of Family Issues, 39*(6), 1523–1544. https://doi.org/10.1177/0192513X17710774

Harris, D. L. & Daniluk, J. C. (2010). The experience of spontaneous pregnancy loss for infertile women who have conceived through assisted reproductive technology. *Human Reproduction, 25*(3), 714–720. https://doi.org/10.1093/humrep/dep445

Hart, R. & McMahon, C. (2006). Mood state and psychological adjustment to pregnancy. *Archives of Women's Mental Health, 9*(6), 329–339. https://doi.org/10.1007/s00737-006-0141-0

Hartrick, G. A. (1997). Women who are mothers: The experience of defining self. *Health Care for Women International, 18*(3), 263–277. https://doi.org/10.1080/07399339709516280

Hayman, B., Wilkes, L., Halcomb, E., & Jackson, D. (2015). Lesbian women choosing motherhood. *Journal of GLBT Family Studies, 11*(4), 395–409. https://doi.org/10.1080/1550428X.2014.921801

Hays, S. (1998). *The cultural contradictions of motherhood.* Yale University Press.

Heideveld-Gerritsen, M., van Vulpen, M., Hollander, M., Oude Maatman, S., Ockhuijsen, H., & van den Hoogen, A. (2021). Maternity care experiences of women with physical disabilities: A systematic review. *Midwifery, 96*, 102938. https://doi.org/10.1016/j.midw.2021.102938

Heinicke, C. (2002). The transition to parenting. In M. H. Bornstein (Ed.), *Handbook of parenting, Volume II, Becoming and being a parent* (2nd ed, pp. 363–388). Lawrence Erlbaum Associates.

Hennegan, J. M., Henderson, J., & Redshaw, M. (2018). Is partners' mental health and well-being affected by holding the baby after stillbirth? Mothers' accounts from a national survey. *Journal of Reproductive and Infant Psychology, 36*(2), 120–131. https://doi.org/10.1080/02646838.2018.1424325

Hertz, R. & Nelson, M. K. (2016). Acceptance and disclosure: Comparing genetic symmetry and genetic asymmetry in heterosexual couples between egg recipients and embryo recipients. *Facts, Views & Vision in ObGyn, 8*(1), 11–22. PMID: 27822347; PMCID: PMC5096423.

Higley, E. & Dozier, M. (2009). Night-time maternal responsiveness and infant attachment at one year. *Attachment and Human Development, 11*(4), 347–363. https://doi.org/10.1080/14616730903016979

Hill, J. L. (1991). What does it mean to be a 'parent'? The claims of biology as the basis for parental rights. *New York University Law Review, 66*(2), 353–420.

Hiscock, H., Cook, F., Bayer, J., Le, H. N., Mensah, F., Cann, W., Symon, B., & St James-Roberts I. (2014). Preventing early infant sleep and crying problems and postnatal depression: A randomized trial. *Pediatrics* 133 (2): e346–e354.

Hodnett, E. D., Gates, S., Hofmeyr, G. J., & Sakala, C. (2013). Continuous support for women during childbirth. *Cochrane Database Systematic Review.* 7, CD003766. https://doi.org/10.1002/14651858.CD003766.pub5

Hoekzema, E., Barba-Mülleret, E., Pozzobon, C., Picado, M., Lucco, F., Garćia-Garćia, D., Soliva, J. C., Tobeña, A., Desco, M., Crone, E. A., Balesteros, A., Carmona, S., & Vilarroya, O. (2017). Pregnancy leads to long-lasting changes in human brain structure. *Nature Neuroscience, 20*(2), 287–296. https://doi.org/10.1038/nn.4458F

Hoffman, L. W. & Hoffman, M. L. (1973). The value of children to parents. In J. T. Fawcett (Ed.), *Psychological perspectives on population* (pp. 19–76). Basic Books.

Hogan, S. (2017). The tyranny of expectations of post-natal delight: Gendered happiness *Journal of Gender Studies, 26*(1), 45–55. https://doi.org/10.1080/0958 9236.2016.1223617

Hokke, S., Bennetts, S. K., Crawford, S., Leach, L., Hackworth, N. J., Strazdins, L., Nguyen, C., Nicholson, J. M., & Cooklin, A. R. (2020). Does flexible work 'work' in Australia? A survey of employed mothers' and fathers' work, family and health. *Community, Work & Family, 24*(4), 488–506. https://doi.org/10.10 80/13668803.2019.1704397

Holditch-Davis, D., Roberts, D., & Sandelowski, M. (1999). Early parental interactions with and perceptions of multiple birth infants. *Journal of Advanced Nursing, 30*(1), 200–210. https://doi.org/10.1046/j.1365-2648.1999.01065.x.

Hollway, W. (2016). Feminism, psychology and becoming a mother. *Feminism & Psychology*, 26(2), 137–152. https://doi.org/10.1177/0959353515625662

Horta, B. L. (2019). Breastfeeding: Investing in the future. *Breastfeeding Medicine, 14*(Suppl 1), S11–S12. https://doi.org/10.1089/bfm.2019.0032

Howarth, A. M., Scott, K. M., & Swain, N. R. (2019). First time fathers' perception of their childbirth experiences. *Journal of Health Psychology, 24*(7), 929–940. https://doi.org/10.1177/1359105316687628

Hrdy, S. B. (1999). *Mother nature: Natural selection and the female of the species.* Chatto & Windus.

Hubbard, F. O. A. & Van IJzendoorn, M. H. (1991). Maternal unresponsiveness and infant crying across the first 9 months: A naturalistic longitudinal study. *Infant Behavior and Development, 14*(3) 299–312. https://doi .org/10.1016/0163-6383(91)90024-M

Huizink, A. C., Mulder, E. J., Robles de Medina, P. G., Visser, G. H., & Buitelaar, J. K. (2004). Is pregnancy anxiety a specific syndrome? *Early Human Development, 79*(2), 81–91. https://doi.org/10.1016/j.earlhumdev .2004.04.014

Hull, E. (2022). *We've got this: Stories by disabled parents.* Black Inc.

Human Fertility and Embryology Authority (HFEA). (2018). Egg freezing in fertility treatment: Trends and figures: 2010–2016. https://www.hfea.gov.uk/

Human Fertilisation and Embryology Authority (HFEA). (2020). Fertility treatment 2018: Trends and figures. https://www.hfea.gov.uk/about-us/ publications/research-and-data/fertility-treatment-2018-trends-and-figures/

Hunter, A., Tussis, L., & MacBeth, A. (2017). The presence of anxiety, depression and stress in women and their partners during pregnancies following perinatal loss: A meta-analysis. *Journal of Affective Disorders, 223*, 153–164. https://doi .org/10.1016/j.jad.2017.07.004

Huth-Bocks, A. C., Levendosky, A. A., Bogat, A., & von Eye, A. (2004). The impact of maternal characteristics and contextual variables on infant-mother attachment. *Child Development, 75*(2), 480–497. https://doi.org/10.1111/j.1467-8624 .2004.00688.x

Huxley, A. (1932). *Brave new world.* Chatto & Windus. Republished in 1998 by HarperPerennial.

Imrie, S., Jadva, V., Fishel, S., & Golombok, S. (2019). Families created by egg donation: Parent-child relationship quality in infancy. *Child Development, 90*(4), 1333–1349. https://doi.org/10.1111/cdev.13124

Imrie, S., Jadva, V., Fishel, S., & Golombok, S. (2020). 'Making the Child Mine': Mothers' thoughts and teelings about the mother-infant relationship in egg donation families. *Journal of Family Psychology, 34*(4), 469–479. https://doi.org/10.1037/fam0000619

Inhorn, M. (2020). Where has the quest for conception taken us? Lessons from anthropology and sociology. *Reproductive Biomedicine and Society Online, 10*, 46–57. https://doi.org/10.1016/j.rbms.2020.04.001

International Labour Organisation (ILO). (2015). *Maternity, paternity at work: Baby steps achieving big results.* ILO. https://www.ilo.org/wcmsp5/groups/public/---dgreports/---gender/documents/briefingnote/wcms_410183.pdf

Jaafar, S. H., Ho, J. J., & Lee, K. S. (2016). Rooming-in for new mother and infant versus separate care for increasing the duration of breastfeeding. *Cochrane Database of Systematic Reviews, 8*, Art. No.: CD006641. https://doi.org/10.1002/14651858.CD006641.pub3

Jacob, S. (2017). Donor and recipient perspectives on embryo donation. Unpublished masters' thesis. Macquarie University, Australia.

Jaffe, J., & Diamond, M. O. (2011). *Reproductive trauma: Psychotherapy with infertility and pregnancy loss clients.* American Psychological Association. https://doi.org/10.1037/12347-000

Jansen, J., De Weerth, C., & Rikson-Walraven, M. (2008). Breastfeeding and the mother-infant relationship – A review. *Developmental Review, 28*(4), 503–521. https://doi.org/10.1016/j.dr.2008.07.001

Jones, K. (2005). The role of father in psychoanalytic theory. *Smith College Studies in Social Work, 75*(1), 7–28. https://10.1300/J497v75n01_02

Jones, J. C. (2012). Idealized and industrialized labor: Anatomy of a feminist controversy. *Hypatia, 27*(1), 99–117. https://doi.org/10.1111/j.1527-2001.2011.01217.x

Jones, R. K. & Jerman, J. (2017). Population group abortion rates and lifetime incidence of abortion: United States 2008–2014. *American Journal of Public Health, 107*(12), 1904–1909. https://doi.org/10.2105/AJPH.2017.304042

Jones, B. & McMahon, C. (2003). Social representations of stem cell research and prenatal genetic diagnosis. *Reproductive Biomedicine Online, 7*(3), 21–22. https://doi.org/10.1016/s1472-6483(10)61864-0

Kagan, K. O., Maier, V., Sonek, J., Abele, H., Lüthgens, K., Schmid, M., Wagner, P., & Hoopmann, M. (2019). False-positive rate in first-trimester screening based on ultrasound and cell-free DNA versus first-trimester combined screening with additional ultrasound markers. *Fetal Diagnosis and Therapy, 45*(5), 317–324. https://doi.org/10.1159/000489121

Karatas, J., Barlow-Stewart, K., Strong, K. A., Meiser, B., McMahon, C., & Roberts, C. (2010a). Women's experiences of pre-implantation diagnosis: A qualitative study. *Prenatal Diagnosis, 30*(8), 771–777. https://doi.org/10.1002/pd.2542

Karatas, J. C., Barlow-Stewart, K., Meiser, B., McMahon, C., Strong, K. A., Hill, W., Roberts, C., & Kelly, P. J. (2010b). A prospective study assessing anxiety, depression and maternal-fetal attachment in women using PGD. *Human Reproduction, 26*(1), 148–156. https://doi.org/10.1093/humrep/deq28l

Karp, H. (2018). *Baby bliss: Your one-stop guide to the first three months and beyond.* Penguin Books. First published in 2004.

Kassa, A.-M., Engstrand Lilja, H., & Engvall, G. (2019). From crisis to self-confidence and adaptation: Experiences of being a parent of a child with VACTERL association – A complex congenital malformation. *PLoS ONE, 14*(4), e0215751. https://doi.org/10.1371/journal.pone.0215751

Keag, O. E., Norman, J. E., & Stock, S. J. (2018). Long-term risks and benefits associated with cesarean delivery for mother, baby, and subsequent pregnancies: Systematic review and meta-analysis. *PLOS Medicine, 15*(1), e1002494. https://doi.org/10.1371/journal.pmed.1002494

Keizer, R., & Schenk, N. (2012). Becoming a parent and relationship satisfaction: A longitudinal dyadic perspective. *Journal of Marriage and Family, 74*(4), 759–773. https://doi.org/10.1111/j.1741-3737.2012.00991.x

Keller, H., Abels, M., Borke, J., Lamm, B., Su, Y., Wang, Y., & Lo, W. (2007). Socialization environments of Chinese and Euro-American middle-class babies: Parenting behaviors, verbal discourses and ethno-theories. *International Journal of Behavioral Development, 31*(3), 210–217. https://doi.org/10.1177/0165025407074633

Kenrick, D. T., Griskevicius, V., Neuberg, S. L., & Schaler, M. (2010). Renovating the pyramid of needs: Contemporary extensions built upon ancient foundations. *Perspectives on Psychological Science, 5*(3), 293–314. https://doi.org/10.1177/1745691610369469

Kersting, A. & Wagner, B. (2012). Complicated grief after perinatal loss. *Dialogues in Clinical Neuroscience, 14*(2), 187–194. https://doi.org/10.31887/DCNS.2012.14.2/akersting

Khanlari, S., Barnett, B., Ogbo, F. A., & Eastwood, J. (2019). Re-examination of perinatal mental health policy frameworks for women signalling distress on the Edinburgh Postnatal Depression Scale (EPDS) completed during their antenatal booking-in consultation: A call for population health intervention. *BMC Pregnancy and Childbirth, 19*(1), 221. https://doi.org/10.1186/s12884-019-2378-4

Kirkman, M. (2008). Being a 'real' mum: Motherhood through donated eggs and embryos. *Women's Studies International Forum, 31*(4), 241–248. https://doi.org/10.1016/j.wsif.2008.05.006

Kishi, R., McElmurry, B. J., Vonderheid, S., Altfeld, S., McFarlin, B., & Tashiro, J. (2010). Japanese women's experiences from pregnancy through early postpartum period. *Health Care for Women International, 32*(1), 57–71. https://doi.org/10.1080/07399331003728634

Kitzinger, S. (1978). *Women as mothers.* Fontana.

Kitzinger, S. (1980). *Pregnancy and childbirth.* Michael Joseph Limited.

Klaus, M. H. & Kennell, J. H. (1976). *Maternal infant bonding.* C. V. Mosby Company.

Klock, S. C. & Greenfeld, D. A. (2000). Psychological status of in vitro fertilization patients during pregnancy: A longitudinal study. *Fertility and Sterility, 73*(6), 1159–1164. https://doi.org/10.1016/S0015-0282(00)00530-6

Koert, E., & Daniluk, J. C. (2017). When time runs out: Reconciling permanent childlessness after delayed childbearing. *Journal of Reproductive and Infant Psychology, 35*(4), 342–352. https://doi.org/10.1080/02646838.2017.1320363

Kohlhoff, J., Eapen, V., Dadds, M., Khan, F., Silove, D., & Barnett, B. (2017). Oxytocin in the postnatal period: Associations with attachment and maternal caregiving. *Comprehensive Psychiatry, 76*, 56–68. https://doi.org/10.1016/j.comppsych.2017.03.010

Korja, R., Nolvi, S., Grant, K.-A., & McMahon, C. (2017). The relations between maternal prenatal anxiety or stress and the child's early self-regulation capacity – A systematic review. *Child Psychiatry and Human Development, 48*(6), 851–869. https://doi.org/10.1007/s10578-017-0709-0

Kowlessor, O., Fox, J. R., & Wittkowski, A. (2015). First-time fathers' experiences of parenting during the first postnatal year. *Journal of Reproductive and Infant Psychology, 33*(1), 4–14. https://doi.org/10.1080/02646838.2014.971404

Kubler-Ross, E. (1997). *On death and dying.* Scribner. First published in 1969.

Kukla, R. (2008). Measuring mothering. *International Journal of Feminist Approaches to Bioethics, 1*(1), 67–90. https://doi.org/10.3138/ijfab.1.1.67

Kuo, P. X., Braungart-Rieker, J. M., Lefever, J. E. B., Sarma, M. S., O'Neill, M., & Gettler, L. T. (2018). Fathers' cortisol and testosterone in the days around infants' birth predict later paternal involvement. *Hormones & Behavior, 106*, 28–34. https://doi.org/10.1016/j.yhbeh.2018.08.011

Lamaze, F. (1972). *Painless childbirth: The Lamaze method.* Pocket Books. First published in 1956.

Lamb, M. E. (2012). Mothers, fathers, families, and circumstances: Factors affecting children's adjustment. *Applied Developmental Science, 16*(2), 98–111. https://doi.org/10.1080/10888691.2012.667344

Lamb , M. E. (Ed.) (2010). *The role of the father in child development,* 5th ed. Wiley

Lamb, M., & Lewis, C. (2010). The development and significance of father-child relationships in two parent families. In M. E. Lamb (Ed.), *The role of the father in child development* (5th ed., pp. 94–153). John Wiley and Sons.

Lamba, N., Jadva, V., Kadam, K., & Golombok, S. (2018). The psychological wellbeing and prenatal bonding of gestational surrogates. *Human Reproduction, 33*(4), 646–653. https://doi.org/10.1093/humrep/dey048

Lampic, C., Skoog Svanberg, A., Sorjonen, K., Sydsjö, G. (2021). Understanding parents' intention to disclose the donor conception to their child by application of the theory of planned behaviour, *Human Reproduction, 36* (2), 395–404. https://doi.org/10.1093/humrep/deaa299

Laney, E. K., Hall, M. E. L., Anderson, T. L., & Willingham, M. M. (2015). Becoming a mother: The influence of motherhood on women's identity development. *Identity: An International Journal of Theory and Research, 15*(2), 126–145. https://doi.org/10.1080/15283488.2015.1023440

Lau Clayton, C. (2016). The lives of young fathers. A review of selected evidence. *Social Policy and Society, 15*(1), 129–140. https://doi.org/10.1017/S1474746415000470

Leach, L. S., Poyser, C., Cooklin, A. R., & Giallo, R. (2016). Prevalence and course of anxiety disorders (and symptom levels) in men across the transition to parenthood: A systematic review. *Journal of Affective Disorders, 190*, 675–686. https://doi.org/10.1016/j.jad.2015.09.063

Ledger, W. (2019). Pre-implantation genetic screening should be used in all in vitro fertilisation cycles in women over the age of 35 years AGAINST: Pre-implantation genetic screening should not be used in all IVF cycles in women over the age of 35 years. *BJOG, An International Journal of Obstetrics and Gynaecology, 126*(13), 1555. https://doi.org/10.1111/1471-0528.15942

Lee, L., McKenzie-McHarg, K., & Horsch, A. (2016). The impact of miscarriage and stillbirth on maternal–fetal relationships: An integrative review. *Journal of Reproductive and Infant Psychology, 35*(1), 32–52. https://doi.org/10.1080/02646 838.2016.1239249

Lee, W.-S., Mihalopoulos, C., Chatterton, M.-L.,·Chambers, G. M., Highet, N., Morgan, V. A., Sullivan, E. A., & Austin, M.-P. (2019). Policy impacts of the Australian National Perinatal Depression Initiative: Psychiatric admission in the first postnatal year. *Administration and Policy in Mental Health and Mental Health Services Research, 46*, 277–287. https://doi.org/10.1007/ s10488-018-0911-9

Leerkes, E. M. & Burney, R. V. (2007). The development of parenting efficacy among new mothers and fathers. *Infancy, 12*(1), 45–67. https://doi .org/10.1111/j.1532-7078.2007.tb00233.x

Leiblum, S. R., Aviv, A., & Hamer, R. (1998). Life after infertility treatment: A long-term investigation of marital and sexual function. *Human Reproduction, 13*(12), 3569–3574. https://doi.org/10.1093/humrep/13.12.3569

Leifer, M. (1977). Psychological changes accompanying pregnancy and motherhood. *Genetic Psychological Monographs, 95*(1)55–96.

LeMasters, E. E. (1957). Parenthood as crisis. *Marriage and Family Living, 19*(4), 352–355. https://doi.org/10.2307/347802

Leon, I. G. (2002). Adoption losses: Naturally occurring or socially constructed? *Child Development, 73*(2), 652–663. https://doi.org/10.1111/1467-8624.00429

Leon, I. (2008). Chapter 81. Helping families cope with perinatal loss. *The Global Library of Women's Medicine, 6*(1), 8. https://doi.org/10.3843/glowm.10418

Lerner, R. M. & Lerner, J. V. (1987). Children in their contexts: A goodness-of-fit model. In J. B. Lancaster, J. Altmann, A.S. Rossi, & L.R. Sherrod (Eds.), *Parenting across the lifespan: Biosocial dimensions* (pp. 377–404). Aldine de Gruyter.

Lester, A. (2018). A mother's lot: at last bliss gets a mention. (22 September). https://www.smh.com.au/lifestyle/life-and-relationships/a-mother-s-lot-at-last-bliss-gets-a-mention-20180918-p504ib.html

LeVine, R. A., & LeVine, S. (2017). *Do parents matter? Why Japanese babies sleep soundly, Mexican siblings don't fight, and American families should just relax.* Souvenir Press.

Levis, B., Negeri, Z., Sun, Y., Benedetti, A., & Thombs, B. D., on behalf of the DEPRESsion Screening Data (DEPRESSD) EPDS Group. (2020). Accuracy of the Edinburgh Postnatal Depression Scale (EPDS) for screening to detect major depression among pregnant and postpartum women: Systematic review and meta-analysis of individual participant data. *British Medical Journal, 371*, m4022. https://doi.org/10.1136/bmj.m4022

Life Magazine. (1965, 30 April). Foetus 18 weeks.

Life Magazine. (1969, 13 June). The life poll: Science and sex.

Lightfoot, J. (2012). *The transition to fatherhood: Attachments and adaptation.* Unpublished doctoral dissertation. Macquarie University.

Lothian, J. (2008). The journey of becoming a mother. *Journal of Perinatal Education, 17*(4), 43–47. https://doi.org/10.1624/105812408X364071

Loughnan, S. A., Butler, C., Sie, A. A., Grierson, A. B., Chen, A. Z., Hobbs, M. J., Joubert, A. E., Haskelberg, H., Mahoney, A., Holt, C., Gemmill, A. W., Milgrom, J., Austin, M.-P., Andrews, G., & Newby, J. M. (2019). A randomised controlled trial of 'MUMentum postnatal': Internet delivered cognitive and behavioural therapy for anxiety and depression in postpartum women. *Behaviour Research and Therapy, 116*, 94–103. https://doi.org.10.1016/j.brat.2019.03.001

Lowyck, B., Luyton, P., Corveleyn, J., D'Hooghe, T., Buyse, E., & Demyttenaere, K. (2009). Wellbeing and relationship satisfaction of couples dealing with in-vitro fertilization/intracytoplasmic sperm injection procedure: A multilevel approach on the role of self-criticism, dependency and romantic attachment. *Fertility and Sterility, 91*(2), 387–394. https://doi.org/10.1016/j.fertnstert.2007.11.052

Lucassen, N., Tharner, A., van IJzendoorn, M. H., Bakermans-Kranenburg, M., Volling, B. L., Verhulst, F. C., Lambregste-van den berg, F. P., & Tiemeier, H. (2011). The association between paternal sensitivity and infant-father attachment security: A meta-analysis of three decades of research. *Journal of Family Psychology, 25*(6), 986–982. https://doi.org/10.1037/a0025855

Luhmann, M., Hofmann, W., Eid, M., & Lucas, R. E. (2012). Subjective wellbeing and adaptation to life events: A meta-analysis. *Journal of Personality and Social Psychology, 102*(3), 592–615. https://doi.org/10.1037/a0025948

Lupton, D. & Barclay, L. (1997). *Constructing fatherhood: Discourses and experiences.* Sage Publications.

Lutjen, P., Trounsen, A., Leeton, J., Findlay, J., Wood, C., & Renou, P. (1984). The establishment and maintenance of pregnancy using in vitro fertilization and embryo donation in a patient with primary ovarian failure. *Nature, 397*(5947), 174–175. https://doi.org/10.1038/307174a0

Lyerly, A. D. (2022). Pregnancy and the origins of illness. *The Lancet, 399*(10323), 428–429. https://doi.org/10.1016/S0140-6736(22)00117-9

MacCallum, F. & Golombok, S. (2007). Embryo donation families: Mothers' decisions regarding disclosure of donor conception. *Human Reproduction, 22*(11), 2888–2895. https://doi.org/10.1093/humrep/dem272

MacCallum, F. & Keeley, S. (2012). Disclosure patterns of embryo donation mothers; with adoption and IVF. *Reproductive Biomedicine Online, 24*(7), 745–748. https://doi.org/10.1016/j.rbmo.2012.01.018

Maddi, S. R., Khoshaba, D. M., Harvey, R. H., Fazel, M., & Resurreccion, N. (2011). The personality construct of hardiness, V: Relationships with the construction of existential meaning in life. *Journal of Humanistic Psychology, 51*(3), 369–388. https://doi.org/10.1177/0022167810388941

Maeda, E., Sugimori, H., Nakamura, F., Kobayashi, Y., Green, J., & Suka, M. A. (2015). Cross sectional study on fertility knowledge in Japan, measured with the Japanese version of Cardiff Fertility Knowledge Scale (CFKS-J). *Reproductive Health, 12*, 10. https://reproductive-health-journal.biomedcentral.com/articles/10.1186/1742-4755-12-10

Maeda, E., Miyata, A., Boivin, J., Nomura, K., Kumazawa, Y., Shirasawa, H., Saito, H., & Terada, Y. (2020). Promoting fertility awareness and preconception health using a chatbot: A randomized controlled trial. *Reproductive Biomedicine Online, 41*(6), 1133–1143. https://doi.org/10.1016/j.

Maher, J. M. & Saugeres, L. (2007). To be or not to be a mother. *Journal of Sociology, 43*(1), 5–21. https://doi.org/10.1177/1440783307073931

Malloch, S. & Trevarthen, C. (2009). *Communicative musicality: Exploring the basis of human companionship.* Oxford University Press.

Malouf, R., Henderson, J., & Redshaw, M. (2017). Access and quality of maternity care for disabled women during pregnancy, birth and the perinatal period in England: Data from a national survey. *BMJ Open, 7*, e016757. https://doi.org/10.1136/bmjopen-2017-016757

Manne, A. (2018). Mothers and the quest for social justice. In C. Nelson & R. Robertson (Eds), *Dangerous ideas about mothers* (pp. 17–33). University of Western Australia Press.

Mansour, D., Gemzell-Danielsson, K., Inki, P., & Jensen, J. T. (2011). Fertility after discontinuation of contraception: A comprehensive review of the literature. *Contraception, 84*(5), 469–77. https://doi.org/10.1016/j.contraception.2011.04.002

Marinelli, K. A., Ball, H. L., McKenna, J. J., & Blair, P. S. (2019). An integrated analysis of maternal-infant sleep, breastfeeding, and Sudden Infant Death Syndrome research supporting a balanced discourse. *Journal of Human Lactation, 35*(3), 510–520. https://doi.org/10.1177/0890334419851797

Markin, R. (2018). 'Ghosts in the womb': A mentalizing approach to understanding and treating prenatal attachment disturbances during pregnancies after loss. *Psychotherapy, 55*(3), 275–288. https://doi.org/10.1037/pst0000186

Markin, R. D, & Zilcha-Mano, S. (2018). Cultural processes in psychotherapy for perinatal loss: Breaking the cultural taboo against perinatal grief. *Psychotherapy, 55*(1), 20–26. https://doi.org/10.1037/pst0000122

Martins, M. V., Basto-Pereira, M., Pedro, J., Peterson, B., Almeida, V., Schmidt, L., & Costa, M. E. (2016). Male psychological adaptation to unsuccessful medically assisted reproduction treatments: A systematic review. *Human Reproduction Update, 22*(4), 466–478. https://doi.org/10.1093/humupd/dmw009

Matthey, S. (2010). Are we overpathologising motherhood? *Journal of Affective Disorders, 120*(1–3), 263–266. https://doi.org/10.1016/j.jad.2009.05.004

Maute, M. & Perren, S. (2018). Ignoring children's bedtime crying: The power of western oriented beliefs. *Infant Mental Health Journal, 39*(2), 220–230. https://doi.org/10.1002/imhj.21700

Mauthner, N. S. (1999). Feeling low and feeling really bad about feeling low: Women's experiences of motherhood and postpartum depression. *Canadian Psychology/Psychologie Canadienne, 40*(2), 143–161. https://doi.org/10.1037/h0086833

Maxwell, A.-M., McMahon, C., Huber, A., Reay, R. E., Hawkins, E., & Barnett, B. (2021a). Examining the effectiveness of Circle of Security Parenting (COS-P): A multi-site non-randomized study with waitlist control. *Journal of Child and Family Studies, 40*, 1123–1140. https://doi.org/10.1007/s10826-021-01932-4

Maxwell, A.-M., Reay, R., Huber, A., Hawkins, E., Woolnough, E., & McMahon, C. (2021b). Parent and practitioner perspectives on Circle of Security Parenting (COS-P): A qualitative study, *Infant Mental Health Journal, 42*(3), 452–468. https://doi.org/10.1002/imhj.21916

McAdams, D. P. (2013). *The psychological self as actor, agent, and author. Perspectives on Psychological Science,* 8(3), 272–295. https://doi.org/10.1177/1745691612464657

McCarthy, M. & McMahon, C. (2008). Acceptance and experience of treatment for postnatal depression in a community mental health setting. *Health Care for Women International, 29*(6), 618–637. https://doi.org/10.1080/07399330802089172

McKelvey, M. M. (2014). The other mother: A narrative analysis of the postpartum experiences of nonbirth lesbian mothers. *Advances in Nursing Science, 37*(2), 101–106. https://doi.org/10.1097/ANS.0000000000000022

McMahon, C. (1997). The transition to parenthood for IVF mothers: A prospective study from pregnancy to four months postpartum. Unpublished doctoral dissertation. Macquarie University.

McMahon, C. A. & Gibson, F. L. (2002). A special path to parenthood: Parent-child relationships in families giving birth to singleton infants conceived through IVF. *Reproductive BioMedicine Online, 5*(2), 179–186. https://doi.org/10.1016/S1472-6483(10)61622-7

McMahon, C. & Saunders, D. (2009). Attitudes of couples with stored frozen embryos to conditional embryo donation. *Fertility and Sterility, 91*(1), 140–147. https://doi.org/10.1016/j.fertnstert.2007.08.04

McMahon, C. A., Ungerer, J. A., Beaurepaire, J., Tennant, C., & Saunders, D. M. (1997a). Anxiety during pregnancy and fetal attachment after IVF conception. *Human Reproduction, 12*(1), 176–182. https://10.1093/humrep/12.1.176

McMahon, C. A., Ungerer, J. A., Tennant, C., & Saunders, D. M. (1997b). Psychosocial adjustment and the quality of the mother-child relationship at four months postpartum after conception by in vitro fertilization. *Fertility and Sterility, 68*(3), 492–500. https://doi.org/10.1016/S0015-0282(97)00230-6

McMahon, C. A., Ungerer, J., Tennant, C., & Saunders, D. (1999). 'Don't count your chickens': A comparative study of the experience of pregnancy after IVF conception. *Journal of Reproductive and Infant Psychology, 17*(4), 345–356. https://doi.org/10.1080/02646839908404600

McMahon, C. A., Gibson, F., Cohen, J., Leslie, G., & Tennant, C. (2000). Mothers conceiving through in vitro fertilization: Siblings, setbacks and embryo dilemmas after five years. *Reproductive Technologies, 10*(3), 131–135. http://ezproxy.sl.nsw.gov.au/login?url=https://www.proquest.com/scholarly-journals/mothers-conceiving-through-vitro-fertilization/docview/228649423/se-2?accountid=13902

McMahon, C. A., Gibson, F. L., Leslie, G. I., Saunders, D. M., Porter, K., & Tennant, C. T. (2003a). Embryo donation for medical research: Attitudes and concerns of potential donors. *Human Reproduction, 18*(4), 871–877. https://doi.org/10.1093/humrep/deg167

McMahon, C., Gibson, F., Cohen, J., Leslie, G., & Tennant, C. (2003b). Parents of five-year old IVF children: Psychological adjustment, parenting stress and the influence of subsequent IVF treatment. *Journal of Family Psychology, 17*(3), 361–369. https://doi.org/10.1037/0893-3200.17.3.361

McMahon, C., Barnett, B., Kowalenko, N., & Tennant, C. (2005). Psychological factors associated with persistent postnatal depression: Past and current relationships, defence styles and the mediating role of an insecure attachment style. *Journal of Affective Disorders, 84*(1), 15–24. https://doi.org/doi:10.1016/j.jad.2004.05.005

McMahon, C., Boivin, J., Gibson, F. L., Hammarberg, K., Wynter, K., Saunders, D., & Fisher, J. (2011). Age at first birth, mode of conception and psychological wellbeing in pregnancy: Findings from the Parental Age and Transition to Parenthood Study Australia (PATPA). *Human Reproduction, 26*(6), 1389–1398. https://doi.org/10.1093/humrep/der076

McMahon, C. A., Boivin, J., Gibson, F. L., Hammarberg, K., Wynter, K., Saunders, D., & Fisher, J. (2013). Pregnancy specific anxiety, ART conception and infant temperament at 4 months postpartum. *Human Reproduction, 28*(4), 997–1005. https://doi.org/10.1093/humrep/det029

McMahon, C. A., Gibson, F. L., Hammarberg, K., Wynter, K., Fisher, J. R. W., & Boivin, J. (2015). Older maternal age and major depressive episodes in the first two years after birth: Findings from the Parental age and Transition to Parenthood Study. *Journal of Affective Disorders, 175*, 454–462. https://doi.org/10.1016/j.jad.2015.01.025

McSpedden, M., Mullan, B., Sharpe, L., Breen, L. J., & Lobb, E. A. (2017). The presence and predictors of complicated grief symptoms in perinatally bereaved mothers from a bereavement support organization. *Death Studies, 41*(2), 112–117. https://doi.org/10.1080/07481187.2016.1210696

Meade, C. S., Kershaw, T. S., & Ickovics, J. R. (2008). The intergenerational cycle of teenage motherhood: An ecological approach. *Health Psychology, 27*(4), 419–429. https://doi.org/10.1037/0278-6133.27.4.419

Mercer, R. T. (2004). Becoming a mother versus maternal role attainment. *Journal of Nursing Scholarship, 36*(3), 226–232. https://doi.org/10.1111/j.1547-5069.2004.04042.x

Mertes, H. (2015). Does company sponsored egg freezing promote or confine women's reproductive autonomy? *Journal of Assisted Reproductive Genetics, 32*(8) 1205–1209. https://doi.org/10.1007/s10815-015-0500-8

Mickelson, K. D. & Biehle, S. N. (2017). Gender and the transition to parenthood: Introduction to the special issue. *Sex Roles, 76*(5–6), 271–275. https://doi.org/10.1007/s11199-016-0724-9

Michaels, M. (Director). (2008). *Baby mama*. [Film] Universal Pictures.

Michaels, P. A. (2014). *Lamaze: An international history*. Oxford University Press.

Middlemiss, W., Stevens, H., Ridgway, L., McDonald, S., & Koussa, M. (2017). Response based sleep intervention: Helping infants sleep without making them cry. *Early Human Development, 108*, 49–57. https://doi.org/10.1016/j.earlhumdev.2017.03.008

Millbank, J., Stuhmcke, A., & Karpin, I. (2017). Embryo donation and understandings of kinship: The impact of law and policy. *Human Reproduction, 32*(1), 133–138. https://doi.org/10.1093/humrep/dew297

Miller, N. R., Cypher, R. L., Foglia, L. M., Pates, J. A., & Nielsen, P. E. (2015). Elective induction of labor compared with expectant management of nulliparous women at 39 weeks of gestation: A randomized controlled trial. *Obstetrics and Gynecology, 126*(6), 1258–1264. https://doi.org/10.1097/AOG.0000000000001154

Mindell, J. A., Leichman, E. S., Composto, J., Lee, C., Bulla, B., & Walters, R. M. (2016). Development of infant and toddler sleep patterns: Real-world data from a mobile application. *Journal of Sleep Research, 25*(5), 508–516. https://doi.org/10.1111/jsr.12414

Miron-Shatz, T., Holzer, H., Revel, A., Weissman, A., Tarashandegan, D., Hurwitz, A., Gal, M., Benchetrit, A., Weintraub, A., Ravhon, A., & Tsafrir, A. (2020). 'Luckily, I don't believe in statistics': Survey of women's understanding of chance of success with futile fertility treatments. *Reproductive Biomedicine Online, 2*(2), 463–470. *https://doi.org/10.1016/j.rbmo.2020.09.026 1472-6483

Mitnick, D. M., Heyman, R. E., & Smith Slep, A. M. (2009). Changes in relationship satisfaction across the transition to parenthood: A meta-analysis. *Journal of Family Psychology, 23*(6), 848–852. https://doi.org/10.1037/a0017004

Mollborn, S. & Lovegrove, P. J. (2011). How teenage fathers matter for children: Evidence from the ECLS-B. *Journal of Family Issues, 32*(1), 3–30. https://doi.org/10.1177/0192513X10370110

Möller, E. L., de Vente, W., & Rodenburg, R. (2019). Infant crying and the calming response: Parental versus mechanical soothing using swaddling, sound, and movement. *PLoS One, 14*(4), e0214548. https://doi.org/10.1371/journal.pone.0214548

Moore, T. G., Arefadh, N., Deery, A., & West, S. (2017). The first thousand days: An evidence paper. https://www.rch.org.au/uploadedFiles/Main/Content/ccchdev/CCCH-The-First-Thousand-Days-An-Evidence-Paper-September-2017.pdf

Moorthie, S., Blencowe, H., Darlison, M. W., Gibbon, S., Lawn, J. E., Mastroiacovo, P., Morris, J. K., Modell, B., & Congenital Disorders Expert Group. (2018). Chromosomal disorders: Estimating baseline birth prevalence and pregnancy outcomes worldwide. *Journal of Community Genetics, 9*(4), 377–386. https://doi.org/10.1007/s12687-017-0336-2

Morse, J. L. & Steger, M. F. (2019). Giving birth to meaning: Understanding parenthood through the psychology of meaning in life. In O. Taubman-Ben-Ari (Ed.), *Pathways and barriers to parenthood: Existential concerns regarding fertility, pregnancy and early parenthood.* Springer. https://doi .org/10.1007/978-3-030-24864-2

Moulet, C. (2005). Neither 'less' nor 'free': A long-term view of couples' experiences and construction of involuntary childlessness. Doctoral Dissertation Australian Catholic University, Victoria, ACU Research Bank https://doi .org/10.4226/66/5a94aeof5e49f

Murphy, D. A. (2013). The desire for parenthood: Gay men choosing to become parents through surrogacy. *Journal of Family Issues, 34*(8), 1104–1124. https:// doi.org/10.1177/0192513X13484272

Murray, L. & Trevarthen, C. (1986). The infant's role in mother-infant communications. *Journal of Child Language, 13*(1), 15–29. https://doi.org/10.1017/ S0305000900000271

Murray, C. & Golombok, S. (2005a). Going it alone: Solo mothers and their infants conceived by donor insemination. *The American Journal of Orthopsychiatry, 75*(2), 242–253. https://doi.org/10.1037/0002-9432.75.2.242

Murray, C. & Golombok, S. (2005b). Solo mothers and their donor insemination infants: Follow-up at age 2 years. *Human Reproduction, 20*(6), 1655–1660. https://doi.org/10.1093/humrep/deh823

Murray, L., Fearon, P., & Cooper, P. (2015). Postnatal depression, mother–infant interactions, and child development. In J. Milgrom & A.W. Gemmill (Eds), *Identifying perinatal depression and anxiety: Evidence-based practice in screening, psychosocial assessment, and management* (pp. 139–164). John Wiley & Sons, Ltd.

Murray, S. L., Seery, M. D., Lamarche, V. M., Kondrak, C., & Gomillion, S. (2019). Implicitly imprinting the past on the present: Automatic partner attitudes and the transition to parenthood. *Journal of Personality and Social Psychology: Interpersonal Relations and Group Processes, 116*(1), 69–100. https:// doi.org/10.1037/pspi0000143

Muzik, M. & Rosenblum, K. L. (Eds) (2018). *Motherhood in the face of trauma: Pathways toward healing and growth.* Springer International Publishing.

Nandi, A., Jahagirdar, D., Dimitris, M., Labrecque, J., Strumpe, E., Kaufman, J., Vincent, I., Atabay, E., Harper, S., Earle, A., & Heymann, J. (2018). The impact of parental and medical leave policies on socioeconomic and health outcomes in OECD countries: A systematic review of the empirical literature, *The Milbank Quarterly, 96*(3), 434–471. https://doi.org/10.1111/1468-0009.12340

National Institute for Health and Care Excellence [NICE]. (2014a). *Intrapartum care for healthy women and babies.* First published 3 December 2014, last updated February 2017. https://www.nice.org.uk/guidance/cg190

National Institute for Health and Care Excellence [NICE]. (2014b). *Antenatal and postnatal mental health: Clinical management and service guidance.* First published 17 December 2014, last updated February 2020. https://www.nice .org.uk/guidance/cg192

National Institute for Health and Care Excellence [NICE]. (2021a). *Antenatal Care*. Published: 19 August 2021. https://www.nice.org.uk/guidance/ng201

National Institute for Health and Clinical Excellence [NICE]. (2021b). *Caesarean birth*. First published March 2021. https://www.nice.org.uk/guidance/ng192/

Nelson, C. & Robertson, R. (Eds) (2018). *Dangerous ideas about mothers*. University of Western Australia Publishing.

Nelson, S. K., Kushlev, K., & Lyubomersky, S. (2014). The pains and pleasures of parenting: When, why, and how is parenthood associated with more or less wellbeing? *Psychological Bulletin, 140*(3), 846–895. https://doi.org/10.1037/a0035444

Nešporová, O. (2018). Hazy transition to fatherhood: The experiences of Czech fathers. *Journal of Family Issues, 40*(2), 143–146. https://doi.org/10.1177/0192513X18806028

Neugarten, B. L. (1979). Time, age and the life cycle. *The American Journal of Psychiatry, 136*(7), 887–894. https://doi.org/10.1176/ajp.136.7.887

Newman, J. E., Paul, R. C., & Chambers, G. M. (2021). *Assisted reproductive technology in Australia and New Zealand 2019*. National Perinatal Epidemiology and Statistics Unit, the University of New South Wales Sydney.

Nilsson, L., Ingel-man-Sundberg, A., & Wirsén, C. (1965). *A child is born: The drama of life before birth in unprecedented photographs; A practical guide for the expectant mother*. Dell Publishing.

Noble, E. (1983). *Childbirth with insight*. Houghton Miflin Company.

Nordqvist, P. & Smart, C. (2014). *Relative strangers: Family life, genes and donor conception*. Palgrave Macmillan.

Norholt, H. (2020). Revisiting the roots of attachment: A review of the biological and psychological effects of maternal skin-to-skin contact and carrying of full-term infants. *Infant Behavior and Development, 60*, https://doi.org/10.1016/j.infbe3h.2020.101441

Nomaguchi, K. M. & Milkie, M. A. (2020). Parenthood and wellbeing: A decade in review. *Journal of Marriage and Family, 82*(1), 198–223. https://doi.org/10.1111/jomf.12646

Nuffield Council on Bioethics. (2013). *Donor conception: Ethical aspects of information sharing*. Nuffield Council on Bioethics.

Oakley, A. (1986). *From here to maternity*. Penguin Books. First published under the title *Becoming a mother* by Martin Robinson, 1979.

Oates, M. (2002). Adverse effects of maternal anxiety on children: Causal effect or developmental continuum. *British Journal of Psychiatry, 180*(6), 478–479. https://doi.org/10.1192/bjp.180.6.478

Ockhuijsen, H. D. L., van den Hoogan, A., Boivin, J., Macklon, N. S., & de Boer, F. (2014). Pregnancy after miscarriage: Balancing between loss of control and searching for control. *Research in Nursing and Health, 37*(4), 267–275. https://doi.org/10.1002/nur.21610

O'Connor, E., Rossom, R. C., Henninger, M., Groom, H. C., & Burda, B. U. (2016). Primary care screening for and treatment of depression in pregnant and postpartum women. *Journal of the American Medical Association, 315*(4), 388–406. https://doi.org/10.1001/jama.2015.18948

Odent, M. (1994). *Birth reborn: What childbirth should be.* Profile Books. First published in 1984.

O'Hara, M. W. & Wisner, K. L. (2013). Perinatal mental illness: Definition, description and aetiology, *Clinical Obstetrics & Gynaecology, 28*(1), 3–12. https://doi.org/10.1016/j/bpobgyn.2013.09.002

Olds, D. (2016). Building evidence to improve maternal and child health. *Lancet, 387*(10014), 105–107. https://doi.org/10.1016/S0140-6736(15)00476-6

O'Leary, M. (2004). Grief and its impact on prenatal attachment in the subsequent pregnancy. *Archives of Women's Mental Health, 7*(1), 7–18. https://doi.org/10.1007/s00737-003-0037-1

Ombelet, W. & Goossens, J. (2017). Global reproductive health – Why do we persist in neglecting the undeniable problem of childlessness in resource-poor countries? *Facts, Views, and Vision in Obgyn, 9*(1), 1–3. https://www.ncbi.nlm.nih.gov/pmc/articles/PMC5506764/

Organisation for Economic Co-Operation and Development. (2019). Information drawn from the OECD family database. http://www.oecd.org/els/family/database.htm

Osborne, L. M. (2018). Recognizing and managing postpartum psychosis: A clinical guide for obstetric providers. *Obstetric and Gynecological Clinics of North America, 45*(3), 455–468. https://doi.org/10.1016/j.ogc.2018.04.005

Oster, E. (2019). *Expecting better.* Penguin Books. First published in 2013.

Osterman, M. J. K. & Martin, J. A. (2014). *Recent declines in induction of labor by gestational age.* NCHS data brief, no 155. National Center for Health Statistics. https://www.cdc.gov/nchs/data/databriefs/db155.pdf

Padovani, F. H. P., Carvalho, A. E. V., Duarte, G., Martinez, F. E., & Linhares, M. B. N. (2009). Anxiety, dysphoria and depression symptoms in mothers of preterm infants. *Psychological Reports, 104*(2), 667–679. https://doi.org/10.2466/PRO.104.2.667-679

Palacios, J. & Brodzinsky, D. (2010). Review: Adoption research: Trends, topics, outcomes. *International Journal of Behavioral Development, 34*(3), 270–284. https://doi.org/10.1177/0165025410362837

Palermo, G., Joris, H., Devroey, P., & Van Steirteghem, A. C. (1992). Pregnancies after intracytoplasmic injection of single spermatozoon into an oocyte. *Lancet, 340*(8810), 17–18. https://doi.org/10.1016/0140-6736(92)92425-f

Palkowitz, R. (2002). *Involved fathering and men's adult development: Provisional balances.* Lawrence Erlbaum.

Palkovitz, R. (2007). Challenges to modelling dynamics in developing a developmental understanding of father-child relationships. *Applied Developmental Science, 11*(4), 190–195. https://doi.org/10.1080/10888690701762050

Papousek, M. & von Hofacker, N. (1998). Persistent crying in early infancy: A non-trivial condition of risk for the developing mother-infant relationship. *Child: Care, Health and Development, 24*(5), 395–424. https://doi.org/10.1046/j.1365-2214.2002.00091.x

Paquette, D. (2004). *Theorizing the father-child relationship: Mechanisms and developmental outcomes. Human Development,* 47(4), 193–219. https://doi .org/10.1159/000078723

Paranjothy, S., Broughton, H., Adappa, A., & Fone, D. (2009). Teenage pregnancy: Who suffers? *Archives of Disease in Childhood,* 94(3), 239–245. http:// dx.doi.org/10.1136/adc.2007.115915

Parikh, N. M. (1999). Cultural expectations from IVF and reproductive genetics in India. In R. Jansen & D. Mortimer (Eds), *Towards reproductive certainty: Fertility and Genetics beyond 1999.* The Plenary Proceedings of the 11th World Congress on In Vitro Fertilization & Human Reproductive Genetics (pp. 441–447). The Parthenon Publishing Group.

Parke, R. D. & Cookston, J. T. (2019). Fathers and families. In M. H. Bornstein (Ed.), *Handbook of parenting, Vol. 3. Being and becoming a parent* (3rd ed., pp. 64–136). Routledge.

Patnaik, A. (2019). Reserving time for daddy: The short and long-run consequences of fathers' quotas. *Journal of Labor Economics,* 37(4), 1009–1059. doi: 10.1086/703115

Patterson, C. J. (2019). Lesbian and gay parenthood. In M. H. Bornstein (Ed.), *Handbook of parenting, Vol. 3. Being and becoming a parent* (3rd ed., pp. 345–371). Routledge.

Patterson, C. J., Riskind, R. G., & Tornello, S. L. (2014). Sexual orientation, marriage and parenthood: A global perspective. In A. Abela & J. Walker (Eds.), *Contemporary issues in family studies: Global perspectives on partnerships, parenting and support in a changing world* (pp. 189–202). Wiley-Blackwell.

Paulson, J. F. & Bazemore, F. D. (2010). Prenatal and postpartum depression in fathers and its association with maternal depression: A meta-analysis. *Journal of American Medical Association,* 303(19), 1961–1969. https://doi.org/10.1001/ jama.2010.605

Petre, D. (2016). *Father time: Making time for your children.* Ventura Press. First published in 1998.

Pleck, E. (2004). Two dimensions of fatherhood: A history of the good dad-bad dad complex. In M. E. Lamb (Ed.), *The role of the father in child development* (4th ed., pp. 32–57). John Wiley & Sons.

Pleck, J. H. (2012). Integrating father involvement in parenting research. *Parenting,* 12(2–3), 243–253. https://doi.org/10.1080/15295192.2012.683365

Polyakov, A. & Rozen, G. (2021). Social egg freezing: Waste not, want not. *Journal of Medical Ethics.* 47(12), 1–6. https://doi.org/10.1136/medethics-2020-106607

Powell, B., Cooper, G., Hoffman, K., & Marvin, B. (2014). *The circle of security intervention: Enhancing attachment in early parent-child relationships.* Guilford Press.

Practice Committee of American Society for Reproductive Medicine in Collaboration with Society for Reproductive Endocrinology and Infertility. (2017). Optimizing natural fertility: A committee opinion. *Fertility and Sterility,* 107(1), 52–58. https://doi.org/10.1016/jfertnstert.2016.09.029

Practice Committee of the Society for Reproductive Endocrinology and Infertility, Quality Assurance Committee of the Society for Assisted Reproductive Technologies, and the Practice Committee of the American Society for Reproductive Medicine (ASRM). (2022). Multiple gestation associated with infertility therapy: A committee opinion. https://doi.org/10.1016/j .fertnstert.2021.12.016

Preisner, K., Neuberger, F., Bertogg, K., & Schaub, J. M. (2020). Closing the happiness gap: The decline of gendered parenthood norms and the increase in parental life satisfaction. *Gender & Society, 34*(1), 31–35. https://doi .org/10.1177/0891243219869365

Prior, S. (2022). *Childless: A story of freedom and longing.* Text Publishing.

Prior, E., Lew, R., Hammarberg, K., & Johnson, L. (2019). Fertility facts, figures and future plans: An online survey of university students. *Human Fertility, 22*(4), 283–290. https://doi:10.1080/14647273.2018.1482569

Provoost, V., Pennings, G., de Sutter, P., Van der Veldt, A., & Dhont, M. (2012). Trends in embryo disposition decisions: Patients' responses to a 15-year mailing program. *Human Reproduction, 27*(2), 506–514. https://doi.org/10.1093/ humrep/der419

Putnam, S. P., Sanson, A. V., & Rothbart, M. K. (2002). Child temperament and parenting. In M. H. Bornstein (Ed.), *Handbook of parenting, Vol 1, children and parenting* (2nd ed., pp. 255–277). Lawrence Erlbaum.

Rafferty, E. (2017). From cultural revolution to childcare revolution: Conflicting advice on childrearing in contemporary China. In A. Gottlieb & J. DeLoach (Eds), *A world of babies* (2nd ed., pp. 71–92). Cambridge University Press.

Raphael-Leff, J. (2005). *Psychological processes of childbearing.* Anna Freud Centre. First published in 1991.

Raymer, J., Guan, Q., Norman, R. J., Ledger, W., & Chambers, G. M. (2020). Projecting future utilization of medically assisted fertility treatments. *Population Studies, 74*(1), 23–38. https://doi.org/10.1080/00324728.2019.1676461

Redshaw, M., Hennegan, J., & Henderson, J. (2016). Impact of holding the baby following stillbirth on maternal mental health and well-being: Findings from a national survey. *British Medical Journal Open, 6*(8), e010996. https://doi .org/10.1136/bmjopen-2015-010996

Redshaw, M., Hennegan, J., & Kruske, S. (2014). Holding the baby: Early mother–infant contact after childbirth and outcomes. *Midwifery, 30*(5), e177–e187. https://doi.org/10.1016/j.midw.2014.02.003

Reitman, J. (Director). (2007). *Juno.* [Film] Fox Searchlight Pictures.

Rholes, W. S. & Paetzold, R. L. (2019). Attachment and the transition to parenthood. In O. Taubman-Ben-Ari (Ed.), *Pathways and barriers to parenthood: Existential concerns regarding fertility, pregnancy and early parenthood* (pp. 291–305). Springer. https://doi.org/10.1007/978-3-030-24864-2

Rholes, W. S., Simpson, J. A., & Friedman, M. (2006). Avoidant attachment and the experience of parenting. *Personality and Social Psychology Bulletin, 32,* 275–285. https://doi.org/10.1177/0146167205280910

Rich, A. (1986). *Of woman born: Motherhood as experience and institution.* W. W. Norton & Co. First published in 1976.

Riggs, D. W. & Bartholomaeus, C. (2018). 'It's just what you do': Australian middle-class heterosexual couples negotiating compulsory parenthood. *Feminism & Psychology, 28*(3), 373–389. https://doi.org/10.1177/0959353516675637

Rijken, A. J. & Merz, E. (2014). Double standards: Differences in norms on voluntary child-lessness for men and women. *European Sociological Review, 30*(4), 470–482. https://doi.org/10.1093/esr/jcu051

Rizvi, J. (2015, 19 November). *Right now, a hug is all it takes to make my son better.* https://www.mamamia.com.au/coping-with-motherhood/

Rizvi, J. (Ed.) (2018). *The motherhood.* Penguin Australia.

Robinson, M., Baker, L., & Nackerud, L. (1999). The relationship of attachment theory and perinatal loss. *Death Studies, 23*(3), 257–270. https://doi.org/10.1080/074811899201073

Roggman, L. A. (2004). Do fathers just want to have fun? Commentary on the father child relationship. *Human Development, 47*(4), 228–236. https://doi.org/10.1159/000078725

Romanis, E. C. (2018). Artificial womb technology and the frontiers of human reproduction: Conceptual differences and potential implications. *Journal of Medical Ethics, 44*(11), 751–755. http://dx.doi.org/10.1136/medethics-2018-104910

Rosario, M., Scrimshaw, E. W., Hunter, J., & Levy-Warren, A. (2009). The coming out dynamic of young lesbian and bisexual women: Are there butch/femme differences in sexual identity development? *Archives of Sexual Behavior, 38*(1), 37–49. https://doi.org/10.1007/s10508-007-9221-0

Rothbart, M. K. (2011). *Becoming who we are: Temperament and personality in development.* Guilford Press.

Rothman, B. K. (1986/1993). *The tentative pregnancy: How amniocentesis changes the experience of motherhood.* WW. Norton & Company. First published in 1986.

Rotkirch, A. (2007). All that she wants is a(nother) baby: Longing for children as a fertility incentive of growing importance. *Journal of Evolutionary Psychology, 5*(1), 89–104. https://doi.org/10.1556/jep.2007.1010

Rouchou, B. (2013). Consequences of infertility in developing countries. *Perspectives in Public Health, 133*(3), 174–179. https://www.tandfonline.com/loi/uajb20

Rowe, H., Holton, S., & Fisher, J. R. W. (2013). Postpartum emotional support: A qualitative study of women's and men's needs and preferred sources. *Australian Journal of Primary Health, 19*(1), 46–52. https://doi.org/10.1071/PY11117

Rowe, H. J., Wynter, K. H., Burns, J. K., & Fisher, J. R. W. (2017). A complex postnatal mental health intervention: Australian translational formative evaluation. *Health Promotion International, 32*(4), 610–623. https://do.org/10.1093/heapro/dav110

Royal College of Obstetricians and Gynaecologists (2010). Termination of pregnancy for fetal abnormality in England, Scotland, and Wales: Report of a Working Party. https://www.rcog.org.uk/media/21lfvloe/terminationpregnancyreport18may2010.pdf

Rubin, R. (1984). *Maternal identity and the maternal experience.* Springer.

Rubin, S. S. & Malkinson, R. (2001). Parental response to child loss across the life cycle: Clinical and research perspectives. In M.S. Stroebe, R.O. Hansson, W. Stroebe, & H. Schut (Eds), *Handbook of bereavement research* (pp. 219–240). American Psychological Association.

Ruffell, D., Smith, D. M., & Wittkowski, A. (2019). The experiences of male partners of women with postnatal mental health problems: A systematic review and thematic synthesis. *Journal of Child and Family Studies, 28,* 2772–2790. https://doi.org/10.1007/s10826-019-01496-4

Salleh, A. (2019). 'Egg timer test' at centre of new IVF conflict of interest claims. ABC News. https://www.abc.net.au/news/science/2019-02-07/egg-timer-test-and-ivf-industry-conflict-of-interest-claims/10781714

Sandelowski, M. (1987). The color gray: Ambiguity and infertility. *Image: Journal of Nursing Scholarship, 19*(2), 70–74. https://doi.org/10.1111/j.1547-5069.1987.tb00594

Sandelowski, M., Harris, B., & Black, B. (1992). Relinquishing infertility: The work of pregnancy for infertile couples. *Qualitative Health Research, 2,* 282–1301. https://doi.org/10.1177/104973239200200303

Sandelowski, M., Harris, B. G., & Holditch-Davis, D. (1993). 'Somewhere out there': Parental claiming in the preadoption waiting period. *Journal of Contemporary Ethnography, 21*(4), 464–486. https://doi.org/10.1177/089124193021004003

Saxbe, D. E. (2017). Birth of a new perspective? A call for biopsychosocial research on childbirth. *Current Directions in Psychological Science, 26*(1), 81–86. https://doi.org/10.1177/0963721416677096

Saxbe, D., Rossin-Slater, M., & Goldenberg, D. (2018). The transition to parenthood as a critical window for adult health. *American Psychologist, 73*(9), 1190–1200. http://dx.doi.org/10.1037/amp0000376

Schmidt, R. M., Wiemann, C. M., Rickert, V. I., & O'Brian Smith, E. (2006). Moderate to severe depressive symptoms among adolescent mothers followed four years postpartum. *Journal of Adolescent Health, 38*(6), 712–718. https://doi.org/10.1016/j.adohealth.2005.05.023

Schurr, C. (2018). The baby business booms: Economic geographies of assisted reproduction. *Geography Compass, 12*(8), e12395. https://doi.org/10.1111/gec3.12395

Scism, A. R. & Cobb, R. L. (2017). Integrative review of factors and interventions that influence early father-infant bonding. *Journal of Obstetric and Gynecological Neonatal Nursing, 46*(2), 163–170. http://dx.doi.org/10.1016/j.jogn.2016.09.

Sedgmen, B., McMahon, C., Cairns, D., Benzie, R., & Woodfield, R. (2006). The impact of two-dimensional vs. three-dimensional ultrasound exposure on maternal-fetal attachment and health behaviours in pregnancy. *Ultrasound in Obstetrics and Gynecology, 27*(3), 245–251. https://doi.org/10.1002/uog.2703

Sellenet, C. (2005). *Les pères vont bien! Comment les hommes affirment et assument aujourd'hui leur paternité.* Flammarion.

Senior, J. (2015). *All joy and no fun: The paradox of modern parenthood.* Ecco.

Sharma, M. (2008). Twenty-first century pink or blue: How sex selection technology facilitates gendercide and what we can do about it. *Family Court Review, 46*(1), 198–215. https://doi.org/0.1111/j/1744-1617.2007.00192

Sharma, R., Biedenharn, K. R., Fegor, J. M., & Argawal, A. (2013). Lifestyle factors and reproductive health: Taking control of your fertility. *Reproductive Biology and Endocrinology, 11*(66), http://www.rbej.com/content/11/1/66

Shaw, R. L. & Giles, D. C. (2009). Motherhood on ice? A media framing analysis of older mothers in the UK news. *Psychology & Health, 24*(2), 221–236. https://doi.org/10.1080/08870440701601625

Sheeran, N., Jones, L., Bernardin, S., Wood, M., & Doherty, L. (2021). Immoral, incompetent, and lacking warmth: How stereotypes of teenage fathers compare to those of other parents. *Sex Roles, 84*(1), 360–375. https://doi.org/10.1007/s11199-020-01172-8

Shenkman, G. & Shmotkin, D. (2014). 'Kids are joy': Psychological welfare amongst gay Israeli fathers. *Journal of Family Issues, 35*(14), 1926–1939. https://doi.org/10.1177/0192513X13489300

Shereshefsky, P. M. & Yarrow, L. J. (1973). *Psychological aspects of a first pregnancy and postnatal adaptation.* Raven Press.

Sheridan, G. & Bain, K. (2020). Living the theory: The complexity of being both a psychodynamic psychotherapist and a mother. *Contemporary Psychoanalysis, 56*(1), 29–56. https://doi.org/10.1080/00107530.2020.1716842

Shonkoff, J. P. & Fisher, P. A. (2013). Rethinking evidence-based practice and two-generation programs to create the future of early childhood policy. *Development and Psychopathology, 25*(4 Pt 2), 1635–1653. https://doi.org/10.1017/S0954579413000813

Shorey, S., Peng Mei Ng, Y., Ng, E. D., Siew, A. L., Mörelius, E., Yoong, J., & Gandhi, M. (2019). Effectiveness of a technology-based supportive educational parenting program on parental outcomes (part 1): Randomized controlled trial. *Journal of Medical Internet Research, 21*(2): e10816. http://www.jmir.org/2019/2/e10816/

Siddiqui, A. & Hägglöf, B. (2000). Does maternal prenatal attachment predict postnatal mother–infant interaction? *Early Human Development, 59*(1), 13–25. https://doi.org/10.1016/S0378-3782(00)00076-1

Skandrani, S., Harf, A, & El Husseini, M. (2019). The impact of children's preadoptive traumatic experiences on parents. *Frontiers in Psychiatry, 18*(10), 866. https://doi.org/10.3389/fpsyt.2019.00866

Slade, A., Cohen, L. J., Sadler, L. S., & Miller, M. (2009). The psychology and psychopathology of pregnancy: Reorganization and transformation. In C. H. Zeanah Jnr (Ed.), *Handbook of infant mental health* (3rd ed., pp. 22–39). The Guilford Press.

Smith, H. (2018). Feisty and childfree. In C. Nelson & R. Robertson (Eds.) *Dangerous ideas about mothers* (pp. 137–147). University of Western Australia Publishing.

Smith, I., Knight, T., Fletcher, R., & Macdonald, J. A. (2019). When men choose to be childless: An interpretative phenomenonological analysis. *Journal of Social and Personal Relationships, 37*(1), 325–344. https://doi.org/10.1177/0265407519864444

Snell, W. E., Overbey, G. A., & Brewer, A. L. (2005). Parenting perfectionism and the parenting role. *Personality and Individual Differences, 39* (3), 613–624. https://doi.org/10.1016/j.[aod/2005.02.006

Söderström-Anttila, V., Wennerholm, U. B., Loft, A., Pinborg, A., Aittomaki, K., Romundstad, L. B., & Bergh, C. (2016). Surrogacy: Outcomes for surrogate mothers, children and the resulting families – A systematic review. *Human Reproduction Update, 22*(2), 260–276. https://doi.org/10.1093/humupd/dmv046

Solchany, J. E. (2000). The nature of mothers' developing relationships with their internationally adopted Chinese daughters. Unpublished doctoral dissertation, University of Washington. *Dissertation Abstracts International, 61*, 2994.

Souch, A.J., Jones, I. R., Shelton, K. H. M., & Waters, C. S. (2022). Maternal child maltreatment and perinatal outcomes: A systematic review. *Journal of Affective Disorders, 302*, 139–159. https://doi.org/10.1016/j.jad.2022.01.062

Sousa-Leite, M., Figueredo, B., ter Koerst, A., Boivin, J., & Gameiro, S. (2019). Women's attitudes and beliefs about using fertility preservation to prevent age-related fertility decline – A two-year follow-up. *Patient Education and Counselling, 102*(9), 1695–1702. https://doi.org/10.1016/j.pec.2019.03.019

Steptoe, P. C. & Edwards, R. G. (1978). Birth after the reimplantation of a human embryo. *Lancet, 2*, 383–5.

Stern, D. (2018). *The interpersonal world of the infant.* Routledge. First published in 1985.

Stoop, D., Cobo, A., & Silber, S. (2014). Fertility preservation for age-related fertility decline. *The Lancet, 384*(9950), 1311–1319. https://doi.org/10.1016/S0140-6736(14)61261-7

St James-Roberts, I. (2007). Helping parents to manage infant crying and sleeping: A review of the evidence and its implications for services. *Child Abuse Review, 16*(1), 47–69. https://doi.org/10.1002/car.968

St James-Roberts, I. (2008). Infant crying and sleeping: Helping parents to prevent and manage problems. *Primary Care: Clinics in Office Practice, 35*(3), 547–567. https://doi.org/10.1016.j.pop.2008.06.004

St James-Roberts, I., Conroy, S., & Wilsher, K. (1998). Links between maternal care and persistent infant crying in the early months. *Child Care, Health and Development, 24*(5), 353–376. https://doi.org/info:doi/10.1046/j.1365-2214.2002.00089.x

St James-Roberts, I., Alvarez, M., Csipke, E., Abramsky, T., Goodwin, J., & Sorgenfrei, E. (2006). Infant crying and sleeping in London, Copenhagen and when parents adopt a 'proximal' form of care. *Pediatrics, 117*(6), e1146–e1155. https://doi.org/10.1542/peds.2005-2387

St James Roberts, I., Roberts, M., Hovish, K., & Owen, C. (2015). Video evidence that London infants can resettle themselves back to sleep after waking in the night, as well as sleep for long periods, by 3 months of age. *Journal of Developmental and Behavioral Pediatrics, 36*(5), 324–329. https://doi.org/10.1097/DBP.0000000000000166

Stroebe, M. S., Folkman, S., Hanssen, R. O., & Schut, H. (2006). Prediction of bereavement outcome: The development of an integrative risk factor framework bereavement. *Social Science & Medicine*, 63(9), 2440–2451. https://doi.org/10.1016/j.socscimed.2006.06.012

Sturrock, R. (2020). *Man raises boy*. Allen & Unwin.

Sussman, A. L. (2019, 19 November). The end of babies. *New York Times*. https://www.nytimes.com/interactive/2019/11/16/opinion/sunday/capitalism-children.html

Swain, J. E., Kim, P., Spicer, J., Ho, S. S., Dayton, C. J., Elmadih, A., & Abel, K. M. (2014). Approaching the biology of human parental attachment: Brain imaging, oxytocin and coordinated assessments of mothers and fathers. *Brain Research*, 11, 78–101. https://doi.org/10.1016/j.brainres.2014.03.007

Taft, A. J., Shankar, M., Black, K. I., Mazza, D., Hussainy, S., & Lucke, J. C. (2018). Unintended and unwanted pregnancy in Australia: A cross-sectional, national random telephone survey of prevalence and outcomes. *Medical Journal of Australia*, 209(9), 407–408. https://doi.org/10.5694/mja17.01094

Taubman-Ben-Ari, O. (2019). *Pathways and barriers to parenthood: Existential concerns regarding fertility, pregnancy and early parenthood*. Springer

Taubman-Ben-Ari, O., Schlomo, S. B., Sivan, E., & Dolizki, M. (2009). The transition to motherhood – A time for growth. *Journal of Social and Clinical Psychology*, 28(8), 943–970. https://doi.org/10.1521/jscp.2009.28.8.943

Thomas, G. M., Lupton, D., & Pedersen, S. (2018), 'The appy for a happy pappy': Expectant fatherhood and pregnancy apps. *Journal of Gender Studies*, 27(7), 759–770. https://doi.org/10.1080/09589236.2017.1301813

Thomas, J., Harraway, J., & Kirchhoffer, D. (2021). Non-invasive prenatal testing: Clinical utility and ethical concerns about recent advances. *Medical Journal of Australia*, 214(4), 168–170, https://doi.org/10.5694/mja2.50928

Todd, S., & Jones, S. (2003). 'Mum's the word!': Maternal accounts of dealing with the, professional world. *Journal of Applied Research in Intellectual Disabilities*, 16(3), 229–244. https://doi.org/10.1046/j.1468-3148.2003.00163.x

Tornello, S. L., Riskind, R. G., & Babić, A. (2019). Transgender and gender nonbinary parents' pathways to parenthood. *Psychology of Sexual Orientation and Gender Diversity*, 6(2), 232–241. https://doi.org/10.1037/sgd0000323

Tresillian. (2018). *The Tresillian sleep book*. ABC Books, Harper Collins Publishers.

Trounson, A. & Mohr, L. (1983). Human pregnancy following cryopreservation, thawing and transfer of an eight-cell embryo. *Nature*, 305(5936), 707–709. https://doi.org/10.1038/305707a0

Turton, P., Badenhorst, W., Pawlby, S., White, S., & Hughes, P. (2009). Psychological vulnerability in children next-born after stillbirth: A case–control follow-up study. *Journal of Child Psychology and Psychiatry*, 50(12), 1451–1458. https://doi.org/10.1111/j.1469-7610.2009.02111.x

Tymstra, T. (1989). The imperative character of medical technology and the meaning of anticipated decision regret. *International Journal of Technology Assessment in Health Care*, 5(2), 207–213. https://doi.org/10.1017/S0266462300006437

Ulrich, D., Gagel, D. E., Hemmerling, A., Pastor, V.-S., & Kentenich, H. (2004). Couples becoming parents: Something special after IVF? *Journal of Psychosomatic Obstetrics & Gynecology, 25*(2), 99–113. https://doi .org/10.1080/17402520400004599

US Department of Health and Human Services. (2021). Home visiting evidence of effectiveness. https://homvee.acf.hhs.gov/sites/default/files/2020-12/ HomVEE_Summary_Brief.pdf

Vandell, D. L., Belsky, J., Burchinal, M., Steinberg, L., Vandergrift, N., & NICHD Early Child Care Research Network. (2010). Do effects of early childcare extend to age 15 years? Results from the NICHD Study of Early Childcare and Youth Development. *Child Development, 81*(3), 737–756. https://doi .org/10.1111/j/1467-8624.2010.01431.x

van den Akker, O. B. A. (2007). Psychological aspects of surrogate motherhood. *Human Reproduction Update, 13*(8), 53–62. https://doi.org/10.1093/humupd/ dml039

van den Akker, O. B. A. (2017). Surrogate mothers. In *Surrogate motherhood families (pp. 79–117).* Palgrave Macmillan. https://doi.org/10.1007/978-3-319-60453-4_4

van der Gaag, N., Heilman, B., Gupta, T., Nembhard, C., & Barker, G. (2019). *State of the world's fathers: Unlocking the power of men's care.* Promundo-US.

Vaughan, D. A., Cleary, B. J., & Murphy, D. J. (2014). Delivery outcomes for nulliparous women at the extremes of maternal age – A cohort study. *BJOG: An International Journal of Obstetrics & Gynaecology, 121*(3), 261–268.

Verhage, M. L., Schuengel, C., Madigan, S., Fearon, R., Oosterman, M., Cassibba, R., Bakermans-Kranenburg, M. J., & van IJzendoorn, M. H. (2016). Narrowing the transmission gap: A synthesis of three decades of research on intergenerational transmission of attachment. *Psychological Bulletin, 142*(4), 337–366. https://doi.org/10.1037/bul0000038

Wadwa, P. D., Sandman, C. A., & Garite, T. J. (2001). Chapter 9 The neurobiology of stress in human pregnancy: Implications for prematurity and development of the fetal central nervous system. *Progress in Brain Research, 133*, 133–142. https://doi.org/10.1016/S0079-6123(01)33010-8

Walsh-Gallagher, D., Sinclair, M., & McConkey, R. (2012). The ambiguity of disabled women's experiences of pregnancy, childbirth and motherhood. *Midwifery, 28*(2), 156–162. https://doi.org/10.1016/j.midw.2011.01.003

Weinraub, M. & Kaufman, R. (2019). Single parenthood. In M. H. Bornstein (Ed.), *Handbook of parenting, Vol. 3. Being and becoming a parent* (3rd ed., pp. 271–310). Routledge.

Wellings, K., Jones, K. G., Mercer, C. H., Tanton, C., Clifton, S., Datta, J., Copas, A. J., Erens, B., Gibson, L. J., Macdowall, W., Sonnenberg, P., Phelps, A., & Johnson, A. M. (2013). The prevalence of unplanned pregnancy and associated factors in Britain: Findings from the third National Survey of Sexual Attitudes and Lifestyles (Natsal-3). *Lancet, 382*(9907), 1807–1816. https://doi .org/10.1016/S0140-6736(13)62071-1

Wessell, M. A., Cobb, J. C., Jackson, E. B., Harris, G. S., & Detweiler, A. C. (1954). Paroxysmal fussing in infancy, sometimes called colic. *Pediatrics*, 14(5), 421–435.

Wilson, N., Le, J. J., & Bei, B. (2019). Postpartum fatigue and depression: A systematic review and meta-analysis. *Journal of Affective Disorders, 246*, 224–233. http://dx.doi.org/10.1016/j.jad.2018.12.032.

Wing, D. G., Burge-Callaway, K., Rose Clance, P., & Armistead, L. (2005). Understanding gender differences in bereavement following the death of an infant: Implications for treatment. *Psychotherapy: Theory, Research, Practice, Training, 38*(1), 60–73. https://doi.org/10.1037/0033-3204.38.1.60

Winnicott, D. W. (1951). Transitional objects and transitional phenomena: A study of the first not-me possession. *The International Journal of Psychoanalysis*, 34, 89–97.

Winnicott, D. W. (1953). Transitional objects and transitional phenomena; a study of the first not-me possession. *The International Journal of Psychoanalysis, 34*, 89–97.

Winnicott, W. D. (1960). The theory of the parent-infant relationship. In W. D. Winnicott (Ed.), *The maturational processes and the facilitating environment: Studies in the theory of emotional development* (pp. 37–55). International Universities Press, Inc.

Whitehead, M.-B. & Schwartz-Nobel, L. (1989). *A mother's story: The truth about the Baby M Case*. St. Martin's Press.

Winston, R. (2015). *The essential fertility guide*. Quadrille Publishing.

Winter, G. M. (2019). New routes to parenthood. *British Journal of Midwifery*, 27(4), 270. https://doi.org/10.12968/bjom.2019.27.4.270

Wojmar, D. M. & Katzenmeyer, A. (2014). Experiences of preconception, pregnancy and new motherhood for lesbian nonbiological mothers. *Journal Obstetric Gynecologic Neonatal Nursing (JOGNN), 43*(1),50–60. https://doi.org/10.1111/1552-6909.12270

Wolf, N. (2003). *Misconceptions: Truth, lies and the unexpected journey to motherhood*. Anchor Books. First published in 2001.

Wolke, D. (2019). Persistence of infant crying, sleeping and feeding problems: Need for prevention. *Archives Disabled Child, 104*(11), 1022–1023. https://doi.org/10.1136/archdischild-2019-316851

Wolke, D., Bilgin, A., & Samara, M. (2017). Systematic review and meta-analysis: Fussing and crying durations and prevalence of colic in infants. *Journal of Pediatrics, 185*, 55–61. https://doi.org/10.1016/j.jpeds.2017.02.020

Wong, F. C. & Lo, Y. M. (2015). Prenatal diagnosis innovation: Genome sequencing of maternal plasma. *Annual Review of Medicine, 67*(1), 419–432. https://doi.org/10.1146/annurev-med-091014-115715

World Health Organization. (2011a). *Disability. World report on disability*. https://www.who.int/disabilities/world_report/2011/report/en/%

World Health Organization. (2016). http://www/who.int/reproductivehealth/topics/infertility.perspective.en./

World Health Organization. (2018a). *WHO recommendations on intrapartum care for a positive childbirth experience*. World Health Organization.

World Health Organization. (2018b). *Protecting, promoting, and supporting breast-feeding in facilities providing maternal and newborn services: The revised baby friendly hospital initiative. Implementation guidance: Protecting, promoting and supporting breastfeeding in facilities providing maternity and newborn services: The revised baby-friendly hospital initiative.* World Health Organization. https://apps.who.int/iris/handle/10665/272943.

World Health Organization. (2020). *Adolescent Pregnancy Fact Sheet.* https://www.who.int/news-room/fact-sheets/detail/adolescent-pregnancy

Zadeh, S. & Foster, J. (2016). From 'virgin births' to 'octomom': Representations of single motherhood via sperm donation in the UK News. *Journal of Community & Applied Psychology, 26,* 551–566. https://doi.org/10.1002/casp.2288

Zaltzman, A., Falcon, B., & Harrison, M. E. (2015). Body image in adolescent pregnancy. *Journal of Pediatric & Adolescent Gynecology, 28*(2), 102–108.

Zegers-Hochschild, F. (1999). Cultural expectations from IVF and reproductive genetics in Latin America. In R. Jansen & D. Mortimer (Eds), *Towards reproductive certainty: Fertility & genetics beyond 1999* (pp. 435–440). The Parthenon Publishing Group.

Zegers-Hochschild, F., Adamson, G.D., de Mouzon, J., Ishihara, O., Mansour, R., Nygren, K., Sullivan, E., & van der Poel, S., on behalf of ICMART and WHO. (2009). The International Committee for Monitoring Assisted Reproductive Technology (ICMART) and the World Health Organization (WHO) revised glossary on ART terminology. *Human Reproduction, 24*(11), 2683–2687. https://doi.org/10.1093/humrep/dep343

Zimon, A.E., Shepard, D. S., Prottas, J., Rooney, K. L., Ungerleider, J., Halasa-Rappel, Y. A., Sakkas, D., & Oskowitz, S. P. (2019). Embryo donation: Survey of in-vitro fertilization (IVF) patients and randomized trial of complimentary counselling. *PLoS ONE, 14*(8), e0221149. https://doi.org/10.1371/journal.pone.0221149

Ziv, I. & Freund-Eschar, Y. (2015). The pregnancy experience of gay couples expecting a child through overseas surrogacy. *The Family Journal: Counseling and Therapy for Couples and Families, 23*(2), 158–166. https://doi.org/10.1177/1066480714565107

Index

9 781108 799287

Lightning Source UK Ltd.
Milton Keynes UK
UKHW021947260123
416045UK00017B/124